Problems of Australian Defence

Problems
of Australian
Defence

Edited by
H. G. GELBER

MELBOURNE
OXFORD UNIVERSITY PRESS
LONDON   WELLINGTON   NEW YORK
1970

*Oxford University Press, Ely House, London, W.*1

GLASGOW   NEW YORK   TORONTO   MELBOURNE   WELLINGTON
CAPE TOWN   SALISBURY   IBADAN   NAIROBI   DAR ES SALAAM   LUSAKA   ADDIS ABABA
BOMBAY   CALCUTTA   MADRAS   KARACHI   LAHORE   DACCA
KUALA LUMPUR   SINGAPORE   HONG KONG   TOKYO

Oxford University Press, 7 Bowen Crescent, Melbourne

© Oxford University Press 1970

First published 1970

Hardbound   ISBN 0 19 550353 8
Paperback   ISBN 0 19 550362 7

Registered in Australia for transmission by post as a book
PRINTED IN AUSTRALIA BY HALSTEAD PRESS, SYDNEY

Contents

Tables

Maps

Introduction

At the beginning of the 1970s Australian defence policies seem about to enter a new and more complex period. South-East Asia remains in flux. The phasing out of some American responsibilities in and around Asia, the probable rise of the economic and political power of Japan, the creation of new foreign and defence policies by China following the Cultural Revolution, all seem likely to change the framework within which Australian defence policies will need to be considered. At the same time technical evolution and economic change import still further complexities. The changed importance of geographic distance, the declining significance of territorial expansion as a condition or a measure of power, the new kinds of international economic exchanges and the ambiguities which they entail for national sovereignty, all these will profoundly affect the world scene. More nations are reaching towards what Professor Brzezinski has called the technetronic age. The circumstances and feasibility of the exercise of military power in the 1970s may therefore be significantly different from the experience of the international community during the 1960s.

This book tries to make a contribution to the continuing debate about Australian defence policies in changing circumstances. No attempt has been made to review these policies comprehensively. Nor has anyone tried to avoid conflicts of view among the contributors or to eliminate every possible overlap between Chapters. The book sets out to explore two main areas. First, in considering Australia's relations with six other nations, it does so from the points of view of those nations and not from the point of view of Canberra. Secondly, it tries to provide some data, and some argument, concerning a number of economic and technical considerations which affect the formulation of Australian defence policies. Much public discussion has so far proceeded unburdened by previous published research on such matters as Australian defence procurement, or the administration of defence or the facts or arguments concerning oil supplies. This book hopes to change that situation. In addition to these two categories, we examine a few area problems, such as a possible design for an Australian naval strategy or how to control smaller wars.

I wish to acknowledge my debt to the contributors for their patience and helpfulness. I am also indebted to Miss Elizabeth McDonald, of the Oxford University Press, who cleaned up and organized a draft which was, at times, even more untidy than it need have been; Mrs J. Smith and Miss B. Newbold, who typed much of the text; and above all to my wife who had to cope with me.

H.G.G.

October 1970

Monash University
Melbourne

Abbreviations

A.B.M.	anti-ballistic missile
A.D.B.	Asian Development Bank
A.E.C.	Atomic Energy Commission
A.I.D.	Army Intelligence Department
A.J.A.S.	Australia-Japan-Asian system
A.L.P.	Australian Labor Party
AMDA	Anglo-Malaysian Defence Agreement
ANZAM	Australia, New Zealand and Malaya
ANZUS	Australia, New Zealand and United States Pacific Security Pact
APEC	Asian Pacific Economic Community
A.P.O.	Australian Post Office
ASEAN	Association of South-East Asian Nations
ASPAC	Asian and Pacific Council
A.S.W.	anti-submarine warfare
A.T. & T.	American Telephone and Telegraph
A.T.S.	Applications Technology Satellite
B.H.P.	Broken Hill Proprietary Ltd.
B.L.F.	bilateral nuclear force
B.P.D.	barrels per day
B.P.S.D.	barrels per stream day
C.A.C.	Commonwealth Aircraft Corporation
C.C.I.R.	*Conseil Consultatif International du Radio* (International Council on Radio)
C.C.I.T.T.	*Conseil Consultatif des Téléphones et Télégraphes* (Advisory Council on Telephone and Telegraph)
CENTO	Central Treaty Organization
C.M.F.	Citizen Military Force
COMPAC	Commonwealth Pacific Cable
C.P.D. (H. of R.)	*Commonwealth Parliamentary Debates (House of Representatives)*
D.E.A.	Department of External Affairs

ABBREVIATIONS

D.L.P.	Democratic Labor Party
D.W.T.	dead weight tons
E.C.A.F.E.	Economic Commission for Asia and the Far East
E.E.C.	European Economic Community
ELDO	European Launcher Development Organization
f.o.b.	free on board
G.A.F.	Government Aircraft Factory
G.A.T.T.	General Agreement on Tariffs and Trade
G.N.P.	Gross National Product
H.E.	high explosive
H.F.	high frequency
H.M.S.O.	Her Majesty's Stationery Office
HUK	Hunter-killer
I.A.E.A.	International Atomic Energy Agency
I.C.B.M.	Intercontinental ballistic missile
I.C.S.C.	Interim Communication Satellite Committee
I.G.G.I.	Intergovernmental Group on Indonesia
I.M.F.	International Monetary Fund
INTELSAT	International Telecommunications Satellite Consortium
I.T.U.	International Telecommunications Union
K.N.I.P.	*Komite Nasional Indonesian Pusat* (Indonesian Central National Committee)
Maphilindo	Malaysia, Philippines and Indonesia, proposed confederative association
M.L.F.	multilateral (nuclear) force
M.M.B.	million barrels
N.A.S.A.	National Aeronautics and Space Administration
NATO	North Atlantic Treaty Organization
N.C.N.A.	New China News Agency
Nekolim	'neo-colonialists and imperialists'
nm	nautical miles
N.P.T.	Non-Proliferation Treaty
O.E.C.D.	Organization for European Co-operation and Development
O.P.E.C.	Organization of Petroleum Exporting Countries
O.P.M.	*Organisi Papua Merdeka* (Free Papua Organization)
O.T.C.	Overseas Telecommunications Commission
P.K.I.	*Partai Komunis Indonesia* (Indonesian Communist Party)
P.M.F.	Pacific multilateral (nuclear) force

P.P.E.	part-privately-erected
R.A.A.F.	Royal Australian Air Force
R.A.F.	Royal Air Force
R.A.N.	Royal Australian Navy
R.I.I.A.	Royal Institute of International Affairs
R.M.A.F.	Royal Malaysian Air Force
S.A.M.	surface-to-air missile
SEACOM	South-East Asia-Commonwealth Cable
SEATO	South-East Asia Treaty Organization
S.L.B.M.	submarine-launched ballistic missile
S.T.D.	Subscriber Trunk Dialling
U.A.R.	United Arab Republic
U.N.	United Nations
U.S.A.F.	United States Air Force
U.S.N.	United States Navy
V.L.F.	very low frequency

CURRENCY SYMBOLS

$A	Australian Dollar
$M	Malaysian Dollar
$US	United States Dollar
£	Pound Sterling
Rs	Rupees

xi

Relationships

CHAPTER 1

Australia and China

JOHN M. H. LINDBECK

Set on the southern rim of Asia, Australia nonetheless has seen Asia with alien European eyes: 'And China, while continuing to loom large and threatening on the horizon of Australian political consciousness to Australians is as baffling and mysterious as ever'.[1] None are more aware of the cultural and perceptual barriers between Australia, essentially an outpost and extension of British civilization, and Asia and of the underlying reasons and policies that have fostered this estrangement and fear than some of her own scholars and publicists.[2] Until the Second World War brought the western imperial political order to an end in Asia, Australia could go its own way, aloof from major involvements with its Asian neighbours, secure in its privileged political, economic, social and military position within the British and European international system. Relieved by other western powers of heavy and critical international responsibilities for developments in the Asian region, it had little need to organize the thoughts and activities of its people and their institutions to take Asia into full account. As western geographers concluded, Australia was a continent by itself. Now regional developments and the further prospective decline of western power and influence in the region are forcing Australians to think of Australia as another island, albeit vast and different, in South-East Asia.

Modern technology has intensified the impact on Australia of the reordering of world and, notably, Asian patterns of power. Excluding Australia and New Zealand, from Pakistan in the west to Japan in the east, some fifteen new states, two divided, have joined three pre-war Asian governments to organize and to direct the activities of the peoples of Asia. In place of European rivalries that were major sources of conflict in Asia prior to the last two decades, regional conflicts have become major sources of tension and threat, often compounded and intensified by trans-regional Great Power struggles for influence and place in a shrunken world. For Australians the new configuration of power that is emerging in Asia has critical importance for its future.

3

There seems to be a feeling among Australians that China could, in large measure, determine this configuration of Asian power and many, perhaps at present the substantial majority, of politically concerned Australians feel that Asia may, in some sense, become in time China's realm. This prospect is not, apparently, reassuring to most Australians.[3] In what ways it is thought that Asia's future will be shaped by China or that China can threaten Australia is not clear. These fears may stem more from Australian uneasiness about Asia and Asian power than from a detached appraisal of China's future role in Asia. China is not an immediate neighbour. Bilateral relationships are rightly recognized even now as essentially matters of economic transactions. It is the undetermined character and intensity of Chinese influence on its Asian neighbours that preoccupy Australians.

What then is China's role in Asia likely to be? There are no unqualified answers to this question. There are, however, a number of trends, domestic and regional, that will affect China's place and influence in Asia and the world during the next few years. After considering some of these, it may then be profitable to raise the question of what actions, if any, Australia can take to influence the course of events in the region.

China's domestic capabilities and international influence

Lessons from history, if not fully reassessed, may be misleading rather than serving to clarify present realities. Yet conserved history, whatever its myths, does shape the values and views of its conservators, providing a corpus of symbols and myths that reinforce national identities and shape motivations. The Chinese, more than many other peoples, have traditionally been captured by their recorded past and traditions. This, in the view of many of its modern leading figures, has been one of the country's major handicaps in adjusting to new potentialities and situations. Reliance upon traditional Chinese self-images in attempting to assess the willingness or the reluctance of China's communist leaders to pursue their avowed aim of reorienting the nation for effective participation in world affairs is questionable. To the extent, however, that the past is still predisposing, it tends to point away from the notion that China can or will readily shape for itself a hegemonic place in Asia. First, neither experience nor traditional political definitions of China's place in the world have prepared the Chinese people to think of themselves in an international environment where power relations between states are contingent and relative, depending on efficient mobilization of domestic power resources and external coalitional and alliance relationships. Secondly, it has been suggested that China's historically recognized and approved

4

frontiers have been intra-Asian, not maritime. This may imply that the natural and general preoccupation of most Chinese is oriented more toward the dangers and potentialities of continental problems than the threats and opportunities of overseas developments—a feeling obviously not shared by the peoples of the South China coast who, in violation of Ch'ing Dynasty laws, sought richer fortunes overseas, in many circumstances with inducements from European colonial developers and administrators. Thirdly, Chinese political and military power has been extended beyond China's boundaries not for eco' nic reasons but only for political and military reasons—and this traditionally in border areas where Chinese and non-Chinese peoples have not been able to achieve social and economic integration. China's rulers and people never felt impelled, nor were they organized, to handle the problems and discomforts of ruling remote transmarine, transmontane or trans-steppe colonial peoples on a large scale. Unlike Alexander of Greece, the Mongols, the Portuguese or the British, they did not think India a prize worth seizing. (This refers to traditional China, but I believe it also applies to the present government. The 1962 attacks by China on India had limited territorial objectives relating to boundaries. Its primary objectives were political.) They neither have nor accept the spirit of conquest that marked the Mongols. Although one cannot for a moment forget that China is in revolution and that the past may not hold for the future, contemporary developments also appear to inhibit for some time to come China's freedom of action as a world and regional power, thus reinforcing traditional social, historical and geographic constraints.

China has had severe difficulties in developing stable and effective foreign policies in the global arena. In the latter part of the nineteenth century China was trapped by the enfeebled Ch'ing Dynasty rulers and bureaucrats into archaic modes of dealing with other powers; during the Republican period Chinese regimes lacked the capacity to reorder China's relations with other states; and in the first ten years of communist rule, China's leaders accepted a relationship with the Soviet Union that subordinated, in important respects, its relationships with other countries to the requirements of the coalition of socialist states led by Russia. In the past twenty years the twists and turns of China's relationships with other countries, including the Soviet Union, suggest the absence of practical understanding on the part of its present rulers of the nature and complexities of the international environment and of the priority of goals and related policies that might be coherently structured to serve China's national interests.

Before many of these international problems can be resolved, China has to work through its domestic problems. These far outweigh its

5

B

international concerns. By breaking with the Soviet Union in 1959-60 China freed itself to develop a new and independent foreign policy. But by cutting itself off from Russian assistance and at the same time seeking to devise its own models of economic development and social change, the pace of China's economic growth was sharply curtailed. In subsequent efforts to reorganize Chinese society to achieve Mao's prescriptions the entire political system has been shaken and perhaps so severely damaged as to require a prolonged process of reconstruction. The last decade, then, has led to increased domestic preoccupations, increased Chinese isolation and a marked decline in China's participation and influence in international affairs. The important consequence of this for other states and external groups has been the relative decrease in Peking's command of political, economic, psychological and, in some respects, military assets. Because the attitudes and behaviour of other nations toward China depend upon their assessment of the power China possesses and is willing to use for or against them, China's domestic weakness and external ineptness have sharply decreased its ability to shape regional and global disposition of resources, to influence the forms of new regional bodies and to define both the issues and the framework around and through which international competition and conflict take place. In a period of extraordinarily rapid social change and availability of new technologies and resources for accelerating economic growth in nations with effective political systems, a decade of fumbling and lack of development delayed and decreased China's capacity to assemble the assets it needs to develop a strong competitive position in Asia.

With respect to foreign affairs China's place in the international system and its role as a participant in Asian affairs will depend greatly upon its international strategies, in particular the importance its leaders assign to maintaining customary diplomatic relations with other states as compared to dealing directly with individuals and groups in such states. If China disregards the claims of other governments to the loyalty of their citizens, it will pay the price of arousing the organized hostility or discrimination of other countries and their leaders. Both traditionally, living with the idea that China was a cultural universe of its own, and currently, operating under Mao's vision of communist China's revolutionary identity with the proletariat of the world, China has not accepted the primacy of the nation-state and of intergovernmental relationships between nations. From its beginning it did not accord other governments the treatment and prerogatives they expected and sought. Perhaps because the Chinese People's Republic entered the world scene during the height of the Cold War and because it was dominated by a revolutionary movement with an

6

ideology hostile to traditional nationalism and the acceptance of nation states with different and competing political systems, the regime established in Peking in 1949 by the communists was, at the same time, not accorded the status it claimed and otherwise might have expected as a government in power. If China's leaders seek to pursue without caution and great restraint ideological and revolutionary interests by encouraging subversive political movements abroad and by using existing domestic pressure groups in other countries to shape international developments along lines they desire, China probably will remain isolated, and for a long time ineffectual as well, hedged in by both the United States and the Soviet Union and all the allies and collaborators they can recruit. It lacks the resources, both human and material, to create and sustain large political movements that are dependent and thus responsive to it. The primary compulsions upon China's leaders to pursue a revolutionary strategy are probably negative, that is, they lack the appeal of alternative courses that involve concessions to the United States and the Soviet Union, as well as to other powers. The premises of China's present policies rest on hopes that appear to be far from realistic to most observers. Their Maoist justification presumably is in the expectation that persistent and unresolved domestic political tensions in many other countries, both communist and non-communist, will lead to a widespread crumbling of existing political orders whose vast disordered population will then be available for mobilization by Chinese-supported ideological groups.

Assuming, however, that there will be before long a relatively stable and coherent restructuring of power in China with the formulation of national goals that command wide public support and a systematic organization of the nation's resources to achieve these goals, then China once again would be likely to move toward the adoption of foreign policies relevant to her purposes and programmes. Alliance relationships, security costs, economic priorities and a host of other issues would again be pondered and appropriate courses of action sought. But could China quickly repair the damage its reputation and power have suffered as a result of the failure of the Great Leap Forward toward the end of the 1950s and the dissipation of its resources in the Cultural Revolution? The answer appears to be in time, a prolonged period of time, depending only in part on the policies pursued. China has lost the effective use of important psychological, political and economic assets as a result of recent events. Its setbacks have reduced for some time its ability to act in relation to other nations with the force and effectiveness that its size and resources might permit. Its political system still has to be reconstituted and, given the

7

strains and tensions as well as organizational and administrative dis-
integration that have occurred, time and skill will be needed to restore
the legitimacy of the regime and its capacities to elicit from the
Chinese people low-cost, non-coerced responses or compliance to its
demands and direction. China's economic and social structures, particularly educational, also have been weakened. This apparently has
seriously set back its economic rate of growth and, at the same time,
has prevented it from fully using the intellectual and scientific-
technological resources it has to extend cultural and intellectual ties
and to expand its international influence, even among groups from
poorly developed countries.

Among nations, China is a giant. But physical size in a world of
over a hundred and twenty states is not directly translated into international power and influence. Claims to Great Power status do not
make a strong case for a major role in world affairs and for having
demands met. Apart from China's development of nuclear weapons,
its actual capacity for influencing the behaviour of its Asian neighbours and for setting the terms under which other peoples carry on
their activities seems to have been diminished during the past decade
by disruptive internal Chinese developments.

The Asian context and Chinese influence

The environment in which China operates has also been changing.
External constraints on China's influence and role in Asia may, in
the long run, be more important than internal constraints. The two,
of course, are related. Important external factors that affect China's
present and future place in Asia are regional economic trends, the
position and policies of the United States, the role of the Soviet Union
and the configuration of power that is emerging in Asia. It is important to try to understand how these developments are seen and evalua-
ted by China's leaders. Regardless of how they are understood in
China, major alterations in the patterns of regional development and
the distribution and character of military power will change, limit or
enlarge the possible range of activities of various countries in the
region, including China.

It is now clear that China is not and for some time cannot be Asia's
dominant industrial and economic power, nor its organizing commercial centre. Within the region this place belongs to Japan. The
ten member countries of E.C.A.F.E. (Economic Commission for Asia
and the Far East) are acquiring a relatively stronger position in the
region and Australia is developing the assets that should enable it to
play a significant role in the area. Table 1 indicates the current dis-

tribution of economic and industrial power (as suggested by Gross National Product) and the distribution of military power.

Of major importance for Asia is the change among various countries in G.N.P. growth rates from 1960 projected to 1975. Lagging behind China in 1960, Japan's G.N.P. was $US44,570 million compared to China's estimated $US50,000 million. By 1968 Japan had passed and far out-distanced China with a G.N.P. of $US140,000 million compared to China's $US70-75,000 million. Some projections suggest that by 1975 Japan's G.N.P. may be $US240,000 million, or more than two and a half times as great as China's projected $US90,000 million. In fact, Japan may then have a productive capacity that exceeds all of the rest of Asia, excluding Australia and New Zealand. With a population smaller than Taiwan, Australia's G.N.P. ($US25,800 million) in 1967 exceeded that of all Asian countries except Japan ($US116,000 million), China ($US65-70,000 million) and India ($US41,000 million).

In looking at the relative ability of the other countries in Asia to achieve the productive capacity to meet the physical needs of their people and to support the political and social structures and programmes necessary for stability and growth, the picture is less clear and far from satisfying. Yet, even here, one estimate is that ten developing E.C.A.F.E. countries from South Korea to Pakistan with a total population of 898 million in 1967 had a combined G.N.P. of $US72,300 million, or about that of China. By 1975 their combined G.N.P. was expected to be $US116-118,000, or some $US25,000 million more than that of China. Too much must not be made of these projections, but they do underline the fact that within the Asian region, Japan to the north and Australia-New Zealand to the south are regional bases of enormous and proven productivity, cultural cohesion and large trading experience. These economic potentialities are affected to some degree by non-economic factors. These countries, partly because of their large non-regional interests and affiliations, have been regarded by other countries as external powers. But this is rapidly changing. Japan needs skill, perception and time to relate itself to its neighbours and to overcome fears generated by its previous imperial ambitions. Australia has perhaps a more complex domestic problem of learning how to bridge a major cultural and social chasm, highlighted by its selective and discriminatory immigration policy with respect to Asia. Domestic political and social factors probably prevent a rapid and radical change in this policy, but clearly its negative features can be progressively modified as they affect Australia's cultural and political relationships with its neighbours. Japan's population pressure and its social mores minimize its problems in this

9

TABLE 1

Distribution of Economic and Industrial Power and Military Power

	Population 1967 (million)	G.N.P. 1967 (million $US)	Military manpower (regular)	Defence Expenditures			
				Gross (million $US) 1968	Gross (million $US) 1967	1967 per capita	1967 % of G.N.P.
China	792	75,000	2,761,000	7,000	6,900	9	9.2
North Korea	13	2,700	384,000	629	467	37	17.3
North Vietnam	19	2,000	444,750	500	450	27	25.0
Totals	824	79,700	3,589,750	8,129	7,817		
Japan	101	116,000	250,000	1,172	1,068	11	0.9
South Korea	31	4,600	620,000	234	180	6	3.9
Taiwan	13.4	3,500	528,000	300	275	21	7.9
N.E. Asia: Totals	145.4	124,100	1,398,000	1,706	1,523		
Australia	12.05	25,800	84,300	1,375	1,278	109	4.9
New Zealand	2.756	5,700	13,170	109	98	36	1.7
Philippines	34.5	6,000	30,000	115	104	3	1.7
Thailand	33	4,800	141,500	125	119	4	2.5
SEATO: Totals	82.06	42,300	268,970	1,724	1,599		

Cambodia	6.5	900	49,000	63	60	9	6.6
Laos	2.7	200	61,900	40	38	15	19.4
South Vietnam	16.8	2,200	410,000	312	193	11	8.8
Protocol states: Totals	26.0	3,300	520,900	415	291		
Indonesia	112	4,500	340,000	113	102	1	2.3
Malaysia	10.1	3,100	33,800	130	128	13	4.1
Singapore	2.05	3,500	4,500	32	32	16	0.9
South-East Asia: Totals	124.15	11,100	378,300	275	262		
Burma	26	1,700	137,500	112	109	5	6.4
India	520	41,000	1,033,000	1,452	1,368	3	3.3
Pakistan	110	13,100	324,000	514	468	4	3.6
South Asia: Totals	656	55,800	1,494,500	2,078	1,945		
Totals: excluding Communist Asia	1,033.61	236,600	4,060,670	6,198	5,620		

Source: *The Military Balance, 1968–1969*, The Institute for Strategic Studies, London, 1968.

regard with respect to most Asians, except Koreans resident in Japan.

For most of these countries the future of their economies will continue to depend on productive relationships with the large economies of Europe and the Americas. The development of regional economic relationships is, however, expected to assume a larger role. These relationships are being fostered now by various regional bodies and associations that promise to be increasingly effective. They may have the result of providing regional structures that further enhance the bargaining power of Asian nations with China in matters of economic importance.

Related to economic trends are the development of the intellectual, social and political skills required to incorporate modern science and its derivative and associated technologies for personal, social and national purposes, and the speed at which these skills are mastered. There is urgent need for assistance to develop these skills. The patterns of regional development and influence may be markedly affected by the scope and character of the 'modernizing' regional role played by different countries in the area. As China has withdrawn from the scene, Japan has been forging ahead. One index of this is that over 10,000 foreign students, mainly from Asia, are now studying in Japanese institutions of higher education, despite the fact that Japanese has never been an intercontinental or international language, as are German, French and English. In contrast to the past, Australia now seeks to make its training resources available to Asians and to enter into a larger range of relationships with Asia but domestic conditions still appear to be a severe check to speedy change. Commonwealth links, however, help to facilitate association. Australia and New Zealand are expanding their relations with Singapore and Malaysia, and taken together these four countries are the most productive in South-East Asia, with a combined G.N.P. in 1967 of $US38,100 million. This is only slightly less than that of India, which has 520 million people compared to a population for the above four countries of about 28 million. In other words, Australia and Japan, as the two most industrially developed countries in Asia, have the economic and technological resources to influence in important ways the form and content of regional economic and other relationships in the area if they find ways of associating themselves effectively at several levels with other nations in the region.[4] As might be expected, the economic relationship between the two countries represents the largest bilateral relationship in the region both in terms of volume of trade and joint ventures in capital investment.[5] Chinese press accounts in the past three years have indicated a growing awareness and uneasiness over Japan's economic role in Asia and the implications this may

have in strengthening that country's influence, especially in South-East Asia.[6] Australia, except for its new security arrangements with Singapore and Malaysia, has received relatively little attention in the Chinese press.

The position and policies of the United States have also placed major restraints on China's freedom of action in the area and in the world, although the actual effectiveness of the policies of the United States in inhibiting China have perhaps been exaggerated by China and by other countries in the area. Such restraints have been the result of direct confrontations between China and the United States in the Taiwan straits and Korea, where American power could be employed effectively to deter the Chinese from obtaining their demands. Vietnam, on the other hand, demonstrates the limitations of modern military power when employed against a politically and militarily mobilized population rather than against conventional military forces operating in open combat arenas. Another factor that has tended to distort and over-emphasize the role of American power in Asia has been communist Chinese propaganda. In order to create an unfavourable political and social international environment for the United States and to mobilize sympathy and support for itself, Peking has depicted the United States as the prime enemy of China and of all the peoples of the world, strong enough to threaten everyone.

The United States has prevented China from obtaining several of its objectives—it does not control Taiwan; the communist governments of Korea and Vietnam that it favoured have been unable to reunite these countries by force; its efforts to extend its influence abroad through co-operation and use of congenial political groups and movements have encountered at times intense and perhaps occasionally effective American opposition. The major failures of the Chinese in promoting their revolutionary influence in South and South-East Asia appear to be attributable more to local developments and Chinese ineffectiveness than to direct American intervention. Saying this, however, is not to conclude that the United States has not had and will not continue to have a powerful influence in the region. At two critical points, Korea and Taiwan, the American military position is and presumably will continue to be determinative of the future. Japan's future security is critically affected by the American presence and policies at these points. As long as Japan desires to continue security arrangements with the United States, the United States can be expected to maintain forces in the area capable of preventing Chinese and other military forces from altering existing political arrangements. Even should Japan assume military responsibility

for its own security as a regional power, American military power will continue to have an important strategic role in the trans-Pacific region, although its forces are likely to be less directly involved and less important in maintaining domestic stability within countries and sub-regions of Asia. For the rest, local rather than Chinese political and military forces are likely to be of primary importance in affecting regional stability. With the constant interplay of competing external economic, political and psychological or cultural influences in every country, the United States, given its present patterns of commitments, its concern with shaping the international environment, and its growing volume and variety of interests, is in no position to withdraw from Asia. It is safe to assume that in a wide variety of ways China and other Asian countries will have to take the United States into account for the foreseeable future.

A third constraint on Chinese regional influence is the Soviet Union. Russia has steadily extended its influence in Asia, partly because of the mutual benefits to be gained, but also in order to check the expansion of Chinese influence and to diminish American and Western European influence. It has achieved this by working with existing governments through developing bilateral diplomatic and economic relations and selective military assistance programmes, notably so far as China is concerned in India, North Vietnam and North Korea. A growing Russian military presence, consisting of the placement of military forces along the Russo-Chinese border, the introduction of a Russian naval presence in the Indian Ocean and the rapid development of Russian sea power in the Pacific, with a fleet of over 750 ships, including more than 100 submarines, 6 cruisers, 50 destroyers, and about 300 naval aircraft, support this influence. Recent arrangements between Japan and the Soviet Union promise to lead to expanded trade and possibly to heavy Japanese involvement in major programmes of economic development in Siberia. Steadily expanding trade is matched by a growing merchant marine.[7]

These developments have prompted the Chinese to issue long diatribes against the Soviet Union, which is accused in the *communiqués* of both the Eleventh and Twelfth Plenums of the Central Committee of the Chinese Communist Party (1966 and 1968) of organizing, together with the United States, an anti-China alliance. Japan is portrayed as an active force in this alliance and its future Asian logistical base.[8] India also is a member. Russia is accused of doing its best to influence both these Asian powers to adopt hostile policies toward China.[9]

The implications of present trends in Asia suggest an emerging configuration of power in which China, whatever policies it may pursue, will not be the dominant power in Asia. Economically it will be far behind Japan. As a trading partner it may become important, but still far behind the United States, Europe and the Soviet Union. Politically, its prospects are limited. Regional bodies are being developed and shaped without its participation; American and Soviet influences continue to remain potent; and China's own retarded pace of development, political and economic, prevents it from making maximum use of its resources.

Militarily, the Chinese decision to develop nuclear weapons at the expense of its conventional military forces may, in fact, decrease its regional effectiveness. The primary consequence for China of undertaking to develop a nuclear strategic deterrent, with modest capabilities, is an alteration of its relationship to the United States and the Soviet Union. Its regional military policies can no longer be dissociated from global strategies. At present its naval forces are paltry and its land and air forces provide it with very limited offensive capabilities. In the meantime, it may try to find ways to make its few nuclear bombs and missiles serve political purposes in Asia by policies of intimidation. There is no evidence of how China thinks this might be done. Aside from this, most Japanese still feel secure from any threat of Chinese conventional military attack and most of China's island neighbours feel that as long as American forces are in the area they are beyond reach militarily, if not politically.

Thus the interplay of regional and external military, political and economic forces seem to create some major obstacles for China's foreign policy makers in advancing China's interests and augmenting China's influence and role in the world. Chinese leaders appear to recognize that Japan could rapidly become a major, and perhaps dominant, military power in Asia again, should it feel impelled to turn its resources to military production. Already the Chinese accuse Japan of becoming the 'arsenal' of Asia—its military supplier.[10] Moreover, China may prefer to see the present Japanese security arrangements with the United States continued so long as conservative political groups control the Japanese government. In other words, given China's limitations, the main thrust of China's Japan policy is long-range and with remote and perhaps unattainable goals, to work on Japan's domestic political cleavages to encourage the rise of pro-China elements. At present this does not mean the Japanese Communist Party, despite its growing size and role as an independent, nationalist party.

Australia's China policy

From the Chinese point of view Australia is still in the position of being a marginal factor in the Asian political and military scene. Politics and economics are conveniently dissociated to the great profit of Australia's wheat growers. Chinese protests over the participation of Australia's 8,000 troops in Vietnam have been almost *pro forma*. Australian links to Taiwan and its emerging security relationship to Malaysia and Singapore have received greater notice. But, on the whole, Australia has not had a place near the centre of Chinese attention, nor do its political and military relationships with the United States seem to affect the wheat trade. Indeed, China does not appear to have had a special Australia policy. China's economic relations with Australia are handled pragmatically, as they are with Canada, West Germany, Argentina and the United Kingdom. Unlike their approach to Japan, the Chinese indulge in very few or no political manoeuvres in working out their trade relations with Australia. To provide China with some footing in the local scene and because of their competition with the Soviet Union for influence among radical and ideologically oriented social and political groups, the Chinese have, it is true, shown some interest in the minor pro-Maoist bodies in Australia. But compared to Japan and most of the countries of South-East Asia, Australia has not been an area in which the Chinese have been active or about which they have shown great concern.

If Australia becomes a more active force in Asia, as it now proposes, relations with China might be markedly changed. The discussions leading to the decision in 1968 to constitute a sub-regional force through co-operative military arrangements between Malaysia, Singapore, New Zealand and Australia appear to have had the effect of alerting China in a new way to Australia as a potentially important actor in the Asian scene. If Australia enters more fully into the arena of Asian politics, then China may well feel compelled to take Australia into account, as it does Japan, as a distinct and troublesome force in Asia. For the present Australia is accused by the Chinese of being the agent or client of Great Britain and the United States. Over 8,000 Australian troops in Vietnam are, from the Chinese view, too minor a factor in a large-scale guerrilla or revolutionary civil conflict to be of political significance in the region. But the same number of troops integrated into a security framework that affects the regional policies and political strength and orientation of other Asian nations is a different matter. Not trade and profits but involvement in Asian political and security affairs may begin to transform Australia's relations to the region. This, it seems safe to predict, will affect China's

attitude. The fact that Singapore has strong cultural ties with China and also is a state with a population and tradition that is imported into South-East Asia may add to the dynamic quality of the relationship and the importance assigned to the alliance by China.

On the surface Australia's and Japan's relations with China are much alike. Both trade, but do not have diplomatic relations with China. Both maintain diplomatic relations with Taiwan and have security ties with the United States. But there appears to be a curious contrast in Australian and Japanese public perceptions of China's threat to Asia and China's proper role in the area. The Japanese public tends to dismiss the view that Peking is a threat to Japan's and Asia's security; Australians have demonstrated by words, actions and policies a real fear that China will injure the interests of other countries in Asia if unchecked. The Australian perception of China stems from a very different background and situation to that of Japan. The differences, on one side, lie in Japan's domestic policies, its cultural affiliations with China, its efforts to detach itself from full identification with the policies of the United States toward China and in Vietnam, its wide range of economic interests in China, the pre-emptive military roles of the United States, Russia and China in East Asia, and its growing self-confidence as an Asian power preparing to strike out on its own independent policy courses.

Australians, on the other hand, have had extremely tenuous ties with China; there are no important cultural links and virtually no resident Chinese in the country; Australians, despite their country's huge geographic size, feel exposed and small in comparison with China and Asia as a whole in terms of population and economic resources; and the South-East Asian context through which Australians approach and see China is markedly different from the East Asian setting of Japan. Australia's Asian neighbours are fearful of China and are vulnerable to external and Chinese influence. The near seizure of power in Indonesia by Chinese-affiliated Indonesian communists made a strong impression on Australians, as did the Chinese-supported revolutionary movements in the region beginning with the Malayan insurgency and extending to the Vietnam war. This sense of vulnerability has been sharpened, presumably, by the steady post-Second World War withdrawal of European powers and their military forces from the region. Australia shows no signs of encouraging China, under its present leaders, to seek and acquire a more influential role in Indonesia, Singapore and Malaysia; nor does it want to weaken political and military forces in such places as Taiwan, Korea, Indonesia and Thailand that actively restrict the extension of Chinese influence in the area. These trends and policies would seem almost

17

certain to lead to growing tension and competition, in due course, between China and Australia. The price of involvement and collaboration with China's fearful neighbours in South-East Asia may be growing strain in relations with China. Australia's temptation, as long as it feels vulnerable in its Asian setting, will be to approach China on lines compatible with those of the United States. It will want to protect the alliance, to formulate policies that are primarily designed to safeguard the independence of its neighbours from external pressure and to mobilize and strengthen forces seeking to reduce Chinese influence in Australia's area of immediate concern.

So far as China is concerned, is it possible for Australia to resist regional parochialization while becoming a regional power? Can Australia seek, as have Great Britain and France, to break down barriers to normal relations with China without remaining aloof from regional interplays of political forces? Thus far the importance of the United States in the region has been a constraining factor in preventing both Australia and Japan from radically altering their China policies. Apart from the difficult problem of Taiwan, however, establishment of diplomatic relations with China is unlikely to affect Australia's regional role or the security and stability of the area. Instead, it could be argued that the long-term welfare of the region calls for measures leading to the reduction of conflict and the formalization of China's relations with its Asian neighbours. Diplomatic relationships may have some but not crucial importance, as is illustrated in the case of Sino-Indian relations, in one day easing China's problems with the world.

The Chinese, in any case, are unlikely to be responsive to Australian overtures at present. The importance of the Australian-Chinese relationship may not really be in its bilateral dimensions, but in the way this relationship helps to shape the attitudes and behaviour of other countries so as to promote or retard the development of a stable and constructive international environment.

CHAPTER 2

India—A Distant but Important Neighbour

SISIR K. GUPTA

It is as easy to underestimate India's international importance as it is to exaggerate it. With its huge population living at the level of bare subsistence and with a host of internal social, economic and political problems demanding urgent solution India is basically an inward-looking country and is likely to remain so for a long time. But for a variety of reasons it is difficult to ignore India in any consideration of the major issues of world politics of our era and it certainly counts for a great deal in the affairs of the region to which it belongs. For one thing, there are more people in India than there are in Africa and Latin America. By uniting them under a single central authority India performs a vital stabilizing role in the world. For another, it is not only trying to solve the problems created by the acute poverty of this vast segment of humanity but is doing so within the framework of a democratic system. Though it is hard to measure it, it is of some importance for peace and stability of the world that a country like India should be trying to solve its internal problems through democratic methods and laying stress on the welfare of its peoples.[1] Again, many historical and ethnic factors have combined to make India some kind of a meeting ground between the east and the west—a non-western civilization which has been exposed to western currents of thought and philosophy and imbibed some western values. Viewed in the context of many long-term problems of the world like the growing gap between the world's north and south, this position of India is a matter of considerable hope for all those who are committed to a peaceful solution of some of such problems.

There are more immediate and tangible reasons, too, for attaching importance to India. Its geographical location makes it an important factor in the politics of all the turbulent regions of Asia; for both West and South-East Asia, India is a country whose attitudes and policies matter. In populous South Asia, India is in many ways the central

state. Whatever the publicly expressed fears and anxieties about India in some of the other states of the region, it is obvious that their welfare, security and prosperity is bound up with India's. Should any disaster befall India none of the other countries in the region can hope to escape its impact, just as none of them can fail to benefit from India's emergence as a stable, united and peaceful country.[2]

In terms of power, India is not great; but whatever tests one might choose to apply, it does qualify as a 'middle power'. It has over a million men under arms; only three other countries—America, China and Russia—have a larger standing army. Its total defence expenditure of about $US1,500 million *per annum* makes it the world's eleventh largest spender on defence. In terms of *per capita* income India is among the poorest nations of the world but it is one of the top ten in terms of G.N.P. Though it is still technologically backward, it has created a complex industrial base and is rated among the advanced nations in certain fields like nuclear technology. Certainly, in terms of the availability of scientific personnel it ranks quite high among the nations of the world. These and other factors, domestic and international, must tend to involve India in the affairs of the world.

The basic national interests that India's foreign policy seeks to promote are not difficult to identify. First, it is in India's interest to create and maintain a pattern of foreign relations conducive to the solution of its internal problems and to the attainment of a reasonably high rate of economic growth. Secondly, Indian foreign policy must ensure the country's security and territorial integrity in the face of various types of challenges. It has also to try to erect a structure of stable peace in the region. Thirdly, it is necessary for India not only to promote a climate of peace among the major powers of the world but also to strive for world reforms. India is interested in world peace and stability and in the creation of a world order which will ensure equity and justice for the underpowered and underprivileged nations of the world. The pulls exerted by these considerations do not always suggest the same course of action nor can all these objectives be pursued with equal vigour at any point of time. In fact, India has in different phases of its foreign policy stressed different aspects of these objectives.[3] But they are the basic considerations which have influenced India's foreign policy in the past and will continue to do so in the future.

In global politics India has pursued its policy of non-alignment with the two major power blocs in order to further its dual objective of world peace and world reforms. India has felt that the non-alignment of a number of countries of the third world helped both to limit the

area of conflict among the major powers and to resolve their out-
standing problems through peaceful means. In remaining non-aligned
India has stressed the need for a measure of understanding and co-
operation among the Great Powers. It has been particularly interested
in bringing about a degree of Soviet-American *rapprochement* and
détente. Its own posture in international politics has appeared to India
to be a significant contribution to the process of mitigation of the Cold
War; not only has it been able to maintain the friendliest relations
with the leading members of the two blocs but it has also become
some kind of an area of agreement between them. It is a distinctive
aspect of India's foreign relations that both the Super Powers have
some stake in India's success in resolving its internal problems and
also in its ability to withstand the pressures from its northern
neighbour.

Indeed, non-alignment has proved to be a useful way of maintaining good relations with both the U.S.A. and the U.S.S.R. To the
extent that the most crucial issue of our times is the relations between
the two Super Powers, this Indian policy has in its own way helped
the cause of world peace. But what is most important from India's
viewpoint is that it has also promoted its national interests both internally and externally. India still regards it as being in its direct interest to
help the U.S.A. and the U.S.S.R. to achieve a higher and more
meaningful level of accord.

World peace has been only one of the goals that India wished to
pursue through its policy of non-alignment. As a newly independent,
economically underdeveloped and militarily underpowered nation,
India has sought not only to ensure world peace but also to secure
such reforms in the structure of world politics as would create the
conditions for a better world order. Its policy of non-alignment was
intended to underline the fact that the Cold War was not the whole
of world politics; in fact, an obsession with Cold War problems could
distract attention from some of the roots of tension and conflict in the
world. Thus India has repeatedly stressed the importance of colonial
and racial problems and the yawning gap between the rich and poor
nations. It has also opposed any concept of world order based on
unconcealed domination of the smaller and weaker nations by the
larger and stronger ones or on patterns of distribution of world power
that tended to create an oligopoly or duopoly in the world. Its opposition to the nuclear Non-Proliferation Treaty in its present form as
well as its emphasis on the need for the reduction of arms at the dis-
posal of the nuclear powers arise partly out of this desire to see structural reforms in the international system. Altogether India has a distinct interest in preventing the emergence of a world order that

tackled the problems of violence and conflict but sidetracked other, equally important, issues.[4]

Nevertheless, in India's view peace is of overriding importance and the solution of all other problems must be sought through peaceful means. This indeed is the essence of the difference between the Indian and the Chinese ways of looking at the world. In some respects, India and China perceive the problems of the present day in identical terms: both are interested in bringing about structural changes in the world, both are concerned about the growing gap between the rich and poor, and both are interested in securing a better position for large but poor nations like themselves in international politics. But their views as to how these problems can best be tackled are diametrically opposed.

India believes that the salvation of the developing countries lies in world peace and international co-operation and that all efforts to resolve their problems must be made within such a framework. It appears to be the core of China's view, however, that it is only through violent struggle and the intensification of conflict that these problems can be solved. India has faith in the conscience of the enlightened and powerful nations of the developed world and its ethos is reformist; China has no such faith and its ethos is revolutionary.

This divergence between the Indian and the Chinese approaches to global problems has brought about a long and bitter conflict between the two largest nations of the world and greatly complicated India's problem of living in peace with its neighbours. India knew that its capacity to ensure its own security by being equally friendly with all the Great Powers would depend on the state of the relationship among them. India was also aware that the denial of its legitimate rights and status to China was, perhaps, the single most disturbing element in inter-Great Power relations. It therefore continuously stressed the importance of accommodating China in the world political system on a basis which would erase the memory of national humiliation from the mind of its peoples.

At one time it appeared that this role of India was a sufficient assurance to Peking that there was no inherent conflict or hostility between the interests of the two countries. By the end of the 1950s, however, India seems to have appeared to China as a major obstacle in the way of its foreign policy goals. It had emerged as an area of agreement among the two powers which China regarded as its long-term adversaries; its world view appeared to be shared by many other countries of Afro-Asia; the Indian tortoise was making slow but steady progress towards economic modernization; without power or resources of any sizeable kind, it had achieved an international status which was not far below China's; and finally its emphasis on peaceful conduct in

international relations appeared to deprive China of one of its major options in South and South-East Asia. Thus the problems of determining their national boundaries which could in different circumstances have been resolved as a relatively minor issue became a focal point of conflict.[5]

With the beginning of the clash with its powerful northern neighbour, regional peace and stability has become the central problem of India's foreign policy. While in the context of global politics India has been a non-aligned middle power which wishes to emphasize the importance of certain issues without being involved in any way in power politics, in the regional context where its own power is more real it has to apply orthodox balance-of-power criteria in order satisfactorily to tackle its problems of security. In the period before its conflict with China, India hoped that it would be possible to erect a political system in Asia which would be qualitatively different from that in Europe.[6] As the India-China conflict began to take shape, it became clear that Asian politics was governed by many of the same rules of the game as European affairs. Ever since 1959, and particularly since 1962, India has assumed that it has a real and serious problem of security *vis-à-vis* China and that it is only by improving its own military strength and building up relations with other countries which are equally interested in preserving the present political map of the area that it may be able to withstand the Chinese challenge. It is India's hope that eventually it will be possible to live in peace and friendship with China; but the lesson it derived from its experiences in 1962 is that in order to create conditions for stable peace in the region it must be demonstrated to the Chinese that they cannot achieve results by the use of force against their neighbours. India's military weakness has been a basic source of violence and conflict in the region and it is only after rectifying this situation that India could begin to think of long-term coexistence with its hostile neighbours.

In the last few years India has taken some steps towards improving its military capability and is probably now better equipped to meet limited Chinese offensives along the Himalayas than before.[7] But in the same period China has manufactured nuclear weapons and is expected to acquire a fully fledged nuclear capability in the near future. This has added a new dimension to the problems of India's defence. One of India's major tasks is to neutralize the effect of this development either by acquiring a capacity to deter China on its own or by maintaining such relationships with the other nuclear powers as would serve the purpose of deterrence. Successive Indian Prime Ministers have made it clear that India does not wish to manufacture

nuclear weapons but they have also drawn attention to the problems created by China's growing power. What shape the nuclear balance in Asia will take remains to be seen. It is India's hope that eventually China will enter into arms control arrangements with the other nuclear powers and that in the meantime the two Super Powers will deter China and deny to it the political gains it might hope to secure by the mere acquisition of a nuclear capability.

Considerations of security have made India move closer to the two Super Powers. Even before 1959 the predominant feature of India's foreign relations was its cordial and intimate relationship with the Soviet Union and the United States. Its conflict with China has further underlined the importance to India of the sympathy and support of the two Super Powers. For a number of reasons, it has laid special stress on its friendly relations with the Soviet Union. First, the South Asian region is geopolitically much more important to the Soviet Union than to the United States and it has higher stakes in resisting Chinese intrusions into the area.[8] Secondly, it has shown greater willingness to assist India's military build-up and has supplied modern conventional weapons on relatively easy terms. Thirdly, India can derive considerable political advantages in the Afro-Asian world by placing the Sino-Indian conflict in its Sino-Soviet perspective. Last, the legitimacy of a Soviet role in South Asia has already been accepted by the western world and the effort to maintain the closest possible relations with the Soviet Union is no longer inconsistent with the maintenance of good and friendly relations with the major western powers. In any event, the United States continues to be the main source of economic aid to India and the parallelism between its interests and those of the U.S.S.R. remains the key to peace and stability in the region. In brief, from India's viewpoint there is at present no conceivable substitute for its relations with the two Super Powers.

All the same, close co-operative relations with other countries are needed as well. For one thing, the ties between India and the Super Powers are ties between unequals and it is only by improving its relations with a number of significant middle powers that India can hope to acquire the leverage it needs to manage its relations with its benefactors. Though these powers might be generous or compassionate, a degree of discomfort is bound to exist in India about the country's growing dependence on them. A diversification of India's international contacts will improve India's position in the eyes of these powers and enable it to deal with them as a less unequal state. For another, it is not improbable that India's interests as a regional power in South Asia will at some future date appear to be contradictory to the interests of the global powers. The United States and the Soviet

Union are *status quo* powers, interested in promoting the stability of the global system they have erected. India has a greater interest in preserving the *status quo* in the region. If it appears to the two Super Powers at some stage that they have to permit the disturbance of the regional *status quo* to promote their global interests, India will have to try to protect its interests on its own. In that case its relations with other powers of the world could prove to be of immense value both in influencing the decisions of the Super Powers and in exploring other ways of protecting its vital national interests.[9]

These factors apart, it is questionable in the light of certain recent developments whether the Super Powers acting individually or even jointly will be able adequately to guarantee peace and security to all the disturbed areas of the world. In the first place, it is still a question whether they will in all cases have the will to intervene jointly to keep peace; even if they have such will, they may find it difficult to develop the kind of organization and institutions that are needed to implement their common designs. In the second place, there are distinct limits to what they can achieve by using their power and it would not be surprising if a sudden awareness of the limits of their power would make them seek short cuts to stability and peace in a region through such methods as the acceptance of a Great Power's right to have a sphere of influence in its neighbourhood.

Finally, the extent to which the Super Powers will be able to provide support and sustenance to a political system in Asia will depend to a considerable extent on the interrelations among the significant powers of the region. It will also depend on how far they are willing to supplement the efforts of these powers to create a stable political system in Asia. It is possible that any scheme of things in Asia which has not been conceived by Asian powers will fail to prove workable. It is probable that unless the Asian powers learn to consult and co-operate with each other, their views on the future of the continent will remain divergent and no common approach to Asian problems, acceptable to the major nations of the area, can emerge.

It is in the context of these considerations that India may view its relations with Australia. It is obvious that for neither country is the relationship with the other a matter of the highest priority; Australia's primary concern is to maintain the closest possible ties with its western allies while India's primary concern is to remain non-aligned in order to maintain its friendly relations with the Soviet Union and the United States. For neither of them will a closer relation with the other be a substitute for its relations with friendly Great Powers. But this does not preclude the improvement of their mutual relations and in fact there are good reasons for both to attach considerable impor-

tance to Indo-Australian relations. It is now obvious that although India remains non-aligned and Australia aligned, the consequences of this difference in their foreign policies need not be any impediment to their co-operation. If both the Soviet Union and the United States are searching for ways and means to achieve a higher degree of stability in Asian politics, there is no reason why their friends and allies in Asia, acting in their national self-interest, should not also find it possible to co-operate.

Although it is hard to judge accurately, the fact remains that, as an English-speaking country, Australia may find it easier to understand India and other former British colonies in Asia than other Asian nations which have not undergone the British impact to the same extent. The Commonwealth link symbolizes this aspect of Indo-Australian relations and no matter what might happen to the Commonwealth itself, this may have a lasting effect on relations between the two countries. Whatever the nature of the Indian government and whatever its political differences with the west, this cannot erase the imprints of two hundred years of British rule on Indian life. A special link between India and the English-speaking countries may continue to exist in much the same way as the French still find it easier to get along with the *élites* of the Indo-Chinese states than do any other European or western peoples. It is of course wrong to attribute too much to this fact but it is easy to overlook this aspect in discussing the long-term prospects of Indo-Australian relations.

Like the Soviet Union in the north-east, Australia is Asia's 'western' neighbour in the south-east. In fact, the Soviet Union and Australia are two 'western' societies which have to concern themselves with the affairs of Asia for sheer geographical reasons and much as many countries of Western Europe or even North America might adopt an attitude of indifference to Asia and decide to allow it to stew in its own juice, this cannot be the attitude of either Moscow or Canberra. Although there is, of course, a vast difference between the power potential of Australia and the Soviet Union, they have an equal interest in Asian affairs and many of their problems of living at peace with Asia may be similar. There are some Australians who may like to wash their hands of Asia and adopt a policy of 'fortress Australia', but it is inconceivable that over a long term Australia can practise 'isolationism' and be indifferent to Asian problems, or to India's role in Asia.

The involvement of Australia in Asian affairs is partly a guarantee that for Australia's sake, if for nothing else, many western powers will continue to take an interest in Asia. It is also certain that Australia will continue to wield some influence in the making of policies in

major western capitals; while some European countries may want the U.S.A. to be more Europe-oriented in its outlook, Australia's interests are in keeping that country involved in the affairs of Asia. If Australia can maintain some degree of influence over America's policies in Asia and if that influence is exerted in a way which is helpful for the economic development and political stability of Asia, many Asian countries may regard this as a matter of great importance.

From the Australian point of view, India may likewise appear as a country whose relations with the Soviet Union are a guarantee that the policies of that Super Power will be directed towards the achievement of a stable order in Asia. Although India's influence on the Soviet Union may be much less than Australia's on the United States, it is still of some significance that the nature of Soviet interests in southern Asia is determined by the terms of Indo-Soviet friendship. India not only wants the Soviet Union to be involved in the affairs of its region but it also wants that involvement to be of a particular kind. India's friendship with the Soviet Union helps to ensure that the power and influence of that country will be exerted for peace, stability and progress in Asia. India may not be able to influence Soviet behaviour in Asia decisively, but there are good reasons to believe that India has succeeded in persuading Moscow that it is in the Soviet Union's own interest to pursue a policy towards Asia which promotes peace and stability in the continent.

Unless a dramatic political change within India alters the country's world view, New Delhi is likely to feel concerned about the extension of the power and influence of any of the Great Powers in the South Asian region. It has already declared that it would prefer the maintenance of peace in the Indian Ocean to be the responsibility of a number of littoral states rather than to see the spread of either Soviet or American influence in the area. It has also made it clear that while it would welcome schemes of regional economic co-operation it would not be a party to any new security pact, sponsored by any Great Power. Although the possibility that India will unwittingly pave the way for the extension of an external power's influence in Asia cannot be entirely ruled out, it is impossible that any Indian government will see this as being in the country's self-interest. Historical factors apart, the very size of India makes it impossible for New Delhi to see itself in a subordinate role to any of the Great Powers.

Again, India and Australia are both middle powers, with a set of interests which are distinct from those of the Great Powers. It is not impossible that in the next few decades the delineation of the role and status of such powers will become one of the major issues of world politics. It is clear that a world order based on artificial division of the

27

nations into Big and Small would be inadequate for solving the broad problems of security and peace. The five Great Powers together would be able to enforce order as little as the two Super Powers have been. It is in the interest of all the middle powers to insert the question of their place in the world on the agenda of world politics. It is not accidental that both India and Australia have had reservations about the Non-Proliferation Treaty and as the world begins to grapple with the problems of structural reforms in the existing international order, nations like India and Australia may find it necessary to adopt similar postures on certain issues.

The most immediate and obvious reason for consultation and co-operation between India and Australia is that the two countries have a great deal of interest in the stability and progress of the smaller countries of South-East Asia. Addressing the Asian Relations Conference in New Delhi in 1947, Jawaharlal Nehru had said:

> We also welcome observers from Australia and New Zealand, because we have many problems in common, especially in the Pacific and the south-east region of Asia, and we have to cooperate together to find solutions.[10]

The problems of South-East Asia have changed since then but the need for Indo-Australian co-operation in that region remains. Both India and Australia wish to see political stability and economic prosperity in that area; both have stakes in the independence and integrity of all the states of the region, particularly Malaysia and Singapore,[11] both have an interest in mitigating local conflicts among these states; and both have indicated their desire to see a greater measure of regional co-operation among the nations of South-East Asia. There are many differences between the Australian and the Indian assessment of the needs of South-East Asian countries; Australia is much more directly concerned with the defence problems of those countries while India's main interest is in economic co-operation. But stability in South-East Asia is regarded by both as of great importance to their own future.

India and Australia would have been greatly interested in South-East Asian problems even if there had been no fear about the future role of China in that area; the fact that such a fear exists in both countries has further underlined the identity of their interests in the area. On the face of it, India and Australia still view the China problem differently. India wants the United States and other countries to recognize China and believes that the problem of dealing with China will be simpler if that country is accepted as an important member of the international community. Australia does not recognize China and shows no public inclination to do so before the United States

begins to review its policies. But in reality the attitudes of the two countries to China is not so dissimilar. India has an immediate and direct threat to its security from China. Australia for her part is quite keen to do business with it. In fact, both India and Australia are interested in coexisting with China; both are prepared to recognize that it has certain legitimate interests as a great power in Asia; but both are interested in preventing the establishment of China's, or for that matter any other power's, hegemony over South-East Asia.

Another area of common interest for India and Australia is the Indian Ocean. It is generally felt in India that the security of the Indian Ocean area should be left to the countries bordering the ocean;[12] both India and Australia are such nations. India wants its own Navy to be capable of guarding the country's long coastline and to protect its islands in the Bay of Bengal; but it has neither the capability for, nor the interest in, any wider role for its Navy in the Indian Ocean. It hopes that the naval forces of the other countries around the Indian Ocean should be able to undertake similarly defensive roles and that in no event will the Indian Ocean be converted into an area of conflict among the Great Powers.

It has been complained by some perceptive Australians that India has been indifferent to Australia in the past and that while Australia continued to attach great importance to India, the latter has tended to regard it as insignificant and irrelevant.[13] It is true that for many years Indo-Australian relations have not been as close or cordial as they could have been. Australia has been regarded by many in India as too closely identified with the major western powers to pursue an independent policy in Asia; its immigration policies were not appreciated by Indians; its role in the U.N. and in the Commonwealth have often been different from India's; unlike Canada, it had not distinguished itself by adopting a liberal attitude to certain issues of world politics like colonial and racial problems. These factors, coupled with the failure of the leaders of the two countries to establish a personal equation, have often proved to be serious obstacles to closer Indo-Australian relations. But it is easy to overlook certain facts which suggest much greater Indian interest in Australia.

India attached a good deal of importance to the participation of Australia and New Zealand in the eighteen-nation conference on Indonesia in New Delhi in 1949, and it found Australia's attitude extremely helpful. It was also felt to be highly desirable to reassure Australia and New Zealand during that period that India's concept of Asian co-operation was not directed against any non-Asian power and had no racial overtones. Similarly, at the time of the Bandung confer-

ence Nehru made a special point of sending 'our greetings' to Australia and New Zealand. He went further and said:

And indeed Australia and New Zealand are almost in our region. They certainly do not belong to Europe, much less to America. They are next to us and I should like Australia and New Zealand to come nearer to Asia. I would welcome them because I do not want what we do or say to be based on racial prejudices. We have had enough of this racialism elsewhere.[14]

In his statement to the Indian Parliament on the Bandung conference on 30 April 1955 he again referred to this part of his speech at the conference and referred to Australia and New Zealand as 'our neighbours ... for whom we have nothing but the most fraternal feelings'.[15]

During this period India had also been co-operating with Australia in the Colombo Plan and had itself received valuable assistance from that country. In fact, India and Australia played leading roles in initiating the Colombo Plan, proceeding from their common assumption that the long-term answer to many of Asia's immediate political problems lay in rapid economic growth and social change. Though in absolute terms the aid from Australia to India's economic development has been much less than that from some other developed countries, it has been noted in India with great satisfaction that India is the principal recipient of Australian external aid, barring the Trust Territory under Australian administration.[16]

It is hoped in India that Australia will be able to help India's development through increased trade between the two countries rather than through aid alone.[17] Although Australia is already one of India's major trading partners, the volume of trade between the two countries has fluctuated between Rs. 350 and Rs. 450 million in the last decade, except in 1966-67 when it rose to Rs. 800 million because of large Australian exports of wheat both under aid and commercial purchases. There is much scope for further expansion of Indo-Australian trade, if the two governments make a concerted attempt to explore ways of doing this. The Australian government has taken the lead in increasing trade relations with developing countries and has initiated special trade preference in their favour. This has greatly improved Australia's image in the developing world and increased India's hopes about trade with Australia.[18] It would be of great help to India if more items were placed on the list of preferential duty free imports. Another field in which Indo-Australian economic co-operation could prove highly beneficial to India is that of joint industrial ventures.

It is true that for some years in the 1950s India appeared much more concerned with the broader issues of world politics, like Soviet-

American relations, than with the regional problems of Asian politics. Its relations with Australia, as indeed with many other Asian countries, were viewed then as only of secondary importance. This imbalance of emphasis in Indian foreign policy was clearly demonstrated after 1962 and India's leaders have shown a great deal of awareness of the importance of its immediate and distant neighbours in Asia and Australasia in subsequent years. The leaders of the Indian government have repeatedly visited the capitals of South and South-East Asian countries. Throughout the country there is now a greater concern about the affairs of South-East Asia. This has also led to an increasing awareness of the importance of Australia, of which the Indian Prime Minister's visit to Canberra in May 1968 was one manifestation. Since 1967 the two countries have held periodic consultations through meetings of their high officials and both governments appear to be satisfied with the results of these meetings.

It is not necessary to pretend that India and Australia have now begun to perceive all major international problems in an identical manner. There are important differences between them on many world issues, and some of these differences are likely to persist for a long time. It is apparent, however, that there has been a perceptible improvement in Indo-Australian relations in recent years and both countries are now more aware of their common problems and interests. It can be hoped that the strengthening of Indo-Australian relations will prove to be one of the helpful factors in the search for peace and stability in Asia.

CHAPTER 3

Indonesia and Australia

J. A. C. MACKIE

Although Indonesia has bulked large in Australian thinking about its security and foreign policies in relation to the South-East Asian region since 1945, surprisingly little attention has ever been given in Australia to the questions of what Indonesians think about it, how they see its role in the international politics of the region or how far their visions of Indonesia's future and Australia's coincide or diverge.[1] Yet the answers to these questions deserve consideration, since they are bound to affect the course of relations between the two states to some degree. One may be sceptical about the importance of popular attitudes and fickle sentiments of friendship or hostility as factors influencing the foreign policies of nations, but it is a truism that one of the significant factors influencing the course of relations between any two countries is the general image each holds of the other and the impressions prevailing in each about the reasons why the other is behaving in the way it is. The case for seeking 'better understanding of our neighbours', that worthy platitude of public speakers, can be supported not only by the idealistic hope that the causes of hatred and conflict may ultimately be extinguished, but also by the more bluntly realistic consideration that the people who make or influence foreign policy in any country should have an accurate perception of how their counterparts in another are likely to interpret or assess whatever they do or say.

Unfortunately one cannot summarize Indonesian views of Australia and its foreign policies briefly, partly because there is rarely any explicit and systematic discussion in Indonesia of its relations with Australia, partly because Indonesian views about foreign policy in general are so diverse. It is tempting to assert bluntly that Indonesians do not give much attention to Australia at all, that what most of them know about this country is as limited and inaccurate as most Australians know about Indonesia, that the contacts between the two countries, whether commercial, cultural or merely social, are so few and tenuous as to be insignificant and that Indonesia's foreign policies have been determined far more by its reaction to those countries which

have concerned it directly (the Netherlands, Britain, U.S.A., Russia, China, Japan) than by any considerations of the relatively slight influence Australia might bring to bear either for or against its interests. But while this is part of the truth, it is by no means the whole truth.

Australia has not been in the past, and probably is not now, a negligible factor in the policy calculations of Indonesia's leaders. Sometimes it has been able to assist their policies in important ways, as in 1945-49 and since 1966, sometimes to inconvenience them, as between 1959 and 1965. On the whole, however, it has not been regarded as a serious threat to Indonesia's interests and aspirations or as a very substantial impediment to them, although Indonesians have felt threatened by other countries from time to time, including those with whom Australia has been closely allied. Indonesians generally have not given much attention to their east and south-east (except when their costly preoccupation with West Irian has drawn their gaze in that direction—and even then to a rather limited extent) : the thinly populated eastern islands of the archipelago are economically underdeveloped and politically uninfluential, far removed from Djakarta's more weighty problems, in rather the same way as Australia's north-west is remote from Canberra's. The two countries are, as it were, facing away from each other in their most pressing domestic and international concerns. But from time to time, each has had to take account of the other in its foreign policy calculations.

What can be said with some degree of certainty is that Indonesian views of Australia have been and will be mainly determined by the general outlines of its foreign policy in the widest sense, rather than by any intrinsic features of the bilateral relationship.[2] Because there are so few particular points of contact and potential friction between the two countries (apart from the special problem of New Guinea, which will have to be examined in due course), so little trade or investment and, at present, no major issues in dispute, Indonesia has no need for 'an Australia policy' with separate parameters from its overall foreign policy. (This is not quite so true of Australia, which must have an 'Indonesia policy' of sorts. In this, as in many other respects, the relations between the two are not symmetrical, that is, not mere mirror-images of each other.) The broad ideological underpinnings of Indonesian foreign policy have always been particularly important in shaping its responses to events, especially in the late Soekarno era, when his doctrine of the 'New Emerging Forces' strongly coloured Indonesian attitudes and reactions to international developments. Fortunately for Australia, however, they did not entirely determine Indonesian views of it even at that time, for some of the goodwill towards Australians accruing from an earlier, more cordial phase of

Australian-Indonesian relations still persisted and Australia was not categorized in quite the same terms as Indonesia's 'neo-colonialist and imperialist' adversaries of that period. There cannot, of course, be any certainty that this will happen again, if there is a major ideological swing in Indonesia away from the present low-keyed policies of the Suharto regime towards something more reminiscent of Soekarno's noisy radicalism; but there are some reasons for being cautiously hopeful that this is unlikely to happen for some time to come.

This Chapter is mainly concerned with the ways in which Indonesian policies and attitudes towards Australia have been influenced by the broader framework of Indonesia's foreign relations at various periods since 1945. It is a prolegomenon to the proper analysis of Indonesian perceptions of Australia, a preliminary sketching of some of the major formative experiences influencing them. It is not a comprehensive study of the various ways in which Indonesians have reacted to Australian actions and statements. Ideally, such an analysis would not only present the problem as seen through Indonesian eyes, from the other side of the Arafura Sea and within the context of Indonesia's broader foreign policy concerns, but it would also include some discussion of the ways in which Indonesians visualize their place in the world around them. For it is quickly apparent that even the most westernized Indonesians do not always share some of the common assumptions that an Australian, European or American might make about the dynamics of international relations in the mid-twentieth century. While many Indonesian diplomats and political leaders have a sophisticated and wide-ranging appreciation of the forces shaping international politics, their sensitiveness and experience have been developed in areas rather different from those which are familiar to the average Australian politician. And even the most cosmopolitan of them finds it very difficult entirely to transcend the patterns of thinking that have been shaped by his cultural background and early consciousness of the kind of world in which he lives. The influence of traditional notions is, of course, much greater among the less thoroughly westernized politicians, journalists, intellectuals and the 'newspaper reading public' in Indonesia to whom their leaders must make their foreign policies acceptable. But we still know far too little about the interaction of traditional and modern perceptions of the world in transitional societies such as Indonesia's. Recent studies have shown how misleading it is to apply modern political terminology to traditional Javanese concepts of the state or of the nature of political power, which belong to a very different universe of ideas.[3] This is not the place to explore such problems but it is to be hoped

that further research will soon give us something more than a flatly two-dimensional representation of Indonesian views of other countries.

It is well known that Australia built up a considerable store of goodwill in Indonesia by the support it gave in various ways during its struggle for independence against the Dutch during the late 1940s, at a point when the newly established Republic had few other influential friends in the international community. Ironically, Indonesian views of Australian sympathy for their cause were probably exaggerated grossly at the time, for neither government policy nor public opinion in Australia were at all strongly committed to the cause of Indonesian independence, despite various gestures which seemed to indicate that they were, such as the Waterside Workers' ban on Dutch ships carrying arms to the Dutch forces there, the Chifley government's mild support for a greater measure of self-government for the former colony, its initiative in supporting the Indonesian Republic at the United Nations after the first 'police action' in July 1947 and the later sympathetic attitude of the Australian representatives on the U.N. Commission for Indonesia, Judge Kirby and Mr T. C. Critchley. It could be argued that these gestures were of relatively minor importance in contributing to the final victory of the Republic in comparison with the pressure exerted by the U.S.A. in 1949, when the U.S. Senate threatened to cut off Marshall Plan aid to the Netherlands if it continued its campaign of military force in Indonesia; and it can easily be shown that the Chifley government's policy was directed towards something far short of the fully independent Indonesia which came into being in December 1949.[4] But few Indonesians seem to have been aware of these qualifications to the general picture of Australia as one of their foremost supporters in the struggle against Dutch colonialism and it came as a shock even to the politicians and newspapermen of Djakarta to find later that not only the conservative Menzies government but also Dr Evatt and the Labor Party bluntly opposed Indonesia's claim to West New Guinea (West Irian).

We do not have enough evidence to reconstruct a picture of how in the years 1945-49 the leading Indonesians of that period visualized Australia's role in the international drama in which they were involved. Presumably there were substantial differences between the views of the Central National Committee (K.N.I.P.) which formally voted a motion of thanks to the Australian people in November 1945, and those of Prime Minister Sjahrir late in 1946, after Dr Evatt had turned down his first request that Australia bring the Indonesia question before the U.N.: or between the assessments of those officials and leaders, including Soekarno, who had close contact with sympathetic

35

and influential Australian representatives at the U.N. or on the Good Offices Commission, and of the orthodox communists of 1948 who saw Indonesia's struggle primarily within the framework of the wider Cold War conflict between the communist and capitalist blocs, wherein Australia was very small beer. We do know that Indonesia's politicians tended to judge the actions of other countries then and now primarily in the light of their bearing upon its own most pressing preoccupations, which at that time meant the struggle against the Dutch. Being anti-colonialist and Marxist in their political philosophies, most of them were strongly influenced in their view of the world by the dichotomy between the capitalist, colonial powers and the communist, anti-imperialist bloc—although neither American nor Australian support for Indonesia could be entirely explained in these terms. Australia had a Labor government at the time which professed socialist principles that seemed to conform closely to the warmly egalitarian and doctrinally eclectic enthusiasm generated by the revolution within Indonesia itself. It would have been easy for Indonesians to believe that both countries were guided by much the same values and principles. Moreover, Australia's policies in the Indonesian-Dutch conflict revealed substantial independence of both Britain and the U.S.A., so it could not be regarded simply as a satellite of one of the Cold War antagonists, as it was sometimes categorized later on. In fact its very independence of the greater powers, as well as its sympathy for a people struggling for independence, commended it strongly to the Indonesian Republican leaders. It was significant that Australia was one of the two countries chosen to sponsor Indonesia's admission to the United Nations in 1950. And while sentiments of this kind are too evanescent to constitute a firm basis for a foreign policy, it is noteworthy that President Soekarno's view of Australia continued to be influenced, even during the crisis years 1963-65, by the picture he built up at that time.

During the decade after 1949, however, the position changed radically. On the two issues which coloured Indonesian thinking about foreign affairs most strongly, the West Irian issue and non-alignment in the ideological struggle between the communist and western blocs, they found that the Menzies government was ranging Australia in opposition to Indonesia time and again. This did not immediately dissipate the goodwill that was still felt towards Australia, which was preserved to some extent by the establishment of personal ties with the *élite* in Djakarta through Colombo Plan scholarships and training schemes. But the realization that Australia was not as 'progressive' in its approach to the newly independent nations as many Indonesians had believed in the palmy days of the struggle for independence

brought a degree of disillusionment in some quarters. Moreover, Indonesian views of the outside world became increasingly stereotyped by Cold War preoccupations as the decade progressed; left-wing parties tended to look upon all SEATO powers as virtual satellites of the U.S.A., while even their opponents clung to the doctrine of non-alignment, in terms of which Australia belonged to the imperialist bloc and Indonesia to the non-aligned. There were many differences of emphasis, of course, as to the depth of Australia's imperialist dye, but in any case this did not much matter, except on the issue of West New Guinea. The main determinants of Indonesian foreign policy and perceptions of the world order were its attitudes towards the leaders of the three great blocs. SEATO was a convenient whipping-boy for all parties in the late 1950s as an instrument of U.S. interventionism. Some of the opprobrium it evoked must have rubbed off to Australia's detriment, particularly at the time of the threat of U.S. intervention in the Indonesian regional crisis of 1957-58.[5] Charges were then made of Australian involvement in some of the cloak-and-dagger operations to assist the rebels, but the Djuanda government did not take cognizance of them and the efforts of the Indonesian Communist Party (P.K.I.) to generate strong antagonism to the SEATO powers were, on the whole, not very successful. More damage was done to Australia's reputation in Indonesia by its increasingly close identification with the Dutch over West New Guinea.

The years 1958-62 constituted a bleak and depressing period of Australian-Indonesian relations, mainly because of the mounting tensions created by the dispute between Indonesia and the Netherlands over West Irian, but also because of a more general Australian distrust of Soekarno's regime and reluctance to have anything more to do with it than necessary. To the Indonesians Australia appeared to be the most fervent supporter of the Dutch cause, although its role in the affair was deemed to be less crucial than that of the U.S.A. whose formal neutrality amounted, until early 1962, to acceptance of the *status quo* which favoured the Dutch. Both Foreign Minister Subandrio and Nasution, the Chief of Staff of the Army, made visits to Australia in vain efforts to induce the Menzies government to modify its policies, apparently in the hope that this might lead the Dutch to abandon their stubborn resistance to negotiations on the issue: but it is doubtful that they ever had very high expectations of achieving much from this direction, since it was realized in informed circles in Djakarta that Australia in fact had relatively little influence with the Dutch government and was not prepared to urge it to negotiate.[6] But in other quarters, where the reasons for Australia's stubborn resistance to the Indonesian claim were not appreciated, the suspicion

37

became current that Australia's motive in the affair must be to gain ultimate control of West New Guinea itself; such suspicions were based upon their interpretations of the 1957 Dutch-Australian agreement on administrative co-operation in New Guinea, on talk in unofficial but influential Australian circles about a 'Melanesian Federation' and on some of the wilder statements of the anti-Indonesian right wing at that time, such as the bizarre suggestion in February 1959 by Mr Killen, M.P., a Liberal Party backbencher, that Australia should buy West New Guinea from the Dutch. Nevertheless, the West Irian issue did not, on the whole, arouse as much antagonism in Indonesia towards Australia as it aroused in Australia towards Indonesia, for the major focus of Indonesian hostility was the Netherlands, and the major fulcrum of its diplomatic leverage the U.S.A., whose policy and interests on this issue diverged considerably from Australia's.[7] Although a furore arose in the Australian press and parliament over the Subandrio-Casey joint statement of February 1959, the episode attracted little attention in Djakarta. The stock Indonesian response to Australian assertions that West New Guinea was in some way vital to Australia's security was simply to point out that Australia's best shield from aggression would be a stable and friendly Indonesia.

Australia's support for the Dutch stand weakened perceptibly in 1959-60 and thereafter the Menzies government was primarily concerned to ensure simply that Indonesia would not resort to force to regain West Irian, as its leaders were threatening in some of their statements. Soekarno and his ministers gave assurances to this effect in response to Australian queries on several occasions—but in 1962 they had no compunction about ignoring them when their campaign for the recovery of West Irian was intensified to a phase of armed incursions and overt military threats, which served Soekarno's primary purpose of inclining the U.S. government towards applying pressure on the Dutch to negotiate a transfer of control over the territory. In the face of Indonesia's more bellicose approach to the West Irian issue, the Australian Minister for External Affairs, Sir Garfield Barwick, endeavoured early in 1962 to extricate his government from its rigid and fruitless anti-Indonesian position before it was too late.[8] Despite clamorous opposition from the Australian press and the Labor Party, he modified Australian policy towards a relatively calm acceptance of the transfer of West Irian into Indonesia's hands just in time to avoid collision courses with Indonesia during the heated controversies of 1962. And as soon as the dispute was settled, Barwick set out to rebuild more cordial relations with Soekarno's government on a new footing by supporting a U.S.-sponsored programme of

foreign aid and economic stabilization which, it was hoped, would turn Indonesia's energies away from 'foreign adventures' towards the more prosaic tasks of national development. Unfortunately, this programme had barely been launched in early 1963 before it was wrecked on the rocks of Indonesia's 'confrontation' of Malaysia.

Indonesia's conflict with Malaysia in the years 1963-66 proved to be an even more tense and dangerous phase of Indonesian-Australian relations, since on this occasion Australia stood firm by its commitment to Malaysia. At one stage Australian troops were directly engaged in military operations against Indonesian infiltrators on the Sarawak-Indonesia border. At the same time, however, both the Australian and Indonesian governments went to some lengths to avoid exacerbating or intensifying the dispute between them. 'Confrontation' was something less than a war (diplomatic relations were not severed between Indonesia and Britain, although British troops bore the brunt of Malaysia's defence and it was Britain's actions as much as Malaysia's which aggrieved the Indonesians), despite occasional raids into Sarawak and, for a brief period, the Malayan peninsula in the hope of stimulating domestic insurgency there. The reasons for Indonesia's campaign were much more complex than in the struggle for West Irian, but one of the most important was the intensely ideological nature of Soekarno's foreign policy at that time, based on the doctrine of necessary struggle between the progressive New Emerging Forces of the world and the reactionary Old Established Forces, especially the 'neo-colonialists and imperialists' (*Nekolim*).[9] Since Britain and its 'puppet', Malaysia, were castigated as dyed-in-the-wool *Nekolim* enemies of the Indonesian revolution, it might have been expected that Australia would be similarly castigated and subjected to the hot blast of Soekarno's displeasure. Curiously—and perhaps significantly—it was not. Australia was included from time to time in Indonesia's ritual denunciations of Malaysia and its protectors, but in a rather perfunctory manner. The reasons for this attitude deserve attention.

In the first place, it was clear that the Australian government was anxious to prevent escalation of the Malaysia conflict, even though it was committed to support for Malaysia. Australian Colombo Plan aid to Indonesia continued and a normal interchange of people and opinions was maintained as long as possible. Although Australia was under considerable pressure from Britain and Malaysia to send more troops to Malaysia, the government was obviously reluctant to provide combat troops who might find themselves shooting and being shot at by Indonesians on the Sarawak border, which would have inflamed public opinion on both sides; not until February 1965 were

39

Australian infantry battalions sent to the Sarawak front. In the early stages of confrontation, Australia had endeavoured to play a peace-keeping role between Indonesia and Britain-Malaysia, urging the latter to take Soekarno's objections to Malaysia more seriously than they were inclined to at a time when there was still a chance that diplomacy might avert the drift towards violence and subversion. Although Sir Garfield Barwick's policy of fence-mending came to nought when Soekarno decided to 'intensify confrontation' after the mob attacks on British and Malaysian embassies following Malaysia's creation in September 1963, Soekarno and Subandrio looked on Australia's support for Malaysia in a very different light from Britain's. The Australians had taken Indonesia seriously and tried to understand its position, in Soekarno's view, whereas the British were bluntly hostile to it and had belittled or humiliated it. Soekarno's attitude towards Australia was one of sorrow rather than anger at that time: Australians were not being true to their national character, as they had been in 1945-49. They were sheltering under the umbrella of British power and allowing themselves to be manipulated by the British imperialists.[10] But Australia was not excoriated as a *Nekolim* power—in fact, Soekarno and Subandrio are said to have admitted in so many words that it was not—and only on one occasion, in April 1965, did Soekarno make a vague threat that Australia might incur Indonesia's displeasure.

One major difference between Australia's position *vis-à-vis* Indonesia and Britain's was, of course, that the Australians could not be forced to go right away, as the British could. One of the few specific objectives of 'confrontation' was to make the British position in Malaysia untenable and so hasten the withdrawal of British forces. But Australia's right to be concerned by what happened in the region was not denied—and there were no advantages to be gained from pin-pricking military raids against northern Australia of the sort that were being attempted in Malaysia. Another factor of some importance was Australia's link to the U.S.A. through ANZUS, which might conceivably have brought about U.S. involvement if the conflict had escalated. But there were few indications that this consideration weighed significantly with the Indonesian authorities in their determination of the course of strategy of 'confrontation', though it may have been a background factor. In short, for a number of reasons it suited Soekarno as well as the Australian government to keep relations between the two countries low-keyed and as cordial as possible in the circumstances.

On the whole, Indonesian press and public opinion took much the same view. The P.K.I. and its allies were occasionally more vociferous

in their verbal attacks on Australian policies, but the main objective of the P.K.I. at that time was to cast the U.S.A. in the role of principal enemy of the Indonesian revolution. Britain and its allies, including Australia, were regarded as comparatively subordinate factors. Among the anti-communists, many of whom were secretly anxious to be rid of a dispute which was working so much to the advantage of the P.K.I., the predominant attitude to Australia was one of dismay and perplexity that it would not use its diplomatic influence, especially with its great and mighty friends, to push Malaysia into a compromise settlement on the basis of a return to the Maphilindo concept.[11] Australia's security, like Indonesia's was threatened primarily by the communist menace from the north, they would argue; why, then, did Australians not recognize that their true national interests lay in promoting a strong, non-communist Indonesia, rather than supporting a weak reed like Malaysia?

After the downfall of Soekarno in 1966 and the ending of confrontation, Indonesia's relations with Australia improved dramatically, in accordance with the radical reversal of the ideological orientations and foreign policies of the Soekarno era. Once again, Indonesian attitudes towards Australia tended to be influenced more by its broader ideological and political dispositions rather than by any particular features of the relationship between the two countries, although the new era offered greater scope than the previous one for building up more significant links between them, links which might in the course of time help to develop a greater degree of interaction and interdependence, or, at the very least, more favourable views of each other among the top policy-makers of both governments.

The Australian government was quick to welcome the new course taken by the Suharto regime in 1966, signalized by its strongly anti-communist stance in domestic affairs, its restoration of Indonesia's earlier 'non-aligned' or 'active and independent' foreign policy and its attempts to curb inflation and rehabilitate the economy in conformity with the financial orthodoxy recommended by the I.M.F.[12] Australian diplomats played an active part on Indonesia's behalf in the negotiations which led to the rescheduling of its debts to the western creditor nations and in inducing them to extend substantial foreign aid to it (rising from $US250 million in 1967 to $US600 million in 1970 (approx. $A225 million to $A545 million)), through the Intergovernmental Group on Indonesia (I.G.G.I.), without which the new regime would have had little hope of stabilizing the economy. Early in 1968 Australia's own foreign aid contribution was doubled, from approximately $A5 million to $A10.4 million, so that its aid to Indonesia came to assume a significantly larger proportion

41

of Australia's total foreign aid than did aid to any other country with the exception of Papua-New Guinea. In 1970 the Australian government undertook a three-year aid commitment to Indonesia amounting to $A54 million, in line with the I.G.G.I. decision to give the Indonesian government an advance guarantee of the total foreign aid it can count on during the period of its five-year development plan. Here again, it is Australia's support for the principle which is noteworthy rather than the comparatively modest sum contributed.

These tokens of good neighbourliness were welcomed by Indonesian officials, and have helped to consolidate more cordial relations. But there is another side of the picture also. The limits of Australian aid, as well as its extent, have attracted attention in Djakarta. Official expressions of gratitude have often been tempered by private indications of puzzlement and disappointment that Australia's financial contribution to Indonesia's economic recovery has not been a good deal greater, in view of the importance Australians say they attach to it. Japan, Germany and the Netherlands have been giving Indonesia substantially more foreign aid—even on a proportional basis—and investing much more private capital there—although their stake in its stability is not nearly as immediate as Australia's. The very hesitant response of Australian businessmen to the Indonesian government's call for more foreign private investment there—understandable though it may be in view of all the circumstances—has seemed also, in the eyes of at least some Indonesians, incommensurate with Australia's obvious prosperity and its obsession with regional defence against the threat of communism.

How far the attitudes of Indonesia's leaders towards Australia have been influenced by these recent developments can only be guessed. One noteworthy feature of the years 1967-68 was the beginning of a mini-discovery of Australia by a number of influential Indonesian visitors, several of whom expressed surprise at its wealth and technological advancement, which they saw as holding out unforeseen possibilities of economic, technical or educational co-operation. The trickle of Indonesian visitors to Australia, while by no means new, has increased perceptibly since 1966; more importantly, the atmosphere on both sides has been much more conducive to attempts at greater international exchange than before. Presumably this has increased the degree of awareness in Djakarta *élite* circles, as compared with the Soekarno era, that there may be practical advantages in building up closer links with Australia and taking some pains to preserve cordial relations in all spheres. More active efforts are being made on both sides to promote trade, although there is not much likelihood of any substantial increase in the immediate future: nevertheless, Indon-

esian businessmen are now more cost-conscious than they were during the years of inflation, so that Australia's proximity could prove a more important factor than hitherto if shipping services can be improved. The recent interest of the Western Australian government in opening a shipping connection with Tjilatjap, on the south coast of Central Java, is one of the most noteworthy developments in this respect, although it is a very modest beginning.[13]

Increased contacts of this kind should presumably help to create sentiments of friendship and bonds of mutual interest, as well as to break down some of the ignorance and misunderstanding that exist in both countries. In so far as the trade and human intercourse it promotes has been a major force for international understanding, one may hope that much more will be done to link the interests and destinies of the two countries more closely in future. But these gains will not weigh very heavily in the balance of factors that influence government policies at a more immediately political level, since there are bound to be issues on which the two governments could find themselves at odds. And they certainly will not weigh in Australia's favour if closer contact merely results in disillusionment and disappointment, in too blatant a discrepancy between Australian niggardliness and affluence, its words and its deeds, or the expectations Australia encourages and the level of achievement it helps to make possible.

There are three sets of issues which might have created friction between the Australian and Indonesian governments since 1966 if either had been disposed to embarrass or inconvenience the other, but which have fortunately been kept safely within manageable proportions, so that more amicable relations could be established in other spheres. They are the problems of regional security arrangements, of the retention of Australian forces in Malaysia and Singapore and of New Guinea, both the eastern and western halves. One may hope that both governments will continue to prevent situations from arising in which they will find themselves committed to conflicting courses of action. But wishful thinking on these matters is a poor substitute for clear-sighted recognition of the circumstances which have made it possible to cope successfully with these potentially abrasive issues and of the different ways in which they have been seen in Indonesia and Australia.

In their approaches to the problem of regional security, the Indonesian and Australian governments have found themselves in much closer agreement since 1966 than during the previous decade, when the respective attitudes to SEATO, to non-alignment and to the immediacy of the communist threat led them into quite different

camps. Because of the strongly anti-communist cast of Indonesia's domestic policies since the downfall of Soekarno and the dramatic deterioration of its relations with China (and, to a lesser extent, the Soviet Union), there has seemed to be a close similarity of interests and views in Djakarta and Canberra regarding the desirable conditions of regional security. The Indonesian government has not been disposed to look critically upon Australia's close association with the U.S.A., or even upon its efforts to encourage the prolongation of an American military presence in the area. In fact these efforts have probably not been unwelcome to some of the more hardened realists and militant anti-communists in Djakarta who regard the Americans in Vietnam as an important counterweight to communist power in the region. This should probably be regarded as a recessive rather than a dominant strain in Indonesian thinking about regional security and it would be a mistake for Australians to draw the inference that the common interest in warding off communist encroachments entails a very deep or abiding similarity of aims. There are still significant differences of views as to how regional security should best be promoted, differences which have been of no great political significance in the years 1966-69, but which could again make for divergent policies if the major issues and configurations of South-East Asian politics changed substantially.

The essential difference between the two approaches to the problem of regional security is most clearly symbolized in the fact that Australia is a member of the Asian and Pacific Council (ASPAC) (and, still, of SEATO), but not of the Association of South-East Asian nations (ASEAN), and that it relies heavily on its bilateral alliance with the U.S.A., through ANZUS, as the sheet anchor for its defence, whereas Indonesia has clung to its more traditional themes of non-alignment and regional co-operation through ASEAN. The Foreign Minister, Adam Malik, has side-stepped attempts to draw Indonesia into ASPAC and resisted pressures to convert ASEAN into a regional security association. His stress upon ASEAN and 'regionalism' as central pillars of Indonesia's foreign policy has so far been couched in rather vague terms of mutual co-operation in economic, cultural and general political matters, but not of specific defence arrangements. Malik has invoked Indonesia's traditional principle of non-alignment to avoid being manoeuvred into entangling alliances or ranged too obviously in an anti-Chinese camp; he has been careful not to exacerbate Indonesia's relations with China more than necessary, despite the suspension of diplomatic relations with it in 1967.[14] Since he appears to be confident that there is no reason to fear any outside attack on Indonesia in the immediate future, the primary aim

of his policy is to minimize the influence of the Great Powers (including Japan) in South-East Asia by stressing that regional co-operation can deal with the so-called 'power vacuum' being left by the withdrawal of British and American forces. In contrast to Australia's concern for security arrangements based on cast-iron guarantees, Indonesia has sought merely to establish a framework within which political solutions may be sought to regional problems. ASEAN represents an aspiration towards regional co-operation, an ideal rather than a substantial structure, but in so far as it provides a stage on which Indonesia can play out its desired role of political leadership in the region, its very diffuseness of aims is presumably an asset to Indonesia. Indonesian politics abounds with instances of the proclamation of desirable principles and ideals which remain to be 'implemented' in unspecified ways, but to which, in the meantime, general assent can be expected. The mode of thought derives from a different intellectual tradition to the Australian, but it suits Indonesian purposes well enough, here and elsewhere.

The Indonesian official attitude towards Australia's policies on regional security since 1966 could best be described as one of tacit acceptance, but certainly not of close association. Australia still belongs too obviously to a different, non-Asian world.[15] The Australian tendency to see questions of security almost entirely in military terms, involving close association with outside powers, is still very far from the Indonesian approach. Consequently, suggestions made in Australia in 1967-68 that perhaps it should seek membership of ASEAN (in the hope of proclaiming its identity as a part of the region, or of staking a claim to a voice in its councils), or that ASEAN and ASPAC should be merged into one greater regional bloc, were never likely to win enthusiastic support in Djakarta. As the matter was put by Soedjatmoko in 1967 when asked a question about Australia's acceptability in regional co-operation arrangements (and he is one of the most amenable of Indonesians in his willingness to contemplate its participation), 'It is not a question of whether we can regard you as part of Asia, but whether you yourselves will be able to feel a part of this continent'. It is probably no exaggeration to say that until Indonesian leaders are convinced on that score (if, indeed, they can be convinced), they will be reluctant to associate very closely with Australia's security policies, although they will no doubt continue to prefer that the two nations' immediate paths run broadly parallel, as they have since 1966, rather than at cross purposes. At the very least, a formal association could leave them vulnerable to criticism at home and limit their policy options if the domestic political situation changed.

45

It was presumably for reasons of this kind that Prime Minister Gorton's rather clumsy bid for an Australian-Indonesian non-aggression pact in June 1968 came to nought. Though it might have been advantageous from his and from Australia's point of view, it offered little attraction to President Suharto—and the very idea of a non-aggression pact seemed to imply a degree of suspicion that one or both parties might be disposed to commit aggression, as one Djakarta newspaper pointed out in an aggrieved tone.[16] The story of that rather ineptly handled episode, and of the suddenly conceived cultural agreement which was offered as an alternative, is still somewhat obscure. But it does suggest that the pattern of Australian-Indonesian relations will probably be made up of a few concrete manifestations of economic and educational co-operation, accompanied by general declarations of goodwill, rather than by formal political engagements, simply because of the substantial differences in outlook upon regional and world politics.

Another issue on which Indonesian and Australian views might prove to be divergent, but so far have not been, is that created by Australia's defence commitments to Malaysia and Singapore. Adam Malik has repeatedly stated that Indonesia has no objections to the stationing of Australian troops in Malaysia-Singapore and their continuation there since he characterizes this as a Commonwealth obligation that is acceptable to Indonesia. Some other Indonesians have been more critical of it, however, and one cannot be entirely confident that Malik's use of the convenient Commonwealth fiction would survive if this aspect of his policy were vigorously challenged at home. In view of the intensity of nationalist and anti-colonialist sentiments in Indonesia over the last two decades and the suspicion attaching to any suggestion of 'neo-colonialist' influence, of which the presence of foreign military forces or bases would be an obvious symbol, it would not have been surprising if the Suharto government had expressed some opposition to the notion that Australia might take over part of the British defence role in Malaysia when the idea was being scouted actively in 1967-68 and it still seemed possible that substantial Australian ground forces might be kept there after 1971, as well as air and naval units. Indonesians were well aware of the answer most commonly given in Australia, Singapore and Malaysia to the embarrassing question: against whom are these forces likely to be required to defend Malaysia or Singapore? The very fact that Australia seemed to be disposing its military and diplomatic resources in the region against Indonesia could easily be held to imply a lack of trust in Indonesia, despite the ending of confrontation. It would not have been difficult for opponents of the Suharto regime—or even for

members of the regime looking for a pretext to attack Adam Malik's policies—to stir up nationalist resentment on this issue, appealing either to the left-wing nationalists who had formerly supported President Soekarno and his anti-western slogans or to fire-eating radicals in the Army. While these groups have not appeared likely to constitute any immediate threat to the Suharto government over the last two or three years, the possibility that they might do so cannot be entirely overlooked. This consideration presumably weighed heavily with Prime Minister Gorton in 1968-69 as he began to back away from the commitment to retain ground forces in Malaysia and, simultaneously, to put more stress on building up good relations with Indonesia. He has, moreover, seemed less enthusiastic than his predecessors about Australia's previously very close association, amounting almost to a 'special relationship' with Malaysia and Singapore. While it must be admitted that the reasons why the Kuala Lumpur and Singapore governments were so anxious for Australian ground forces to be retained there after 1971 were both mixed and diffuse (having as much to do with their desire for psychological reassurance and for tangible evidence of having allies as with an actual need for either combat troops or a 'trip-wire' force to act as a deterrent against invasion or subversion), it can hardly be denied that apprehensions about Indonesia and the possibility of a reversion to confrontation-type hostility to its neighbours constituted a factor in their calculations, particularly after the deterioration of Singapore-Indonesian relations in October 1968.

To explain the lack of Indonesian protest at the stationing of Australian forces in Malaysia and Singapore one has to go beyond the formal reason given, the Commonwealth connection, and notice several other possible hypotheses, none of which can be assessed with any great precision. First, the very smallness of the Australian forces involved, at least of the ground troops, is probably an important factor.[17] They can hardly be regarded as a potential threat to Indonesia's security in the same way as the much larger British forces could, or even as a very significant symbol to affront nationalist susceptibilities. From the Indonesian government's point of view, there would hardly have been sufficient political benefit in a move to hasten the ending of an Australian presence to balance the diplomatic costs it would entail. Secondly, it has been very much on the cards that Australia's military role in the region may have to be reduced and would almost certainly not be maintained in the face of any substantial Indonesian hostility. Finally, some Indonesians of a less strongly 'anti-colonialist' stamp, or a more anti-communist one, appear to have had a much more favourable view of the Australian military

presence on the grounds that its links with the U.S.A. through ANZUS helped to ensure that the American military umbrella would be maintained between Indonesia and China.[18] It is hard to estimate how widely held or influential this view was, but one should beware of attaching too much weight to it. Probably more important was the realization in Djakarta in the early years of the Suharto government that Indonesia needed to maximize its neighbours' goodwill and to avoid arousing suspicions among potential creditors by a reversion to Soekarno-type policies. A few straws in the wind have suggested that Adam Malik's attitude on this issue may be changing slightly. Some of his recent statements have seemed less acquiescent than before, more inclined to regard the Australian presence in Malaysia-Singapore as a temporary and short-term expedient. As Indonesia begins to feel its way again more confidently towards a role of regional leadership (and to establish a more secure relationship with its creditors and aid donors), its complacence regarding the stationing of foreign troops in an area which it looks upon as in some way its own 'sphere of influence' through the ASEAN and ethnic connection must be expected to diminish. While further evidence will be needed to clarify Indonesian official attitudes in this matter, it would be short-sighted not to take account of such factors.

Finally, there is perhaps the thorniest problem which will affect the relations between Australia and Indonesia over the next few decades —the vexed question of New Guinea. Although the tensions and incidents that arose prior to the 1969 'act of free choice' in West Irian were dealt with in such a way as to avoid any serious strain between Djakarta and Canberra, there are still potential causes of friction over matters of border delineation, of refugees from West Irian seeking political asylum in the Australian half of the island and, in the longer term, of pan-New Guinean sentiment developing in both parts of the island. (It should be emphasized, however, that there have been very few manifestations of the latter sentiment so far; it is little more than a possibility, not an imminent prospect). The progress made since 1966 towards defining the border between the two halves of the island has helped to reduce the dangers, and underlined the desire of both governments to eliminate potential sources of friction before they arise; the work of the joint teams engaged in delineating the border has proceeded amicably and effectively.[19] There are people in both countries who realize that the real danger in New Guinea is likely to arise not so much from the ill will of the other government as from situations which might be engineered by discontented elements on either side seeking to put pressure on the authorities, either by embarrassing them (as in the matter of political refugees) or by

embroiling them in awkward international incidents. But one cannot be at all sure that either the Indonesian or Australian government (quite apart from a future government of independent Papua-New Guinea in the eastern half of the island) will be able to exercise sufficient control over events to prevent trouble from developing, even if they have the desire to do so. The processes of political mobilization are only just beginning on both sides of the New Guinea border and their dynamics are far from clear. The one prediction that can be made with some confidence is that the pace and direction of socio-political change in the two halves of the island will almost certainly be very different, and that this will probably create difficult problems for all parties concerned, particularly if pan-New Guinean sentiments are aroused in either territory.[20]

It would be absurd to claim that any clear pattern of Indonesian perceptions of the problems of New Guinea is discernible either among the *élite* of officials and intellectuals or among the wider 'political public'. But, as far as these affect Australia, two rather obvious generalizations may be made from which further refinements will follow. First, there is probably still a considerable legacy of distrust or misunderstanding among most Indonesians about the role Australia has played in the saga of West Irian, not only in the years before 1962 but also in the subsequent period leading up to the 1969 'act of free choice' there. Secondly, the Australian role in eastern New Guinea is generally regarded as a last lingering manifestation of colonialism, and hence is seen in much the same light as other examples of colonial rule elsewhere, with the same defects and presumed motivations. It is highly doubtful if many Indonesians see it as a form of benevolent trusteeship or regard the substantial Australian governmental expenditure in New Guinea as either altruism or generosity. With their strongly anti-colonialist sympathies, the central issue to them is simply that independence should not be withheld or delayed because of the old excuse that the people concerned are not ready for self-government. Whatever may be said against this in favour of Australia's administrative record in Papua-New Guinea, and bad though the record of Indonesian rule in West Irian may seem to Australian eyes, it is improbable that more than a tiny handful of Indonesian officials and intellectuals would regard rapid social or economic progress as counting for more than political freedom. To this extent, if troubles arise in the eastern half of New Guinea, Australian motives and achievements are likely to be seen in an unfavourable light by most Indonesians. Their point of view may change in time, as their own experience of the singularly difficult problems of

developing West Irian increases their awareness of the difficulties involved, but that is likely to be a slow process.

Fortunately for the course of Australian-Indonesian relations, the last chapter of the saga of West Irian was finished in 1969 without creating serious friction between the two governments. Some criticism was directed at Australia by the Djakarta press when various West Irian refugees were granted asylum in eastern New Guinea and some allegations were made that the anti-Indonesian Free Papua Organization (*Organisi Papua Merdeka* or O.P.M.) was finding support in Australia, as well as in the Netherlands and elsewhere. Australian press comment on the situation in West Irian and on Indonesian actions there was certainly critical, frequently sensational and in several instances distinctly hostile, reflecting the instinctive fears and ignorance of Indonesia that lie just below the surface of so much Australian thinking about that country. (In fairness, it should also be recorded that the better newspapers gave a much more balanced account of the problem than in 1962, reflecting their much greater awareness of the political realities.) Australian press comment on the extent of West Irian discontent with Indonesian administration probably attracted as much attention in Djakarta as the fact that the Australian government had no desire to see the West Irianese cast their choice against Indonesia. In fact, the Australian government's attitude to the whole episode was based upon a determination to avoid offending the Indonesian government or raising false hopes that it might support an independent West New Guinea, so much so that the Minister for External Affairs, then Mr Freeth, was accused by some Australian critics of having gone beyond his duty in the matter and having condoned a mockery of the principle of self-determination. It was clear from the government's cautious handling of the problems created by several episodes on the New Guinea border involving refugees from West Irian and, on at least two occasions, alleged violations of the border by Indonesian security forces, that the Australian authorities were acutely aware of the dangers of such episodes escalating and inflaming public opinion on both sides.[21] Fortunately they did not, so the 'act of free choice' was completed without serious complications. It may be premature to predict that the last has been heard of the dissidents in West Irian, but their most favourable opportunity for attracting international attention or involving Australia in a dispute with Indonesia over the principle of West New Guinea's self-determination has probably passed.

The greater danger in New Guinea will come in a few years, however, when East New Guinea advances further towards independence,

if the indigenous political leaders there decide to take up the cause of their brethren in West New Guinea. Two types of situation are readily conceivable which could create strained relations and possible conflicts of interests between the Djakarta and Canberra governments. One is the likelihood of intensified discontent and secessionist sentiment in West Irian if there is too blatant a discrepancy in the levels of economic, political and social advancement in the two halves of the island. Rapid development in East New Guinea is to this extent a source of potential trouble to Indonesia, and its reaction to it is not easily predictable. Several quite different responses could be imagined. Another contingency fraught with dangers is the possibility that the emerging political leaders of Papua-New Guinea may seek to put pressure on Canberra either by looking towards Indonesia for diplomatic support, if they fear that their progress towards self-government is unduly delayed, or by attempting to embroil Australia in conflict with Indonesia against its will by stirring up trouble over the plight of the West Irianese. A paradox is that the latter eventuality is more likely to arise if Australia pushes East New Guinea forward too slowly and the former if it does so too rapidly. Skilful timing, tact and foresight will be needed if friction with Indonesia is to be avoided.

Indonesian perceptions of Australia's aims and motives in New Guinea will obviously be an important influence on its response, but so far too few Indonesians have been to the eastern half of the island for any clear outlines of an 'Indonesian view' of Australian New Guinea to develop. It has been alleged that some of the most senior Indonesian officials who have visited Papua-New Guinea have paid more attention to the traditionally colonial aspects of white rule there, which they readily recognize and understand, than to the more prosaic evidence of economic development and gradual social progress.[22] Others have politely expressed their admiration for Australia's achievements there—achievements which they must realize are in some respects a reproach to their own record in West Irian and which for that reason may need to be rationalized out of sight and mind— but there is no way of knowing whether they are reporting back to Djakarta that Australia is just another colonial power to be criticized whenever opportunity arises or an enlightened trustee burdened with a peculiarly difficult set of problems in New Guinea. One can all too easily imagine that the anti-colonialist view could be propagated readily in Indonesia if it suited the government or some political group to focus hostility on Australia. Conversely it will not be easy for Australia to spread a realization in Indonesia of the complexities of New Guinea's problems—especially as the Australian govern-

ment has so far been extremely suspicious of Indonesian requests for an exchange of permanent liaison officers in the two halves of the island.

The crux of the problem here is not just one of perceptions, of course, but of the will and the ability of the Djakarta and Canberra authorities to prevent conflict situations arising in New Guinea. If an Indonesian government, or powerful elements seeking to change the policies of that government, wanted to let a 'confrontation'-type situation develop in New Guinea, it would not be difficult to find opportunities and rationalizations for it. So long as the Suharto regime is set upon avoiding international incidents, it will presumably endeavour to prevent friction with Australia developing to such a point. But it may not always be able to do so if events get out of hand in New Guinea, even though it may want to damp down excitement. The 'confrontation' of Malaysia was an object lesson in this respect, although the combination of causative factors was different in many respects. The key to such situations does not lie solely in Djakarta and Canberra, though it is to be hoped that the capacity of the two governments for crisis management will prove equal to the strains likely to arise in New Guinea itself. It is easy to become excessively pessimistic about the hypothetical complexities New Guinea could create in Australian-Indonesian relations simply by anticipating the worst. On the other hand, it would be foolish to ignore the problems that might arise or hope that they will disappear if there is enough goodwill and mutual confidence on both sides. They will be a constant thorn in the sides of both governments for years to come, no matter what the political outcome in the two halves of New Guinea. For this reason, if for no other, Australia and Indonesia need to know much more than they do about the views prevailing in each other's country regarding the nature of these problems and the solutions being attempted.

CHAPTER 4

Australia and Japan

MAKOTO MOMOI*

The Japanese view

For most Japanese people, Australia is a vast white man's continent, 21 times as large as, and 88% less-populated than Japan. Beyond that, the Japanese man in the street is generally no better informed about Australian than Australians are about Japan. This is indicated, for example, by the small number of Japanese books and articles, published between 1960 and 1968, which deal solely with Australia. The catalogue of Japan's largest archive, the Parliamentary Library, has a total of eleven published by either government or semi-governmental organizations and only one published by a commercial firm—on the subject of Australian swimming. There is not a single book on Australia's defence; though there are three magazine articles by Japanese authors dealing with Australia's national security.[1]

On the other hand, for many industrialists Australia today is one of the best sources of raw materials, including iron ore and oil. During recent years, Japan has been Australia's most important customer, at times importing almost twice as much as the total of Australian exports to the United States. Such a close trade relationship is reflected in an increase of news about Australia as carried in major Japanese newspapers: a rise from some 85 articles in 1968 to 125, or one every three days, in 1969.[2]

Even the physical distances have begun to look shorter today, as freighters shuttle between Port Hedland and Hirohata, Japan's iron and steel industrial complex, in less than ten days.[3] Indeed, for Japan, Australia has emerged as one of the most reliable and attractive trade partners in the world in the 1960s, particularly after the discovery in 1961 of oil deposits in Moonie, Queensland, and the conclusion of various long-term billion-dollar iron ore export contracts with Japan. Australia's annual coal exports to Japan are also expected to average

* This paper contains the personal views of Professor Momoi and does not reflect the opinions of any Japanese government agency or of the National Defense College.

53

E

seven million tons or more before 1975. All this indicates the degree of reliance of Japan's iron and steel industry on Australia. No industrialist in Japan today doubts that the Australian-Japanese trade relationship will and must remain close throughout the 1970s.

In fact, the iron ore imports, present contracts for which run until 1990, assume and depend on the political stability and strategic security of Australia. If that stability were threatened by either internal Australian or by external factors, Japan's iron and steel industry itself would be seriously affected. Australia's internal political situation, however, is and will remain one of the most stable in the world. So will its booming economy which gives it a leading role in the development of the Asian-Pacific region, with its vast reservoir of natural resources and potential industrialization.

Yet Australia is seldom mentioned as a potential defence partner in official Japanese documents or statements. For one thing, Japan's interest in South-East Asian (and *a fortiori* Australian) national security problems has been strictly limited. Over a quarter of a century the U.S. has been too dominant a presence in the region to encourage Japan's interest in Asian defence affairs. More basically, Australia does not look like a prospective target of aggression by any power. It is, in Japanese eyes, simply difficult to imagine a contingency in which Australia would be directly threatened or attacked.

Yet Australia's geopolitical condition does not necessarily ensure its invulnerability to external threats. T. B. Millar rules out Japan as a potential threat to Australian security, unless Japan 'comes under Chinese influence, has her foreign and trade policies limited accordingly, and perhaps eventually turns into a vast factory and arsenal for China'.[4] This is an extremely interesting observation since it (a) singles out China's influence on Japan as a threat, and (b) emphasizes an adverse effect on Australia of Japanese production for, or on behalf of China. He does foresee a possibility, albeit a remote one, of major Japanese rearmament 'if the United States does wholly withdraw from the Japanese mainland' and of Japan's threatening Australia if Japan did become a major military power. But for him, the possibility of Japan's 'rapprochement with Communist China' looks 'no less disturbing'.

From a Japanese viewpoint, Australia has never been and will not be a direct threat to Japan. For most Japanese, it is simply inconceivable that Australia will ever come under communist influence and have its trade policies limited accordingly. They would agree with Millar who believes China is 'not likely to threaten Australia outside the context of a major war'. The close trade partnership, the crux of economic development for both nations, might, however, be

affected by any one of several potentially dangerous factors, though some of these are purely hypothetical. Among them are (a) domestic instabilities in either country, (b) an economic-political conflict between the two, (c) an armed conflict in Asia involving either of them, (d) threats to air and sea communications between them or between either and the rest of the world, and (e) a partial or total breakdown of their alliances with the U.S.

Threats to trade partnership

1 Of the five factors, internal political instability in Australia is one of the least probable phenomena. So is social insecurity. The Australian parliamentary system is solid and living standards are high. It is free from racial and unemployment problems. Pollution and other urbanization problems will sooner or later make themselves seriously felt, but probably in a far less degree than in Japan. There is in fact not a single Australian domestic problem that makes the Japanese feel really uneasy about Australia.

On the other hand, Japan's domestic politics may well undergo considerable structural changes around the mid-1970s. But no drastic changes in trading patterns are expected. The country must live with, through the 1970s, a series of domestic problems inherent in the modernization and urbanization of a small, densely populated, highly industrialized island nation. In a relative sense, Japan will remain Australia's best customer for its mineral and other natural resources. The two nations will continue to 'mutually complement their vertical trade relationship of a 19th century pattern'.[5]

2 These trade patterns, however, are undergoing a change to 'horizontal patterns' which may well force the two nations to vie for the same natural resources.[6] If escalated, such a competition would create, by way of chain reaction in Australia, unfavourable public sentiment toward Japan.

'A victor of the World War II who today enjoys the first class living standard, Australia is just too proud to come under strong Japanese influence while willing to positively contribute to economic and political stability in Asia', a Japanese economist warns.[7] 'Australia's nationalism symbolized in its national efforts for industrialization and regional development', he points out, 'might lead to a revulsion against foreign goods that threaten indigenous products, or against foreign capital that drains natural resources'.

Japan's overseas investments are not announced on a country-by-country basis. A research institute report estimates that Japan's capital inflow into Australia stood at about 10% of total foreign investment in Australia in 1963-64.[8] In future, the report suggests, this

investment flow will increase as an 'insurance to protect Japan's share in a large scale development project'. Such an increase might create a series of frictions with other foreign and local investors. That in turn could arouse Australia's economic nationalism and eventually lead to a breakdown of the complementary trade relationship between Japan and Australia.

Extreme discretion and strong self-restraint would be needed to keep the two from reacting excessively and, above all, emotionally. Otherwise the trade partnership would deteriorate, with great loss to both partners and to the region as a whole.

3 Australia's involvement in a protracted local conflict would not adversely affect Japan's national security, if Japan were not so dependent both on Australia's natural resources and on sea communications through the Indonesian archipelago. Such a conflict, however, would inevitably affect (a) first and foremost, safe passage of Japanese merchant shipping, (b) over time, Japan's imports of those Australian resources which Australia might need for war purposes, and (c) sooner or later, Japan's exports to the countries with which Australia is engaged in a conflict.

If, on the other hand, Japan is involved in a direct conflict with its neighbours, Australia would suffer less than Japan, simply because it does not rely on Japan so much as Japan does on Australia in an emergency. In either case, Japan must face serious situations (a), (b) and (c). Some of them might be manageable if Japan could successfully find alternative sources of imports or markets for exports, or could simply give up trade activities for the duration of the conflict. Situation (a) would be an exception. Any conflict that involved either Japan or Australia would immediately create difficulties in high sea communications.

4 Such difficulties might escalate to a major crisis if air and sea communications between the two countries were threatened by external forces. The threats might come, at least theoretically, from (a) Indonesia if it came under an external influence and imposed restrictions on, or otherwise harassed, the freedom of sea lanes close to its islands, (b) pirates, and (c) foreign naval powers such as the Soviet Union or, in future, China. Outside powers might also affect the safety of Japanese and Australian merchant ships if threats were directed at the Strait of Malacca or its alternate routes.

The countries whose ships were threatened would then be left with two basic options. The first, to retaliate immediately, might lead to a further escalation. This is an option which Japan does not really have, due to its lack of naval power and its domestic constitutional restric-

tions. In cost-effectiveness terms Japan might prefer the second option of taking no action since 'cold calculation shows Japan will be better off by giving up a few tankers then by retaliating or even operating prohibitively expensive long distance escorts'.[9] Japan then could send its ships through alternate routes, even at the cost of extra time and money.

The second option presupposes an absence of extreme emotional reaction at home and, more importantly, an absence of threat (c), the involvement of foreign naval powers, which can theoretically preclude the use of the alternate routes or escalate the threat. They can do so, however, only if they were prepared to face a major showdown with the U.S. That in turn assumes a continued U.S. commitment to the two allies and a U.S. reaction, more or less automatic and immediate, to an armed attack on the vessels or aircraft of a U.S. ally.

Theoretical proposals

This analysis of potential threats to the two trade partners reveals a need to examine a series of security arrangements, present and future, conventional and nuclear.

1 A unilateral posture

A basic principle here would be the adoption not so much of a unilateral or fully independent position by either Japan or Australia as a combination of reliance on the U.S. for nuclear protection with the relatively independent defence posture in other matters which is appropriate for an ally. The posture would, however, assume a continuation of the U.S. alliance. As such it would provide the Australian merchant marine with a greater measure of protection than its Japanese counterpart.

The U.S. Security Treaty with Australia and New Zealand (ANZUS) states, as part of Article 5:

> . . . an armed attack on any of the Parties is deemed to include an armed attack on the metropolitan territory of any of the Parties, or on the island territories under its jurisdiction in the Pacific or on its armed forces, public vessels or aircraft in the Pacific.

No similar clause can be found in the Treaty of Mutual Co-operation and Security with Japan. Article 5 of this refers merely to 'an armed attack against either Party in the territories under the administration of Japan'. Thus even under a continued U.S. commitment, it is not certain whether a potential harasser on the high seas would be convinced of a semi-automatic U.S. reaction to an armed attack on Japanese ships.

Consequently, Japan's options are limited to (a) no action (or an acceptance of a loss), (b) a sizeable naval build-up, or (c) a new maritime safety agreement with either the U.S. or Australia. If no action (a) is ruled out as impractical (as suggested above), Japan's options will be narrowed to (b) or (c).

The option (b) involves an insurmountable problem: manpower shortage. The number of eighteen-year-old youths in 1966 was 1,240,000. This figure will decline to a mere 770,000 in 1974. Industry and higher education will further drain young manpower which otherwise would go to the all-volunteer self-defence forces. Even if money and technology are not serious problems, the naval build-up would create major difficulties in terms of software and manpower.[10] Besides, even if undertaken, the build-up would take a good deal of time. Japan needs other options to supplement or substitute the naval build-up option.

Option (c) would then be attractive if the U.S. were willing to help Japan and Japan were ready to pay the price. The domestic political climate in both countries, however, will most probably make this option—either a new U.S.-Japanese maritime safety agreement or a modification of the existing treaty in the direction of the ANZUS treaty—impractical. But an Australian-Japanese agreement is not necessarily inconceivable. For one thing, Australia cannot physically disengage itself from Asia. For another, it can hardly ignore the threats which, if left unchecked, might involve Australia sooner or later.

2 A bilateral system

A bilateral system would be primarily intended to secure safe operations of Australian and Japanese tankers, freighters and other 'public vessels' shuttling between the two countries. The system might be useful even if the U.S. partially and covertly decommitted its conventional presence from Asia while publicly keeping its nuclear commitment to its allies.

(a) The system could supplement a decreased U.S. naval presence by the build-up of the Australian Navy, with or without Japan's co-operation. Japan's contribution might be a limited one, due to various restrictive factors. It could perhaps contribute to the system some hardware items, such as vessels and equipment. Some merchant marine could be earmarked for the use of Australian shipping firms in exchange for Australia's naval protection of Japanese ships. Another alternative might be a direct or indirect financial contribution. Japan might also offer to provide Australia with special trade terms designed to boost Australia's foreign exchange reserves, with consequent benefits

to the Australian defence potential. Such measures would of course have to be formulated in ways acceptable to Australian opinion, and without carrying an implication of Japanese payments for the provision of Australian forces.

(b) If, however, the U.S. disengaged openly, Japan might be forced to augment the system with some physical or direct contribution such as the deployment of its own naval power, if this were available and could be spared from other duties. That eventually would require a constitutional revision,[11] which will remain politically impossible for many years. Even if the deployment were made possible, Japan would continue to suffer from the shortage of suitable manpower. As a practical matter therefore, a second-best option would be a combination of a lend-lease type hardware contribution and of an indirect financial arrangement.

3 A multilateral system

In the bilateral systems Australia would play a major role and Japan that of an indirect contributor. Together, the two could expect to supplement the decreased presence of U.S. conventional power. If the U.S. should withdraw farther back into a Fortress America concept, a potential aggressor might assume that the U.S. had become both indecisive and inactive in dealing with a non-nuclear conflict and/or a limited nuclear attack on its ally.

An option which might then be open for both Australia and Japan would be either to replace the U.S. presence, or to improve the credibility of the remaining U.S. commitment, by organizing a collective security system, either conventional or nuclear or both. This theoretical option would be more similar to a B.L.F. (naval bilateral nuclear force) as referred to by Fred Greene[12] than to an M.L.F. or a P.M.F. (Pacific multilateral nuclear force), in that it would be in a sense a bilateral arrangement between the nuclear power (the U.S.) and a group of two (Australia and Japan) or more non-nuclear nations. The system might work if a 'double veto could satisfy both nuclear and non-nuclear partners and relieve the fears of others that Japan would gain a strategic force of its own'.[13]

(a) An Australia-Japan-U.S. (B.L.F.) syste 1

Both Australia and Japan could, for instance, increase their naval and air capabilities in order to replace the role of the U.S. 7th Fleet, effectively to counter maritime guerrilla activities and to protect U.S. merchant marine in the Pacific. In turn, they would still rely on the U.S. nuclear umbrella to deter nuclear attacks on their homelands.

One delicate question would then be how to apply the double veto power within the non-nuclear group. If the deterrent failed and one

59

of the non-nuclear partners was attacked, it might become difficult for all the partners to identify the attack as one directed at the group as a whole. This would be more due to the absence of an economic-geopolitical identity such as that which exists in Europe, where member states of NATO and of the formerly proposed M.L.F. are located closer to each other, than would be the case for a Pacific membership of a B.L.F. In a sense, the success of the B.L.F. system depends on the solution in advance of this identity problem.

(b) An Australia-Japan-Asian system (AJAS)

Such a problem may not be so serious in an AJAS formula primarily designed to maintain, by collective action, peace on the high seas in Asia. An essentially regional 'policing' system, it could be applied to a limited area, more widely or with a limited contribution from member states. Suppose, for instance, the case of a 'Malaccan Straits Maritime Patrol Force'. The area it would cover could be limited to the strait and its vicinity. Its patrol boats could be provided by Japan, crew and port facilities by Asian members and their training by Australia. Its operation and finance might be jointly managed primarily for rescue, counter-piracy and counter-smuggling operations.

The presence of the force itself might function as a deterrent to a nation which might contemplate launching a premeditated, centrally-controlled, high sea guerrilla warfare campaign. A similar patrol force could theoretically be organized in other parts of the Pacific region, without the participation of any non-Asian or non-Pacific nation, if necessary.

The AJAS formula is primarily for an Asian system in which Australia and Japan would confine themselves almost solely to a logistical role, with Asian members playing operational parts. It would be a far cry from a regional collective security system, unless its equipment were made highly sophisticated and sufficiently numerous. The force might, however, constitute a module around which a full-scale collective security system could later be built, if and when a need arose.

Conclusion

The suggestions sketched here remain not so much a policy proposal as a theoretical analysis. They also reveal, among other things, the sorts of requirements—and limitations—which Japan might eventually face in the field of national security as its economic commitment to Asia increases and its trade partnership with Australia expands, although at present the two nations appear not to feel a pressing need to examine their mutual security problems.

From Tokyo's point of view, however, the requirements of such

situations and the probable limitations upon action should be examined carefully and well before a need arises. A clear limitation on both Australia and Japan, for instance, is manpower shortage. A common need for both is expansion of trade. The former limits the level of military manpower and hence the extent of deployment overseas. Neither Japan nor Australia can rely completely on the other in terms of manpower. They can only take care of security situations within or near their respective territorial waters and, perhaps to a lesser degree, of their own vessels farther afield.

On the other hand, as trade expands, more merchant ships shuttle between Sydney and Tokyo. Neither the Japanese nor the Australian navies can protect all these ships in a crisis. They must rely either on the U.S. or upon the co-operation of Asian nations.

This, in turn, points to the need for a regional or multi-national arrangement which might broadly rest on Japan's hardware and Australia's software contributions. Perhaps an immediate need will be an AJAS-type regional maritime police force, of a kind less provocative and more practical than a full-scale collective security organization.

In Japanese eyes, furthermore, Australia looks like a potential substitute for the U.S. nuclear umbrella if, however unlikely that now seems, this should either completely lose its credibility or be declared no longer applicable to the Pacific area. In such a situation Australia might be in a better position than Japan to go nuclear and restore a measure of nuclear protection. Theoretically, if one of the two countries did so, it ought to be Australia, not Japan which has no strategic ability to survive since its land is too small and too densely populated. If Canberra should go nuclear, it would not be unthinkable to devise a new security arrangement between the two nations, or an Asian M.L.F. with Australia as member. It must also be remembered that a nuclear Australia might be less provocative to others than a nuclear Japan which has a past record of militarism.

Finally, in the most unlikely event that Japan should decide to go nuclear without U.S. help and in spite of all the strategic and diplomatic negative factors, Japan might still need Australia's co-operation, if only for obtaining a testing area which does not exist in Japan.[14] This in turn means that Australia does in fact hold a veto power over Japan's nuclear programme. If it refused to co-operate with Japan, the programme would end either as an abortive attempt or an 'untested system', which would have very little credibility.

This mainly theoretical analysis indicates clearly that the two nations are and will be largely interdependent. Their co-operation thus will be the core of peacekeeping in Asia, with or without an actual U.S. military presence.

Alliances

CHAPTER 5

Great Britain and Australia

PETER LYON

Great Britain and Australia have shared a considerable amount of common history. In general this history is much better known by Australians than by the British. There has not been even a single study of any significance written by an Englishman about Britain's relations with Australia in the twentieth century.[1] It is prodigious how little the British really know of Australia.

And yet paradoxically enough the British public is told and sees more about Australia these days than ever before. Australia's near-domination of a variety of sports, the mining boom, Prince Charles at Timbertop, Sydney harbour and Opera House, Aboriginals, flying doctors, kangaroos, bronzed beach guards, vast desert, sheep, pine-apples, cattle galore—such are some of the many words, images, flooding the kaleidoscopic mental pictures the British have of Australia and Australians. Such are the stereotypes conjured up by the fleeting casual impressions of the British people in an age of instant communications, if not of instant understanding. Surely this British-Australian relationship is truly symbiotic? This situation remains unaffected by the political colour of the party in power in London.

There may well be different British regional attitudes to Australia; but, in this essay, Australia deals with an almost United Kingdom, even if this incorporates elements of optimism and simplification. Though popular impressions may be important, there are more substantial sinews linking the two countries. For present purposes three will be singled out: immigration, trade and diplomatic/defence ties.

Immigration

Of every ten Australians one is a post-war immigrant, and about four in ten of these immigrants are British. A majority of Australians are of British stock, and Britain is still the main single source for new immigrants. After a few months in office the new Australian Minister for Immigration, Mr Phillip Lynch, hurried around in Europe in June

65

1970, like his predecessors in the same office, looking for the 125,000 best emigrants a year from the Australian government's point of view.

'Britain is still our corner-stone', Mr Lynch told a British journalist.[2] 'We want at least 350,000 from the United Kingdom in the next five years. In the last twelve months we have had 68,000 most of whom got to Australia on the £10 assisted-passage scheme for less than it would cost them to call on relatives at the other end of Britain.'

There has been a post-1945 revival of British migration to Australia.[3] Total net immigration (mainly British and Irish) fell in the 1930s to about 30,000, having been just about ten times that in the 1920s. In the 1960s rather less than 700,000 British emigrants (about half of all emigrants) arrived in Australia. The Australian Department of Immigration apparently hopes for up to a quarter of a million British settlers every year by the end of the 1970s. The notion that there is a high reverse flow of homesick Englishmen from among the recent immigrants is often exaggerated, as Mr Lynch explained during the same interview:

> The percentage of British migrants quitting Australia is only fractionally higher than the number from other countries. The main reasons are homesickness, commitment to families back home, bereavements, sickness, and those cases where we took on somebody who would be no more a success in Australia than he ever was in Britain.

Migration is perhaps only the most prominent of a host of personal and institutional connections between the two countries. The tradition of looking to London for a lead is over for Australia. The habits and practices of maintaining, renewing, expanding and creating multifarious links with Britain continue. Despite the fact that Anthony Sampson's *Anatomy of Britain* (published in 1962) made but one perfunctory reference to Australia, there is between Australia and Britain a profound interpenetration of *élites* and classes,[4] especially of professional *élites* (university teachers, accountants, stockbrokers, bankers, engineers, officers in armed forces, leading sportsmen and entertainers). What the precise impact of these linkages are on governmental policies it is impossible to tell.

A random reading of British newspaper and magazine comment about Australia in the past year would strongly suggest that British writers amply confirm their previous expectations and stereotypes when writing about Australia. Left-wing writers regard Australia as increasing its dependence on the United States, not only in military and political terms, but especially economically, so that from this perspective Australia is rapidly becoming a neo-colonial dupe of the Americans. Right-wing writers extol the rugged individuality, the

energetic private enterprise and consequent, or so it seems, economic growth of Australia, untrammelled by excessive governmental intervention.

Such confident judgements tell more about the people making them than about Australia. Even so, when such a devoted Anglophile as Sir Robert Menzies writes an article entitled 'Australia and Britain Drift Apart',[5] and the Australian High Commissioner in London says, 'with great sorrow that the voice of Britain is listened to less and less in the world',[6] it is worth remembering that the British still use— sincerely, if often superficially—the language of duty, obligation and affection more for their ties with Australia and New Zealand than for their relations with any other country in the world, not excluding the United States or Canada.

Foreign policy has never been merely what foreign offices do. If detailed refutation of this dead idea is ever needed, then the record of past and present British-Australian relations could provide ample evidence. Foreign policy does mean relations between foreigners, and British and Australian governments so far have never quite regarded their relations in this light. They seek to disguise or diminish their differences, even though they are nowadays two undoubtedly independent and individual countries. It may be that eventually Australians will come to regard Britain as just another Western European country; and the British to think of Australia as so undeniably antipodean as to be beyond their spheres of principal interest and concern. Such trends are not inevitable, though there are already some who take this attitude. In times of growing complexity prediction becomes more desirable, and more difficult.

It cannot seriously be said that Edward Heath's enthusiasm for some continued British military presence on stations East of Suez (at about £100m. p.a. as an integral but not predominant part of a Commonwealth package) is explicable in terms of improving his public image at home. His mostly apathetic and neo-isolationist public is not inclined to state precise and sophisticated requirements in overseas affairs. What public opinion polls in Britain reveal about membership in the E.E.C., the Commonwealth, links with Australia, military commitments East of Suez, will be irrelevant to government unless and until ministers choose to make it so. As a man who successfully defied the dire predictions of the pollsters that his party would not win the 1970 general election, Heath is unlikely to be greatly deterred by any new adverse oracular pronouncements by the pollsters.

Popular opinion is not of much, if any, value in the production of practical answers to problems of foreign policy. Acceptability to popular opinion, even if only in the sense of tacit assent, must be a central

67

presupposition of the conduct of foreign policy by any democratic government. Britain is better regarded as a polyarchic than as a populistic democracy.[7] Here this means parliamentary government by freely and popularly elected members of parliament, regarded as representative and responsible; and a national politics of freely competing groups and oligarchs, not by a single sovereign people. Referenda and plebiscites have not been the practices of the U.K. (Australian government seems also to be polyarchic, but with more populistic trimmings—including an occasional referendum—than in Britain.) So far as domestic decisions will determine matters, Britain's membership of the E.E.C. and its residual East-of-Suez military policies will depend mostly on the state of the economy and upon executive initiatives and skills much more than upon public opinion and moods. Indeed, national opinions and moods are principally shaped by the former factors. The British have become hypochondriacs about their national economy (lurching along with each month's trade returns); whereas the Australians are now, rightly, the reverse of valetudinarians about their increasingly robust economy. Foreign and defence policies in each country are subsidiary branches of political economy.

Trade

Australia has always had close trading and financial links with Britain. Current Australian fascination with Japan may cause the British and Australians to undervalue the fact that their countries are still very important to each other economically.

Britain's share in Australia's trade has fallen from first to third place in recent years; but there is no single country close behind Britain in fourth place. Japan has become Australia's main marketing outlet (in particular for Australia's chief export commodity, which is still by far the largest earner of foreign exchange—wool). The United States recently has displaced Britain to become Australia's main supplier of imports. If, however, account is taken of all types of payments, including invisibles, Great Britain still remains one of Australia's two most important partners.[8]

Australia shares with Britain a global trading nation's interest in the stability of the international monetary system, and in the fortunes of sterling as an international currency, or its satisfactory replacement. The Treasurer in the Australian government, Mr Leslie Bury, M.P., told an audience of the American Chamber of Commerce in Australia, in Canberra on 5 December 1969, that Australia's present holdings of sterling total about $A540 million.

It is arguable that Britain and Australia have in common the in-

terest of seeing that globalism and regionalism are complementary and not competing features of contemporary international economic life. But there is not much evidence of hard thinking, lobbying and close accords on this as yet. Regional organizations, whether one examines the lures of the E.E.C. and of O.E.C.D., or of ASPAC and the A.D.B., are each and all seen in very particularist and individualistic ways by each member government, including those of Great Britain and Australia.

This is very clear when one looks at the respective attitudes of Britain and Australia to the E.E.C. Writing in the American quarterly journal, *Foreign Affairs*, in October 1969 Edward Heath said little about his ideas for Britain's future military deployments in Asia, except to state again his active interest in a joint five-power Commonwealth force for Malaysia and Singapore, and to reassert that 'the economies promised as a result of the [Labour government's] policy of withdrawal are false in the sense that they expose British interests and the future of our friends to unacceptable risk'. We must here leave aside the question whether Britain really could remove or reduce the level of unacceptable risks.

Mr Heath's most interesting point was his insistence that,

> Britain is now less able than she was in 1961-2, or even in 1967, to assume without special arrangements the obligations of full membership [of the E.E.C.]. The increase in Britain's international indebtedness and the underlying weakness of her balance of payments make more formidable the heavy short-term burden which a Common Market and the Common Agricultural Policy as it now stands would inevitably impose.

What Mr Heath understandably did not also say on this occasion was that the £100 million a year (give or take a margin of £10 million) he soon afterwards estimated as the extra cost, as compared with the Labour Party's, of his East-of-Suez military policy might be accounted as of some immediate psychological and material disadvantage in Britain's negotiations for membership of the European Communities. Such it will surely be in the negotiations from July 1970 onwards. Two main points need to be made. Britain's trade East of Suez is much more important for it as a proportion of its total trade (in which of course an Australian component looms large) than is trading in this region for other Western European countries as an aspect of their total trade. Secondly, though German, French and Dutch trade drives in Asia may be active and burgeoning in the early 1970s (and in many respects their recent gains are much greater than those of the British), there is not and probably will not be any overt West European enthusiasm for European military presences in Asia and the Pacific in

69

the early 1970s. Trade no longer follows, or necessarily needs, the national flag.

The immediate short-term interest of gaining membership of the E.E.C. might well jeopardize Britain's long-term interest of maintaining close trading and other ties with Australia. In 1970, and immediately beyond, undoubtedly British negotiators for entry into the E.E.C. will feel even less impelled to safeguard specifically Australian interests, as an aspect of the acceptable terms of British entry, than they did in 1961-63.

There is more awareness in Britain in 1970 than there was in the early 1960s of the increasingly close relations Australia has with Japan and with the United States, not least because their trade links have become even closer since then. If Britain joins the E.E.C. the question of deciding comparative advantages for Australia as between Japan, the U.S.A. and Britain within the E.E.C. will become more acute and pressing. The loss or even further diminution of Australian preferences in Britain surely will tempt Australians to cancel British preferences in Australia, and replace them, if they are replaced at all on a bilateral basis, with preferences to Japan, who has become too good a customer to disappoint. Although British entry into the E.E.C. would certainly stimulate further Australian efforts to trade with the E.E.C. and with Europe as a whole, it would also strengthen existing Australian determination to find better markets in the Pacific Basin rainlands, and especially in the United States and in Japan.

Terms of trade are not irreversible and unchangeable. But in the immediate future the relative decline in British-Australian trade as a proportion of their total trade seems unlikely to be reversed. Nevertheless, the value of certain British-Australian trade sectors (perhaps, e.g., machinery from Britain, mining and mineral products from Australia) may increase. The two countries are going to, or at least should, regard each other as mutually important trade partners into the foreseeable future.

Diplomatic and defence ties

It seems appropriate to regard British-Australian relations as not so much an alliance as a multi-purpose and adjustable but enduring *entente cordiale*. It is not that there are no formal ties of alliance: even puny SEATO provides some, and there are other institutionalized or at least quasi-formalized military links (such as ANZAM).[9] But these in no way really reveal the full substance of the connections between the two countries in military and diplomatic matters.

Even in military matters alone, Staff College interchanges, weapons research and development, recent comradeship in arms, and similari-

ties in equipment and training result in intimacies and workaday mutual understandings more far-reaching than those between countries ostensibly linked in much more onerous alliances.

Australia faces both the Indian and the Pacific Oceans as well as northwards to the turbulence and rapid change of contemporary southern Asia. Britain was the predominant military power in the Indian Ocean and in South-East Asia from 1815 to 1945, and in some senses even after 1945.[10] Its active interest and military involvement in parts of these vast areas has been maintained patchily (despite the significance of its withdrawal from India in 1947) right up until the present time. For better or worse this has brought Britain and Australia together: diplomatically over Ibadan in 1951, over Suez in 1956, in offering material support to India in late 1962, in support for Thailand in 1961-62, and, above all, in Malaya (later Malaysia) and Singapore ever since 1949. Australia's active assistance to the United States in Vietnam since 1966, and Britain's refusal to offer similar support, has been one of their most significant points of departure in recent years. Australia was thus a subsidiary supporter and beneficiary so long as there was a Pax Britannica in the Indian Ocean, so long as the Indian Ocean was in effect a British lake. Now, with Britain's former military eminence in the Indian Ocean almost entirely at an end—with a rapidly growing (and increasingly variegated) Russian naval presence in the Indian Ocean; with local turbulence brewing and burgeoning along the East African littorals, in and around the Persian Gulf, and in South and South-East Asia; above all, with a United States determined to disengage from Vietnam—Australia has been forced to ponder and explore the consequences for itself of an Asia without a major British military presence, just when the United States, the first and most powerful of its friends, is causing many more uncertainties for Canberra, and for other capitals. Metaphorically as well as literally from Simonstown to Suez to Singapore to Subic Bay to Sydney and back to Simonstown the present situation is very fluid.

Britain never has been the predominant military power throughout the Pacific Ocean, even in the most palmy days of its world naval supremacy from 1805-1905. In 1905 the British government withdrew the British Far Eastern squadron from patrols off the East Asian coasts, as a consequence of the rewritten terms of the British-Japanese alliance. Henceforth British naval power concentrated on Singapore, on other British interests and colonies in South-East Asia and those others in and around the Indian Ocean generally. The war against Japan was for Britain only marginally a Pacific war (a fact which Curtin's famous plea to the United States in 1941 recognized). For

71

Britain the war against Japan was fought from the Indian Ocean, from India and South-East Asia. These perspectives and priorities have prevailed ever since, despite Britain's interests in Hong Kong, and Fiji, despite Britain's alleged exclusion or original unwillingness to join ANZUS, and despite the common membership Britain and Australia have in SEATO. Australian leaders initially reacted to the prominent presence of the United States in the Pacific rather tardily, but close concordance with the United States whenever possible has been a major plank of policy ever since 1951, and in this respect connections with Britain have been either largely irrelevant or slightly distracting.

It is not necessary here to repeat the tediously familiar story of the latest stages of Britain's long military recessional from Asia. It is a story already many times told[11] and capable of several different glosses, in Australia as in Britain. Something of its prevarications and improvisations can be deduced from reading British Defence White Papers seriatim from 1967-70. But two features of the recent situation do seem worth outlining in a little detail. These are the Labour government's actual legacies to the new Conservative government, and the avowed policies and likely actions and opportunities open to Mr Heath's new government.

A plausible, clear, and almost the last sophisticated rationale for the Labour government's intended policy of complete withdrawal of permanently stationed troops from anywhere in Asia (apart from a slightly strengthened garrison in Hong Kong) by the end of 1971 was given by Mr Denis Healey in the debate on the annual Defence White Paper in the House of Commons in March 1970. This is worth quoting from at some length because it draws attention very clearly to problems with which his ministerial successors also unavoidably have to grapple:

> . . . operations even against external subversion and infiltration are very expensive in troops and very difficult to control. In Borneo, when dealing with external subversion and infiltration, we had to use 55,000 men over three years. In Vietnam, the United States had to use 500,000 men and the war is not over yet.
>
> The real question is that of the nature of the commitments of the Government. We, as I said yesterday, are getting rid of all our automatic commitments to give assistance in the Persian Gulf and the Far East. The right hon. Gentleman plans to keep them, and this is the crux of the matter. It is no good talking about Mekong or Laos. We never had the commitment to intervene there and we never had troops on the spot who might have been involved whether we had commitments or not. We have a commitment now in the Anglo-Malaysian Defence Agreement, but I put

this to the right hon. Gentleman, because its implications go far outside the confines of this House: the Agreement in its present form involves an automatic commitment. It gives to the other signatory of the Agreement a blank cheque to call on British troops. It is a commitment which applies to Britain alone. It does not apply to the Australian and New Zealand Governments, and there is no chance that they would accept a commitment of this type. Therefore, this commitment would provide no basis for the presence of their forces once we have gone. This is why the Government are seeking release from the commitment and intend to do so before our forces finally retire next year; and we are seeking a new form of political framework within which the four Commonwealth countries could cooperate in the area and which Australia and New Zealand would be prepared to accept. But even if the right hon. Gentleman changed the commitment, given the presence of British forces and his declared intention to commit them to counter-insurgency operations, it means that he must have a reinforcement capability or he is putting the lives of our own soldiers at risk. That is why to cover the cost of what the right hon. Gentleman proposes we must double the £100 million to which I referred earlier. Of course he does not like that and maybe he is appalled by it; but it simply illustrates the danger of jumping into commitments without any clear idea of their full implications.

I come next to the question of the manpower implications in the right hon. Gentleman's policy. To run on the carrier force alone would require another 8,000 men. No presence of less than 6,000 in the Gulf would be safe for the British forces who composed it. If the right hon. Gentleman intends a presence of even about half the size of our present force in the Far East—and they are only half what they were in 1964—that means about 20,000 men; and he must have 20,000 men at home to reinforce them or he is exposing them to unacceptable risks.[12]

The nature of commitments and manpower problems undoubtedly are two major perplexities which will worry the Conservative government just as it did its predecessor. But there are some other more specific features of the Healey legacy to the new government which should be mentioned.

By April 1970 total British troops in South-East Asia were down to 30,800 from their pre-1968 level of 47,300. There was a reduced fleet but still a commando brigade, and there were six squadrons of aircraft where there had been ten before 1968. Thus a marked reduction in 'teeth' arms already had taken place, and the next stage of the main run down was to be of support elements and local employees. The cliff edge of the run down (to employ a Ministry of Defence phrase) was to be from April 1971. All families were to be out by October 1971. The final withdrawals were to be the carrier group and the amphibious group including the Marine Commando Brigade by 1972.

All this meant that by the end of 1971 any British military opera-

tion, apart from the defence of Hong Kong, was to be mounted from the U.K. as part of 'the general capability'. Much depended then on the size, efficiency and time periods in which Britain could expect to provide reinforcements by sea and by air as a part of the general capability. The eastabout, or trans-CENTO air route is by way of Cyprus, Bahrain or Masira, and Gan to Singapore. The westabout air route is via Canada, the U.S.A. and U.S.-controlled Pacific islands to Hong Kong and Singapore-Malaysia. The sea routes are via the Suez Canal (when it is open) and around the Cape of Good Hope.

Under the Labour government's plans no specifically British commitments were to continue after 1971 except to dependent territories (which means Hong Kong, though how it might be defended by Britain has never been explained; and perhaps Fiji). Britain's military support for Brunei was to lapse in November 1970 and to be replaced, perhaps, by a Treaty of Friendship, an instrument which has been for Britain very specific and limited hitherto. Britain was to retain its membership in SEATO, but not to earmark and declare specifically any of its forces after April 1971. Even so, Britain was to continue to participate in SEATO exercises, to maintain a full U.K. staff of SEATO headquarters, and to consider possible uses of its general capability for SEATO operations. ANZAM was to continue as a forum for consultation and joint planning only, though its interests were expected to change depending on what new five-power Commonwealth arrangements were made. The Labour government had not got around to abrogating or renegotiating the hitherto automatic commitment of the Anglo-Malaysian Defence Agreement (AMDA), or to clearly defining its commitment to Singapore, in the light of the post-withdrawal situation.

Even after the completion of the envisaged run down by 1971 Mr Healey had planned that there would still be a British presence of sorts, and rather strong in training terms. It was to involve British participation in the Commonwealth jungle warfare training school in Johore, with 3,000 British troops being flown out and trained there annually, a detachment of some 30 R.A.F. aircraft-servicing personnel at Tengah airbase in Singapore and some naval vessels almost continually in the vicinity.

This was hardly complete withdrawal. The real difference between the Labour and Conservative military policies East of Suez is between an intermittent presence mounted from general capability and only serviced locally, and a small permanent combat-ready presence which can be reinforced from general capability. But the important difference between the two positions is that the first was called, and widely believed to be withdrawal, and the second is not. Diplomatically and

militarily, then, Conservative policy probably will involve slowing down or forestalling certain aspects of Britain's disengagement rather than actual reversals.

What Conservative policy will be from July 1970 onwards cannot be foreseen in detail. But enough indications have been offered by Mr Heath[13] and Sir Alec Douglas-Home[14] to make their general outline and preferences fairly clear. When Mr Heath visited Singapore and Malaysia in January 1970 (when it seemed as if an election might not take place until early 1971), he made three basic promises: to stop any complete British military withdrawal, to retain some British presence and to affirm that this presence would not be as the locally predominant military power but only as one part of a five-power Commonwealth defence arrangement.

A complete British withdrawal militarily from East of Suez may now be postponed for some years. But those military arrangements which have accompanied the era of decolonization in Asia for Britain are now over and thus almost entirely anachronistic. Only a Britain determined and demonstrably capable of being a military power of some consequence in Asia can convey credibility, and it is now questionable whether any present or future British government really can or should assume a major East-of-Suez role. A small British contribution within a five-power mix in South-East Asia is something slighter. The still remote prospect of a British contribution as part of an enlarged E.E.C. is something very speculative.

It was a fairly common Whitehall and Westminster assumption of three or four years ago that Australia should and would step into Britain's shoes militarily in South-East Asia as Britain disengaged and perhaps a number of leading Americans were misled by these mistaken British hopes. The vision, popular among some American policy makers in the late 1960s, of Australia taking a more active and onerous role in South-East Asia already has dimmed and expectations about Australia in Washington seem much more modest. Even so the view is still held in some quarters that 'Australia is America's second most important ally in Asia after Japan'.

On present indications the most that can be expected from Britain militarily in Asia in the immediate future is the reduction of its Malaysia-Singapore presence into a co-partnership in a Commonwealth five-power arrangement, some continuing garrison duties in Hong Kong and perhaps even small presences in Brunei and the Gulf. Only a major catastrophe or very dramatic local occurrences prompting Britain to unplanned reactions and reinvestments (such as happened in response to Indonesia in 1963-66) could reverse this trend.

Present Conservative party intentions were well conveyed by Sir

75

Alec in his article in the *Daily Telegraph* of 20 April 1970. Having earlier in the article said that 'it is timely that Australia should take a lead in the defence' of Malaysia and Singapore, Sir Alec continued:

> There is a strong case for reconstructing the framework of collective defence but new alliances are not in fashion and until confidence has been restored it is probably better to concentrate on improved contingency planning between the different military organizations already in being. There is much in that field which could be done . . . A modest [British] presence will be enough to give confidence and to enable the four Commonwealth countries in the area to develop their full potential.

It is not difficult to imagine situations and scenarios in which Britain and Australia might be thrown together militarily in some joint peace-making or peace-keeping endeavours. In policy making (and especially in policy planning), however, it is generally advisable to avoid complexity and subtlety, lest the government itself and one's domestic public and foreign friends become befuddled. For, as Edmund Burke once well said, 'Refined policy ever has been the parent of confusion —and ever will be so, as long as the world endures'. Ingeniosity can be overdone.

The partnership which Britain has enjoyed with Australia in the twentieth century so far has not been merely a partnership in trade and military alliance but one deeply tinged by shared sentiments, much common culture and many personal affections and affinities. One well-known passage from Burke has an abiding relevance to the past, the present and, it is hoped, to the future of British-Australian relations, with or without British membership of the E.E.C., with or without common memberships in military alliances or arrangements:

> We lay too much weight upon the formality of treaties and compacts. We do not act much more wisely when we trust to the interests of men as guarantees of their engagements. The interests frequently tear to pieces the engagements; and the passions trample upon both. Entirely to trust to either, is to disregard our own safety, or not to know mankind. Men are not tied to one another by papers and seals. They are led to associate by resemblances, by conformities, by sympathies. It is with nations as with individuals. Nothing is so strong a tie of amity between nation and nation as correspondence in laws, customs, manners and habits of life. They have more than the force of treaties in themselves. They are obligations written in the heart. They approximate men to men, without their knowledge, and sometimes against their intentions. The secret, unseen, but irrefragable bond of habitual intercourse holds them together, even when their perverse and litigious nature sets them to equivocate, scuffle, and fight, about the terms of their written obligations.

Amen.

CHAPTER 6

The U.S.A. and Australia

H. G. GELBER

The broad objectives of United States foreign and strategic policies have remained remarkably steady over the last fifteen to twenty years. They can be summed up as the triple aims of preserving the security of the United States together with its vital lines of communication, maintaining a stable balance of power in two crucial areas of the globe, Europe and East Asia, and preventing a nuclear war. All three have implied the prevention of strategic changes which were undesirable from Washington's point of view and in any case of violent change. They have also implied some measure of containment of the Soviet Union and of China for so long as either of them continues to be an actual or potential opponent, as well as, more recently, the containment of each by the other.[1] This has meant the maintenance of a nuclear balance between the United States and the Soviet Union which should preferably be favourable and at least invulnerable to attempts by third parties to destabilize it. In pursuit of such policies the U.S. has sought the support of local coalitions in both Europe and Asia. These have helped to reconcile local and U.S. wishes and efforts; relieved the U.S. of some of the economic and military burdens of these global policies; and made the U.S. effort more acceptable within the United States, both because of the smaller costs involved and because the role of American leadership of a coalition has traditionally been more acceptable to Americans than the notion of unilateral American action. In Europe NATO has for twenty years fulfilled such a purpose, as well as others. The failure of SEATO to fulfil a similar role in Asia[2] has been followed by attempts to encourage regional groupings, in part perhaps under Japanese auspices. As the leader of coalitions, the U.S. has claimed to provide not merely general military support but nuclear protection. This in turn has been intended to help stabilize and consolidate the general balance of power; enlist the military and economic potential of allies in support of policies shaped, in considerable part, to suit American purposes; make the American umbrella essential to those allies and decrease the pressures for nuclear

77

proliferation by them and others, with the complications which proliferation would bring for the maintenance of the Soviet-American nuclear balance and the costs entailed in establishing some new framework of nuclear power and arms control on terms acceptable to additional nuclear powers.[3]

In the Pacific and South-East Asia the American interest has been interpreted, more specifically, in terms of the security of U.S. territory in Hawaii and Guam as well as the continental United States, the security of the sea and air approaches to North America and the maintenance of an East Asian balance which would prevent any large power in that area from acquiring a degree of dominance which could spill over into a threat to these U.S. interests.[4] In method the U.S. has usually veered between two kinds of approach: stress on an offshore presence, both to contain mainland power and to exercise influence there, and involvement on the mainland for limited and *ad hoc* purposes. The tendency of U.S. policy in 1968-70 has clearly been towards a reversion from the second to the first. Though the communist world was never regarded as entirely monolithic, the evidence that disputes between major communist countries can lead to open warfare is new. It clearly points towards a looser U.S. containment of China, a limited mending of fences with Peking and an even-handed aloofness from Sino-Soviet disputes. The rise of Japan, equally, both permits and compels some draw-down in the U.S. presence in East Asia. Developments in military technology and the lessened need for overseas bases point in the same direction. There has also, of course, been Vietnam, and the limited effectiveness of a major exertion of American military power.

In some ways the most important factors of all have been associated with the urgency of American domestic problems. Irritation with foreign involvement has, to a significant extent, reflected less a judgement on the merits of the case than annoyance with a distraction from domestic problems which were believed to be more urgent. There is a paradox here. Concentration at home has been fed, in part, by the irritating intractability of an outside world of assertive nation states. Yet it is the very success of American power in making the world safe for America which has allowed Americans to regard so many foreign problems as pale and insubstantial by comparison with more real concerns at home.

'This is not', as Denis Brogan has remarked, 'just a matter of renewed "isolationism" in the old sense. It is a stocktaking of the American domestic situation and especially of the clash between generations.'[5] While the problems are real enough, their effects have been compounded by the demands of American domestic politics. The

social and economic changes of the last two decades may have begun to alter the basic political landscape. The first two years of President Nixon's term brought intensive discussion as to whether the old Democratic coalition, which has dominated American politics since Franklin Roosevelt, is breaking up or being superseded, possibly by a Republican majority. It is clear that such phenomena as the attempted reassertion of the role of the Senate in foreign affairs, or the call for such inherently impossible policy goals as the imposition of racial and social tolerance by legislation, or the support for student dissent are deeply entwined with the party political opposition to President Nixon. Even on Vietnam it seems clear that, were the affair to end less disastrously than President Nixon's opponents suggest it will, those opponents would be in a poor electoral position. From this point of view the frantic character of some of the dissent reflects less the depth of the substantive problems than a despair over a Republican trend which suggests some parallels with the despair of Senator Robert Taft over the Truman victory in 1948, or the no less frantic character of some of the opposition to Franklin Roosevelt during the New Deal period.

Domestic dissent in general, and its foreign policy aspects in particular, have several highly traditional characteristics. The emphasis upon moral criteria in judging the foreign and strategic policies of states is a staple attitude. The New Left notion that America, having done evil abroad, must withdraw, is merely the obverse of the view that an America morally restored should resume its role as the exemplar of the world. This, in turn, can be compatible with a renewed interventionist role as often as with the view that America should stand aloof. The most vocal of America's domestic critics, indeed, have scarcely moved beyond these obvious ideas. 'Having come to maturity in a Vietnam world where America seems the "bad guy", campus liberalism's foreign policy suggestions do not go beyond the demand that the United States cease being bad.'[6] Partly in consequence, they have offered no serious amendment to the principles which have underpinned U.S. foreign policies for the last twenty years. The more responsible critics of U.S. China policies, for example, insist that China is no threat to the larger Asian balance of power. They do not say that the U.S. should be indifferent to a Chinese threat if it were to arise. In South-East Asia it is said that U.S. interests have been exaggerated, misinterpreted and defended at disproportionate cost. The argument is that the area is unimportant to the U.S., not that important interests should be disregarded.[7] More generally, it could be argued that the relative caution displayed by both China and the Soviet Union in recent years is due, to a signifi-

79

cant degree, to constraints imposed by U.S. power. If so, the absence of threats to the U.S. might be due at least as much to the success of American security policies as to any lack of realism in threat analyses in Washington. In such a situation, large concessions to public impatience with the allegation of persisting threats might encourage the reappearance of the very difficulties which past policies have managed to avoid.

In such circumstances President Nixon's Guam doctrine is necessarily an exercise in ambiguity, designed to reflect a mood without needlessly narrowing operational possibilities. Its main thrust, developed over several years,[8] is a reversion to an offshore policy in Asia, smaller U.S. responsibilities in the region, and greater security efforts by local powers. In mood, it is a response to the contemporary intolerance of far-off, difficult and ambiguous problems. But it also reflects a line of thought which goes back to George Washington and holds that:

> The destiny of Europe and Asia has not been committed, under God, to the keeping of the United States; and only conceit, dreams of grandeur, vain imaginings, lust for power, or a desire to escape from our domestic perils and obligations could possibly make us suppose that Providence has appointed us his chosen people for the pacification of the earth.[9]

The 1970 version is that America has no business being the 'world's policeman'. In strategic geography the Guam doctrine harks back to General Douglas MacArthur, who declared in 1949 that 'our line of defense runs through the chain of islands fringing the coast of Asia. It starts from the Philippines and continues through the Ryukyu Archipelago, which includes its main bastion, Okinawa. Then it bends back through Japan and the Aleutian Island chain to Alaska.'[10] It also echoes President Eisenhower who, following the Korean stalemate, thought that:

> United States security policy should take into account the need for membership in a system of alliances. Since our resources were and are finite, we could not supply all the land, sea and air forces for the entire Free World. The logical role for our allies along the periphery of the Iron Curtain, therefore, would be to provide (with our help) for their own local security, especially ground forces, while the United States . . . provided mobile reserve forces of all arms, with emphasis on sea and air contingents.[11]

Mr Nixon's view that never again must another country's security be more important to the U.S. than to that country's own citizens and neighbours is an obvious comment upon the political difficulties which the United States has encountered in Vietnam. But it also echoes the

opinion of Secretary of State Dean Acheson some twenty years earlier: 'it is not the function of the United States nor will it nor can it attempt to furnish a will to resist and a purpose for resistance to those who must provide for themselves'.[12] U.S. support has not been withdrawn, but in its new form the American insurance policy carries a sizeable deductible clause.[13] Moreover, though the Guam doctrine was originally intended to apply primarily to Asia, both its reasoning and its underlying mood had clear global implications. In a sense the Mansfield Resolution for a reduced American presence in Europe was always complementary with the Guam doctrine. During the early months of 1970 that complementarity became explicit as indications multiplied that American ground forces in Europe were almost certain to be reduced during the next few years.

For nuclear strategy the implications of the Guam doctrine are two fold. The United States, according to Mr Nixon, will 'provide a shield if a nuclear power threatens the freedom of a nation allied with us, or a nation whose survival we consider vital to our security and the security of the region as a whole'.[14] At the same time the draw-down of conventional military power associated with the disengagement in Vietnam will necessarily decrease America's ability to respond in non-nuclear fashion to a military challenge even at the non-nuclear level. Yet the history of American decisions in the crises of the nuclear era cannot encourage smaller states, or those not vital to American security, to have much faith in American nuclear protection, least of all in cases where the opponent is a Soviet Union which not merely commands an assured destruction capability against the continental United States but has moved towards parity with the U.S. in some forms of nuclear weaponry.[15]

This is not to say that American policies in Asia, or elsewhere, can be interpreted simply as a return to an older tradition, or that the presence of traditional elements must make future U.S. policy-making more predictable. The situation is complicated by a number of new, or newly important, factors. One of the more important is the uncertainty surrounding the outcome of the Vietnam war, and the consequences which this will produce within the U.S. itself. It is, for example, not impossible that Vietnamization may fail and the entire U.S. effort in South-East Asia be seen to have been wasted. Prediction about such a situation, unprecedented in U.S. history, is foolhardy. But the appearance of far-reaching withdrawal symptoms cannot be excluded. It is already clear that the dissenters of 1969-70 include some of the very groups who, for the last twenty years, have supported American engagement and intervention abroad. Many of them are liberals. Opposed to them have been administration supporters often

more concerned to deflate the liberals than to support foreign commitments. Up to mid-1970 it was not clear what policies could be constructed on the basis of such changed domestic support. Furthermore, the impact of liberal disillusionment was increased by the growing influence of an academic-media complex with its identifiably liberal political centre of gravity, considerable opinion-forming influence and a tendency to regard itself as the conscience of governments and the proper guide of public policy. At the same time liberal dissent was connected with the increasing importance of international public opinion in impressing, not so much the U.S. decision-maker as his domestic constituency. This was so less because foreign criticism was interesting *per se* than because the communications industries, with their considerable domestic political clout, had become in important senses part of an international fraternity, subject to considerable influence from outside the nation's boundaries.

These developments may, indeed, form part of a decline in the nation-state principle in its old sense.[16] A variety of groups in the advanced countries have moved farther away from a view of the world in which the nation-state is the primary focus of loyalty, and towards the consolidation of sub-national and trans-national loyalties. Some of the most notable have been the sub-national groupings of students[17] and the trans-national network of new left radicalism. This redefinition of the terminology of community accords with a number of new organizational, institutional and economic developments within and between these advanced countries. As the role of national government becomes both more complex and more uncontrollable, so individuals have come to look for units which are at once more comprehensible and more responsive to their own wishes. At the other end of the scale, the connections between the advanced industrial countries over the last twenty years have created economic, cultural and communications infrastructures of quite a new kind. An increasing number of rules of international or trans-national behaviour are made otherwise than through governments. These range from international credit and credit information organizations to international air transport affairs and market sharing or insurance arrangements. The constantly increasing flow of money and goods between nations is qualitatively changing, and in some respects eroding, the self-determination of states. Money, credit and investment capital have ceased to be national, at least in their provenance and organization, if not in their targets. The activities of the international corporation are becoming at once more influential in the lives of individual states and less subject to the control of single governments.[18] While, therefore, the central position of the United States in the pattern of economic inter-

change between advanced countries, and the functions of the $US, give America a unique role, even for it the degree of interdependence with others is increasing. Together with these ambiguities has come the devaluation—real or apparent—of such traditional criteria for national action as 'superiority' and 'victory'. It has proved hard, both for public opinion and for the traditionally-minded in the services and in government, to accept either the notion that military victory is only the beginning of a political process, not the end,[19] or the belief that a war without an apparently conclusive victory is worth fighting at all.[20] Shifts of opinion and loyalty of this kind have aggravated the abrasiveness of domestic division, if only because they have tended to make the old regulators of sectional differences irrelevant and therefore ineffective. This, too, has necessarily weakened the nation as an actor in international politics.

Yet these factors, too, point to no single or firm conclusion. The focus of liberal opinion may have turned towards disengagement in Asia and concentration at home. It is less clear how far it would like the renunciation of responsibilities to be permanent, and how far it looks to restoration at home as a necessary condition for the fulfilment of America's role in the world. The liberal view may in some ways be reinforced by the media and by foreign opinion. Yet as the political influence and role of the media has increased, so they have also become more vulnerable to political attack. At least some sections of American society have displayed considerable sales resistance to the media and to the kind of political comment which appears to imply that voters are either retrograde or predictable.[21] Television may make a minor radical into a national figure, or a local brawl into a national event. But it may also tend to make the revolutionary ineffective. It can give him a national audience; but it also gives him an aura associated with show business. And once he has attained public notice, the very constancy of television's demand for the new story and the novel cause deprives him of the sustained attention and support which is a prerequisite for successful political action. These handicaps may be surmountable if he has a real and urgent issue which compels attention. But this is merely another way of saying that issues matter in spite of the public's jaded television palate rather than because of its hunger for novelty. Again, the American voter or Senator may hear or see more of the world than ever before. But it has not necessarily become easier to perceive the real world through the fog of conflicting words, with the result that both judgement and action relevant to real and concrete situations have become in some ways not easier but more difficult. Even the decline in patriotic values has its ambiguous aspects. For one thing, patriotism

has rarely been the solely dominant strand in American thinking, even in wartime. According to one investigating group the average American soldier in the Second World War 'gave little concern to the conflicting values underlying the military struggle . . . Although he showed a strong but tacit patriotism, this usually did not lead him . . . to subordinate his personal interests to the furtherance of ideal aims.'[22] It may be, therefore, that what happened during the later 1960s was less a decline in patriotism than a relative upgrading of sub-national or cross-national loyalties; and that this was made possible at least in part by the apparent disappearance of immediate external threats. It seems significant that the devaluation of patriotism by some groups led, almost immediately, to a countervailing reassertion of national loyalty by others. And neither doubts about patriotism nor disappointment with inconclusive military involvements would necessarily survive the appearance of a cause which aroused moral fervour and a renewal of national pride as did the Second World War and the opening stages of the Korean War. Even the development of trans-national and supra-national ways of doing things is to some extent contradicted, and may yet be reversed, by an increasing tendency towards national separatism and self-determination, and economic protectionism, in various parts of the world. In terms of economics and technology, indeed, the developments of the last decade have probably increased the role of government as much as they may have weakened the state in other ways. Emmanuel Mesthene has concluded that:

> What is actually happening is best described as a mixing up of social institutions. Put more positively, what we are seeing is the forging of new partnerships between governmental and non-governmental forms, as all institutions in the society become aware of the increasingly public character of the problems they face. In these new partnerships, government finds a new dimension, a new role, that we have not normally associated with it. No longer is government either the simple arbiter of conflicting interests between business, labor, farmers, or whatever, or the agent to whom all social action should be delegated. Instead, government—however haltingly as yet—is taking on the function of social pioneer and leader of a team.[23]

The tendency towards American withdrawal in 1969-70, therefore, was not unambiguous. It remained unclear how far it was a temporary phenomenon, associated with Vietnam warweariness or how far it reflected, or would come to reflect, a permanent change in the U.S. view of the world. In spite of the desire to concentrate on domestic problems it remained true that 'in a certain elusive but nonetheless operative sense the world is the American neighbourhood'.[24] Even

more, with the withdrawal of European responsibilities in the outside world Washington seemed increasingly convinced that it alone had a truly global view. All other powers associated with the western alliance were in essence regionally oriented.[25] Yet the sheer intractability of a world where smaller states seek escape from the constraints of Great Power dominance at the same time as they look to Great Power strength to further their own purposes, whether in defence or development, has also led to a decline in the belief in world order. The world may be America's neighbour, but the recent tendency has been to be chary about using U.S. power far afield; to accept a greater degree of local turmoil; to shift policy emphasis from the establishment of world order to the containment of such regional disorder; and to accept that peace is, after all, not indivisible and that in some areas the U.S. and the U.S.S.R. may jointly abstain from involvement.[26] At the same time the major parameters of the global situation, as seen from Washington, remain relatively unchanged. Western Europe remains vital, and NATO a binding commitment, for all Mr Nixon's emphasis on do-it-yourself where possible. The need to maintain a balance against the Soviet Union and China remains imperative, as does the U.S. commitment to the security of Japan.[27] In East and South-East Asia, while some American withdrawal has begun, much may depend upon the success of consolidation efforts within the individual countries of the area during the last half dozen years. If President Nixon is right in saying that 'others now have the ability and responsibility to deal with local disputes which once might have required our intervention',[28] a measure of U.S. withdrawal may be compatible with the maintenance of stable relationships. If not, America may in future face fresh dilemmas quite analogous to those which led it away from an offshore strategy and into Vietnam a decade ago. Withdrawal, then, may or may not be adequate in particular situations in the future. It may or may not permit a continued belief by others in a measure of American protection. Towards the rest of the globe, including much of the third world, the U.S. is displaying a degree of friendly disinterest, except perhaps for some economic and technical aid.[29]

At the military level, in America, as in other advanced countries, the pressures for a reversion to fully professional forces have increased. These pressures include not merely public resentment of conscription but the services' own needs for longer-serving personnel to cope with the increasing technical sophistication of modern weaponry. At the same time, while modern weapons technology and transport developments have made overseas bases less essential for some purposes, they have also made it possible to conduct some kinds

G

of far-flung operations based directly upon the U.S. Increasingly, therefore, it has become possible to tailor weapons systems and deployment to particular situations rather than for generalized purposes. It may be that this tendency will continue for military action to be carefully calibrated for particular situations, carried out by professional forces, and with a minimum of either domestic public involvement or overt prior political commitment. In some situations where there seems no danger of major escalation, small 'police actions' might be fought by professionals (especially sea and air power) amid comparative public indifference. It seems conceivable that, as during the 1950s and 1960s America sometimes waged peace so that it was almost indistinguishable from war, so it may in future sometimes wage war so that it will be as much as possible like peace.[30]

In these circumstances it seems likely that, while the broad framework of principle which underpins U.S. policies will change only slowly, detailed policies for particular problems will continue to be worked out in comparatively pragmatic, indeed *ad hoc*, fashion. The emphasis on 'keeping options open' which has characterized so much of American policy-making since John F. Kennedy is, after all, merely another way of saying that it is better to have no policies at all than ones which may turn out to be undesirable or irrelevant. Decisions on such matters are also usually determined by the peculiarities of the Washington decision-making structure. In this context two of its characteristics deserve mention. The first is the constant tension between the disposition not merely to activism but to novelty, and the need for those long-term and consistent policies which almost always underlie success in foreign affairs. The second is the degree of competition in decision-making as between departments, with the result that on secondary matters decisions are taken, often in conflicting fashion, by separate agencies; while on major issues decisions are difficult to arrive at, largely the result of domestic compromise, and rarely susceptible of amendment through the urging of foreigners. A professional comment on the first has been given by one of America's greatest Secretaries of State, Dean Acheson:

> The simple truth is that perseverance in good policies is the only avenue to success, and that even perseverance in poor ones often gives the appearance of being so . . .
> The great exponent of perseverance, William the Silent, Prince of Orange, never wavered in the face of every hardship and disaster from striving for the unity and independence of the Netherlands. The immortal sentence in which he epitomized his life cannot be repeated too often: 'It is not necessary to hope in order to act, or to succeed in order to persevere'.[31]

86

The second factor has been explained as follows by Alastair Buchan:

. . . the United States Government itself has the characteristics of an alliance and the process of evolving decisions on high policy is probably more difficult for it than in that of any other government in the world. Yet American public servants are perhaps the most open-minded in the world, are less hampered by traditional conceptions than the European counterparts and are closely linked to a system of academic discussion and research on public policy of great vitality. This means that in the preliminary states of the evolution of a new policy or strategy, or reaction to an external challenge, the discussion is a relatively free one and one in which the views of allies are welcome. But so difficult is the process of reconciling the views of different departments, agencies and branches of the government that the further it moves up the chain of authority the more inflexible positions become. By the time the President has made 'a determination' on a particular policy, there is little that an allied government, however powerful, can do to change it. The President can, of course, short-circuit or bypass the system, but it is unwise for allied governments to rely on being able to persuade him directly in a crisis. . . . For the same reason, American repesentatives abroad often lack the authority with which the material power of the United States should endow them, simply because they cannot keep closely in touch with the Washington debate and cannot therefore present a clear picture of the evolution of their government's policy until it is clarified into a decision which they can only present as a fait accompli.[32]

Washington's view of its relationship with Australia is therefore likely to be more a function of its domestic preoccupations, of America's major political and strategic interests to Australia's north, and perhaps most of all of the general drive and momentum of U.S. policies at the time, than of any policies clearly focussed on Australia *per se*. Within this stream the custom of friendship and the habits of alliance, undoubted as these are, play a role which some Australian writers have probably underrated. Friendship has been accompanied, and probably sustained, by a considerable degree of mutual ignorance.[33] This ignorance may have highlighted the real and remarkable similarities in the public philosophies and attitudes of the two countries while obscuring the equally real but less obvious dissimilarities. It is not merely that in Australia, as elsewhere, radicals have aped the causes, even the phraseology, of American dissent;[34] or that Australian television watchers are more familiar with some aspects of American than of Australian life; or that Australian shops sell American-style goods. It is that Australians and Americans have quite parallel attitudes to material benefits, economic growth and

87

engineering enterprise. Both have an optimism based on a deep belief in their own destiny, on evidence of wealth and, by comparison with other advanced countries, an inexperience of public suffering, of invasion or defeat or even violent revolution. Australians have gone almost as far as Americans in accepting a deeply rationalist approach to social organization and progress, based perhaps on the pioneering influences which have helped to shape both nations.[35] The Australian emphasis on competition and achievement, especially achievement measured in material terms, has begun among many social groups to match the American example.[36] At any rate a significant number of Americans find Australia a likely place to invest, and sometimes even to settle. They are apt to think of Australia as yet another open frontier to the west; an extension of the American experience, with very similar compulsions to tame desert and wilderness. Partly as a result political friendship with Australia creates few problems within the U.S. Nor is association with successive democratically elected Australian governments likely to arouse moral or political criticism in the U.S., or to entail external difficulties.[37] The point is not that these intangibles of alliance and friendship compel official American support, still less that they can guarantee American political or military backing in particular situations. It is rather that they provide an environment in which America's disposition to consider Australian interests is enhanced and action (or abstention from action) in accordance with those interests becomes much easier and politically more acceptable than it otherwise would be.

More concretely, there is a tradition of mutual obligation and support. This has ranged from the Second World War, through the Korean conflict, the formation of ANZUS and the SEATO treaty, to the involvement of both nations in Vietnam. The alliance with the United States has solid bipartisan support in Australia, for all the occasional differences on details and emphasis. The Australian role in Asia, though inevitably small, has been generally helpful from Washington's point of view. This is so in spite of a series of disagreements. The Australians initially resisted the American wish to begin to move Japan from occupation to alliance. They refused to follow the American lead over Quemoy and Matsu in the mid-1950s. They did not join in the complete American economic boycott of China. They deeply resented the American position on Indonesia's acquisition of West Irian during the early 1960s. Until the middle of that decade they maintained a defence effort which was not only small in absolute terms but which, as a proportion of the Australian G.N.P., seemed incommensurate with the claims which Australia was making on U.S. support. But Australians have also, and apart from direct in-

volvement with and support for the U.S. in South-East Asia, helped to maintain a position in Singapore and Malaysia which buttressed the general American effort in the region. Their diplomatic and aid efforts have often also been compatible rather than incompatible with American intentions and efforts there.[38]

The United States enjoys Australian co-operation in a variety of other ways. Much of Australian military planning, training and procurement has been based on the assumption of actual or potential co-operation with the United States. Standardization of some weapons systems upon American models helps Australia, but also makes Australian support for the U.S. easier to give, makes some forms of involvement dependent upon U.S. co-operation and support and gives the U.S. some leverage in influencing Australian strategic decisions.[39] Co-operation in intelligence matters means that the U.S. gives more than it receives. But there are important pay-offs, too. Once the flow of information is established, it is likely to have one or more of three kinds of result. The flow of intelligence can be used as subtle flattery of those to whom it is made available. Moreover, since the information received in Canberra will tally with that received by American decision-makers, it is likely to make Australians more sympathetic to American difficulties and actions.[40] And given the general political disposition of the government in Canberra, even if the intelligence is ignored, this is likely to lead to a mere reversion to customary Australian stereotyped opinions, which include reliance upon the U.S. In any event, once the flow of information is established, the Australian official apparatus is likely to be highly sensitive to any action which might result in having the flow limited or interrupted. Beyond that, Australia serves as a base for important elements of the U.S. military and space effort. This ranges from the availability (and popularity) of Australia as a rest and recreation centre for American troops in Vietnam to U.S. National Aeronautics and Space Administration tracking stations and military installations including the communications base at North West Cape for the Polaris submarine fleet.[41] It seems highly likely that at least some of these stations are relevant to the monitoring of observation satellites and certain other kinds of orbital device, both from the United States and elsewhere, the monitoring of nuclear testing and the detection of shipping movements in important quarters of the southern hemisphere.

Australia also has an economic role of some significance from a United States point of view. It is not that Australia is indispensable as a market for U.S. goods, or even that by 1965 the accumulated total of U.S. investment in Australia had reached some $A5,000 mil-

lion, or well over 40% of total foreign investment in Australia.[42] For the U.S. these figures are hardly of major significance. But Australia plays an important role in the economic patterns of the Pacific region, most importantly perhaps as a supplier of raw materials for Japan.[43] The political and strategic relationship between the U.S. and Japan, itself one of America's central concerns in the Pacific, is bound to be influenced by the degree of Japanese dependence upon Australian iron and coal, derived from deposits in a country allied with the United States, owned and developed by companies in which U.S. interests have an important stake.

The strategic centrepiece of the alliance is, of course, the ANZUS treaty. It is also one of the few American treaty relationships in the Pacific region which have not been seriously questioned during the U.S. internal debates of recent years. In terms of U.S. public opinion no doubt this has something to do with the comparative obscurity of its obligations and the absence of past or present costs. Yet the fact remains that America's acceptance of its formal obligations, including ANZUS, has been repeatedly reaffirmed over the years by a variety of officials including President Nixon.[44] The idea of American nuclear protection for non-nuclear allies has also been reaffirmed; and this must have important implications for U.S. involvement in the management of any conflict which might escalate to nuclear levels. At the same time ANZUS, like other treaties, involves ambiguities. The two most obvious concern the area covered by the treaty and the precise character of the help which the parties would give to each other in case of need.[45] The chief operational provisions of the treaty, Articles IV(I) and V, run as follows:

> Each party recognises that an armed attack in the Pacific Area on any of the Parties would be dangerous to its own peace and safety and declares that it would act to meet the common danger in accordance with its constitutional processes.

and

> For the purpose of Article IV, an armed attack on any of the parties is deemed to include an armed attack on the metropolitan territory of any of the parties, or the island territories under its jurisdiction in the Pacific or on its armed forces, public vessels or aircraft in the Pacific.

It is evident that the treaty does not specify the kind of action to meet a common danger which any of the parties to it would actually take. Nor could any government so bind itself in advance on events whose character and surrounding circumstances are necessarily unknown. There is also some uncertainty as to what the 'Pacific Area'

includes for the purposes of this agreement. In 1955, for example, the
Australian Prime Minister, Mr Menzies, sought assurances of 'effective co-operation' from the U.S. before agreeing to send Australian
troops to Malaysia. He was told that such co-operation was implied
by the SEATO pact,[46] but this was probably a less substantial undertaking than he had sought. During later years, and particularly in
1963-65, there were repeated signs of uncertainty as to whether
American protection under ANZUS could be taken to apply to Australian troops in Malaysia and North Borneo.[47] While the Australians
clearly wanted to be able to use U.S. backing, or at least the threat of
it,[48] to avoid trouble, Washington was uneasy about an Australian
attempt to extend American responsibilities by interpretation. Ambiguities of this kind can also confer considerable diplomatic leverage
upon one of the contracting parties, in this case the U.S.A. Washington is likely to make a distinction between the central obligation of
support for Australia in a case of direct attack, and support for less
central Australian interests further afield. Beyond the defence of the
Australian continent the invoking, let alone the exact interpretation,
of ANZUS is essentially a matter of bargaining. This helps to explain
the Australian tendency to operate so as to build up political credit
in Washington and place the U.S. under a moral or political obligation to Australia which could be cashed in case of need. 'The American commitment anywhere', Mr McGeorge Bundy has written, 'is
only as deep as the continued conviction of Americans that their own
interest requires it'.[49] Successive Australian governments have tried to
ensure that the interpretation of the American interest shall include
the most important of their own concerns. No doubt it is true that
Australia joined SEATO, became involved in Malaysia and supported the American containment of China for reasons of its own.
Still, the Australian wish for American support in New Guinea and
over Malaysia probably made it more difficult for Australian governments to avoid U.S. requests for troop support in Vietnam. No doubt
Australia desires, in its own interests, to further some kinds of collective action within the region. But this is surely reinforced by the fact
that the U.S. looks to Australia to play such a role and that U.S. support for Australia itself is connected with these expectations. As Mr
Percy Spender explained as long ago as 1950: 'Before the United
States can be expected to assume responsibilities in connection with
the defence of Pacific countries, some of those countries at least must
themselves give evidence of their willingness to unite in their own
defence'.[50] It is a corollary of Australia's role in this respect that
some Asian countries themselves have a direct interest in the Aus-
tralian-U.S. link as a way of attracting U.S. support to themselves.

These considerations must not be taken too far. Australian doubts about the U.S. have increased in recent years. Among some groups which were formerly among the firmest supporters of the alliance, even within the Liberal-Country Party government coalition, disappointment at the American withdrawal in Vietnam has led to new doubts about the value and reliability of U.S. friendship. Australian opinion is probably more volatile on such matters than in the past. Yet Australians are probably still reluctant to assert a degree of self-centredness or unco-operativeness within the alliance which would deprive the arrangement of its success, and therefore its substantive value, in American eyes. As with all relationships, to declare it useless is to go far in making it so. Australians have so far been reluctant, on the whole, to go to such lengths.

This reluctance may have been reinforced by the fact that the U.S. is in any case not committed to Australia's support in every circumstance where such support might be desired by Canberra. In particular, the relationship does not bind the U.S. to give priority to Australia in every situation where its requirements clash with other American interests or where the Australian view springs from a different focus upon the problems of the world. These may be highly important limitations. The U.S. has, for example, displayed a lively interest in the development and consolidation of Indonesia, in part as an element in the containment of China and a prop of a future South Asian security system. If Australian and Indonesian interests were to clash, for example in New Guinea, it is by no means clear that Canberra could count upon unhesitating U.S. support. The matter of general focus may be even more important. Many of the issues of most acute concern to Australia, especially those concerning the Indonesian archipelago and Pacific trade, are of entirely subordinate importance to Washington. Conversely, there is not much evidence that Australia has, or wishes to have, anything significant to say on such major U.S. concerns as the Middle East problem, or the achievement of a U.S.-Soviet understanding on limiting strategic armaments. Of the major American foreign policy problems of 1969-70 it is probably only on Vietnam that the Australians have, from time to time, had something to say that was not merely important but couched in terms which would ensure it a serious hearing in Washington. Australia is not often a source of important new ideas for American foreign policy-makers.

On the other hand, the maintenance of a strong relationship with Australia seems essential if America looks to the fulfilment of its plans for redeployment in Asia in the form in which these have developed during 1968-70. Strategically, Australia remains the great land bridge

between the Indian Ocean and the Pacific, and guardian of some of the major sea passages between them. It is a geographically convenient and politically secure southern base for pro-western influences in southern Asia, from the rendering of economic aid to the provision, in some situations, of military support. The main thrust of American planning for the post-Vietnam period has been for an offshore presence, combined with a continued containment of China, for which Australia is a secure southern anchor. The emphasis upon regional action is furthered by the presence of a state which is unimpeachably local as well as a traditional friend. An American presence in East or South-East Asia, in whatever form, is likely to continue to depend for its political acceptability upon evidence—indeed increased evidence—of allied effort.[51] The American interest in the shipping lanes of southern Asia, both direct and by consequence of the U.S. relationship with Japan, will depend upon the presence of a friendly rather than an unfriendly Australia. There is also the Indian Ocean. The U.S. has been reluctant to undertake any deployment in this area. But if the Soviet Union were to secure a reopening of the Suez Canal, with consequently easy passage from the Black Sea to the Arabian Sea, counteraction might be thought necessary. If so, this might take the form of a U.S. presence or a deployment by more directly interested parties. In either case the importance of Australia for the United States would be enhanced. In the further future, the creation of nuclear forces by India and perhaps Japan could equally upgrade Australia's importance, both as a monitoring base and for purposes of non-nuclear containment. In sum, the U.S. may wish to shift the focus of its actions in these regions away from direct American participation and towards local arrangements of a sort acceptable to it. But arrangements in East Asia are bound to be influenced by the economic and strategic relationship of Japan and Australia, while South-East Asian stability—assuming that it can be achieved—is even harder to visualize without Australian support and perhaps a measure of participation. Australian foreign and defence policies are likely to retain their dual character of ties with the advanced countries and the U.S., and an intimate concern with southern Asia. So long as this is so, Australia is likely to be a valuable, and upon occasion essential, partner of the United States.

Some Area Problems

Malaysia and Singapore—Their Strategic Implications for Australia

ROBERT O'NEILL

Malaysia and Singapore comprise one of the traditional areas of concern for Australia's defence and foreign policy. They have received
so much emphasis in the period since 1920 that one tends to take for
granted their legitimacy as foci of Australian attention. The events of
December 1941 proved the validity of the earlier Australian appreciation of their potential influence on the security of Australia itself.
The growth of the Super Powers, of the nuclear deterrent and of the
multi-national alliance system, however, have changed the assumptions by which the construction of the Singapore base was justified.
Under present conditions, it may be asked whether the interests of
Australia are to be served better by adherence to the old notions of
involvement with and commitment to both Malaysia and Singapore,
or whether a Fortress Australia policy would be preferable.

It is tempting to say that one of the most vital and unchangeable
factors in the strategy of the Malay Peninsula is its shape. In the days
of the *Dreadnought* British strategists were hypnotized by the sea
which encompasses seven-eighths of the circle around Singapore. The
Imperial Japanese Army, however, emphasized the weakness of
ignoring that vital one-eighth—the 400-mile-long peninsula down
which they marched in under eight weeks. The development of air
power and the general increase in mobility both by land and by sea
has weakened the old Japanese concept and hence there are some
serious shortcomings in the notion of stopping the 'yellow hordes' at
the point where once the narrow strip of red began on the map.

One might also suppose that the common bond of inherited British
attitudes which links Australia, Malaysia and Singapore will ensure
mutual sympathy and rapport for some considerable period. The
strength of such a link has been shown elsewhere as by the community
of former French possessions in Africa. This example, however,
ignores the potentially destructive force of racialism. The former

97

French colonies in Africa are peopled largely by indigenous Africans. Australia is inhabited largely by the non-indigenous scions of the former imperial power. Malaysia and Singapore can win some recognition as members of the third world. Australia is identifying itself more and more with the capitalist world of the 'haves', led by the U.S. Hence it would, on balance, be unwise to hope for much continuance in the strength of links based on imperial, cultural and political heritage.

The location of Malaysia and Singapore with respect to Australia is another factor working for a permanent link. Only 1,800 miles separate Darwin and Singapore, and hence it is difficult to conceive of a threat to Malaysian security which would not cause major concern in Canberra. Yet the idea of a close relationship between Malaysia, Singapore and Australia depends a great deal on the attitude of Indonesia towards the question. When only the docile Netherlands East Indies were interposed, this problem did not arise. Dutch neutrality during the First World War was of only minor inconvenience to Australia and co-belligerence during the Second World War eliminated the problem. Since 1945 Indonesia has developed its own interests and it can no longer be taken for granted that these interests are going to coincide with those of its neighbours, any more than one would assume such coincidences in a European context. Confrontation typified this problem.

The factor of location has been changed also by the new significance for Australia of the nations beyond Malaysia—Thailand, Vietnam, Cambodia and Laos. Because of the decreasing significance of distance as an obstacle to military operations, the arguments for Australian-Malaysian defence co-operation could be applied with greater force to the nations of the SEATO area. By this reasoning Malaysia is of secondary importance to Australia while Thailand and South Vietnam are not communist, and it is of little importance should these countries become communist.

In the light of these three factors it is apparent that the future attitude of Australia towards Malaysia and Singapore will not be easy to determine. The Australian forward defence theory stresses Thailand and Vietnam more than Malaysia and Singapore; the importance of close relations with Indonesia for Australia makes a binding commitment to Malaysia and Singapore unwise; future political instability in those two countries could draw Australia into internal political disputes which she should avoid.

What can be deduced from the more changeable economic and demographic factors in the composition of Malaysia and Singapore? Singapore with a population of 2,025,000 and a Gross National Pro-

duct of $US1,200 million[1] relies on trade and manufacturing for its income. Confrontation placed some stress on Singapore's economy but since 1964 its G.N.P. has increased by almost 50%.[2] Singapore's major economic problems are how to increase national income in step with population growth, how to replace dwindling *entrepôt* income through earnings from manufactures and how to create jobs for the growing labour force to compensate for the reduction or withdrawal of the British military establishment.

These problems may be formidable, but they are not as difficult as those confronting Malaysia, whose economy rests on the unsteady pillars of rubber and tin. Rubber earns nearly 35% of the Malaysian export income and hence there is a pressing need for diversification. The fall in world rubber prices and the increasing competition from synthetics has amplified this need. The average export price for rubber sold in Singapore and Malaya in 1960 was 106.6 cents (Malaysian) per pound. By 1967 this had fallen to 55.4 cents per pound,[3] and official estimates anticipate that the 1970 price will fall to less than 50 cents, a price which will make uneconomical many of the small holdings which together produce 42% of the Malayan output.[4]

The problem of finding a suitable additional export earner is one of the first magnitude. The market for Malaysian timber is growing and great hopes have been built on expanding the oil palm plantations. The price of oil palm has not fluctuated wildly and demand is strong, but, in 1960, this commodity earned only 2% of the Malaysian export income, and by 1967 it was earning only 3%.[5] Massive conversion of plantations from rubber to oil palm is severely complicated by the latter's greater sensitivity to soil types, the social problems in changing the living patterns of the small holders from the easier routine of rubber to the more demanding culture of oil palm, the need to re-educate small holders in crop management and the very heavy capital outlay necessary for oil extraction factories. Other crops, tea, cocoa, pineapples and rice, are faced with difficulties of similar magnitude.

Of the remaining 65% of Malaysian export income which is not earned by rubber, nearly one half is earned by minerals, chiefly tin and iron. Malaya produces low-cost tin and supplies one-third of the world's demand. Tin prices and output have fluctuated severely, however, partially due to the cessation of U.S. strategic stockpiling of tin. The long-term outlook for Malayan tin is gloomy, with current estimates of exhaustion of the tin deposits occurring before 1995. New tin-bearing lands are being sought energetically, but with little success. Iron ore, which produces approximately one-sixth of the

99

export earnings of tin, faces a more extreme predicament because of uncertainty regarding the extent of reserves.

Hence, from economic considerations, Malaysia's importance to Australia as a supplier of raw materials is likely to decline and Malaysia's overall economic difficulties seem likely to threaten its ability to maintain both economic progress and the strength needed to make an alliance of reciprocal benefit. The outlook for Singapore, while not so acute from an economic standpoint, is nonetheless fraught with difficulties which are being complicated by the second category of changeable factors—those relating to demography.

With a population of over 2 million and an area of 225 square miles, Singapore is an overcrowded island. Its population density approaches 9,000 persons per square mile, by comparison with Malaya's 153 and the low 17 persons per square mile for Sabah and Sarawak.[6] The acute housing deficiency and labour surplus problems thus created are being compounded by a high, although decreasing, rate of natural increase. The death rate in Singapore, 5.7 per thousand in 1964, and 5.5 in 1968[7], seems to have stabilized and hence the Singapore government has emphasized birth control measures which have reduced the birth rate from 42.7 per thousand in 1957 to 23.5 in 1968.[8] The racial composition of Singapore's population in 1968 was 74.4% Chinese, 14.5% Malay and 11.1% other races, and of these the Chinese are increasing the most rapidly.[9]

Although the yearly rate of increase of Malaysia's population is only three-quarters of that of Singapore[10] Malaysia faces an acute racial problem. Approximately 50% of the population of Malaya is Malay, 37% is Chinese and 11% is Indian and Pakistani.[11] Hence attempts by the Malays to dominate the Chinese have encountered very strong resistance, and unusual delicacy in internal politics is called for, but not always found. The higher Chinese birth rate is tending to complicate and perpetuate the problem.

Despite the relatively few Europeans living in Malaya and Singapore, the European financial interest in these countries is of considerable importance and poses further difficulties for the future. Overseas capital has played a major part in the development of both countries, particularly through the plantation and mining industries. Of large rubber estates which produce half of Malaya's output, 60% are European- and American-owned. Both American and British ownership control much of the oil palm plantations, extraction and marketing. The mining industry has attracted both European and Chinese capital. Most dredge-operated mines, producing 54% of the output, are British-owned, and Chinese ownership prevails amongst the gravel pump mines.[12] Hence any Malay attempt to oust the non-

Malay owners could cause serious international trouble and economic loss to all concerned.

Consequently the stability of Malaysia and Singapore, both economically and racially, could be severely threatened in many different ways, ranging from population pressure to attempts by ethnic groups to alter significantly their conditions and status. Australia's interests in Malaya and Singapore could meet with sudden reverses, but clearly the situation is one in which Australia's assistance is needed from the more long-term view of regional stability if not for short-term selfish gains.

Having considered the anatomies of Malaysia and Singapore in isolation from Australia, it might now seem appropriate to examine problems and interests shared by Australia with either or both of the other two. Paramount amongst these is the desire to contain China and communist influence. Malaysia and Australia are ruled by moderately conservative governments and that of Singapore, now moderately socialist, has moved gradually towards the right over the last few years. Each of these governments has a strong vested interest in denouncing communism as an ideology, and all feel insecure in the face of China's numerical superiority over each. The period of the Malayan Emergency, 1948-60, was one of acute anxiety for all nations interested in South-East Asia. In 1950 Australia sent two air squadrons, and in 1955, after it was free of its Korean War commitment, Australia contributed small naval, military and further air forces to aid the British and Malayan authorities. The original purpose for which these forces were sent to Malaysia has been achieved, but they have been maintained there ever since, in the interests of both regional and local stability.

The Australian participation in the Malayan Emergency has established a tradition of close co-operation in many fields—diplomatic, economic, cultural and military being some of the more important. It is necessary, however, to recognize the dependence of this link on ideological and national considerations. Should any of the three nations no longer feel insecure because of communist insurgency, then a slackening in mutual interest would appear inevitable.

In the context of ideology Vietnam has also played an important role in the three-nation relationship. Malaysia and Singapore have not made any direct military contribution to the war in the way that Australia has, and on occasions they have even been critical of some aspects of American involvement. Both Malaysia and Singapore have, however, expressed privately, if not publicly, considerable support for American policy in Vietnam and are hoping for a continued American military presence in South-East Asia for many more years.

H

The increasing role of Indonesia in international affairs, particularly during the last years of the Soekarno regime, has given the three nations another common concern. Just as Russia has been a natural ally for France because they are on opposite sides of a potentially hostile major power, Soekarno's chauvinism brought Kuala Lumpur and Canberra into close alignment in their policy towards what appeared to be a common menace. Indonesian confrontation of Malaysia followed the emergency so closely that there were considerable institutional factors making for Australian support of Malaysia, rather than for neutrality, or even support of Indonesia in the spirit of the early post-war years. In addition, the decision to hand Dutch New Guinea over to the Indonesians rankled in Canberra. It took only a few hints of a wider Indonesian interest in New Guinea, which Soekarno seemed only too willing to provide, to harden the resolve of the Menzies government against confrontation. The consequences of this decision have been of the utmost significance for the course of Australian foreign policy ever since.

One Australian reaction was a quest to obtain an American guarantee, in terms of the ANZUS agreement, to cover Australian operations against the Indonesians during confrontation. This assurance had certainly never been intended under the original anti-Japanese conception of ANZUS, but once it had been given by the Americans, Australia was in the position of owing a favour. In order to stiffen the American resolve to support its smaller ally, the Australian government may have stressed to the Americans the importance of resisting communism whenever it tried to expand and thus generally 'out-hawked' the American administration, which was still attempting to maintain a good relationship with the Indonesians. The American guarantee was given either in late 1963 or early 1964.[13] As confrontation turned out, Australia did not need to call upon America for assistance. Eighteen months later, however, when the U.S. was making its big increase in commitment of ground troops to Vietnam, the time came for Australia to return the kindness— only with men rather than guarantees.

The Menzies government had shown considerable caution in becoming involved in Vietnam, despite appreciable American pressure. By early 1965 Australia had barely 100 men in Vietnam, and these acted purely as instructors. When President Johnson decided that America would have to bear a much greater war burden, it was unlikely that the Australian government could have ignored Johnson's call for assistance and still hope that the U.S. government would define its responsibilities under ANZUS to the full extent of Australia's wishes. Thus the Australian government was placed eventu-

ally in the position of having to conscript men for the Vietnam war. Had the debt to the U.S. been somewhat smaller, it is difficult to believe that the Australian government would have committed more regular troops than could be maintained by voluntary enlistment.

The other major consequence of the Australian reaction to Soekarno's foreign policy in 1963 was the F-111 aircraft, bought presumably to give Australia a retaliation capacity against Indonesia. Since General Suharto ousted Dr Soekarno, the role of Indonesia in Australian-Malaysian relations has changed fundamentally.

The chances of an Australian-Indonesian military confrontation in New Guinea have faded and the two nations have largely reconciled their interest. Indonesia has also done much fence-mending with Malaysia. But the execution in late 1968 of Indonesian commandos captured in Singapore during confrontation caused much ill-feeling in Indonesia. Difficulties over Sabah or Sarawak could easily grow into major points of contention for Malaysia and Indonesia, should there be a change of heart in Djakarta. If Australia is firmly committed to the Malaysian side of any such dispute, then its own good, and increasingly important, relations with Indonesia could be seriously damaged. Hence any Australian government must look very closely at the effect on Indonesia of any aid or commitment which it gives to Malaysia and Singapore. Indonesian leaders ought not to be exposed to the same feelings of encirclement which the Germans felt before 1914.

Another problem shared by Singapore, Malaysia and Australia is that of military weakness and hence of the need to keep Britain and the U.S. interested in, if not actually involved in, South-East Asia. Britain's economic circumstances suggest that little fruit will reward efforts to maintain its defence interest in the Malaysian area. Whether the U.S. under Richard Nixon will suffer a severe post-Vietnam reaction has yet to be seen, but it seems unwise to plan on the basis of massive American support to solve any local South-East Asian problems. There seems little of a specific nature which small powers such as Singapore, Malaysia and Australia can do to retain the interest of the larger powers in the region, apart from simply being on good terms with them.

Dependence on international trade is another common link. Thus control of the seas around Malaysia and Australia, and of the sea routes to America and Europe, is vital. Should either the Soviet Union or, later, Japan gain a naval ascendancy in these waters, the independence of the three countries, in an economic sense at least, could be jeopardized. Consequently there is incentive for a regional naval forces agreement between Malaysia, Singapore and Australia but the

size of each country's navy would rob such an agreement of any significance greater than that of somewhat increasing the likelihood of American support.

Close similarities between the problems facing the armies of the three countries have led to appreciable co-operation between them since 1955. Although Singapore has sought aid from outside the British and Australian forces and relies appreciably on Israeli military advice and assistance, Malaysia has requested and received increasing Australian aid, principally in the field of training, as replacement for the dwindling British role as Malaysia's military mentor. The three armies share a common concern in counter-insurgency warfare in a tropical environment and in view of Australia's relative expertise and experience in this field and the need for the Australian army to have continuous training facilities available in an Asian country, there would appear to be firm foundations for prolonged military co-operation with mutual benefits to each of the three partners.

The inclusion of Australian forces in Malaysia within an integrated command structure has been possible in the past because of the British Commonwealth strategic reserve, consisting mainly of the 28th Commonwealth Brigade, which has been stationed in Malaysia and Singapore. With the removal of most British forces some delicate questions of command and control, previously handled by the British, will have to be answered. The size of any force Australia is likely to keep in Malaysia would hardly qualify it for the title of strategic reserve, and therefore Australia would not be entitled to any major role in the exercise of joint command except in the case of small-scale operations employing only a few battalions of troops. But whether the Australian government would be inclined to place its forces in Malaysia directly under Malaysian command is, to say the least, a very open question, because of the military weakness of both Malaysia and Singapore.

The armed forces of Malaysia, with 44,750[14] men, number a little over half of the Australian regular forces. Singapore has fewer than 15,000 men under arms. The Malaysian army of 38,750 includes twenty infantry battalions, two reconnaissance regiments and two artillery regiments. The Australian regular army of 43,000 men supports only nine infantry battalions. The comparison supports the evidence that the Malaysian army is heavily deficient in supporting and logistic elements. The Singapore army numbers 10,000 men organized into nine regular battalions. The naval and air forces of Malaysia and Singapore are very small and can do little more than provide light operational support for their respective armies. The Malaysian forces, however, receive additional support from 23,000 paramilitary field police, and thus Malaysia's strength in a counter-

insurgency role is a great deal more than that suggested by the size of its army.

It may be argued that criticism of the present military weakness of Malaysia and Singapore is not justified because, as newly independent countries, both have many more urgent matters to be dealt with. The magnitude of the economic and political problems facing both countries suggests that it will be very difficult for Malaysia to lift its annual *per capita* defence spending from $US13, the 1968 figure, towards the Australian figure of $US107.

Therefore in any foreseeable situation in which an alliance between Malaysia, Singapore and Australia would be invoked, Australia would be bearing considerable costs for, at best, indirect gains. The types of situation which could precipitate such an invocation are numerous. The internal situations in both Malaysia and Singapore could become unstable due to a number of causes: communist insurgency, racial violence and economic collapse could occur, either singly or combined. Another period of hostility towards Indonesia could arise. The Borneo states of Malaysia could provoke a civil war over the issue of secession. The Sabah dispute could lead to hostilities between Malaysia and the Philippines.

The degree of Australian interest in the outcome of any such trouble is as variable as is the probability that any one instance will actually come to pass. Australia is interested in the suppression of communist insurgency, but not necessarily in the promotion of Malay domination of the Malaysian Chinese. A situation could well arise in the event of renewed Malaysian-Indonesian hostilities in which Australia preferred to stay closer to Djakarta than to Kuala Lumpur. Australia would definitely not be interested in aiding Malaysia against Australia's own SEATO partner, the Philippines.

Therefore any defence agreement between Malaysia, Singapore and Australia, particularly one covering the stationing of Australian troops in these countries, ought to define closely the circumstances under which Australia would be prepared to render assistance. In Australia's interest, it would seem unwise to attempt to cover more than the question of communist insurgency.

There are, of course, many other ways of conducting relationships apart from an alliance. One obvious means is the provision of Australian economic support to enable Singapore to find jobs for its expanding population and to help Malaysia during the transitional period from reliance on rubber and tin to a diversified, industrial economy. Unless these problems are solved, Malaysia and Singapore will be weak states, easily blackmailed by any greatly superior force detrimental to Australia's interests. Educational, technical and medi-

cal assistance are clearly important means for Australia to employ in this regard.

The most fruitful military contribution which Australia could make to Malaysia and Singapore, should the latter become less dependent upon the Israelis, would be the provision of training facilities and instructors both in Australia and Malaysia or Singapore as appropriate. There seems to be no reason for limiting such training to the armies, particularly when Malaysia and Singapore possess such embryonic air and naval forces.

Because of the advantages in training which accrue to the Australian services through the use of the facilities of Malaysia and Singapore, each service should exercise its elements in these countries. Care ought to be taken in determining the numbers of Australians to go to Malaysia and Singapore, not only from the standpoint of Australian operational and financial commitments but also because of the possibilities both of causing displeasure in Djakarta when this is not desired and of losing a degree of control over whatever Australian forces are present in the two countries if one of the above-mentioned crises occurs.

Malaysia and Singapore both face futures which are overshadowed by some serious problems. Australia shares a great number of common interests with these two countries. In some, but not necessarily all of these issues, Australia can play an important role, but the individual interests of Malaysia and Singapore, coupled with their military weakness, ought to incline Australia towards caution in the conduct of relationships which were entered into in the now superseded circumstances of the 1950s. In particular, Australia ought not to encourage hopes that it can render the two countries military assistance of other than a marginal kind.

CHAPTER 8

An Australian Maritime Strategy

DAVID HAMER

Strategy is usually defined as the efficient application of national power to achieve the object of war. This definition is not, however, an adequate explanation of strategy in time of peace, when the enemy may not be clearly identified, and the proportion of national resources which is allotted to military power is limited.

Peacetime strategy might be better, although less succinctly, explained as the use of diplomatic and economic means to prevent potential enemies gaining positions from which they can threaten vital interests, and the provision of sufficient military power to make the political pressure effective.

Further, sufficient military forces must be kept in being, or be capable of being created in the necessary time scale, to enable attacks on vital interests to be defeated. Since strategy deals with the application of national power, it follows that there can be no independent naval strategy; nevertheless, the defensive and offensive uses of the sea must always be important components of the strategy of an island country such as Australia.

What forms could direct threats to Australia's vital interests take? The first is disruption of its coastal and overseas trade; the second is bombardment, probably with nuclear missiles; and the third is invasion and occupation. Each of these will be examined in turn to establish the likelihood of the threat becoming a reality, and the counteraction it might take.

Australia's economic life depends on overseas trade by sea, which in 1967-68 amounted to more than 60 million tons;[1] this was more than double the quantity of ten years earlier. The discovery of oil in Australia makes it unlikely that this rate of increase will be maintained, but certainly a continued increase can be expected.[2] (For comparison, the movement of cargo by air was less than six *thousand* tons including mail.) The ownership of the ships engaged in Australia's overseas trade might in some circumstances be of great im-

portance, so it is worth enumerating. In 1967-68, the last year for which statistics are available, the 3,972 vessels entering Australian ports from overseas were registered as follows: Britain 966, Japan 612, Norway 456, Liberia 424, Greece 197, Holland 179, New Zealand 174, Sweden 139, Panama 93, West Germany 93, France 86, Italy 83, Denmark 83, Australia 71, U.S.A. 44, Hong Kong 39, India 34, others 199.[3] The proportion of Australian-owned shipping may be expected to rise slightly in the next few years, but it will remain true that an overwhelming proportion of Australian exports and imports will be carried in shipping over which Australia has little or no control. The coastal shipping trade is more under Australian control. Of the 129 vessels engaged solely on coastal trade (which in 1965-66 amounted to more than 34 million tons) only two are owned and registered overseas.[4]

Important though this sea-borne trade obviously is, it does not necessarily follow that it needs protection. Two questions need to be answered: is the shipping threatened and, if it is threatened, would the merchant ships continue to come to Australia? If the risk were small, neutral ships might continue to trade to Australia—albeit with greatly increased insurance premiums—but, if the risk became significant, they would surely cease coming to Australia. This country has no exports which cannot be replaced from elsewhere in the world, and shipping companies are in business to make a profit. In the event of a serious threat to shipping the only ships on which Australia could rely would be its own and those of its allies. In this connection it should be pointed out that about 45% of the shipping registered in Panama and Liberia is wholly or partly American-owned, and the U.S. Department of Defense has—with the approval of the governments of Panama and Liberia—made agreements to ensure that most of these ships would be available to the United States in time of emergency.[5]

The question of whether this trade is threatened is more complex. Since the Second World War the prime role of the Australian Navy has been the defence of trade against submarine attack, but the actual enemy has never been specified.[6] Until about 1955 it must have been the Soviet Union, because no other conceivable enemy had any submarines. By 1955, as the Soviet Union's nuclear power developed, the idea of a non-nuclear global war between the U.S.S.R. and the West became less likely, and it was perhaps fortunate for Australian naval planners that by this time the communist Chinese were beginning to build up a submarine fleet, with Russian assistance. Although Soviet assistance has long been withdrawn, the Chinese submarine force now consists of more than thirty submarines.[7] In the early 1960s

Indonesia, too, began to build up its submarine fleet, again with Russian assistance. By 1962 Indonesia had twelve ex-Soviet submarines[8] and must have been considered as a possible adversary during the 'confrontation' between Indonesia and Malaysia.

The mere possession of submarines does not make them a threat to Australia's trade. The Soviet Union possesses nearly four hundred submarines, of which probably over sixty are nuclear-powered.[9] It is just conceivable that they might be used against NATO shipping in the North Atlantic in conditions short of general nuclear war but it seems quite inconceivable that Australian trade would be selected as a pressure point against NATO. Although the Soviet Navy will remain significant as a source of equipment for possible enemies, the possibility of a direct clash with Soviet submarines is too remote to warrant further consideration.

Although the ANZUS treaty covers attacks on Australian shipping only 'in the Pacific',[10] the treaty might effectively deter Indonesia from engaging in open warfare with Australia. If a further deterrent to Indonesian submarine attacks on shipping were needed, it would be the fact that submarines have great difficulty in identifying the nationality of their targets and most of the shipping in Australian waters is not Australian-owned; the probability of provoking retaliation from third countries would therefore be obvious to the Indonesians.

There remains communist China. The communist Chinese have been bellicose in speech but, since the Korean armistice, have been most cautious in any actions which might provoke American retaliation. If, through miscalculation, the Chinese did become involved in a war with the United States, it seems highly likely that nuclear weapons would be used, and the significance of a submarine campaign against trade would be negligible. Before such a campaign could be significant, we must imagine a situation in which the United States, with Australia as one of its allies, was engaged in a war with communist China, and that this was a war in which nuclear weapons were not used. This may seem most improbable but the importance of overseas trade to Australia perhaps justifies examination of the possibilities.

Communist China now has thirty anti-shipping submarines and at least one capable of carrying ballistic missiles. None is nuclear-powered.[11] The anti-shipping submarines do not seem to have the range to operate in the focal shipping areas off eastern and southern Australia from bases in China,[12] and in any case the Chinese have shown no signs of grasping the full potentialities of the submarine. Its great quality is that it can operate in an area where its enemy has

surface and air superiority, and by its elusiveness and mobility can force a wide dispersal of the defending forces. It can attack shipping directly with torpedoes, or it can lay mines. Mines, however, have the disadvantage of being completely undiscriminating in their operation, sinking friend or neutral as readily as foe. The Chinese, who have no modern maritime tradition, seem likely to use their submarines purely defensively, which is the most ineffective way possible to use submarines.

Before the Chinese submarine force could be considered a threat to Australian trade, they would have to build a large number of long-range submarines, train the crews in distant operations, and set up powerful radio stations (similar to North West Cape) so that the submarines could receive messages while submerged.[13] It would also be desirable for them to acquire a reconnaissance system able to locate shipping targets, for without such reconnaissance submarines are forced to operate in the focal areas, where shipping can easily be found; this would simplify considerably the task of the defending forces (see map on opposite page). The most attractive method of providing this reconnaissance is by satellite, but there are considerable technical problems here for the Chinese to overcome—and no sign that they have yet attempted to tackle them. It can be seen that the development of an effective submarine force would take the Chinese many years,[14] and so far there have been no reports which suggest such development.

Although the strategic employment of Chinese submarines is likely to be defensive, they must be expected to attack allied shipping in the vicinity of China itself, and if, in a war with China, Australian troops were deployed on the mainland of Asia, their supply shipping would need protection. This problem is minor compared to that of protecting Australian coastal and overseas trade. In the Second World War Japanese submarine strength never exceeded 100,[15] and faced with the immense power of the United States, they were never able to deploy more than five submarines at a time in Australian waters. During the whole war there were only twelve individual submarine missions on the Australian east coast, yet this minuscule effort compelled the employment of twelve Allied convoy escorts on the east coast, and in May 1943 convoy frequencies had to be halved so as to provide a reasonable escort for each convoy.[16]

Even if the Chinese managed to build their long-range submarine force to a strength comparable to that of the Japanese, and decided to embark on an anti-shipping campaign, they would be unlikely to dispose more of their strength in Australian waters, for they too would have their attention fixed on the might of the United States.

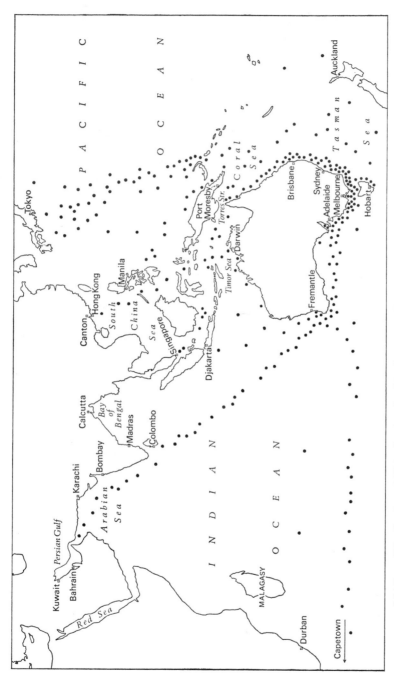

MAP 1   Distribution of Shipping involved in Australian Trade—18 March 1968 (Suez Canal closed)
(Each black dot represents one ship.)

The submarine's biggest advantage is its ability to strike in unexpected areas, and the size of the anti-submarine forces thus depends largely on the amount of shipping to be defended, as well as the quality of the individual anti-submarine units. No submarine has fired a torpedo in anger since 1945—a quarter of a century ago—and when a weapon has not been used for so long its capabilities are bound to be obscured by myths and propaganda. Despite immense research efforts by the western powers, no breakthrough in submarine detection has yet occurred, and the advances which have been made have barely kept pace with the improvements in conventional submarines.[17]

The problem of anti-submarine warfare is exceedingly complex but a few observations may help to indicate the type of forces which might be required. The first point to be made is that convoys remain the only effective way of defending shipping. The convoy escort would consist of sonar-fitted destroyers and helicopters, but sonar echo ranging has serious range limitations. Reliable detections at more than a few thousand yards are unlikely, and even this performance can be seriously degraded by the varying temperatures of the sea. Thus escorting ships and helicopters can rarely even attempt to provide a watertight screen around a convoy, and convoy battles inevitably become a battle of attrition between the submarines and the defending forces.

In peacetime a feeling always seems to grow up that convoy protection is too defensive, and that forces should be used aggressively to seek out and destroy the submarines.[18] This is excellent in principle, but is only likely to be fruitful if the means of location match the offensive spirit. This is far from true at present, although there was a period in the Second World War when these tactics were effective. During the Battle of the Atlantic Hunter-killer (HUK) groups, usually consisting of an aircraft carrier screened by about six destroyers, operated aggressively against the German submarines. They were very effective, because at this period the submarines had to surface in order to use their diesel engines or refuel from a tanker submarine and they did not have an efficient search receiver to give warning of the approach of a radar-fitted aircraft. The submarines had to use their diesels—and therefore be on the surface—whenever they wished to concentrate to attack a convoy, for their range using electric batteries was not more than 100 miles at very slow speed. Moreover, while on patrol, they had to spend about four hours a day on the surface re-charging their batteries. In these circumstances, the HUK groups made many kills, but conditions are very different now.

All modern non-nuclear submarines are fitted with 'snort' breath-

ing tubes, so that they can use their diesels with no more than a few feet of steel tube projecting above the surface. Moreover, nearly all submarines are now fitted with efficient search receivers which will detect the presence of radar transmissions from an aircraft before the snort is detected by the radar set. It is true that aircraft have other means of locating submarines, notably sonobuoys, which are hydro-phones dropped in the sea to pick up the noises of the submarine and relay the sound by radio to the aircraft. But although some detections might be made by sonobuoys, or by operating radar intermittently in the hope of surprising a submarine, it remains true that the detection means are grossly inadequate to the task of finding a submarine which does not wish to be found. A properly handled submarine should have little difficulty in evading the blind thrusts of a HUK group. Indeed, if the sonar conditions are poor, and the submarine captain is aggres-sive, the result is more likely to be the torpedoing of the aircraft carrier than the sinking of the submarine.

For the same reasons that HUK operations are not likely to be very effective, attempts by shore-based aircraft to attack the submarines on passage to their operating areas are not likely to be fruitful, unless the submarines have to pass through a narrow strait. Most aircraft will have to concentrate their efforts closer to the convoys they are supporting. They can perform a very useful role by harassing the submarines to prevent them from getting into position to attack the convoys, by operating radar to prevent the submarines from using their snorts and by using sonobuoys to prevent the submarines from going fast on their electric motors. The defensive pattern must be one of co-ordination between the close escort of destroyers and heli-copters, and the more distant support of shore-based aircraft.

So far there is no sign of China producing nuclear-powered sub-marines, but the rapidity with which nuclear and thermo-nuclear devices have been produced suggests that nuclear propulsion for sub-marines is within the range of their technology. A nuclear submarine has enormous advantages over the conventional diesel-battery sub-marine. Its range is virtually unlimited, conditioned only by the expenditure of weapons and the fortitude of the crew. It need never show anything above the surface, and thus is immune from radar detection. Its speed is as great as the fastest aircraft carrier or de-stroyer, and considerably faster if the weather is at all rough. It would be fair to say that, in the anti-shipping role, a nuclear submarine would be at least six times as effective as a conventionally powered submarine.

There is one other possible threat to Australian shipping that must be mentioned, and that is from the air. Within two or three hundred

miles of the coasts of China, ships would have to be prepared for attacks from the air, either direct bombing attacks or more probably by cruise missiles launched by aircraft or surface ships, guided or homing onto their targets. Defence against these attacks must come from fighter aircraft, which can shoot down the bombers or destroy the ships launching the missiles; and from the missiles in the defending ships themselves, to deal with approaching cruise missiles.

To summarize: Overseas and coastal shipping are vital to Australia's economic survival, and if this shipping were seriously threatened, very large forces would be required for its protection. The only foreseeable threat to this shipping is from communist China, but a non-nuclear war with China is a cumulation of improbabilities. Moreover, China has shown no signs of developing an anti-commerce submarine force, and development of such a force would take many years. Until there are some signs that it is being developed, Australia need not maintain more than a nucleus of an anti-submarine force,[19] which could be expanded if the need arose. If, in such a war, Australian troops were committed to the mainland of Asia, their supply convoys would be subjected to air and submarine attacks when close to China, but the likelihood of such a war is so low, and the significance of the Australian troops in such a cataclysm would be so slight, that it would be quite unwarranted to provide special naval forces for such an eventuality.

Defence of Australian territory against air or missile attacks is not primarily a naval responsibility. Australia is remote from possible enemy air bases. It seems highly unlikely that bombers would be sent to attack Australia with H.E. bombs; the effect would simply not be worth the effort. It is conceivable that missiles with nuclear or thermo-nuclear warheads might in some circumstances be fired at Australia, and this could be a naval problem if the missiles were fired by submarines. The Soviet Navy possesses over 20 nuclear powered and 35 conventionally powered missile-firing submarines,[20] and the Chinese at least one conventionally powered missile-firing boat.[21] The range of the Soviet missiles is probably between 1,500 and 2,000 miles,[22] and as all important Australian targets are on the coast, the area from which the submarine could fire would be more than 6 million square miles. With existing detection devices, to find a nuclear submarine in such an area would be like searching for a needle in a hundred haystacks. The suggestion of having each missile-firing submarine shadowed by another nuclear submarine does not take into account the fact that the performance of a submarine's hydrophones is degraded rapidly as the submarine's speed increases, and for one submarine to shadow another of comparable performance for weeks at a stretch

would only be possible if the crew of the missile-firing submarine showed almost unbelievable incompetence.[23]

One possible system to give warning of the presence of a submarine is to lay sensitive hydrophones on the sea bed, and connect them to receivers ashore. This is quite an effective warning device in shallow water, but the narrow continental shelf around most of Australia, and the deep water beyond, make it ineffective against missile-firing submarines, although such a system might be effective in defending oil drilling rigs against submarine attack.

It can be concluded that, in the present state of submarine detection devices,[24] it would be a waste of effort to attempt to locate missile-firing nuclear submarines.

The threat of invasion is a constantly recurring bogey, but most accounts fail to recognize the enormous problems there are in mounting an overseas invasion against a determined adversary, for not only must a substantial initial force be landed by sea or air, but an enormous amount of equipment would have to be supplied—almost certainly by sea—over a prolonged period. Even when Japan was at the height of its power, in early 1942, the Japanese General Staff considered that the invasion of Australia required more force than they could possibly muster.[25] Whether a future invasion of Australia was to be sea-borne or air-borne or both, it is safe to say that it would be quite impracticable unless bases were available in the Indonesian archipelago. The future of Indonesia is thus of paramount importance in Australia's strategic planning.

A hostile regime in Indonesia might possibly cause trouble in Australian New Guinea. Overt intervention, or attacks on the mainland of Australia, are most unlikely in the near future because of the fear of provoking American intervention under the ANZUS treaty. It is not that the ANZUS treaty gives Australia a cast-iron guarantee of American aid, but the consequences for Indonesia of American intervention would be so grave, both militarily and economically, that it seems highly improbable that any non-communist Indonesian government would dare to take the risk. The level of attack is therefore likely to be kept down to the infiltration of small groups into Australian New Guinea to stir up trouble. The long common border with West Irian makes overland infiltration the obvious route, but it is possible that attempts might be made to infiltrate small parties along the coast in fast fishing boats. In calm weather it is possible for a canoe driven by an outboard motor to reach speeds of more than 30 knots, so the defending forces must have a proportion of fast craft, either hovercraft or patrol boats. Apart from providing patrol forces,

sea power could contribute little to the defence of New Guinea against such small-scale infiltration. There would be no requirement for bombardments or amphibious assault operations, and the low level of the threat would mean that airfields would not need large static garrisons. In circumstances where the threat to airfields is negligible, an aircraft carrier is not an economic alternative to basing tactical support aircraft ashore, provided of course, that the airfields are already there.

Although the ANZUS treaty seems an effective guarantee against the invasion of the Australian mainland at present (when in any case there is no possibility of such a thing happening), it would be rash to believe that the United States will necessarily protect Australia indefinitely. A nation's strategy must be based on what it conceives to be its own best interests and the United States is no exception to this. In its strategic thinking Australia must face the possibility that at some future date—probably at least a decade or more away—the ANZUS treaty may be no more than a memory.

A hostile Indonesia would not only be able to cause trouble in Australian New Guinea but, if not inhibited by the ANZUS treaty, could pose an invasion threat to Australia's northern coasts.[26] Australia certainly lacks the power and—one hopes—the desire to impose an unwelcome regime on the Indonesian people, but it would be in its interests to assist a potentially friendly Indonesian government to suppress an insurrection or 'War of National Liberation' through which a minority group attempted to overthrow the government. If such an insurrection broke out, and the situation became critical, the Indonesian government might welcome Australian assistance.[27]

Although diplomatic and economic efforts should be made to prevent such a situation developing, it is only the military requirements that concern us here.

How could Australia assist militarily? The Indonesian archipelago consists of more than 3,000 islands, and sea power can be used to isolate these islands and prevent the infiltration of men and equipment between them. The only successful campaigns against 'Wars of National Liberation' have been those where it has been possible to isolate the insurrection area from external assistance, as in the Philippines in 1949-54, or as in Malaya at about the same time. But although sea power can isolate islands, it requires very considerable forces to be effective and Australian efforts would be a valuable supplement to the Indonesian Navy. As a rough guide, a patrol boat would be needed for every ten miles of patrol front. A proportion of these boats must be fast enough—probably 40 knots—to catch their fastest adversaries, and they must have within call a more heavily

armed ship such as a destroyer, to cover them while they board a suspect. The guns of these destroyers would also be useful as mobile artillery for the forces ashore, although they would be limited to targets within about ten miles of the coast. The patrol forces must be efficient, because detecting infiltrators among legitimate trading craft and fishing boats is far from easy. From the defensive point of view the ideal solution would be the elimination of the fishing boats, but these boats are of vital economic importance to their communities. Attempts to control and marshal them are never completely satisfactory, and some always stray, to the confusion and irritation of the patrolling ships.

It is most unlikely that there would be, in such a situation, much opposition to the operation of the patrolling forces. Infiltrating craft which were detected would probably fight, but there would be no air or submarine opposition. It is possible that some mines might be laid clandestinely by fishing craft, but the risk would not be great, although it would be necessary to use minesweepers to check the areas in which valuable ships were operating.

Apart from interdicting enemy sea-borne movement, what else could Australia's maritime forces do? Indonesia has a very large army, which would hardly require much military assistance in anti-insurgency operations for unless the Indonesian government succeeded in retaining the loyalty of the great mass of the people, the counter-insurgency struggle would be hopeless. Specialized forces with great mobility would, however, be very useful in quelling incipient troubles. An assault helicopter carrier would be worth considering for this role. Such a vessel[28] could carry up to two battalions of troops, and land them by helicopter in any spot where trouble threatened, with a reaction time and speed of build-up which would better anything which could be achieved by parachute forces. This bald assertion must be qualified by pointing out some of the limitations of such a ship. The quick reaction time would only be achieved if good intelligence enabled the ship to be in the right place at the right time. Further, the assault helicopter carrier must be supported by at least one other ship to carry the supporting arms and other equipment and, if these cannot be lifted by helicopter, they would have to be landed over the beaches with some loss of tactical freedom. Nevertheless, despite these limitations, an assault helicopter carrier would provide a capacity for flexible response which might be invaluable.

What of the value of aircraft carriers in such a situation? Many comparisons have been made to assess the relative cost-effectiveness of fixed airfields ashore and mobile airfields afloat,[29] but all seem to have been vitiated by biased assessments of unavoidably subjective

I

factors, or refer to situations which are very different from that of providing tactical air support to counter-insurgency forces in the Indonesian archipelago. It seems fair to say that, in situations where there is no threat to the ship, and an insignificant threat to the airfield, the use of shore airfields—if they are available—is certainly the more economical way of deploying tactical air power. On the other hand, in a situation where there is still no threat to the ship, but where there is a substantial threat to the shore airfield, necessitating the use of a large static garrison, the advantage would lie with the aircraft carrier. It must be pointed out, though, that this comparison assumes an aircraft carrier of optimum size, which is certainly in excess of 50,000 tons; smaller carriers have a substantially lower cost-effectiveness.[30] Moreover two aircraft carriers are needed to maintain one on station, because the ships have to be withdrawn periodically for replenishment, repairs and overhaul, and it is very difficult to achieve an operational availability significantly in excess of 60%. This has of course been taken into account in the cost-effectiveness comparison; a single carrier cannot be considered as a serious alternative to a shore airfield, if the requirement for tactical air power is expected to last for more than thirty days.

It is unlikely that there would be air opposition to tactical support aircraft and, if the sea blockade was effective, anti-aircraft missiles and sophisticated guns would not be encountered in any numbers. The tactical support aircraft could then be much less complex and of lower performance than those needed to attack heavily defended targets.

The question of manning the aircraft in the carrier also deserves serious consideration. The provision of tactical support to the army has little relation to the other activities of a naval aviator, and if an aircraft carrier is to be provided and used primarily as a base for army tactical support aircraft, it would seem logical that the aircraft should be manned by the Air Force.[31] The aircraft could then be based ashore or afloat, whichever better met the requirements of the tactical situation.

It is very difficult to quantify the naval requirements for a counter-insurgency campaign, for so much depends on the location and extent of the insurgent activity. The available patrol forces of the Indonesian Navy consist of one cruiser, eighteen destroyers or similar types and seventy smaller patrol vessels.[32] Most of these are, however, obsolescent ships of Russian origin, and the Indonesians are facing increasing difficulties with spare parts. It is certain that, if the insurgency were at all widespread, the Indonesian Navy would require substantial external assistance, for there is little else of value in

the Indonesian Navy. There are some Second World War amphibious ships,[33] but they are too old, slow and unreliable to be a useful part of a quick-reaction amphibious force.

The sort of forces that would be of most assistance to the Indonesians would be:

Fast patrol boats

Destroyers, heavily-gunned

An amphibious group

At least two large (50,000 ton) aircraft carriers (Fewer or smaller carriers would be of little value.)

At least two tankers and two store ships, so that one of each would always be available in the operating area; or, alternatively two very large 'all purpose' supply ships.

All the ships would have to be capable of operating with Indonesian ships although the largely Russian origin of the latter would cause great problems.

It is of course evident that these forces could not be provided by the existing Australian Navy. The sole carrier (the *Melbourne*) is too small.[34] There are no amphibious ships, and the patrol boats, with a top speed of 24 knots,[35] are probably too slow. There are no store ships and only one tanker. The only area in which the requirement could be met, in quality if not in quantity,[36] is in destroyers, and even these were designed primarily for anti-aircraft or anti-submarine tasks, and it would be extravagant to use them to intercept infiltrators in small boats; but at least they could do the job.

There is another force which might have a great impact in the area, and that is the Soviet Navy. Since the confrontation with the United States over the missile bases in Cuba, the Soviet Union has realized the value of oceanic power. Soviet warships are beginning to appear on most of the seven seas, and the Soviet Navy is beginning to develop the techniques which can keep ships fuelled, stored and efficient, when far from their main bases. Soviet ships are uninvited guests at all the major western naval exercises, and a powerful Soviet fleet is operating in the Mediterranean, which has long been regarded as a NATO lake. The Soviet Mediterranean fleet has at least one assault helicopter carrier, and these days smart Soviet marines may be seen strolling through the streets of Beirut or Alexandria. Soviet ships have passed through the Indian Ocean, and it seems inevitable that a Soviet fleet will soon be operating there. The formation of this fleet has been delayed by the closure of the Suez Canal, but it would be possible for a fleet to be deployed to the Indian Ocean from the Soviet bases in East Asia. Once such a fleet is formed, it would have

considerable nuisance value. Their remoteness from their bases and their lack of integral air power would make Soviet ships no match for the Americans if it came to a fight. But no one except the Americans would possess such superiority over the Soviet fleet, and it may well be that the chief, and indeed the only, role that the American Navy will be able to play in the Indonesian archipelago will be to neutralize the Soviet fleet.[37]

So far, Indonesia has been considered in isolation. The Philippines to the north-east and the Malay Peninsula to the north-west have shielded it from direct contact with communist countries. Both these countries have experienced communist insurgency, and if they succumbed to communism the position of Indonesia would probably become more difficult. But the Philippines are not an easy area for communist insurgents, because it would be possible to isolate the areas of insurgency by the use of sea power. The United States has historical and emotional links with the Philippines, and it is reasonable to assume that it would use its sea power to contain any insurgency situation that arose there.

The problem of Malaysia and Singapore is more complex because they are part of the mainland of Asia. Britain may still withdraw from the area and once the Vietnam war is settled, the United States is likely to be even more reluctant than in the past to enter into any new military commitment on the Asian mainland. These events place the future of the non-communist countries of mainland South-East Asia in considerable jeopardy. Perhaps the best way to assess their strategic importance to Australia in the long term would be to consider the worst case—that in which the whole of mainland South-East Asia was communist. In such circumstances, some strategic materials —principally rubber and tin—might no longer be available; Australia might lose certain export markets; the Malacca Strait might be closed to non-communist shipping; communist infiltration into Indonesia would be greatly facilitated; and finally, Singapore might become available as a base for Soviet and other communist fleets.

Two of these consequences can be dismissed at once as of minor importance. Other sources of supply of tin and rubber are readily available, and the loss of Malaya as a source of supply would not be crippling. It is also by no means certain that Australia would lose its export markets in the area; it has been found possible for Australia to trade with China, even though Australia does not recognize the communist regime there.

The question of the freedom of the Malacca Strait is more complex. This strait, lying between Sumatra and Malaya, is one of the

great waterways of the world. It is, by definition, an international strait, through which ships have a right of innocent passage, even though parts of the passage must be made through Singapore and Malaysian territorial waters. But not all communist countries are signatories of the International Convention on law of the sea,[38] and if Malaysia and Singapore fell into communist hands, it is quite possible that they would resort to harassment or outright refusal of passage to non-communist ships. The possibility is sufficiently real to justify examination of the consequences.

Although the Malacca Strait is a great waterway, it is of primary interest to the countries of East Asia, and those trading with them through the Indian Ocean. It is little used by ships trading with Australia, and its closure would therefore not be of any great direct consequence to Australian trade. The greatest loser would be Japan, because almost a third of its overseas trade passes through the Malacca Strait.[39] Yet there is an alternative route, through the Sunda Strait between Sumatra and Java. Although this route increases the passage between Japan and the Persian Gulf by 400 miles, it is already in use by the super tankers which are of too deep draught to use the shallow Malacca Strait. As more of these ships are built,[40] the importance of the Malacca Strait will inevitably decline. The closure of the Malacca Strait would therefore only be a minor irritant to the non-communist trading countries. Indeed, it might have positive advantages, if the threat of possible closure made Japan realize its stake in the stability of South-East Asia. At present Japan, under its American-imposed constitution, is forbidden to use its armed forces for anything other than self-defence, and a major constitutional amendment would be necessary before Japan could use its military forces to help defend South-East Asia.

The strait between Singapore and the Riau islands of Indonesia is less than 8 miles wide at its narrowest point, and the Malacca Strait between Malaya and Sumatra is 400 miles long and varies in width from 20 miles at its southern end to 150 miles at its northern end. During the 'confrontation' between Indonesia and Malaysia, the Indonesians made rather half-hearted attempts to infiltrate raiding parties into Malaya and Singapore, and the prevention of this infiltration necessitated the use of the Malaysian Navy, practically all the available ships of the British Navy, and contributions from Australia and New Zealand. It is true that some of these ships were being used in Borneo, and that the size of the Royal Navy's contribution was intended to overawe Indonesia but, even discounting this, the forces required to prevent infiltration were substantial. Unfortunately no statistics have yet been released on the success of these patrols in

preventing or deterring infiltration. Nevertheless it can be said that the forces required to prevent infiltration of arms and agitators from a communist Malaysia and Singapore into Sumatra and the Riau islands would be far in excess of anything the Indonesian Navy has at present.[41]

The final consequence of this worst case—all of mainland South-East Asia being communist-controlled—would be the danger of Singapore becoming a fuelling and repair base for the Soviet fleet. Such a base would make it much easier for Russia to maintain an effective fleet in South-East Asian waters, but it seems very unlikely that this would force a direct clash with western warships. The dangers for Russia of such a high risk policy would be far greater than the potential gains.

On balance, therefore, the loss of South-East Asia to communism would have little direct effect on Australia's interests, but it would probably increase the danger of successful communist insurrection in Indonesia.

Although Australia has a treaty commitment with Thailand through SEATO, and intends to maintain token military forces in Singapore,[42] it is almost inconceivable that Australia would become involved in significant military operations on the mainland of Asia except as an ally of the United States. If America decided to continue to give active military assistance to the non-communist countries on the mainland of South-East Asia, this would have to be done in the knowledge that the counter-insurgency struggle would be in an area where it would not be possible to make full use of U.S. superiority in sea power. But this does not mean that maritime power has no part to play. The military air lift into South Vietnam has been by far the largest ever organized, yet all the millions of tons of petrol and oil, and 98% of the dry cargo has been brought in by sea. The reason is not difficult to see. An aircraft is a magnificent method of transporting men, and small cargo items of high value, but as a carrier of bulk cargo it is hopelessly inefficient compared with a ship. A single example will suffice: 6,000 tons of bulk cargo from Australia to, say, Bangkok could be carried by a tramp steamer in a single voyage lasting three weeks. It could also be done by a squadron of twelve C. 130 Hercules aircraft—working steadily and unremittingly for ten months. And for every ton of cargo carried to Asia by the Hercules, a ton of fuel would have to be brought into Asia by sea so that the Hercules could make the return flight.

It does not seem likely that these cargo ships will be under any threat while on the high seas. In both the major wars in East Asia

between the communists and the United States and its allies, the communists have refrained from attacking ships on the high seas, although it would not have been difficult to have provided either the North Koreans or the North Vietnamese with submarines. The danger of using submarines is that the inevitable retaliation against the real or supposed submarine bases will spread the conflict, and this is a risk that the communists have not been prepared to take in the past, nor does it seem at all likely that they will change their policy in the future. This immunity on the high seas does not mean that the ships will not be attacked while unloading in port. Clandestine mining and sabotage attacks by underwater swimmers must be expected but in sum it can be said that the naval effort necessary to protect sea transport will be relatively trivial.

The effort required from the patrol forces will be far from trivial. Although sea power cannot isolate the area of insurgency, it can assist by preventing the smuggling of men and supplies along the coast. The forces required are patrol boats, assisted by radar-fitted aircraft and covered by gun-armed destroyers. The latter can on occasion be used as mobile artillery in support of the army. An extension of the coastal patrol force concept is their use on the rivers and canals. The French used this idea with their 'Dinassauts' in Indo-China, and the Americans have copied the idea with the Riverine forces in South Vietnam albeit at great cost and with dubious results; in each case the purpose of the forces was to prevent the use of the waterways by the communists, and to launch attacks on communist base areas. It is really no more than a modern version of the old-style river gunboat.

In the Vietnam war more than half the air attacks on North Vietnam were launched from aircraft carriers.[43] The heavy communist attacks on airfields made the aircraft carriers an attractive alternative to land bases, particularly as the carriers could replenish with fuel and ammunition at sea or in distant ports, thus reducing the strain on the already overloaded ports of South Vietnam. Of course, aircraft carriers, even if enough were available,[44] can never be a complete substitute for airfields ashore. Helicopter airfields should not be more than 50 miles from the troops they are supporting and close support airfields not more than 100 miles away,[45] if reaction times are to be sufficiently short. Since all of Malaya and the southern half of Thailand are within 100 miles of the sea, aircraft carriers could play an important role in their defence, even in a close support role.

The naval forces which Australia might usefully contribute to a war on the mainland of Asia are thus very much the same as those needed to combat insurgency in the Indonesian islands: patrol boats,

gun-armed destroyers, aircraft carriers as bases for close support aircraft and possibly helicopters, some mine clearance vessels and the necessary logistic support ships. All of these ships should be capable of using American supplies—particularly ammunition—to avoid having to try to provide special Australian stores[46] to ships on dispersed operations.

One of the major difficulties in strategic planning is that of time scale. Intelligence experts are only prepared to commit themselves a few years ahead, but equipment planners have to look much further into the future. It takes something like seven years between the time a new piece of major equipment is first thought about until it is in service, and it will then remain in service for perhaps twenty years. Major items of equipment being considered now are therefore unlikely to be in service before the late 1970s and will remain in service until nearly the year 2000. With most of the men enrolled on long-service engagements, it also takes many years to change the personnel balance in the armed services. Opportunism is an excellent tactical approach, but it is quite inappropriate as a basis for strategy, for here it may be impossible to implement a desired change quickly because of equipment or manpower decisions made years before. The armed services need a long-range, clear strategy on which to base their deployments, equipment and personnel programmes—with all three armed services as well as foreign policy planners working to the same strategy.

It is here suggested that Australia's armed forces should be shaped so that they can assist a potentially friendly Indonesian government to resist insurrection, and so as to provide a small nucleus of an anti-submarine force which could be expanded if a threat to its sea-borne trade ever became apparent. These forces would be available as a contribution to the defence of mainland South-East Asia—Thailand, Malaysia and Singapore in particular—if enough reliable allies could be found to make this defence practicable.

The result would be a very different Navy from its present one.[47]

Editor's Postscript: At the end of October 1970 the Federal government approved the construction of the second stage of the proposed naval base at Cockburn Sound near Perth. The base is expected to be capable of supporting four escort vessels and three submarines for up to one year without dry-docking.

CHAPTER 9

Anti-Submarine Warfare—A Comment

ARLEIGH BURKE

In the development of a general thesis on anti-submarine warfare, it is helpful to review briefly the fundamental strategy of sea power, within which A.S.W. is an essential element.

The definitions of the nature of sea power are many and complex. But, however it is defined, no nation in modern history has achieved determining influence without it. Nations which have not had ocean commerce, or which have been unable to protect the free movement of their mercantile fleets, have usually failed to gain, or to maintain, a position of strength in the economic and political affairs of the world.

Sea power has three essential ingredients. First, an instrument to carry on essential ocean trade—the Merchant Marine. Secondly, an instrument to protect that commerce—a Navy. Thirdly, the ability to project the national political will through mobile military forces conveyable across the world's oceans.

There is also a fourth ingredient, hard to define but perhaps the most important of all. This is the will of a nation to exercise its enterprise on the sea. Without this, fleets of commerce and defence cannot be built, or, if built, cannot be used or sustained.

The major nations of our civilization have consistently complied with these fundamentals of maritime power, though each has naturally tailored the details of strategy to its own era and national objectives. The principal engine of change, both in strategic approach and in tactics, has been the logarithmic advance of technology.

Technology has permitted the development, by the start of the 1970s, of high-quality submarines. This weapons system wrought vast devastation on shipping in two world wars, even with its then existing severe operational limitations, many of which today's more advanced technologies have removed. The modern submarine is one of the most sophisticated weapons of war. In consequence, there is an urgent need for the development of anti-submarine warfare systems. For the protection of naval forces, in the preservation of free and

peaceful trade, in guaranteeing essential ocean communication between the United States and its military and trading partners, anti-
submarine warfare capability may well be of pivotal importance.

The United States requirement for an A.S.W. capability must be
considered in relation to the potential threat, possible U.S. strategies
and budgetary problems, U.S. capabilities, the use of A.S.W. specialists within the Navy, and U.S.-Allied co-operation in A.S.W. matters.
The Soviet Union has begun to challenge supremacy of U.S. sea
power and to project Soviet strategic and political power across the
oceans. Visible evidence of this Soviet drive has been provided by the
increasing Soviet naval deployment in the Mediterranean, the recent
extension of operations by Soviet surface and submarine task forces
into the Caribbean and Indian Ocean and cruises by submarines in
the South Atlantic and South Pacific. Attention-getting as they are,
these visible operations reveal only the less significant forces comprising the new Soviet challenge at sea and the least threatening
aspect of Soviet naval power. The primary offensive force constituting
this challenge and posing this threat—the Soviet submarine force—
remains relatively invisible.

It is the world's largest submarine force. It poses a triple threat to
the United States, to U.S. naval task forces at sea and to its lines
of communications. Currently, the Soviet submarine force consists of
some 350 units of which at least 65, or 18%, are nuclear-powered.
Of that total submarine force, about 12%, including 15 nuclear-
powered units, are equipped with ballistic missiles capable of strategic
attack against the United States. Another 16%, including 30 nuclear-
powered units, are equipped with 400-nm anti-ship missiles designed
primarily for a stand-off attack against U.S. naval task forces and
convoys but also having some capability against land targets. All
Soviet submarines, including some twenty nuclear-powered attack
boats, are armed with torpedoes or mines. All Soviet submarines are
under fifteen years old. The existing diesel-powered and the earliest
nuclear-powered units have received modifications and improvements to their propulsion and weapons systems. More important,
however, has been the addition of a new class of nuclear-powered
ballistic missile-firing submarine and several new classes of nuclear-
powered attack units to the submarine force during 1968-69.

The new class of ballistic missile submarine is similar to U.S. Polaris units and is equipped with sixteen missiles. These can be
launched from beneath the surface to an estimated range of 1,500nm,
thus extending the Soviet potential for strategic attack over much of
the earth's surface not formerly targeted by their inter-continental
ballistic missiles (I.C.B.M.). The new classes of attack submarines

are faster and quieter than their predecessors and carry improved weapons systems. These increased capabilities have made them more difficult to locate and destroy and have increased their ability to threaten U.S. naval forces and sea-borne commerce.

The appearance of these new classes of Soviet submarine presages the development of a Soviet submarine force with still greater capabilities. In recent years great capital investment has been put into expanding and modernizing Russian shipyards. The U.S.S.R. now has the largest and most modern submarine construction facilities in the world. In the past the Soviet Union has built some five nuclear submarines a year. It is believed that they are now building up to double that number. Moreover their nuclear submarine construction capacity is estimated to be some twenty units a year and, with a crash programme having no restraints on manpower or materials, they could produce a considerably higher number. It is estimated that by 1978 the Soviets will have constructed from 100-150 new submarines. From 80%-100% of these will be nuclear. Thus, as they replace their older diesel-powered units, they are expected to have by 1978 a submarine force of some 300-350 units, of which as many as 50% could be modern nuclear-powered units.

The Soviet submarine force has also been improving its operational capabilities. Today Soviet submarines operate outside their home waters for longer periods, in greater numbers and at greater distances than ever before. At the same time the expansion of operations by the Soviet fleet in general can provide support for submarine operations. An underway support group to tend Soviet submarines in the central Atlantic has already been in operation. Were this concept extended on a regular basis to both the Atlantic and Pacific, it could greatly increase the patrol areas which Soviet submarines could cover, and prolong their time on station. The Soviet Union typically has about 4%-6% of its submarine force deployed. Recently this number of deployed submarines has begun to increase and to include units of the new classes. The U.S. typically deploys about 33% of its submarine force. If the Soviet Navy decides to operate at a similar rate it has the capability to deploy over 100 submarines regularly.

Thus a force of some 300-plus submarines, half of which will be nuclear-powered and one-third of which could be continually maintained at sea, is the Soviet submarine challenge to be faced by the U.S. A.S.W. forces of the future. To meet this power, which will be poised for strategic attack over wide areas of the globe and threaten to cut off the U.S. from its allies, will be the role of those future A.S.W. forces.

While developing the power of its own submarine force, the Soviet Union has also tried to encourage development of similar forces which might pose a threat from other corners of the world. The U.S.S.R. has disposed of some of its older diesel-powered boats to various nations like Albania, China, Indonesia and the U.A.R. Political and economic problems have, so far, prevented these forces from becoming an active and co-ordinated supplement to the Soviet submarine force or from constituting a significant independent threat. The most powerful of those nations, communist China, has not yet indicated, by an expansion of its force or the scope of its operations or by the development of a missile for its one ballistic missile-capable submarine, that it intends to pose a serious challenge on the seas of the South Pacific. Thus, without dismissing the possibility of threats from other corners of the world, the U.S. Navy has concentrated its A.S.W. efforts on the primary threat—the Soviet submarine force.

Any strategic plan for the defence of U.S. and allied interests must include the meeting of the submarine threat. This would be true even with the adoption of a minimum strategy: defence of the homeland (Fortress America). For in that case, as well as in any broader strategy, the requirement for some minimum level of protected sea communication between the U.S. and other nations would continue to exist. A.S.W. therefore occupies a vital part in the effective prosecution of war and the major portion of the contest for the use of the sea and its communications will probably remain what it has been—a battle of attrition. There is, however, no agreement on the right strategic concepts for A.S.W. One school of thought favours a 'defensive' A.S.W. strategy, dismissing what they term 'offensive' anti-submarine warfare as an idea only for peacetime. Should one, in sum, wait until the enemy is poised to attack before attempting to destroy him, or should the defender search him out in the oceans before he becomes a direct threat to vital forces? The U.S.N. at any rate has rejected an exclusively perimeter defence, for new technology has made offensive A.S.W. strategies very attractive. Although the submarine has the initiative in battle, the proper strategy appears to be the pursuit of counter-submarine operations based on broad ocean search-and-destroy missions. The ultimate measure of A.S.W. effectiveness can be given in ton-miles of successfully protected forces, both naval and merchant. The U.S. Navy's A.S.W. strategy is founded in part on the certainty that ton-miles percentages will increase to the extent that forward, offensive A.S.W. operations are able to reduce the numbers of enemy submarines which threaten the defending force perimeter.

The key element of anti-submarine warfare strategy, then, is the

conduct of offensive operations, attacking enemy units as close as possible to their points of origin, continuing to hunt down those which may reach the open sea or which were on station before hostilities began, destroying them as far from the defenders' lines of communication as possible. Naturally, this is to be combined with operations against any boats which may get to attack positions in the vicinity of U.S. convoys or strike forces. The strategy is implemented by attack submarines and A.S.W. aircraft, both land and sea-based, operating largely in response to advance intelligence on enemy movements. Thus, an in-depth deployment of A.S.W. forces which includes the establishment of forward barriers across probable enemy routes of ingress-egress and open-ocean Hunter-killer groups, as well as escort units for the close-in defence of formations.

The recent development of a Soviet Polaris-type submarine will, of course, have an impact on strategic planning. Some argue that with the present capability of submarine detection devices it would be a waste of effort to attempt to locate ballistic missile-firing submarines at sea. The U.S.N. view of the problem is different. The task of countering the submarine-launched ballistic missile is formidable and underlines, in principle, the need for defence in depth.

In support of this strategy, the U.S. Navy has developed a multi-platform system for the detection, localization and destruction of hostile submarines. These platforms are the A.S.W. surface ship, A.S.W. aircraft, both land and sea-based, attack submarines, and the long-range surveillance system. The U.S. Navy possesses a significant long-range surveillance capability. While the details of the system are highly classified, the role of the system is to detect and localize potentially hostile submarines with sufficient precision to 'hand-over' the target to other members of the A.S.W. team. The system is constantly upgraded to handle new generation targets. In addition, the U.S. Navy is developing a family of mobile and quickly deployable surveillance systems. The mix of systems will give the U.S. Navy the ability to increase the levels of surveillance in any given ocean area, and to provide surveillance in other areas at very short notice. These vital systems make possible the more effective employment of the other platforms—air, submarine and surface ships. Any one member or all of the team may be employed in classification and tracking a contact developed by the system, rather than conducting a long-range, broad-ocean search in large basins.

The U.S. Navy's newest nuclear attack submarines—the Permit-Sturgeon class—are the most advanced in any navy. In view of the continuing, rapid qualitative improvement in Soviet nuclear submarine technology, however, a new class, the SSN-688, is being

developed by the U.S.N. which will have increased speed and more effective sensor and weapons systems.

The aircraft, which began to prove its capability in an A.S.W. role towards the end of the Second World War, has become increasingly effective in the localization and attack functions of A.S.W., as well as in broad area search. The refinement of air-borne detection equipment, sonobuoys, and air-dropped A.S.W. weapons is now approaching the point where the aircraft may become the deadliest (and most deceptive) enemy of even the nuclear submarine. New integrated attack systems in long-range patrol aircraft, now entering service, are providing vastly improved capabilities. Similar systems, mounted in long-endurance sea-based aircraft for Hunter-killer groups are being developed.

New classes of A.S.W. surface ships—destroyers and destroyer escorts—are continuing to join the U.S. fleet. These, like the new attack submarines and A.S.W. aircraft, are designed to meet the modern nuclear submarine threat. With long-range sonars, high data rate systems, longer range weapons, and later, perhaps, small manned helicopters for distant weapons delivery, the destroyer will perform its traditional escort role in much expanded form.

Each of these platforms also has its limitations. Although an individual platform may by itself detect, localize and destroy a hostile submarine, it is much more probable that a combination of means will be needed. This requires teamwork. Intelligence is the keystone of successful anti-submarine warfare, the foundation for co-ordinated action by air, surface and sub-surface units. Individual ships, aircraft and command centres must be tied together with an elaborate command-control network supported by a number of electronic computers. Each ship and aircraft must in turn operate complex sensors and weapons systems.

All of this also requires highly skilled personnel with long experience in A.S.W. A large modern navy is torn between two conflicting requirements: the need for technical specialists capable of operating and maintaining complex equipment and the need for all-rounders for broader tasks. Beyond that, the close co-operation which exists among the scientific community, the engineers in industry and the various operating forces in the Navy is perhaps the most important factor in the development of U.S. A.S.W. capability. There is a constant feedback among all elements which is the heart of the American system. The basis of the new U.S. A.S.W. developments is the Navy laboratory system. Many government and private laboratories are almost entirely devoted to developing and improving A.S.W. equipment and techniques. Although manned primarily by

civilian specialists, each has a number of Navy personnel on its staff.

The U.S. Navy has a long history of co-operation with the navies of the Commonwealth and NATO. Meeting the increasing Soviet submarine threat, both the strategic threat and that to the vital supply lines which link the free world, is placing an increasing burden on present American A.S.W. forces. As this threat becomes greater and as fewer resources are being made available for U.S. A.S.W. efforts, allied nations, having a vital interest in maintaining freedom of the seas will necessarily assume greater roles in the A.S.W. defence of their continents and supply lines. There are solid foundations for developing such a co-operative defence. There is a NATO Standing Naval Force. U.S. and Australian A.S.W.-capable forces are serving side by side in the South China Sea. Further, joint A.S.W. exercises with numerous other nations, such as those conducted during Operation UNITAS each year, have formed a world-wide co-operative basis for building such a combined defence. In the area of research and technological development the U.S. has bilateral and special information exchange agreements for the joint exploration of technical areas of A.S.W. interest and the joint development of A.S.W. equipment. The future is likely to see closer co-ordination and an expansion of these varied operational and technical relationships into a more cohesive A.S.W. defence upon the oceans of the non-communist world.

Editor's Postscript: Towards the end of 1970 it was reported that some of the latest types of Soviet nuclear-powered submarines were capable of submerged speeds of up to 35 knots.

Controlling Small Wars

CHARLES WOLF, JR*

In almost every year since the Second World War at least one insurgency has been under way in the less-developed areas. In chronological order such insurgencies have appeared in Greece, Burma, Malaya, the Philippines, Vietnam, Kenya, Laos, the Congo, Algeria, Cuba, Yemen, the Dominican Republic and Thailand. Not surprisingly, nearly half of the 'small wars' on this list have occurred in South-East Asia.

One can think of several reasons for expecting this high frequency to diminish in years to come. For example, 'lessons' have been learned from Vietnam by both internal and external participants, and the termination of alien rule in most of the world has removed a major stimulant for many insurgencies.[1] One can also think of reasons for expecting the frequency to remain the same or to increase: again, the 'lessons' learned from Vietnam (the lessons are, in other words, ambiguous and opposite inferences can be drawn from them); the persistence of deep frictions, grievances and inequities in the less-developed countries, and the heightened frustration that is likely to accompany unconstrained promises and limited success in producing remedies. In sum, the reasons for expecting this frequency to diminish are not obviously stronger than the reasons for expecting it to remain the same or to increase.

Each major insurgency is, in some sense, unique as suggested by the diversity of areas and circumstances in the list. But most of them have shared many common features—organization and disorganization, tactics, violence, coercion, persuasion, ideology. The common features make insurgency a proper subject for more general analysis. The diversity warrants caution in pushing generalizations too far.

What are the sources and causes of insurgency? How are the

* Any views expressed in this paper are those of the author. They should not be interpreted as reflecting the views of The Rand Corporation or the official opinion or policy of any of its governmental or private research sponsors.

sources and causes combined and converted into an effective insurgent organization and operation? What concepts and doctrines can help in understanding insurgency, from either the side of the initiator or the opponent? How can an insurgency be made to wax and win, or to wilt and wane? What programmes can be formulated to deter or anticipate it, or to control or suppress it once it has started? These are the sorts of questions with which this essay will be principally concerned.

An essay on insurgency and counter-insurgency might appropriately begin by considering the words themselves. Both terms have been used so loosely that their meaning is unclear. And frequently strong feelings are evoked by them despite, or because of, their ambiguity. In much of the underdeveloped world the term 'insurgent' more often denotes the 'good guys' than the 'bad guys'. (In Mexico City, for example, a main boulevard is the *Avenida de los Insurgentes.*)

For these reasons we shall generally use instead two terms that are probably more accurate, certainly fresher and perhaps less partisan: 'rebellion' and 'authority'. The dictionary defines rebellion as 'open, *organized,* and often *armed,* resistance', whereas insurgency is defined as a revolt *'not reaching the proportions of an organized* revolution' [emphasis added]. Since it is precisely the organizational aspects that are central to its strength, as well as to its analysis, 'rebellion' is a more useful term.

'Authority' is a legal and legitimized right and capacity to command. Of course, authority can be employed for good or bad purposes, and for purposes that are congenial or hostile or indifferent to American or other interests. These purposes should be of first importance in policy formulation—that is, in the choice of whether and how to support or oppose or remain neutral toward a particular authority structure—but they are not the primary concern of this essay. In principle, the analysis of what makes rebellion succeed or fail can be used by those interested in its success or those interested in its failure. In deterring or fighting rebellions, or in helping them emerge and advance toward victory, what needs to be made central to the discussion is the structure of authority, and how to strengthen and maintain it, on the one hand, or how to undermine, destroy and supplant it, on the other. (In the following discussion, I shall frequently use the letter 'R' to stand for rebellion or insurgency, and 'A' to refer to authority.)

Let us now turn to some specifics concerning the concepts and conduct of counter-insurgency. In so doing, I do not mean to imply that insurgencies should invariably be countered wherever and when-

ever they arise. The question of whether and when to oppose, or to support, or to ignore an insurgency does not permit an easy or a general answer, neither from the Australian nor the U.S. point of view. General Suharto's rebellion against Soekarno, following the attempted *coup* of 30 September 1965, provides one instructive example of the wisdom of non-involvement by both countries. Nevertheless, when the controlling of an insurgency does emerge as a policy goal, as it has and no doubt will, questions of concept and technique are important to ask and to answer.[2] They are the principal concern of this paper.

Politics and force in counter-insurgency

According to a frequent assertion, in successful counter-insurgency politics is primary and force is secondary. In this respect, counter-insurgency is supposed to differ from conventional war, where the order is reversed.

Belief in the primacy of politics over force characterizes the familiar slogans and priorities of a set of views I shall refer to as the 'hearts-and-minds' approach to the problem. But advocacy of the primacy of politics is not confined to civilians. Sometimes the views expressed by professional military men also stress the primacy of politics in counter-rebellion, although probably the typical military view would have it otherwise.[3] While the view that politics is primary is both frequently expressed and widely accepted, is it true?

One difficulty in answering this question arises from the unclear meaning of 'politics' and 'force'. Tautology often lurks behind such strongly drawn but loosely defined dichotomies, and this is a case in point. Frequently, perhaps usually, the political effectiveness of an A is judged by whether or not an R is suppressed (deterred), while the suppression (deterrence) of rebellion is construed to depend on the political effectiveness of A. Thus, if Magsaysay was indeed successful in suppressing the Huks, he was politically 'effective' (thereby demonstrating the primacy of politics over force), and if Batista was notably unsuccessful in suppressing Castro, it was because of his political ineffectiveness, thereby demonstrating the same point!

However, if an effort is made to define the concepts so that each can be observed independently of the other, it is highly questionable whether the commonplace assumption about what is primary and what is secondary is right. If 'politics' is construed as the domain of non-violence, persuasion and consensus, and 'force' as the domain of violence, coercion and constraint, then the biggest contrasts between counter-insurgency and other types of war probably lie within these categories, rather than between them. The main differences (and

they are significant ones) between counter-insurgency and other wars should probably be put, not in terms of the commonplace view, but in other terms. The types of force, and the types of political actions that are most relevant and most effective in determining outcomes, are likely to differ significantly between counter-insurgency and other wars. Military techniques that work effectively in counter-insurgency are not likely to be effective in other wars, and political techniques and strategies that work in counter-insurgency are likely to differ from those that work in other kinds of wars.

But 'politics' is not necessarily more important in counter-rebellion than in conventional wars—particularly, recent and future conventional wars. In its influence on the outcome of the Battle of Britain, for example, Churchill's political ingenuity played as decisive a role as that played by the Royal Air Force. To mobilize (manoeuvre) the British populace into such intense resolution that compromise became unthinkable was an act of great political dexterity, comparable in its influence on Britain's stamina and on the outcome of the war with the military effectiveness of the R.A.F. The contrast with the role of domestic politics in influencing military outcome in the Battle of France is obvious and notable. The importance of Syngman Rhee's political ingenuity in freeing the North Korean prisoners of war in 1953, and thereby influencing the outcome of the Korean war, is another case in point.

Moreover, politics does not seem to be less important in contingencies closer to the nuclear end of the spectrum. Thus, in the Suez crisis of 1956 and the Cuban missile crisis of 1962—in both of which nuclear threats arose with differing degrees of imminence—political manoeuvring was singularly important in influencing military outcomes. For example, recall the profound political importance of the militarily almost valueless Jupiter missiles in 1962.

Of course, politics is equally significant in insurgent conflicts. But the ingredients of effective political action are different from those suggested by the previous examples. From A's standpoint, effective politics require that A demonstrate—by adhering to and enforcing law and order, by maintaining discipline within and between its agencies, and by completing announced programmes visibly and expeditiously—a growing capacity to govern. Demonstrating competence and acquiring a reputation for effective action constitute A's political task. Political actions that strengthen A are synonymous with political actions that expand A's capacity to absorb and offset harassment from R.[4] Elections, political organizing, government probity and development programmes are contributors to this end.

If, on the one hand, politics is important in other kinds of conflict

135

besides rebellions, so, on the other hand, the application of force and violence is important in rebellions and counter-rebellions as well as in other wars. Thus, Magsaysay's reorganization of the Philippine Constabulary into smaller, more decentralized and mobile units, combined with the altered incentive structure created for the Armed Forces of the Philippines to reward effective application of force against the Huks,[5] was not less important in suppressing the Huks than were the *political* moves (for example, the relatively free elections of 1953 and reduced corruption in the civil administration) instituted by Magsaysay at the same time.

The military measures, forces and capabilities that are best suited for counter-insurgency are apt to be different from those that are best suited for other types of contingencies. Thus, if the forces of Asian countries are designed to meet major conventional invasion by China or North Vietnam or North Korea, or if Latin American forces are designed for hemispheric defence, their capabilities for deterring or meeting insurgent threats may be considerably less (for a given budget) than if they were specifically designed to meet these lower-level threats. A capability to prevent R—that is, a deterrence capability requires a highly developed intelligence system, enlarged and improved paramilitary and police forces, and expanded engineering and medical units for 'civic action' in remote areas, rather than conventionally armed and trained military units with heavy firepower and armour. A capability to wage effective counter-insurgency warfare—that is, a 'war-fighting' capability—is likely to require forces (as does nuclear war) with a high degree of surface mobility, airlift and aerial reconnaissance, as well as a capacity for operating effectively in small units for long periods of time while retaining good communications with higher-echelon headquarters. On the other hand, forces to meet a major conventional aggression are likely to stress not these capabilities, but rather armour, artillery, fighter aircraft and air defence, as well as highly centralized operations by large, division-level units. And the use of forces trained, commanded and equipped for major conventional contingencies in unconventional, insurgent conflicts is likely to entail both high costs and low effectiveness. The war in Vietnam is the most obvious and glaring example.

Defence capabilities for deterring Rs, as well as for fighting them in their earliest stages, should emphasize police and militia forces rather than military ones. Such forces are apt to be more closely associated with civil than with military administration, because their primary mission is preserving law and order and protecting the population. Fulfilling these missions depends critically on an intimate knowledge of local happenings, people and organizations—in other

words, on police intelligence, rather than the order-of-battle, 'counter-force' type of intelligence with which the military tends to be preoccupied.[6]

Thus, the requirements in an insurgency context for both deterrence and war-fighting capabilities are likely to differ sharply from the requirements for deterring or meeting large-scale conventional aggression. The ingredients of effective force in counter-insurgency are not less important than, but just very different from, the ingredients of effective force in other contingencies. A decision to base force structures on one set of contingencies is thus likely to mean reducing capabilities for other contingencies.

In sum, politics typically plays a powerful and often undervalued role in military confrontations at the higher levels of the spectrum, including nuclear as well as conventional contingencies; and the use of force plays a highly important and also often undervalued role in lower levels of conflict, including counter-insurgency. The differences between counter-insurgency and other conflicts relate to the content and conduct of political and coercive roles, not to their relative importance. In analysing and specifying these roles, the systems view of counter-insurgency differs as sharply from the conventional military emphasis on counter-force (attrition) as it does from the hearts-and-minds emphasis on sympathy.

Contrasts between counter-insurgency and other conflicts

While it is, as we have suggested, expedient for A to join closely politics and force—civil and military instruments—in counter-insurgency, this point is hardly a distinguishing one. Still, there are important contrasts between counter-insurgencies and other conflicts as traditionally analysed and practised.

Traditionally, wars between As have been waged and analysed as counter-force and pro-territory, aiming at the destruction of the enemy's forces and the occupation of his territory. Consequently, the location and movement of the 'forward edge of the battle area' (FEBA) were viewed as providing a relatively clear indication of success.

By contrast, counter-insurgency is primarily a counter-production effort, rather than an effort to annihilate forces or acquire territory. The aim of successful counter-insurgency is to counter R's ability to produce and reproduce forces, as well as to 'harden' the structure of government authority so that it can withstand R's attacks while the essential counter-production effort is gaining momentum.

In conventional war destroying the enemy's forces (counter-force)

is a means of acquiring his territory. Destroying his forces and acquiring his territory, in turn, provide the means of coercing the adversary to accept a desired outcome. In counter-insurgency, by contrast, the adversary may have no territory in the earlier and usually critical stages. (In contrast to A's doctrine, to eschew territory, to retreat, to evaporate and to accept local setbacks are fundamental attributes to R's operating doctrine.)[7] Instead, A's aim should be to attack R's organization; that is, to attack the apparatus by which the forces and outputs of the system are produced. Counter-force is part of the process, but not the most important part. R's military forces are a part of the target system, but not necessarily the major part. In addition, A must target both the population and the exogenous sources of R's support: the former, in order to influence the population's behaviour so as to limit the inputs available to R internally; and the latter, in order to restrict external resupply of key inputs.

Force ratios in counter-insurgency

An important point of contrast between counter-insurgency and conventional wars arises in connection with the much discussed 'force ratios' between counter-insurgents and insurgents. Sir Robert Thompson has properly characterized much writing on this matter as 'nonsense' and 'one of the myths of counter-insurgency'.[8]

Part of the nonsense arises from the fact that the data are so ambiguous. It is never quite clear what is in the numerator and denominator of the ratios cited. Do they include only active combatants? And what about guerrillas who are only part-time combatants—should they be expressed in terms of some 'full-time' equivalents? And should the counter-insurgents include the police and air and naval patrol forces, or only active ground combat forces?

Although the familiar ratio of ten counter-insurgents to one insurgent has often been cited as prerequisite to successful counter-insurgency, two important qualifications need to be attached to this ratio, apart from the ambiguity (as noted) of the numerator and denominator. First, widely different ratios have prevailed in different insurgencies: the range extends from one or two to one in the Philippines, to twenty or thirty to one in Kenya, to perhaps forty to one in Malaya, at least toward the end of the campaign. The second qualification is that the ratio itself is sensitive to the stage in the conflict at which it is computed, and to whether a given ratio comes about by a build-up of the counter-insurgents, or by a reduction in the insurgency's ability to produce forces. To the extent that A is successful in its efforts to disrupt R's production mechanism, the ratio will be drastically raised by the decline in R's production capability toward the end of a

counter-insurgency effort. A rising ratio brought about by the reduction of R's forces thus has quite a different meaning from, and—from
A's point of view—a more auspicious significance than, one brought
about by a rise in counter-insurgent forces.

Still, as noted earlier, an important contrast exists between force
ratios in counter-insurgency and in conventional wars. The contrast
arises from the fact that where there is a front line in the battle area,
the defender generally has a strong advantage, one further strengthened by defensive fortifications. Consequently, although there are
major exceptions—Israel's rout of much larger Arab forces in the
six-day war of June 1967 is a striking example—the familiar planning factor of two or three to one in favour of the defender reflects
this advantage. Where there is no front line, as in counter-insurgency,
this model no longer applies, and it is more appropriate to use an air
defence model. The defender does not know where an attack may
come. Hence, even if he is able to keep an advantage by maintaining
a high-level alert at each of the targets, there are so many targets to
defend that the aggregate force ratio becomes much larger than that
of the attacking force.

Putting the problem this way underscores an important influence
on the force ratios needed by A. The better A's information about
where and when an attack may come, and the shorter his response
time[9] (as through aerial surveillance and lift), the smaller force ratio
that he needs. Therefore, A's intelligence and information system will
play a central role in influencing force ratios.

Moreover, it is probably at least as important to stress the kinds of
forces that A needs as the numbers. As noted earlier, A's mobility,
weapon training and communications are likely to be different from,
and considerably less expensive on a unit cost basis than, those associated with military forces equipped for fighting large-scale conventional wars.

Indicators of success in counter-insurgency

One of the distinguishing characteristics of counter-insurgency is
the difficulty and complexity of finding reliable indicators of success.
After the fact, it is easy to put things in their places: to say that at
such and such a time it became clear that the insurgency was going
up or down hill, or that the force ratios were decidedly moving in the
right direction, or that a decisive turn was taken toward A's success
or failure. But during a counter-insurgency campaign, it is hard to
be clear about 'winning' and 'losing'.

The difficulty of identifying reliable indicators of success is related
to the previously noted points about the unsuitability of indicators

normally used for evaluating success in conventional war: destruction of the enemy's military forces and acquisition of his territory (that is, casualties and movement of the FEBA). Counter-force and pro-territory indicators are not appropriate in counter-insurgency.

Further, to measure the warmth of popular support, and its shift from R to A is not a reliable indicator of success, even if we had a good calorimeter for this purpose (which we do not). Genuine popular support in transitional societies is multifaceted and heterogeneous; perhaps more important, it is rare in any durable sense. And when it appears to be most genuine, it is as likely to be a manipulated appearance as a deep-rooted conviction. (This is not to deny that genuine support is desirable in principle, or that successful manipulation of its appearance is an important quality to cultivate, whether by A or by R.) Nevertheless, as I have suggested elsewhere, Rs or As can wax in the face of popular dislike and wane in the midst of popular sympathy.[10]

Rather, the difficulty of assessing successes and observing the process of winning and losing in counter-insurgency arises from the complex political-military tasks of counter-insurgency previously alluded to. Observing each task accurately is difficult, and observation is complicated by the possibility that progress in one task may be accompanied by regress in another.

To be confident that the process of winning in counter-insurgency is actively under way, we need to know several things: that R's access to inputs is becoming more difficult (the 'prices' at which inputs are available are rising, and the quantity available is diminishing); that R's organization is experiencing increased difficulties in converting its inputs into insurgent activities (there is growing evidence of lassitude, friction and misunderstanding within the R organization); that R's forces are being destroyed (and faster than the conversion mechanism is producing new ones); and that A's efforts to strengthen local defensive capabilities (by hardening, relocation, fortification and the build-up of a responsible and effective police force) are making progress.

That such an assessment is difficult, demanding an active and competent intelligence system, is evident. If there is a single indicator that is more reliable than any other it probably is the rate at which middle and higher-level officers and cadres in R's organization are acquired by A—whether by defection or by capture. Given the high regeneration coefficient of the intact infrastructure, this is the crux of R's strength and stamina. Depleting the core of the organization is the aim; acquiring cadres is the key to the core. In both Malaya and the Philippines, this indicator was—retrospectively—a good predictor.

And it has never been deceptively high in counter-insurgencies that have been unsuccessful, probably because it is harder to falsify than other indicators.

The selection of appropriate indicators is further complicated by two problems which, though they also operate in conventional conflicts, play a more critical role in insurgent wars. One problem is possible distortions in the actions of members of A as a result of the selection of a particular indicator. If casualties inflicted on R's forces become accepted as an important indicator of success, incentives facing A's personnel are changed. The reporting of R's casualties may be inflated as a result. Or the threshold of reliability for distinguishing R's forces from the general population may be lowered so that a higher proportion of actual casualties may be imposed on the population than before.

A second problem is that accurate observation of success requires the indicators relating to R's own behaviour to be known as well. For example, if one is concerned with judging the process of winning or losing, it would be useful to know how an external sponsor of R might be viewing the same process. If R is concerned with strengthening its control in one part of the country by executing local officials, then combat undertaken by R in other parts of the country may be considered successful even in the relative casualty rate is highly unfavourable, because such combat diverts A's attention and resources from the area in which control by R is being strengthened. The first problem makes concentration on pure counter-force indicators of success unreliable and misleading, and the second makes the use of territorial indicators inapplicable.

Judging the process of counter-insurgency requires, in other words, intimate knowledge of R's organization and of the impact on that organization of various tasks and measures undertaken by A. What A must be after is to suppress R's capacity to undertake disruptive acts to some tolerable (to A) level, so that eventually the continued effort and sponsorship of the residual R will not seem worth the costs. When a given package of measures (or costs) undertaken by A buys a greater current and expected future suppression of R's capacity, then the process of winning is under way.

Finally, it is important not to specify an unrealistically high suppression level in concluding that a win has been obtained. The normal level of dacoity, disorder and illegal activity in less-developed countries is usually high. Efforts to establish an unrealistically stringent suppression level may have the effect of vitiating relationships between A and its own external support, thereby turning allies into suspicious and disaffected adversaries.

Intelligence and information: needs and dilemmas

Improved intelligence and information capabilities are central to nearly all aspects of insurgent conflict, both for R and for A, as already noted. Yet achieving this improvement is most difficult in the environment of the less-developed countries. In general, the costs of timely and accurate information vary inversely (and probably non-linearly) with the level of development. Thus, it is much harder for A to obtain timely and accurate information in less-developed countries than in more-developed countries. In advanced countries, A's intelligence is usually much better than R's, while in the less-developed countries the situation is reversed.

A corollary can be drawn from this hypothesis concerning differences between more-developed countries and less-developed countries with respect to the types of violence likely to be encountered there. In the former, 'hot' violence—which implies spontaneity, hence a shorter preparatory period, and hence less time for possible pre-emption by A—is more likely to occur. On the other hand, in less-developed countries, 'cool' violence, accompanied by greater preparation and a longer lead time, is more likely; the resulting increase in the risk of being observed may be small and the chance of being detected remains low.

While an improved capacity to obtain and make use of intelligence information is central to virtually all the tasks of counter-insurgency, its role is nowhere more crucial than in connection with the controlled use of coercion. Indeed, there is probably nothing more likely to enhance the legitimacy and respect of an A in the eyes of the people than a demonstrated capacity to make the punishment (as well as the reward) fit the crime, both in severity and in timeliness. Such discernment requires a capacity to ascertain who is doing what and when, with a speed and reliability seldom found among the As of the less-developed countries. Consequently, improved intelligence capabilities are likely to be of great importance in insurgent conflicts, probably at least as important as the judicious distribution of benefits to the population at large.

The components of such enhanced capabilities involve (a) collecting, processing and retrieving information; (b) communicating clearly and regularly with the population; (c) observing behaviour and responses accurately and continually; and (d) relating the foregoing components to the allocation and control of subsequent programmes and action.

Although the cost of information—broadly construed—is negatively correlated with most other characteristics of economic and

social development, this does not necessarily mean that the problem of improving information flows must be merged with all other development problems. To some extent, the information and intelligence problem can be approached and solutions found, separately from other development problems. There is, of course, a profound risk in attempting to do so—namely, the risk that improvements in information and intelligence capabilities may be used to bring about or to entrench repressive despots. The dilemma is a real one, not to be overlooked or dismissed lightly. On the other hand, it is in some ways only a more acute instance of a phenomenon applying generally to advanced technology and modernization in the third world—to the internal combustion engine, to the jet engine and to nuclear explosives, as well as to intelligence capabilities. Programmes and techniques that can widen opportunities for choice may nevertheless result in undesirable consequences. Precautions can and should be taken, and some degree of control should be maintained to reduce the risk of abuse. But the dilemma remains: reducing the risk of insurgency may carry with it an increase in the risk of abuse of capabilities that have been created with this aim in mind.

One need not be apologetic about this dilemma, nor should one view its acceptance as 'reactionary' and its denial as 'liberal'. Without more effective information and intelligence capabilities—indeed, without more effective capabilities for dealing with rebellion and subversion in general—authorities that are genuinely disposed toward freedom and progress can still be destroyed by oppressive rebellions. Such rebellions may then establish themselves impregnably with precisely those capabilities whose absence from the authorities' arsenal contributed to their arrival to power.

CHAPTER 11

Australia and the Nuclear Balance

A. L. BURNS

The nuclear context of Australia's foreign policy is not a regional one: world-ranging thermo-nuclear vehicles ignore the regions' imagined boundaries. But the universal nuclear context can be seen from a distinctively antipodean perspective, in which northern-hemisphere readers may descry unnoticed facets.

Australia has lagged behind in nuclear technology, both military and civilian, yet it played a subsidiary part in its early development. Australian scientists worked from the outset in the United Kingdom's wartime project. British atomic weapons were later test-exploded on Australia's Monte Bello Islands, 30 October 1952, and at Woomera and Emu Fields, 15 and 26 October 1953. Throughout the 1950s British rockets were tested on the Woomera Range, and research establishments were located at Salisbury Plains.

American interest in Australian locations was first brought to public attention in 1963, through the North West Cape Station issue.[1] Arranged between Washington and Canberra by late 1961, the establishment on the Western Australian coast of a Very Low Frequency Signalling Station, for communication principally with nuclear submarines, was announced by the Federal government in late 1962, and amplified in March 1963. The ensuing political crisis revealed to ordinary Australians how momentous such issues could be, and how significant their continental location could become for nuclear strategy.

Late in 1968 the Joint Defence Space Research project at Pine Gap near Alice Springs began to be a subject of the speculation that in April and May 1969 again precipitated a political crisis over U.S. control of defence space facilities in Australia—perhaps unwarrantedly since, after the 1963 North West Cape debate, Australia had already cast in its lot with the American strategic deterrent system. The Australian Labor Party (A.L.P.) Opposition had in 1963 been manoeuvred by its political opponents into appearing totally opposed (which it was not) to allowing any Australian facilities to be used for

any aspect of the American deterrent system. But it was for the most part not drawn in the same way in 1969, though it objected to the extreme secrecy insisted upon by the twenty-year-old Liberal-Country Party government and to alleged abrogations of Australian sovereignty.

The political parties had taken up their distinctive positions about nuclear armaments in the 1950s. The coalition government had welcomed first British, then American, research and testing installations, then the U.S. signalling station, the British V-bombers and finally the highly secret Pine Gap installation, all in the name of connection with, in that famous phrase of Sir Robert Menzies, 'our great and powerful friends'.

The A.L.P., on the other hand, had declared reservations about being 'all the way' with any power (except the U.N.) as early as its crucial 1955 conference, which followed upon the schism from it of the largely Catholic Actionist and strongly anti-communist Democratic Labor Party (D.L.P.). In May 1962—following Sweden's 1961 resolution in the U.N. General Assembly calling for the abjuring of nuclear weapons—the A.L.P.'s Federal Parliamentary Party executive proposed a nuclear-free zone in the Pacific, which the executive of the party's Federal Conference later extended, on the analogy of the Antarctic Treaty, to the whole southern hemisphere. In March 1963, urged on by radical rank-and-file denunciations of the North West Cape Station proposal, the opposition debated the matter in Parliamentary and Conference subcommittees, eventually referring it to the Federal Conference of State Delegates. On 21 March this Conference pronounced the station to be compatible with Australian Labor Party policy provided six conditions—among them, joint U.S.-Australian control and operation, no automatic involvement in war, and no nuclear stockpiling on the Australian continent—were met.

The coalition government immediately took up the gage, and this issue of Australia's commitment to an American nuclear weapon system caught public attention. The Coalition and the Democratic Labor Party hoped either to split the A.L.P. on the question, or to force it into outright rejection of the North West Cape Station. The government's case was that joint operation and control of technical facilities was not feasible; the opposition's that what they sought was joint political control analogous to the mutual consultative arrangements obtained by the United Kingdom in regard to flights from British aerodromes after the RB-47 incident in 1960. The Federal parliament late in May 1963 debated the proposed agreement with the United States to establish the station. After the government vic-

tory by a majority of one, the opposition stated that if elected it would seek to re-negotiate though not to repudiate the agreement.

Acquisition by Australia of a nuclear deterrent is policy only for the D.L.P.[2] At least since 1965 D.L.P. supporters have advocated an Australian deterrent in response to China's nuclear weapons programme, to the expected withdrawal of the U.K. from East of Suez, and now to a likely contraction of U.S. commitments in South-East Asia—a 'region' with which the D.L.P. has long been concerned. This clause of D.L.P. policy was most loudly advocated in late 1967 and early 1968 when the Non-Proliferation Treaty (N.P.T.) began to look practicable. Less on the subject has been heard from it since—perhaps because the government, by its reservations first about signing and later about ratifying the N.P.T., and its recently implemented peaceful nuclear-reactor programme which may exclusively employ Australia's indigenous atomic fuel, has given some evidence of tacitly seeking an option on nuclear capacities.

The first two reactors acquired by Australia, HIFAR and MOATA, are at Lucas Heights (the station was opened in 1958) and are wholly experimental. But studies were reported in April 1962 (then due for completion in about 1967) for a 'centrifugal isotope separation plant with a capacity of one or two metric tons a year' which 'could probably meet the whole of Australia's fuel enrichment requirements until the end of the century'. 'The development of the gas-centrifuge method of isotope separation promises smaller countries such as Australia a means of producing enriched uranium without very large capital investment.' This suggests that HIFAR and MOATA were intended amongst other purposes to give the Australian Commission experience which might enable it to initiate a gas-centrifuge production of enriched uranium, and at the same time to build, or at least to operate, a power reactor which could also be fuelled by enriched uranium for industrial purposes.

Australia's tardiness in civilian nuclearization is explicable by local conditions. Thermal sources have been known for decades to be plentiful and easily accessible; they yield cheaper electricity than the vast Snowy River hydroelectric scheme, which in turn produces it more cheaply than the earlier nuclear reactors. Again, the 'archipelago' of the Australian population, clustering about the isolated State capitals, has until now made superfluous the feeding into the characteristic State power grid of the 500-megawatt quantum produced by the type of reactor which Federal government policy demands. By 1968, however, technological journalists were arguing that both disadvantages of nuclear-generated power (its comparative costliness; and the unsuitability to the Australian grids of such large

146

increments) would disappear in the 1980s, when the new generation of fast breeder-reactors would generate cheap power which could be fed into the grids at an accelerated pace, reaching the output of one new reactor a year by the end of the century.

By mid-1969 the Federal government's rather more defined intentions about the acquiring of options on nuclear weapons, its distinctive conceptions about the methods most suitable to Australia for developing civilian nuclear power, its interest in the technology of peaceful nuclear explosions, and its reiterated doubts (overcome by February 1970) of the prudence of even signing the Non-Proliferation Treaty had been brought together to form the grounds for a novel diplomatic posture, almost wholly contrary to that of the Holt government. With India, also doubtful of the N.P.T.'s merits, a new common concern was found. Conflicting interests within American and United Kingdom governments responded in contradictory ways to the Australian position. Internally, the impression of Canberra's new and 'nationalistic' obstinacy about the country's nuclear future coalesced with that later formed by its equally novel response to Russia's feeling out towards South-East Asia and the Indo-Pacific waters, to create an image of a Gorton government policy quite at odds, not only with the views of the A.L.P., but also with the previous policies of the Liberal-Country Party coalition itself. Several of its features, e.g. the attitude to Russian expansion and, though much less so, the reservations about the N.P.T., startled public opinion and may have contributed to the Coalition's loss of seats in the Federal elections of October 1969.

Canberra remains interested in the technology of peaceful nuclear explosions, and continued in 1969 to seek exemption for them from the provisions of the N.P.T. and from the competence of International Atomic Energy Agency (I.A.E.A.). But it decided not to press ahead with an early employment of Project Plowshare, viz. the creation by nuclear explosion of a harbour on the northern coast. The Australian Atomic Energy Commission, estimating this as likely to cost $US8 million, had turned against it the Sentinel Mining Company which would have used the harbour. Though the cost probably was decisive, rumours were heard that disarmament agencies in the U.S. government and the disapproval of non-American sources concerned for the N.P.T. had also been influential.

On 14 August 1969 Mr Freeth, then Minister for External Affairs, indicated four things Australia would 'wish to know' before reaching a 'final decision' on the N.P.T.: (a) what other, especially nuclear and pre-nuclear nations, would support it; (b) what safeguards agreement with the I.A.E.A. would be required of signatories; (c) the

N.P.T.'s effects on development of peaceful nuclear energy and of peaceful explosives; and (d) the effects of the treaty upon Australia's economic and commercial developments.[3]

Of these, the first may have partly referred to France which, if it had not agreed to act as though it complied with the treaty, would have been in a position to supply nuclear weapons to non-weapon states; it certainly referred to, e.g., India and Japan, countries which, like Australia, were known or believed to be concerned about China's nuclear potential and of whose interests the treaty-proposing powers took less note than those of, say West Germany, whose decision on the treaty was also of interest to Canberra. The second was a concern that on the one hand safeguard methods might be so lax as to permit espionage or something approaching it, and on the other hand that implementation of the safeguards might disadvantage the peaceful industries of non-nuclear signatories. The latter also provided the gravamen of (c) and (d).

That concern for independence in civilian nuclear industry was interpreted in Australia, especially by academic critics, as a mere disguise for the machinations of the 'Australian bomb' advocates, which included an eminent scientist-public servant, who had indeed spoken out for acquisition of the most effective modern armaments, recently instancing chemical and biological weapons. Nevertheless, the critics may have quite misinterpreted the government's and the Australian Atomic Energy Commission's intentions: economic, and not primarily strategic, autarchy appears to be the first objective. Australians of the Second World War generation and immigrant scientists from the United Kingdom have nursed ambitions since the 1940s for a great nuclear industry which could help transform the continent. Promises of technological advance, notably those of the fast breeder reactors, began to articulate these ambitions during the 1960s, and the outlines of a strategy for independent civilian nuclear development were not long in emerging.

However that may be, Australia is now clearly bent upon making up its late start in peaceful nuclear technology. A 500-megawatt reactor will be built at Murray's Beach, Jervis Bay, about 100 miles south of Sydney but in the Australian Capital Territory and thus under the control of the Federal government[4] which is inhibited by the Constitution from most kinds of industrial enterprise elsewhere in Australia. This will be the first of a series of reactor-constructions. As part of the present sudden expansion of the country's exploitation of its continental resources, the peaceful nuclear programme should go to make it an industrial power of some consequence by the end of the century, a condition which alone could transform its present place

in the strategic nuclear system. And if, as appears to be government policy, a technology based on the country's own sources of uranium and on nationally controlled means of enrichment is also developed, Australia will have begun to acquire an option on nuclear and thermo-nuclear explosives in the same year as it has signed the Non-Proliferation Treaty: the kind of step that in 1967 could be foreseen to be taken by signatories around the world as a more-or-less direct effect of that ambiguous international instrument itself.

This recent widening of expectations about civilian nuclear technology, though partly a result of innovation abroad, also accords very well with the Australian mining boom of the last few years. More importantly, the unexpected vision of an Australian resource-potential comparable to that of the North American continent will tend within the next few years to transform its outlook upon its place in the world. Evidence thus far available that the Japanese in the 1930s or the Chinese communists in the 1950s cast hungry eyes upon Australia's open spaces has been—though a little of it does exist— quite *recherché*. By the end of the century, on the other hand, 20 to 30 million Australians may be exercising sovereignty over resources and territory of something like the dimensions and the promise of continental United States: over a terrain that only ten years ago appeared—except for the eastern and southern seaboard and a few fertile pockets—a beautiful but unprofitable salmon-pink desert; and then powers with populations in the hundreds of millions, each disposing perhaps of an invulnerable deterrent, may consider it worth owning.

A new sense of such possibilities contributed to a certain questioning of the reliability of the American alliance which became evident amongst some government M.P.s and even those of the moderate A.L.P. in the late 1960s. But the government's change of policy in signing though not yet ratifying the N.P.T. is probably to be explained (a) by West Germany's doing so in November 1969; (b) by Japan's signing, while foreshadowing severe conditions for ratifying, in the first week of February 1970; and (c) possibly by an interesting development in the peaceful nuclear situation reported at the time in the better-informed Australian press.[5]

The Australian A.E.C.'s policy of sole national control of Australia's nuclear fuel had raised the question whether to persist in seeking reactors using natural uranium (e.g. the Canadian CANDU), or whether, instead or also, to look for an enriched-fuel reactor complete with the means for Australia to enrich its fuel itself, i.e. with the Anglo-Dutch-German gas-centrifuge technology.[6] Canberra's probing for the latter alternatives had by mid-1969 already caused a diplo-

matic upset in and with Whitehall. Non-official Australians were surprised to be attacked by English officials concerned for the success of the N.P.T. who assumed them to be privy to Federal government policy on this matter. Apparently other official interests in the United Kingdom were in favour of selling a British reactor to Australia along with the gas-centrifuge technology in some form.

The A.A.E.C.'s years of investigation into the latter had put the country in some position to negotiate with the tripartite consortium for direct participation in the new technology. In March 1970 there appear to have been official visits and explorations, made possible by Australia's signing the N.P.T. and thus overcoming the anti-proliferation concerns of one of the consortium's members. In June, the Lucas Heights establishment, in a Sydney exhibition 'Power for To-day', revealed some of the extent of its work with gas centrifuges. Thereafter, as tenders for the Jervis Bay reactor came in and the choice narrowed between CANDU, the British steam-generating heavy-water reactor (SGHWR) and pressurized-water reactors from Germany and the U.S.A., Australia's strategy clarified: if CANDU, using natural uranium, were not the choice, it would require, as a side-payment for buying any enriched-fuel reactor, the provision of a technology for enrichment. Preliminary success was reported in late August: the tripartite consortium would grant access to the gas-centrifuge technology by a written government-to-government guarantee provided (a) Australia undertook not to use the output of any enrichment plant or of the technology to make nuclear weapons, and (b) enrichment would be subject to I.A.E.A. safeguards. As Alan Wood pointed out, both conditions could be met by Australia's ratifying the N.P.T.[7]

Thus, whether CANDU or the British reactor is chosen, the Australian government seems to have settled for the economic rather than the strategic form of nuclear independence for some time to come. But one does not wholly preclude the other. As Ian Bellany shrewdly suggested,

> If it is recognised that Australia might one day wish to acquire its own nuclear weapon force, the balance of advantage does seem to lie with Australia's signing and ratifying the treaty, and at the same time building up its level of competence in nuclear engineering and delivery vehicle technology, the latter being totally unrestricted by the treaty. The aim should be that if Australia felt it had to leave the treaty, it could be in possession of a nuclear force of some kind as soon as possible thereafter.[8]

Bellany's publication should become a landmark in Australian discussion of nuclear acquisition. He makes it clear, first, that the outlay

in money and in skilled manpower for a modest but not ineffectual force using plutonium war-heads was markedly reduced in the last decade, is financially well within Australia's capacities now, and in manpower terms could be so by the 1980s. (But uranium rather than plutonium may become the preferred material for weapons, and the present Australian policy seems wide enough eventually to provide both materials in the years ahead.) Secondly, he has canvassed the feasibility for Australia of a sea-launchable force, and considers a non-ballistic cruise missile to be the cheapest alternative, and a far from ineffective one. The terms of Australian debate on nuclear weapons are quite changed by Bellany's analysis, and also by the developments in peaceful nuclear exploitation mentioned before.

If then, within the next few decades, Australians are likely to see themselves as subject to threat in an old-fashioned way by unnamed Great Powers avid for the continent's resources, the response of nuclear armament would not be impracticable. Another old-fashioned counter-measure to such apprehensions is now probably out of the question: Australians are unlikely to propose a 'peaceful internationalization' of their own and others' underemployed national resources, as a means of forfending the temptation to wars of conquest. Furthermore, the promised 'nuclear guarantees' (annexed to the Non-Proliferation Treaty and quite possibly liable to be made conditional in their application upon adherence to that treaty) are in any case regarded as workable only against nuclear aggressors of the quality represented at the time of this writing by communist China; that is: against the very powers whose capacity to threaten Australia is what might make a nuclear guarantee significantly helpful, any guarantee is apt in practice to run out as such powers so increase the range and quality of their nuclear armaments that the guarantor-powers' capacity to limit damage after having punished the threatening power becomes questionable. These all-too-likely emerging factors of the late 1970s appear, as suggested, more obvious and ineluctable from the antipodean angle than from within one of the present Super Powers.

A tacit assumption (for example) of many American strategic projections has been that even pre-eminent nuclear capacity is pretty well irrelevant to a power's capacities to invade, to conquer and to occupy non-nuclear or barely nuclear countries and groupings of countries; and therefore, on the other hand, that to the non-nuclear power(s) nuclear forces would be useless or worse against the threat of invasion from a Super Power. Extraneous considerations—including of course the wish to halt or delay proliferation—have encouraged pro-guarantor strategists not to question those quite implausible

assumptions. One says 'implausible', for would European NATO be actually more secure from invasion if denied its own or its main ally's nuclear potential, whether strategic or tactical? Or would India really gain no security from a Chinese invasion if it had nuclear weapons?

The 'nuclear context' for Australians is, and may be expected to be, constituted by their imagined projections of the future as they become more sharply defined and more widely diffused to the public. An early projection, very little disseminated, was current in the middle and late 1950s amongst Australian services staff who had been on exchange in the United Kingdom: a major thermo-nuclear war, though believed to be quite unlikely, would be largely confined to but would devastate the civilizations of the northern hemisphere; equatorial air current would insulate the southern hemisphere from the worst of the fallout; of the three surviving outposts of advanced production—southern South America, South Africa and Australasia, the last would predominate and would have great responsibilities as a base for reconstruction and as a force for a new world order. This possible role, it was then thought, would be prejudiced if Australia, before the possible catastrophe, had acquired—or more plausibly had been willing to accommodate its allies'—strategic nuclear forces. Divulging the scenario could also be prejudicial; so when the film *On the Beach*, with an utterly contrary scenario of global destruction, was made in Melbourne, the few better-informed staff and civilian students of nuclear affairs had no special reason to expose its technical impossibilities.[9]

Left-wing radical opinion outside the A.L.P. still maintains that the 'end of the earth' will not be subject to nuclear attack provided no nuclear forces are based on it, and provided (to make doubly sure) it renounces its present alliances. The right-wing radicals, many of them supporting the D.L.P., work upon Australians' deep-seated anxiety about being deserted by their allies, and have made much of the possibilities of nuclear attack, since 1964 from China, to some extent since 1967 from Soviet forces beginning to deploy in the Indian Ocean and the South-East Asian Archipelago, and quite recently from a Japan nuclearized in the late 1970s.

Successive Liberal-Country Party governments under Menzies and Holt gave every appearance of an 'end of the earth' complacency about the country's nuclear environment even though, at least until the British government's cancellations of the Blue Streak project, Australia had co-operated closely in the development of the United Kingdom's national deterrent. But this had been managed very much out of the public gaze and with no overt indication of official belief that Australia's strategic situation might have a nuclear component.

The small-scale civil defence effort of the 1950s projected the possibility of a single-weapon strike of a few kilotons on some Australian seaboard city and laid plans for only a partial evacuation—of mothers and children—and for largely extemporized rescue and reconstruction. These measures were based explicitly upon a strategic estimate that nuclear attack was 'unlikely'; and, indeed, that estimate still stands. Throughout the 1950s the attitude of government remained (and in 1969-70 the attitude of much A.L.P. leadership still remains) that Australia was not and within the foreseeable future would not expect to be 'in the nuclear-power league'. At the same time it had 'great and powerful friends', so that nuclear guarantees for Australia were in any case implicitly provided by the 'umbrellas' of the American and British strategic nuclear forces. At the end of the 1950s, with spending on defence a little over 2% of the nation's G.N.P., the Commonwealth government had small need to engage in the academic exercise of surveying an imaginary Australian nuclear procurement that might then have made the figure something over 8% for five years or 6% for ten years.

An early sign of preoccupation with nuclear weapons appeared in 1962, when a strike aircraft was being sought for the Royal Australian Air Force (R.A.A.F.) : it was not taken as an irrelevancy if one asked whether Phantoms or TSR2s had 'dual capacity'. A little later, when the United Kingdom deployed V-bombers in the Indonesian-Malaysian confrontation, at one time flying them from near Darwin, commentators pointed out that the aircraft 'could' carry nuclear weapons. No-one thought they would deliver them in that affair; nevertheless, it was recognized that they did impose a limit upon escalation by the Indonesians, at the time supplied by the U.S.S.R. with armaments, including nuclear bombers still in Soviet use. The Australian services were of course quite at home with ideas of such military or tactical deterrence.

At the first major post-war civilian seminar on Australian defence in January 1964 Sir Garfield Barwick, then Minister of External Affairs, presciently declared:

It has to be accepted that China will develop not merely a nuclear explosive device but also a weapons delivery system, however inferior it may be militarily to that of the advanced nuclear powers. I should like to see our academic community paying increasing attention to this question, of which I define two main aspects. The first relates to the political and psychological reactions within the Asian area to these developments. The second relates to the possible decisions of those major Asian countries which may be looked upon as interacting powers with China. They will presumably face such questions as whether they will develop nuclear

153

capacity of their own, rely upon support of existing nuclear powers, or look to other international arrangements or principles. It is, in short, by no means unlikely that the kind of complex issues over nuclear weapons that have arisen in Europe will in due course appear in Asia with a series of repercussions that have still to be analyzed.[10]

The Minister's remarks were made when his government's external situation was most felicitous: espousing a policy of 'forward commitment', the government found both its great and powerful friends committed in the forward area, the one in Malaysia, the other in Vietnam. Yet its own relations with Indonesia were for the time being quite cordial, and it was fostering other minor *ententes*, e.g. with Cambodia. The complex unfolding and present dissolution of its major allies' positions has since occupied its attention, so that even the emergence, sooner than expected, of China as a thermo-nuclear power has not been sufficient to bring the nuclear context to the fore in the strategic debate. But the Commonwealth government's position on the acquiring of nuclear weapons is now more articulated than before.

It is hardly surprising that the government should be reserving its decision whether or not to ratify the Non-Proliferation Treaty: as Herman Kahn has pointed out, generalized disarmament negotiations put ideas into statesmen's heads they would not otherwise have had. The terms of the N.P.T. have suggested to many governments two questions. If we sign, and if we then go on to ratify, how close all the same might we be to having a nuclear option? From what important prospects would our signature or our subsequent ratification preclude us? There is now evidence of consideration by the government as to whether Australia might develop civilian nuclear resources so as by the 1980s to have entirely within its own control the semi-processed materials for a nuclear-weapon programme (this with no specific 'threat' in mind, merely with the likely prospect of nuclear proliferation).

It is not policies of acquiring an Australian nuclear capacity, but the provision of facilities for nuclear allies that has actually involved the Australian continent in the nuclear military networks of the U.S.A. and, to a lesser extent, the U.K. Britain still retains, though it is now running them down, facilities at the Woomera range and elsewhere. British aircraft capable of delivering nuclear weapons have several times flown from Australian airfields. Fixed installations for Skynet, the U.K.'s system for communication with and between its remaining forces around the world, may be sought in Australia.

As well as the North West Cape facility mentioned above, America's N.A.S.A. has sited in Australia a number of receivers of

signals from space satellites, several near Canberra. The amount of $US225 million is alleged to have been invested since 1967 in the experimental outfit at Pine Gap, said by the Minister of Defence to be concerned with 'deep space' investigations of possible military significance and therefore highly secret. In 1969 a U.S. facility at Woomera, for possible tactical communication by military satellite, was announced in the Lower House. Though they are represented by the Federal government as designed to perpetuate U.S. protection of Australia, it is not easy to see precisely what these arrangements do to increase Australia's security, whether nuclear or conventional; and not difficult to imagine several circumstances in which they might reduce it in both regards.

Such conflicting considerations are reflected in the attitudes of the Australian government. There has been a consensus neither on the nature of the threat facing the country nor on the measures required to meet it. In August 1969 the Minister for External Affairs displayed, for the first time, a less hostile Australian disposition towards the efforts of the Soviet Union to promote its influence in the Indian Ocean area.[11] This was an exceptional view. The government made a determined effort, during the following weeks and before the elections of late 1969, to mitigate that stand. And at the election the Minister, Mr Freeth, lost his seat.[12] For Australia's strategic-nuclear situation, that *démarche*, though later withdrawn, indicated that the government still conceived China as the significant source of a nuclear threat to the country, and was little concerned about the U.S.S.R. in that role, despite the fact that the U.S.A.'s substantial military installations in Australia were elements in a system directed largely against the U.S.S.R. as potential enemy.[13] This single-minded apprehension of China as the nuclear danger is likely to be confirmed, at least in the public mind, by its mid-1970 advances in rocketry—if so, an unwarranted confirmation, at least for the short run of a decade or so in which China will build its still small stockpiles for targets now more accessible to it, and always more desirable, than any in Australia. In the longer run the possibilities mentioned above of invasion under cover of nuclear threat, or of nuclear blackmail, by communist China appear less implausible, and nuclear guarantees against them also less credible. Australians who feel compelled to argue against acquiring nuclear weapons as a deterrent against China will have to do so more and more upon sheer moral grounds. These have at least the advantage of immunity from changes in military technology.

With regard to nuclear perils incurred from the Soviet Union by virtue of America's strategic deployments in Australia, the technological possibilities create and complicate political issues much more. It

is possible to imagine the U.S.S.R. blackmailing Australia on account of its hospitality to American facilities and that therefore an attempt should be made to rid the continent of them, though not necessarily to press on toward full-blown neutrality. It is also possible to imagine the whole world's deterrent balance depending entirely upon the United States's maintenance of a capacity for global surveillance; and then the arguments for hospitality to the bases are supportable on many grounds. Politically, the likeliest direction of development by Australia at the moment seems to be (a) retention of facilities owned by or shared with the United States; (b) an Australian option on a bomb and on long-range means of delivery; (c) continuing perception of China as the principal threat. Australians not in favour of all three probably comprise no more than a divided middling minority of the politically concerned. Where the Gorton government led in 1969, Australian opinion in the 1970s is likely to follow. A contrary if rather unlikely possibility—the A.L.P. electorally victorious before or during 1972—might well reduce the prospects of (b), but otherwise would make little difference. How urgently Australia seeks an option, and how quickly it realizes upon it, will depend upon how Australians perceive the external world, and not upon deliberate and meditated internal decision.

Later in the century, a predatory nuclear Super Power might issue nuclear threats and even launch nuclear attacks in an attempt to occupy the continent and to acquire its now impressive natural resources. This would be feasible only for a predator disposing of a thermo-nuclear deterrent sufficiently invulnerable against all comers. In the nature of the case, if Australians were then to look for nuclear support from friendly powers, only the friend whose government regarded Australians as, in effect, its own people could be thought at all likely to help. There is little reason to suppose that a U.S. government might so regard the Australian people. If, then, this is a future nuclear danger worth considering, the current American-Australian alliance gives little evidence of providing a significant counter to it. But amongst non-allies only the U.S.S.R. has at present the Super Power attributes with which thus to threaten Australia; and it is likely to remain for some time preoccupied with China and with its disintegrating Eastern European empire. Thus Australia at this moment, and perhaps for a decade, does not run that danger of conquest-by-nuclear threat.

During the next five or ten years, then, global nuclear war is by no means the only conceivable occasion upon which nuclear threats or attacks might be directed against Australia. If it does occur, however, several of the State capitals, as well as some U.S. defence facilities, are

liable to be targeted by the U.S.S.R.—the Russians being however, the less likely to be able to destroy targets in Australia, the prompter and more effective are the West's damage-limiting strikes against Soviet missile bases on land and sea. There is some evidence that U.S. military installations in Australia might contribute significantly to the effectiveness of such forfending strikes by the Americans. (They would do so, presumably, by facilitating *inter alia* surveillance and other information-gathering as well as communications and control.) At another remove, the recognition that the system of which they are part can perform such functions is counted upon in western strategic doctrine to deter the U.S.S.R. from attempting nuclear war or from otherwise worsening a conflict with the U.S.A. This is a double means by which American facilities in and around the continent may be contributing to Australia's own security from nuclear attack.

Nevertheless their location on its territory, together with the ANZUS treaty, ensures that they themselves and some Australian cities are likely to be made Soviet nuclear targets: and the cities at least would have been much less subject to attack in the course of a U.S.A.-U.S.S.R. nuclear war, even as late as 1969, had there been no ANZUS treaty and no important American military installations in Australia. (A desperate and three-quarters-destroyed U.S.S.R. might expend some of its remaining war-heads on unaffected countries of all kinds, so as not to leave them heirs to international predominance in the post-Third-World-War situation.) Yet whether, if Australia were now to turn to complete neutrality, its being out of the nuclear arena would give it a better chance of avoiding nuclear attack within the next ten years is a question that cannot be answered with a conclusive strategic calculation even on the best available military intelligence. The fundamental issues are political. Furthermore, alliance and neutrality each invite distinctive perils other than nuclear attack. So again a political and not merely quantitative judgement is called for as to whether the nuclear peril is so great as to override all other diplomatic considerations. It is clear to Australians, however, that among such issues the nuclear one is now of much greater moment than in 1962, and yearly grows more so.

An unlimited nuclear war between Russia and America is usually held to be the least likely of feasible nuclear conflicts provided both parties remain prudent and controlled, and provided the coming escalations of the deterrent arms races between these two countries do not wholly restore such a premium upon striking first as would set them at each other out of desperation. Unfortunately, the less chance (because of a relatively stable nuclear stand-off to which Australian hospitality to U.S. facilities may be making a modest contri-

bution) of such an unlimited war, the more are opportunities and motivations apt to arise for limited Russian-American conflicts, despite or even in part as a result of movements toward *détente* between the two countries (the Soviet multi-megaton tests followed an informal moratorium upon testing; Russian anti-aircraft weapons were destroying U.S. aircraft over North Vietnam while the two countries were settling the Non-Proliferation Treaty). It is not impossible that some such conflict would bring upon Australia a nuclear attack which the U.S.A. was being spared—a possibility considered in later paragraphs.

In an unlimited conflict between the U.S.A. and China, the consequent nuclear dangers for Australia would depend in a complex fashion upon both those nuclear countries' and the U.S.S.R.'s then-current deployments. If China's deployments were such as to ensure it being able to launch a significant retaliatory second strike against the U.S.A. itself (a situation about which civilian strategists' expectations vary greatly, some saying that China will never have it, and others that it could begin to do so by 1975) the implications for Australia would be quite like those of unlimited Russian-American war, except that (a) a desperate and devastated China would have fewer war-heads to expend in reducing countries like Australia and (b) U.S. facilities here would be even more significant than in the Russian case for helping a conclusive American counter-force strike and for detecting any Chinese deployment in Indo-Pacific waters. Though generally similar to the implications for Australia of U.S.A.-U.S.S.R. nuclear war, those of U.S.-China war when China comes to be able to hit continental U.S. centres, are likely to be less serious.

Perhaps surprisingly, nuclear dangers to the U.S.A.'s allies may well be greater for so long as China cannot retaliate against the U.S.A. itself; for in that period it will 'make hostages' of the allies and, quite possibly, of Soviet populations also. The Peking statement on the day in 1964 of its first successful atomic test can be interpreted as such a threat to Japan. 'Hostage-taking' was, of course, practised by the U.S.S.R., before it was able to promise retaliation upon continental U.S.A., against the Western Europeans. It is a measure taken by the desperate. From the hostage's viewpoint, its incidence is very different from that of 'nuclear blackmail' inappropriately so-called. If China's current restricted nuclear capacity were invoked by Peking, at a time when China was not directly threatened by the U.S.A., to 'blackmail' Australia into destroying the U.S. facilities there, an American preventive strike, at least upon Chinese nuclear sites, would very likely follow; (and would certainly follow any Chinese strike on the cities of Australia, whether or not it was neutral) ; and similarly

if China were currently to attempt a conquest of Australia by nuclear threat. In contrast, hostage cities in Australia or elsewhere amongst America's allies would fall victim (if at all) to Chinese nuclear strikes only after the U.S. had struck at China.

Thus one could hardly be taken as nuclear hostage by China if one were completely neutral or were opposed to the U.S.A. (and to the U.S.S.R.). On the other hand, neutral or not, one may become vulnerable to Chinese 'nuclear blackmail' or similar selective nuclear threats, when China has come to have some small chance of destroying American populations and/or clearly vulnerable hostages located amongst the U.S.A.'s remaining allies.

Australia in ANZUS and taken by China as nuclear hostage might nevertheless derive some protection of a directly defensive kind from the alliance and from the functioning of the global U.S. system of which the facilities here are a part. There would be at least a chance that Chinese I.C.B.M.s aimed at Australia would be destroyed before launching (notice, however, that since all of Europe as well as major Canadian and American centres of population are as much within range of any rocket capable of reaching Australian cities, China would almost certainly prefer to target the former, unless they were defended by a thick anti-ballistic missile system). In practice far more important, U.S. surveillance systems would have some probability of pinpointing, for destruction before they were fired, Chinese submarines or unconventional delivery vehicles off Australian cities. But that direct U.S. protection is not utterly certain—it is at best, a probability.

Is there then no great source of security for Australians in a nuclear guarantee against possible Chinese threats, both particular through ANZUS, and general as in the assurances of the U.S.A., U.S.S.R. and U.K. annexed to the Non-Proliferation Treaty? For so long as China's nuclear forces can be almost completely disarmed by a U.S. and/or Soviet pre-emptive strike, any Chinese nuclear threat to non-nuclear powers is apt in any case to provoke such pre-emption. But when Chinese forces are no longer disarmable, and when either or both the Super Powers' own territories are likely to be open to a Chinese second strike, the Super Power guarantors will hesitate to risk such reprisal on behalf of any people or region which they do not regard as their own, or as essential to their vital interests (e.g. as, in past or perhaps even present circumstances, Western Europe is essential to the U.S.A.). Formal nuclear guarantees are then apt to be either superfluous or inadequate. It would be a different story if what was 'guaranteed' were the transfer to, say, Australia's sovereign control of an adequately invulnerable nuclear deterrent strike force (and, per-

haps, surveillance system), immediately upon its asking in the event of any nuclear threat to it, and if such a 'crash proliferation' were known by the potential enemy to be practicable.

In short: at present and for some time to come, Australians do not avoid but incur nuclear danger from China by adhering to the ANZUS treaty, housing the American deterrent system's facilities, and otherwise co-operating militarily with the U.S.A. On the other hand, the U.S.A.'s deterrent system itself certainly promises to reduce significantly some of the dangers thus incurred, by assisting the location and destruction beforehand of the vehicles possibly threatening Australian cities. The risk of Australia's becoming China's nuclear hostage on account of its American connections is imminent and increasing, and may be expected to be so for years; but, because many other hostages are also available to China, it may not be a very high or probable risk.

In an all-out war between the U.S.S.R. and China—by no means an impossible development—Australia may seem to be quite uninvolved. But a major war of that kind might spread, for many reasons; specifically China could well try to deter a Russian preventive attack or to withstand it if launched, by putting itself in a demonstrable position to involve the U.S.A.—thus capitalizing, as it were, upon that primary deterrent balance between Russia and America perpetuated by their reciprocal fears. One way of involving the U.S.A. would be to make clear both to Moscow and to Washington that Russian nuclear strikes on China would cause Chinese strikes upon America's European allies, or, better, upon continental U.S.A. (and *vice versa* to deter the U.S.A. from striking at China: paradoxically, one's best 'hostage' may be the other Super Power). Another way to involve America would be for China to take hostages amongst America's allies. This would be an even more sensible Chinese stratagem if an American-Russian *détente* were to lead to their combination against China and, say, to some resultant understanding between the Russians and the Australians.

The U.S.S.R. could present nuclear risks to Australia in several kinds of situation other than unlimited war between it and the U.S.A. We here assume that the primary deterrent balance is still reliable: the two Super Powers are able in effect to conduct more or less vicarious limited warlike operations against each other—as ostensibly in Cuba 1962, and explicitly in Vietnam. For objectives less vital than Russia's survival, Australia might still be made to serve as a kind of hostage. The Russians' increasing interests and deployments in the Indian Ocean and around southern and eastern Asia, though doubtless primarily against China, focus Australia and its co-operation with

the U.S.A. much more than before within the Soviet's area of attention. A dependent ally such as Australia, offering hospitality to
elements of a major ally's deterrent, runs nuclear risks as an emergent
strategic feature within the rival Super Power's field of vision that it
would not as a neutral living at the end of the earth.

An atmosphere of *détente* between Super Powers does not always
prevent a perilous crisis between them a few months later, though it
may make less likely the deepening of that crisis into a Third World
War. These sudden conflicts are usually played out by the Super
Powers in or around the territories of one or another's allies. In these
conflicts conventional armed force, not nuclear weaponry, has been
used. It is also far more likely that some Super Power should use
nuclear weapons in a limited way and outside his major opponent's
home territory, than that he should fight a nuclear Armageddon with
his major opponent.

A limited Russian use of nuclear weapons against Australian territory within five or ten years is not likely; but it is not impossible. The
U.S.S.R. may have occasion to take reprisals for some unacceptable
American action by eliminating the U.S. facilities here with nuclear
weapons. It may foresee urgent strategic reasons for eliminating the
facilities. In these cases, too, therefore ANZUS and subsequent agreements would have proved to be at least the pretext for nuclear dangers
from the U.S.S.R., even though they would also provide some means
toward mitigating the effects of those dangers after having given rise
to them.

Beyond the naive declared aim of building up a credit of future
gratitude in Washington—a justification also employed on behalf of
the sending of Australian forces to Vietnam—the deeper and more
statesmanly object in offering hospitality to the U.S. strategic facilities
seems to have been to make Australia's co-operation indispensable,
and not merely convenient, to America's deterrent system. An indispensable Australia really would be liable to nuclear attack if, but only
if homeland U.S.A. were also. But American practice has more and
more avoided strategic dependence upon any single set of facilities
or systems; indeed, the developing state of the art may preclude any
ally's becoming indispensable.

Moreover, the notion that Australian facilities had become indispensable to the U.S. system could technically make them objects of
gravest concern to the Russians. (One's caution at accepting this
corollary of indispensability as universal truth arises from there being
certain categories of information, which surveillance facilities provide for one party, that the other will feel safer for his potential
enemy's receiving. Both might thereby avoid 'nuclear war by inad-

vertence'.) A not unlikely situation even worse for Australians would obtain if the facilities came to be a dispensable element to the Americans in a crisis, but a provoking anxiety to the Russians—like some U.S. missile deployments in NATO countries.

Australian laymen have recently been asking whether they would be worse off than they are with the present U.S. facilities, if Australia were also to give hospitality to American I.C.B.M.s and nuclear bombers. A reasonable answer is that, on the one hand, the U.S. might be thereby somewhat more committed to defend such strategic resources in Australia; but on the other, that the missile sites and bomber-bases would invite a lot of megatonnage, and therefore a great deal of fallout, in a global war. This is possibly an over-simplification of the general case. Successive Australian deployments of U.S. facilities can add marginally to the dimensions (but not necessarily to the probability) of a possible Soviet nuclear attack upon them, and consequently to the incidence of resultant fallout. They do not add to the indispensability to the U.S.A. of those Australian-located facilities, for indispensability is a yes-or-no condition depending on the way in which the facilities fit into the total American deterrent system; nor do they add to any conviction a potential enemy may have about the indispensability to the Americans of their Australian facilities.

The two current Super Powers are about to ascend another spiral in the strategic arms race, which could quite possibly destabilize the primary deterrent stand-off between them; not only would anti-ballistic missiles (A.B.M.s), if used in order to give thick protection to cities, make it harder for the other side to ensure a 'credible' strike; but, much more seriously, increased accuracy of missiles and deployment by both sides of MIRVs and MRVs would tend to make a disarming first strike more tempting and the surprised power's strike in response to it even less feasible.

The homelands of both the Super Powers, nevertheless, will probably remain secure because of the overriding balance of terror—the prudent recognition that even the most promising surprise attack might somehow misfire. But the Soviet Union, being rather more likely to fall behind in this new turn of the arms race, and having tended when thus behind to make dangerous moves in third-power regions (e.g. the Berlin blockade; the regional missiles and bombers targeted on Western Europe from the mid-1950s; the Cuban adventure) might create nuclear dangers for U.S. allies—Australia included, so long as it, like the Europeans, were housing significant elements of American strategic systems—in the early and middle 1970s.

What nuclear dangers would Australia incur by acquiring its own strategic deterrent nuclear forces? The answer turns again upon 'What kind of forces?' and 'How acquired?'. If Australia were under some predatory nuclear threat, but were instantly presented with an invulnerable second-strike force by some fairy godmother of an ally, that would secure it from the threat in the best possible way—better, for instance, than by its ally's pre-emptively attacking the threatener. The alleged destabilizing effects of gradual proliferation would not attend this instant variety. If Australia started now to build its own force—which might take four to ten years—it would in the interval remain more or less vulnerable. And even afterwards, at the very best it could be no safer from nuclear attack than the present lesser nuclear powers: the safety offered by nuclear deterrents is contingent upon the political decisions, as well as upon the sanity and scruples of the other nuclear powers.

Even non-nuclear neutrals have nuclear problems. The U.S.S.R. might well have as much of an interest in locating its strategic facilities on the Australian continent if it became neutral, as the U.S.A. has now, and might be willing to compel Australia to accept them. That would put it in something like Cuba's situation of 1962—i.e. a nuclear threat from the U.S.A., though quite unlikely, would no longer be unthinkable. (Twenty years after abrogation of the Anglo-Japanese alliance, Britain was at war with Japan.) But could Australians not 'denuclearize' their continent while retaining ANZUS as a conventional alliance, or even, while remaining in ANZUS, withdraw also from conventional military co-operation with the U.S.A. in the way that France remains in NATO?

Though that policy might avoid abrogating ANZUS, it would entail renouncing all the agreements for U.S. military-communication facilities, from North West Cape on. At the same time, the Federal government could commit itself to denying such facilities to all other powers, quite probably including the United Kingdom. Even so, the U.S.A. might well conclude that in the circumstances ANZUS itself was not worth retaining; to separate the nuclear from non-nuclear strategic systems—a possibility upon which most schemes for nuclear-free zones have implicitly depended—nowadays seems technically impracticable. Furthermore, America's rivals may yet be willing to risk U.S. intervention here as a price for coercing Australia into conceding their facilities a location on the continent.

To summarize: ANZUS and—much more—Australia's hospitality to U.S. strategic installations assist to some degree in keeping America's own deterrent system credible. By helping supply the U.S. with astonishingly detailed and world-ranging intelligence, they also

serve to stabilize the primary balance between the U.S.A. and the U.S.S.R. By the same token, they would help detect and interdict submarine and unorthodox nuclear delivery vehicles deployed by enemies of the U.S.A. to make hostages of Australia's cities or to blackmail it. On the other hand, the U.S. installations and ANZUS have brought and continue to bring upon the antipodes nuclear perils that would not impend without them. Finally, neutralism itself would not necessarily guarantee Australia against all other nuclear dangers.

Longer-term possibilities of nuclear threats to Australia (e.g. in the 1980s from Japan, which may have the potential to become by then a thermo-nuclear Super Power) are hardly touched upon in this Chapter. The aim has been to estimate possible nuclear dangers in the shorter term, and in the context of present power-political relations, current Australian policy, and currently canvassed alternatives to the latter. The estimates arrived at do not warrant Australians' taking to the bush: they are not recognizably in worse peril than continental Europe, or than Japan, or than France which has some deterrent capacity of its own, or even than the United Kingdom which has a significant capacity. No one danger by itself is probable; and though some are cumulative, some cancel one another out. One can hardly, for example, be blackmailed by a power that at the same time is making one its hostage in order to deter another nuclear power; nuclear threats to a neutral Australia would be alternatives to those now brought upon it through the American alliance.

Nevertheless, the country is already in nuclear dangers that in 1962 were only just arising. Moreover, no stratagem or policy has revealed itself that would eliminate each and every kind of nuclear threat to it. The perils, though not likely, are by no means out of the question; and there seems no way of nullifying one set of them without evoking another.

Australia's geography modifies the impinging upon it of the global nuclear situation, which otherwise affects it very much as it does the rest of the U.S.A.'s western allies. ('Regional' location is an unimportant item in the geography: for example, given thermo-nuclear ranges now possible, neighbourhood with Indonesia is likely to become significant for Australia at the nuclear level only if that archipelago were to play host to Soviet or to Chinese—or, in the distant and hypothetical future, perhaps to Japanese—nuclear forces, and only if Australia and Indonesia were already in power-political conflict.) Furthermore, the universal nuclear context connects in a single web of relations a large minority of the states of the globe—not only the five nuclear powers with their allies and dependencies.

Within this web several strands may nevertheless be distinguished.

The main one, upon which the whole fabric depends, is the Russian-American nuclear confrontation. We have seen, for example, that the expected new spiral in the deterrent arms race between them could greatly increase the risk to Australia of involvement in nuclear conflict, especially should the U.S.S.R. begin again to fall behind in the next lap of the race. Contrariwise, a high level of mutual surveillance (to the American side of which satellite-communication facilities in Australia may contribute) could reduce risks for all other parties, not only by making a Third World War less likely, but also by making it harder to wage unscrupulous limited wars against the allies of the enemy Super Power. We have also noticed that the more stable the dominant deterrent balance between Russia and America, the greater the motives and opportunities for other kinds of limited operations against non-nuclear states.

Inextricably tied into the main strand are those of the other thermonuclear powers, Britain, China, and France, and of the 'threshold' powers. Short of general nuclear war, many situations are possible in which two, three or more of these powers could be dangerously and complexly implicated together. This emergent 'multi-polar' environment by no means restores the classic balance of power, nor does it yet amount to Morton Kaplan's hypothesized 'unit veto' system,[14] in which the nuclear retaliation of any one of a number of powers could destroy many or all of the others. It is rather a novel power structure in which are woven strands we have not yet distinguished, for example, those of countries like Australia, which play host not to the nuclear weapons but to certain communication systems in their allies' deterrent forces.

The issue of policy apt to confront the latter kind of power within the next five or ten years has been most clearly anticipated, so far, by France. This is the issue whether to acquiesce in further involvement with and dependence upon one's Super Power allies, or whether to strive to disengage at least from the thermo-nuclear aspects of one's alliance. Australia, since 1950 an over-eager client of the U.S.A., may set about quite soon to debate that issue.

M

Some Economic and Technical Considerations

CHAPTER 12

Oil and Defence

ALEX HUNTER*

Australia's dependence on petroleum products

Approximately 48% of Australia's primary energy, including transportation energy, (1970-71) is derived from petroleum products.[1] In
the main, this degree of dependence is unavoidable. Any sizeable
decrease in the supplies of crude oil products coming to this country
would have a catastrophic effect on the operation of the economy,
including its capacity to provide the *matériel* of defence. It may
appear surprising, but personal consumption, including motoring and
domestic heating, account for only about 22% of the total consumption of petroleum products; trade and transportation take around
43%; agricultural and pastoral activity about 11%; and building and
construction about 7%. The remaining 17% goes into manufacturing industry and some exports of refined products, one-third of which
is in the form of ships' bunkers. Clearly there is little scope for a
straight economizing exercise in order to reduce dependence on
petroleum products. It could only hinder economic growth.

Nor is there much scope for developing substitutes for petroleum
products. Over three-quarters of Australian electrical energy is
already generated in thermal stations employing brown or black coal.
Coal instead of oil burning is of course technically feasible for furnace
heating in a wide range of industry; also for heat processes in foun-
dries and metal work, for extrusion, for food processing and bakeries,
in cement, ceramics and in chemicals. But considerations of thermal
efficiency, cleanliness, relative advantage in terms of air pollution, as
well as in maintenance-free convenience in operation, have progressively predisposed industry towards employment of the heavier petroleum products as fuel. The same processes are at work in railway transportation. And today no ships are built which burn coal as fuel. In
the future nuclear fission may provide substantial electrical energy
for the grid systems of Victoria and N.S.W. But this development is

* This is a revised version of a *Canberra Paper*. See note 1.

likely to displace black and brown coal, not oil fuel. Natural gas, an indigenous fuel now in process of intensive development for Sydney and recently arrived in Melbourne, Adelaide and Brisbane, will have a more formidable impact, reducing the share of energy produced by petroleum products from 48%-46% by 1975 (coal from 44%-42%).[2] But here again it is industrial uses and, to some degree, electricity generation which will benefit from the employment of this high quality fuel. Consequently, while the 'black oils' (furnace oils and heavy industrial diesels) will be rather less in demand, natural gas will do nothing to diminish Australia's dependence on the 'white oils' (motor spirit, kerosines, automotive distillates, and lubricants) for transportation. These latter categories constitute almost 55% of refinery production and their manufacture requires a certain input of crude oil, regardless of whether all of the inevitable joint production of black oils can be utilized. Until a revolution in transport technology occurs, petroleum products will retain their unique function.

In the manufacture (refining) of petroleum products Australia is virtually self-sufficient. Its refineries have produced for some years 95%-98% of all petroleum products requirements. Small quantities of aviation spirit—a declining market—are imported; also some cargoes of solvents; and some 1%-2% of consumption around the north and north-west coastal area is satisfied from Malaysia-Singapore and Indonesian refineries. Petroleum refining in Australia, its main components established since 1951, is a modern, efficient industry— the only major manufacturing industry without benefit of tariff protection. Of the crude oil required for the industry, most, however, comes from abroad. Table 2 gives some comparisons over time of the crude oil supply coming from the Middle East, Indonesia and Malaysia-Brunei. In 1966-67 indigenous production from Australia was only 4%; in early 1970 it was 12%-13% of refinery inputs. This proportion will rise as exploration and development of Australian oil fields reveal further reserves. We return to this point later.

Thus Australia's special problem is that its refinery industry, and with it almost all of its transport industry, most agriculture and a large part of manufacturing industry, at present depends on foreign supplies of crude oil. There is no danger of a physical shortage of crude since the Persian Gulf area and Indonesia, both East of Suez, account for rather less than 60% of all world reserves while supplying only 28% of world production. The real danger, of course, is that there could be some form of interruption of supplies for political reasons or because of war or war-like episodes. It is important to note, therefore, that the strategic problem, if it should arise, is less one of availability of supply sources than of possible dangers to the trans-

portation of crude oil. About fifty to sixty tankers are currently engaged all the year round in bringing crude 4,000-5,000 miles from central Sumatra and Brunei and 7,000 miles from the Persian Gulf to Australia. This is rather less than 2% of the world's ocean-going tanker fleet.[3] Any shortage of tanker capacity because of events in other parts of the world (the Suez Canal closures of 1956 and 1967-70 for example), interdiction of supply routes, or any sinking of tankers, can as easily affect Australia's supply position as a stoppage of the crude supplies themselves.[4]

TABLE 2

Supply Sources of Australian Crude Feedstock (%)

Refinery throughputs	Middle East	Indonesia	Malaysia –Brunei	Australia	Others
1966–67					
133 M.M.B. p.a. or					
365,000 B.P.S.D.	68	23	4.8	4	1
1970–71					
194 M.M.B. p.a. or					
530,000 B.P.S.D.	24	10		65	1
1976–77					
274 M.M.B. p.a. or					
750,000 B.P.S.D.	20–40	9	0	50–70	1

M.M.B. = million barrels; B.P.S.D. = barrels per stream day.

Note: The percentages for 1966–67 are calculated from actual imports. The 1970–71 proportions represent a reasonable expectation based on plans contemplated at the time of writing (early 1970) by local producers and refiners in view of the government's compulsory purchase policy for indigenous crudes. And the 1976–77 percentage distribution is designed to show how uncertain the position is beyond 1971. (It is not clear when new fields will be discovered and brought into production—the present reserves can supply only 50% of expected demands in 1976–77. The policies of Australian governments in compelling compulsory absorption of local crudes could change. And the refining and market characteristics of Australian crudes yet to be discovered are unknown.)

Source: Department of National Development, *Forecasts: Primary Energy and Petroleum Fuels* (1970).

Possible emergencies

Once the international character of the oil industry and the distances over which crudes must be transported are appreciated, one is compelled to take a very wide view of the range of emergencies which can significantly influence the supply of petroleum products in Australia. The sources of crude oil supply and tanker fleets can be affected by a variety of events around the globe.

TABLE 3

Proportions of World's Ocean-Going Tanker Fleet by Main Voyages (%)
Voyages from:

Voyages to:	U.S.A.	Caribbean	Middle East	North Africa	Others	Total
	%	%	%	%	%	%
U.S.A.	3½	3½	2½	½	1	11
Canada	—	1½	1	—	—	2½
Other Western Hemisphere	—	1	1½	—	½	3
W. Europe, N. & W. Africa	—	3½	41½	7½	3	55½
E. & S. Africa, S. Asia	—	—	1½	—	½	2
Japan	—	½	16½	—	1½	18½
Other Eastern Hemisphere	½	—	5½	1	½	7½
Total	4	10	70	9	7	100

Source: The British Petroleum Co. Ltd., *Statistical Review of the World Oil Industry* (1968); and Petroleum Information Bureau, *Oil and Australia 1969*.

We must therefore consider not only (a) the defence of Australia in the strict sense of resisting aggression, and (b) involvement of this country in military and/or naval engagements in South-East Asia, in the Pacific or the Indian Ocean, but also (c) war in all parts of the globe, and (d) war-like episodes arising out of insurrection, rebellion or revolution in the more unstable parts of the world. Indeed it is necessary to look beyond military or quasi-military events. Supply areas or tanker routes may also be influenced by (e) political penetration of underdeveloped countries. China, Algeria, Egypt, Syria, France and the Soviet Union are some of the countries having ambitions which could lead them to influence the oil affairs of other states in the Middle East and Africa.[5] Besides, there may be (f) internal political developments leading to intervention in the oil industry— the nationalization of oil fields, the takeover of the Suez or Panama Canals, embargoes on foreign exploration on shore or in continental waters, the closure of important shipping routes and so on.

This list of possible episodes is formidable. For systematic examination it is convenient to categorize the various possibilities which may affect Australian supplies of crude oil in terms of the geographical areas which might be the source of the dislocation. Consider the following:

The western hemisphere: In the South American continent and the Caribbean insurrections, revolutions and political actions affecting

the oil industry are quite likely to occur from time to time. Mexico expropriated foreign oil companies in the late 1930s; Argentina, Brazil and Peru intervene substantially in the importation of oil and the control of local production; Cuba took over the refineries from international companies after Dr Castro's successful revolution and now uses crudes from distant U.S.S.R.; and Venezuela, a militant member of the Organization of Petroleum Exporting Countries (O.P.E.C.), could conceivably inherit a government eager to disfranchise American and British-Dutch oil companies. Leaving aside Venezuela which supplies itself and exports considerably to the U.S.A., however, the South American countries are not large consumers of oil. There is some indigenous supply in Colombia, Peru and Argentina; and the state of industrial development, and therefore demand, is low in others. Only a small part of world oil movements, involving 4% of the world tanker fleet, goes to the South Americas (see Table 3). The North American continent is stable enough. The U.S.A., the world's largest consumer of petroleum products (34% in 1968), imports, net, around 21% of its crude oil inputs. Almost two-thirds comes from Venezuela but that country would not willingly interfere with exports to the U.S.A., its largest market, no matter what internal political changes occur. In the event of cessation of supplies the U.S.A. could in any case fall back on expanded Texas, Louisiana and now Alaskan production. The main effect of such an event would therefore probably be to release international tankers for use in other parts of the world. Looking at the western hemisphere as a whole, only the involvement of the U.S.A. in a global conflict could have a serious effect on world supply sources or the disposition of the world tanker fleet. Otherwise the U.S.A., because of its size, actually provides something of a stabilizing factor. Its reserves and tanker fleet can be deployed to meet emergencies in other parts of the world—as was done successfully during the 1956 Suez crisis, for example.

Western Europe: Until there is a settlement of the German question, the involvement of Western European countries in war, which is also likely to bring into the arena the U.S.A. and the Soviet Union, is always a possibility despite the determination of all groups concerned to avoid it. A conflict in Europe would not affect Australia's supply sources directly. But it could absorb and cause the sinking of a large proportion of the world tanker fleet. This would be most serious. Around 55% of the world's ocean-going tankers are employed in taking crude oil to Western Europe and the United Kingdom refineries (see Table 3). Thus even distant Australia could have its tanker fleet depleted.

The Soviet bloc: Even if the Soviet bloc countries became involved

in Great Power struggles in Europe or elsewhere, this factor would affect Australia's oil supply sources or the availability of tankers very little. The U.S.S.R. is not an unimportant exporter (5%-6% of international oil and product movements). But over two-thirds of this travels on relatively short sea routes and in pipelines to North-Western Europe and Italy (more than half in the form of residual oils and low grade motor spirit); only one-twentieth goes to distant Japan; and small quantities go to Cuba, Ceylon and certain South American and African states. The Soviet international trade is not, and cannot be, substantial enough to have significant repercussions on other world oil movements (surplus reserves are small); and any disagreements within the bloc are insulated from world trade since each of the countries (other than China) is connected to an internal network of pipelines fed mainly from U.S.S.R. oil fields.

The Middle East: Emergencies in this area are always liable to affect one or a number of the principal crude-oil-exporting countries of the world. Seventy per cent of all international oil movements by sea originate from the Middle-East group (see Table 3). It is therefore certain that events internal to the Middle-East oil economies would affect Australian supplies at least marginally. Consider some possibilities. Another Arab-Israeli war seems a probability. And the British have declared their intention to withdraw armed forces from the Persian Gulf and South Arabia. This could lead to an increase of U.S.S.R. influence in Egypt, Iraq and Syria. Without much encouragement from the Soviet Union, Egypt itself could attempt to dislodge the regimes controlling Saudi Arabia, Kuwait and the minor Persian Gulf sheikdoms. Thus, in the worst case view of the prospects of instability in this area, the oil economies could be so involved in war, or revolution, as to become ineffective suppliers. But there are solid reasons, (to be discussed later) based on political and commercial considerations, for believing that the damage to Middle-East supply-effectiveness will not be of anything like these dimensions. Meanwhile, it should be noted that, in the twenty politically eventful years since 1949, the only serious decreases in the flow of oil from the Middle East have been caused by the closure of the Suez Canal and not by direct interference with oil production facilities.[6] And Australia is, of course, on the right side of Suez.

South-East Asia and the Pacific: In this area close to Australia several types of war or war-like activity could occur: (a) Insurrectionist activity created by nationalist or religious groups (Indonesia, Cambodia, South Vietnam, Laos) or by local communist parties (Malaysia, Indonesia and the Philippines). These could result in continuous 'brush-fire' wars over quite long periods. (b) Regional

wars on a greater scale, because of border issues, nationalistic regional ambitions, or ideological disagreements (Indonesia and Malaysia, Malaysia and Singapore, Indonesia and the Philippines, Thailand and the Indo-China group of countries). (c) Great Power wars. They could originate in the United States's involvement, and the Soviet Union's interest, in Vietnam. China must also be classified as a Great Power in this area. Some of its traditional preoccupations—to have control over Formosa, to influence border countries such as Burma, North Vietnam and Korea, and possibly to accomplish an ideological revision in Japan—could well bring this country into conflict with other Great Powers, at first on regional-type disputes, but possibly developing into conflicts in which nuclear weapons are employed. Serious disputes with the Soviet Union concerning mutual border areas in North China and Outer Mongolia are particularly dangerous in view of the ideological schism between the two powers.

The first two types of belligerency, on recent past experience, can be expected to take the form of guerrilla and partisan activity principally. These must be small-scale land wars, in the main, with only insignificant coastal activity requiring small naval vessels and not major fleet units. Therefore insurrectionist activity or regional wars will not spread out to such an extent as to interfere with supply routes from the Persian Gulf across the Indian Ocean. Indonesian crude, ex Dumai in Central Sumatra, could possibly be prevented from passing through the Java and Arafura Seas to the east-coast refineries of Australia; and the longer passage westabout the continent could become necessary. (The larger tankers already take this route.) On past experience the supplies themselves are unlikely to cease. Although, since 1946, Indonesia has experienced revolution, civil war, 'confrontation', and the attempted *coup d'état* of September 1965 with its counter-coup, Indonesian governments have never permitted these episodes seriously to interfere with the valuable foreign exchange earnings involved in crude exports to the markets of Japan, Australia, the Philippines and the Pacific.

The prospects latent in the third type of conflict—Great Power wars—are altogether more serious. One cannot plausibly indicate any specific danger to Australia at this point in time; nevertheless, it would be foolish to discount the idea that future events might bring this country more clearly within the sphere of disputes between the Great Powers. In the South-East Asia and Pacific regions Australia has already aligned itself firmly, possibly inextricably, with the foreign policies of the U.S.A. So long as the United States continues to maintain self-assumed, substantial naval and military obligations in the region (a willingness to undertake mainland engagements such as

Korea or Vietnam and the retention of a major fleet presence to support the *status quo* in Korea, Japan, Formosa, Indonesia, etc.), the results of Australia's alignment are held at arm's length. But events may not permit Australia to maintain this relatively safe and pleasant posture in foreign policy. In a resurgence of isolationism the U.S.A. could withdraw and/or other Great Powers may attempt to replace the American hegemony in the region. Looking well ahead one can see that the third industrial power of the world, Japan, may well wish to fill the role. Although, currently, Japan secures all its needs through trade, its almost total dependence on foreign supplies of metallic ores, oil, raw chemicals and coal may compel Japan to become, once again, a major Pacific naval and air power. The Soviet Union may be another long-run candidate although it displays at the moment no disposition to interfere in what is *de facto* an American bailiwick. Such permissiveness may not last; consider the emergence, over a long period, of the Soviet Union as a naval power in the Mediterranean and its more novel interest in the Indian Ocean. China could constitute a proposition of more immediate importance. It borders on South-East Asia and one must keep in mind its traditional policy of controlling, or strongly influencing, border countries as well as its current enthusiasm for the export of revolutionary fervour. As it develops military nuclear capacity it may well effectively become one of the group of Great Powers. China may have in view a more active political and military phase of activity in which it resumes some of its ancient hegemony over South-East Asia. In the event of nuclear attacks Australia may be one logical target. It is an active, not a passive, ally of the U.S.A.; it provides a useful base for certain naval and air force purposes; and it is the location of a communication centre for American nuclear submarines. In short parts of Australia, including some or all of the capital cities, could become at least ancillary targets in a Great Power conflict.

Solutions

Individually examined, each of these emergency situations liable to interrupt crude oil supplies can easily be interpreted as only remote possibilities. Even in South-East Asia, of Australia's neighbouring regions the most vulnerable to political dislocation, it is difficult to foresee within the next five years anything more substantial than border incidents, local insurrectionist activity sponsored and led by nationalist, religious and communist forces, possibly a civil war or two or a minor regional conflict over territory. Looking at all the emergencies possible in the aggregate, and combining their incidence across the world over a longer, say, ten-year period, one becomes less

confident. It seems likely that one or more of these emergencies will emerge to disconcert Australia. For consideration of events over this longer period three background factors are to be stressed: (a) the probable increase in proliferation of nuclear weapons among small powers and the relative inability of either the United Nations or the Great Powers to control this development; (b) the fact that tankers are around 38% of the gross tonnage of the world's ships and carry cargoes which constitute more than 50% by volume of the world's internationally traded goods; and (c) the increasing size of the submarine fleet of the Soviet Union and, perhaps to become more significant later, that of China which, if ever they are used, will find their principal targets in oil tankers.[7] Since the combined Soviet Union-Eastern Europe-China group of countries have only a minor tanker fleet (around 4% of the world total), and a small movement of oil (internationally about 6.5% of the total), they have much less to lose than most countries from wars which become general enough to extend into naval conflicts. In short, oil tankers are the most important as well as the most numerous targets available for submarines.[8]

To achieve security in oil supplies we can think in terms of two desirable objectives. Each can be pursued separately but in a complementary fashion. These are:

1. A short-term solution, or solutions, to meet a temporary scarcity of crude oil caused by political upsets, nationalization of oil fields, interruptions of supply routes due to a regional disturbance or a shortage of tankers created by wars elsewhere. (*In essence what is required for emergencies of this duration is storage capacity of some type.*)

2. A long-term solution, or solutions, to offset in a more permanent manner Australia's dependence on oil sources in the potentially unstable areas of the Middle East and Indonesia and to remove its reliance on a specialized form of transport, oil tankers, over lengthy and undefended ocean routes. (*To be free of these kinds of uncertainties over the next ten years calls for the discovery and development of further alternative sources of supply in order to spread the risk of disruption; a more adequate supply of tankers under Australian influence or control; or, best solution of all, adequate reserves of indigenous oil so placed that lengthy tanker hauls around the difficult-to-defend perimeter of Australia are unnecessary.*)

Short-term solutions

Since short-term solutions turn on additional storage it is as well to know the present position. On mainland Australia and Tasmania,

seaboard storage capacity totals 61 million barrels—mainly holdings of petroleum products for distribution. At a refinery throughput of 460,000 barrels per stream day (B.P.S.D.), roughly the 1969-70 figure, and assuming that all tanks are full, this quantity would last for 132 days or four and a half months. If inland storage is added one can safely assume that total storage is of the order of five months' normal consumption. It is impossible, however, to maintain a 100% capacity in all storage at all times. Stocks must be distributed; and refills must take place at intervals which ensure that economic loads are transported. Industry sources suggest that, allowing for these logistic factors, aggregate inventories of products and crude held in company tanks are about 60% of total storage capacity, that is, sufficient to carry industry and private consumption for about three months.

Some of this seaboard storage is in crude oil awaiting manufacture into products. Practice varies but most companies have available crude oil tankage sufficient for between four to five and a half weeks depending on throughput. But only occasionally is this storage completely full. Depending on the size of tanker employed, tanker schedules and current production rates, the crude oil tanks could be carrying at any one time anything from as much as thirty days throughput to as little as five days throughput. Thus in an emergency affecting crude supplies, some of the unluckier refineries might easily be compelled to curtail and then cease production within ten to twenty days. As against this, industry and the community could continue to operate for so long as the supply of finished products remained available —for about three months. With rationing of the private consumer —who absorbs rather more than one fifth of refinery products—and curtailment of exports, perhaps stocks could be made to last four months.

The most efficient method of extending the period for which stocks can be made to last would seem to be an increase in crude oil storage capacity. Crude is a cheaper medium in which to hold inventories. It is less liable to contamination or deterioration in quality or to the hazards of fire. And it has the advantage that a sufficient size of holding will avoid the necessity of closing down refinery operations too soon if and when crude supplies are cut off.

Several possible methods of storing crude in bulk deserve consideration:

(a) *Steel tanks* of the pattern conventional in the industry. Remembering that the larger the vessel the lower the unit costs of providing the storage, tanks as large as may be technically feasible should be selected. For the oil industry the optimum size is now in

the region of 500,000 barrels. Each tank of this size would cost around $A1 million to fabricate and erect. To gain thirty days additional throughput for Australia, assuming a required importation rate of 400,000 B.P.S.D. (12 million barrels or 87% of 1970-71 needs), a total of 24 such tanks would be required at a capital cost of $A24 million. To gain sixty days additional supplies 48 tanks would be needed at a capital cost of $A48 million. Ninety days storage would require a capital outlay of $A72 million. And so on. Then there is the cost of the stocks to be held. At an average landed cost for foreign crude of $A1.80 per barrel (the probable mid-1970 prices allowing for discounts on Middle East crudes) each 500,000-barrel tank would cost another $A1 million to fill. To fill 24 tanks—thirty days consumption—would cost $A21.6 million; 48 tanks filled—sixty days supply—would cost $A43.0 million; and 72 tanks filled—ninety days supply—would cost $64.6 million. To summarize, the total capital cost of buying an additional thirty days crude is around $A46 million; and for sixty and ninety days it is respectively $A91 and $A137 million.[9]

Storage in conventional tanks may seem expensive. But an outlay of $A46 million (or a *per annum* charge of $A6 million) to gain one month's uninterrupted operation of the refinery industry (and a further period added to the operation of the remainder of the economy which depends so much on vital supplies of petroleum products) is not a high price to pay for this form of insurance. Then, if and when the need to cover emergencies recedes, the tanks can, where not required for defence purposes, be integrated into oil company assets. Conventional tankage of this sort probably is the most economical form of storage construction. But admittedly they are not ideal. They are easily located and are vulnerable to bombing, sabotage and fire dangers.

(b) *Old tankers* can be used as storage containers. They are, however, smallish and not too freely available at the moment (1970). If the average size could be taken as 35,000 D.W.T. (i.e. each holding 250,000 barrels) then 48 would be required for thirty days storage; 96 for sixty days; and 144 for ninety days storage. At $A1.5 million per ship, which if anything underprices a twelve-year-old 35,000 D.W.T. tanker, the cost of storing oil would be nearly three times as expensive as it would be by using conventional land tanks. There are other obvious disabilities. Maintenance costs to keep down marine deterioration could be greater than on land. There is the risk of oil escaping into coastal waters. And such vessels would be stationary, conspicuous and vulnerable to air, and possibly sea, attack.

(c) *Nylon-reinforced rubber bags* may also be used to store oil.

They can be held in tidal waters, in bays and lagoons around the coast, and have mobility advantages in that they can be towed around from one location to another and eventually alongside a refinery wharf. But they also have some of the disadvantages—contamination, vulnerability and fire hazard—of old tankers. They can be used on land if suitably supported in a watery medium (large excavations partly filled with water). Certain stronger varieties do not require support; and are so used by military forces as bulk-storage containers in base areas. The cost of purchasing and maintaining nylon-reinforced bags large enough to hold, say, 250,000 barrels is not known (oil companies use them in much smaller sizes as oil and product barges). And estimates would be required for the additional cost of preparing suitable sites and/or anchorages. It seems certain, however, that, for a short-term solution, they are cheaper and more rapidly prepared than conventional steel land tanks.

(d) *Underground storage* should also be examined. In some countries natural gas is stored in porous rock formations. It is more difficult to store oil in this fashion since it is not compressible. A special study could possibly yield some knowledge of appropriate structures. But it is unlikely that suitable and conveniently located formations could be found without considerable diversion of scarce geological talent. Underground caverns excavated from hard rock are used in Sweden for storing oil and products—an unusual and expensive method and not too easily available in Australia reasonably adjacent to refineries. A depleted oil field makes very suitable storage since the wells, pumps, separating plant, oil-gathering lines and valve equipment are already in place. Further, oil so stored is almost completely safe from sabotage, fire and nuclear contamination. A corollary of this point is that oil in existing, proved reservoirs is stored in very suitable and economic conditions. All that is required—a point to be remembered—is a decision to leave the crude in the ground for emergencies.

Long-term solutions

(a) *Diversification:* One long-term solution is to diversify oil supply sources to take in areas other than the Middle East and Indonesia. This policy is scarcely practicable. The nearest alternative supplies are in Libya, 8,500 miles away, and Venezuela, 8,000 miles. Each of them is on the wrong side of the Suez and Panama Canals, possibly the subjects of international dispute and interruption of supplies. Further, oil from these areas is expensive ($US2.10 per barrel in Libya as against the Arabian discounted price of $US1.30; and in Venezuela $U.S.2.80 per barrel as against the Indonesian

equivalent at $US1.62. Including the extra tanker freight—about 25 cents per barrel—Libyan is around $US1.05 per barrel and Venezuelan $US1.43 more expensive than their Indonesian and Arabian counterparts. Only in a serious emergency can their use be contemplated.

In any event one should handle the idea of diversification of sources with care. To refer to the Middle East, from which come two kinds of Australia's crude, as one single source of oil is misleading. In the Persian Gulf there are in fact four large suppliers: Saudi Arabia (71% of world production); Kuwait (6.0%); Iran (7.2%); and Iraq (3.3%). In addition there are a number of small producers —mainly coastal sheikdoms such as Abu Dhabi, Bahrain, Qatar, the Kuwait Neutral Zone and others which between them export almost 4.0% of world production. These tiny countries produce in fact close to one-half as much as Venezuela, the major exporter of the western hemisphere; three times as much as Indonesia; and almost three times as much as is required for Australian needs.

These Persian Gulf producers cannot be expected to act together for long. Consider Iran. Although a Muslim country, it is an outsider in the ethnic sense (Aryan, not Semitic), a foreigner, almost an enemy to the Arab group, particularly Iraq. It is a bitter commercial rival of the main Arab oil producers. It has fought strongly, through the consortium of foreign oil companies and its own national oil company, to regain the leadership in production from Saudi Arabia and Kuwait which it lost during the attempt to expropriate British Petroleum in 1951-54 and take over the running of the industry in Iran. Iran would now almost welcome a shutdown, for political or other reasons, of any of the three major Arab oil-producing countries in order to appropriate a share of their markets. Among the four large producers, Iraq is farthest to the left of the political spectrum. A republic run by a military junta, it is the most likely to nationalize its oil fields regardless of commercial consequences. (Syria, through which passes 70% of Iraq's oil, encourages such aspirations.) And recently, Iraq unilaterally took over from the international Iraq Petroleum Company a large part of its concession-exploration areas in order to explore these itself with the assistance of French and U.S.S.R. state companies. Because of its anti-imperialist-cum-socialist views Iraq is strongly distrusted by Saudi Arabia, an ultra-conservative dynastic monarchy. Kuwait also has reason to fear Iraq. In 1963 Iraq laid claim, ignoring a past history of independence, to the whole of this tiny but incredibly oil-rich sheikdom and would have succeeded by military means had not Britain moved a mobile defence force into Kuwait at short notice. Also, Saudi Arabia and

181

Kuwait are wary of the motives of the United Arab Republic (Egypt). Its mildly socialist policies are distasteful to them, and they have sound reason to believe that Egypt is attempting, by means of the infiltration of pan-Arab ideas, and until recently in Southern Arabia by direct military assistance, to acquire political hegemony over most of the Arabian peninsula including its Persian Gulf shore.

A further factor which tends to disrupt the solidarity of oil producers' policy is the enormous excess capacity which persists in the area. The Middle East accounts for around 60% of world oil reserves as against its 28% of world production. The whole area has proved reserves in the ground giving 66 years of production as against 31 years for the world. And these Persian Gulf countries are far from being fully explored. In this respect the area is only an extreme case of a world-wide phenomenon. As the result of the intensity, and success, of exploration over the past decade the reserves which have been proved and the further reserves which can be inferred, give almost 100% excess capacity over expected refining requirements at least until 1975. Indeed, if the pipelines and marine terminal facilities existed, Middle East output could, if required by world demand, be doubled very rapidly. Further, since 1957 Persian Gulf crudes have had to be sold to independent refiners (and subsidiaries) at larger and larger discounts (for example 44 cents per barrel from the $US1.59 f.o.b. price for 31° crude in 1968-69). And, to confound the Arab producers again, new areas of oil production have developed in Africa (Nigeria, Algeria and Libya) more advantageously placed to serve the world's largest market area, Western Europe and the United Kingdom.

In sum, whatever occurs in the Middle East and North Africa, whether it be insurrection, nationalization, revolution or war, the international oil companies can always count on a few dissident or commercially opportunistic producer-countries to supply. Each of them is now unwilling to risk Iran's mistake of 1951-54 thereby losing markets to competitors, lowering production and permanently lowering income from oil. The vulnerability of oil supplies from the Middle East to Australia is a defence *cliché* particularly favoured by politicians when discussing the need for Australian self-sufficiency in oil production. It is at best only partially true. And the prospect of a total or even substantial embargo has been, and is, almost completely bogus.[10]

(b) *Control over tankers:* Rather than seek diversification of supply sources a more realistic and cheaper solution would be to obtain some substantial control over the disposition of tankers on the runs from the Middle East and Indonesia to Australia. Given access

to tankers and assuming there remain some well-defended or suffi-
ciently-isolated ocean routes to Australia, even if some of the normal
supply sources are cut off, there may yet be oil available at a high
price and transportation cost from such exporting areas as the Caribbean, Canada, Mexico, Texas, Nigeria, Algeria, Libya and the Soviet
Union. To this list will soon be added Alaska, Portuguese West Africa,
Thailand, Madagascar and perhaps even South Africa and the
Pacific island of Tonga. Control of tanker facilities could mean government ownership.[11] Providing they were efficiently managed—preferably by an experienced shipping company—on behalf of the
government, a fleet of twelve modern, turbine-engined, 16-knot tankers each of 100,000 D.W.T., purchased in Japan, could deliver nine
million tons of crude oil *per annum* (180,000 B.P.S.D.) from the
Persian Gulf—or 37% of present Australian throughput. The capital
cost of this investment would be around $A100 million; effectively
managed the fleet would require no operating subsidy; and, over a
ten to twelve-year period, would repay its cost if normal tanker
freight rates were charged.

But there is probably little need for government intervention in
tanker arrangements. The same seven companies which dominate
the Australian refinery industry are also its major owners and the
charterers of the world's ocean-going tankers. At any given time
these companies, along with one other (the Gulf Oil Corporation of
U.S.A., not represented in Australia) control around 70% of tanker
tonnage. Normally it would seem to be in the interests of the international companies to find, in defence emergencies, the tanker tonnage necessary to maintain the operation of their Australian assets.[12]
One can, however, think of situations in which the scarcity of tankers
would compel the companies to choose between supplying refineries
in Australia as against larger and more valuable installations elsewhere. The parent companies may also be under strong pressure
to give priority in tanker operations to American, British, French or
Dutch interests. In such circumstances Australian government ownership of a tanker fleet could be advantageous. It is salutary to remember, however, that in an emergency affecting directly the security
of ocean routes to Australia (as distinct from a general scarcity of
tanker tonnage) it is not obvious that a government ship is any more
useful than a company ship. Both are sinkable.

(c) *Indigenous supplies:* The best long-term solution for the oil
supply problem is, of course, to secure self-sufficiency from indigenous
fields. What can be said of the prospects in Australia? At present
(early 1970) only 12%-13% of oil requirements come from Australian fields—about 8,000 barrels per day (B.P.D.) from Moonie in

Queensland, 40,000 B.P.D. from Barrow Island and some 20,000-25,000 B.P.D. from Gippsland. The Esso-B.H.P. group has, however, made a confident announcement that it plans to produce 250,000 B.P.D. or more from Gippsland fields by early 1971. (Total production will probably be around 320,000 B.P.D. by 1971-72.) Thus, together with the planned 1971-72 production from Moonie (7,000 B.P.D.) and Barrow Island (45,000 B.P.D.), indigenous production will be around 69% of the expected refinery throughput (550,000 B.P.D.) in that year. This proportion of self-sufficiency, so quickly acquired, looks very promising.

Moreover, if one examines the prospects beyond 1971-72 in the broadest possible way, with no precise time limit in mind, it would seem that Australia is assured of self-sufficiency in oil at no very distant date. Contrast Australia with the U.S.A. That country has a land area, and a sedimentary basin area, close to that of Australia. The U.S.A. produces 10,601,000 B.P.D. of crude for its refinery industry (and imports another 2,449,000 B.P.D. from Venezuela, Canada, Mexico and the Middle East). Thus U.S.A. production is twenty-one times Australia's present needs. Even allowing for the fact that import controls and pro-rationing keep in being a 30% proportion of U.S. production which is high cost and uneconomic it appears more than reasonable to suppose that, in time, Australia will discover, if not commensurate quantities, at least a few major fields, and will be in a position to meet all its requirements from indigenous resources. Indeed, quite probably it will become a substantial exporter of crude.

But there are serious defects in this apparent self-sufficiency by 1971. The first concerns a technical point. All indigenous crudes so far discovered are high-specific-gravity, sulphur-free, paraffinic, rather waxy crudes. Their yield is high on petrols, moderate on kerosines and with a wide range of middle distillates. But it is low, almost negligible, on heavy industrial diesel, furnace oils, bitumen and lubricating oil. Thus, even if by 1971-72 the physical output of indigenous fields corresponded to the then 550,000 B.P.D. requirements of Australian refineries, no more than about, say, 70% of this can be processed in the refinery industry. On present refinery design, constructed for foreign crudes but modified in order to absorb indigenous crudes, the remainder of the crude throughput must be made up of heavy, low-gravity crudes with a high yield of furnace oil, bitumen and lubricating stock. The Middle-Eastern fields of Kuwait, Arabia and Iran are the most suitable suppliers of this component. This is a situation which holds even if Australia produces crudes in excess of requirements. On economic grounds any production over a 70% absorption ratio therefore should go to export. The relinquish-

ment of some equipment (vacuum distillation and desulphurizers) and the further acquisition of certain other types (catalytic cracking and reforming) can and will ease the problem to some degree. Also, consumers can be induced to take unusual specifications of fuel oil. Even so, it seems most unlikely that, on present types of indigenous crudes and completely modified refineries, Australia can ever better a 70% self-sufficiency on crude without undue sacrifice of an important component—flexibility in refinery operations.[13]

The second major blemish on the self-sufficiency picture from 1971 onwards turns on the remoteness of many of the potential petroleum-bearing areas of Australia and the exposure of the lengthy 12,000-mile Australian coastline. It could well be, and in recent years has become increasingly likely, that the largest Australian reserves will be found along the north-west and northern arc of the continental shelf. In one sense these are convenient enough locations since, except for unusually large flows of oil through an inland pipeline, 100,000 B.P.D. or better, tanker transportation is by far the most economical and flexible method available for bringing oil to refinery centres. (In any event, a trans-Australian land pipeline to south-east Australia is too lengthy to be contemplated.) But oil bought by tanker from these areas to, say, Sydney and Melbourne undertakes an expensive journey. Australian flag tankers, now compulsory on coastal voyages[14] are rather more than twice as expensive to operate as foreign flag tankers. (Thus a tanker haul, Darwin to Melbourne, costs over 80 cents per barrel as against 40 cents to Japan). More important, remoteness creates a defence problem of considerable importance. Oil supplied through onshore pipelines is fairly secure. Supplied from the underwater collecting lines of an offshore field it is less secure (a mine laid by aircraft or submarine at the appropriate point on the collecting network could put most of the Gippsland fields out of operation) but is at least concentrated in a circumscribed area easily monitored by anti-submarine listening devices and patrolled by aircraft and anti-submarine vessels. But where the crude travels some 5,000 miles along the coast from, say, Bonaparte Gulf to Melbourne, it is altogether more vulnerable to enemy action if Australia should be involved in a war with a foreign power which possesses ocean-going submarines. Coastal monitoring systems would assist enormously in the protection of these vulnerable vessels; but a twenty-four-hour vigil on each convoy along a 5,000-mile journey (greater than a trans-Atlantic crossing) would be an impossible drain on defence resources.

Fortunately, the largest discoveries so far, the Gippsland offshore fields, are so placed as to supply Melbourne through a 140-mile pipeline. If another line to Sydney, 350 miles, were constructed these two

main refining areas of Australia, containing 66% of refinery capacity, would then be directly, and fairly securely, connected to their main source of crude supply. Assuming successful supply of one-quarter proportion of foreign crude in the throughput, close to two-thirds of Australian refinery capacity could be supplied from this one source alone in times of emergency. But the foreign supply may not be easy. And the position of the other refining centres is certainly less happy. Adelaide is 500 miles from Western Port bay and 7,000 odd miles from the Persian Gulf. Brisbane's two refineries, with 70,000 B.P.D. capacity, can obtain only 10% of their combined requirement from Moonie fields; the remainder must come 1,000 miles from Western Port bay or 4,500 miles from Indonesia. And the 100,000 B.P.D. refinery at Fremantle can count on only 40% of its throughput coming from Barrow Island (itself an exposed 800 miles to the north along the coast) ; while the other sources are Western Port bay, 2,000 miles, and the Persian Gulf, 5,000 odd miles away. Thus for the near future perhaps less than 50% of refinery throughput will, from a defence point of view, be securely based on local crude oil fields. The remainder must come from abroad or travel difficult-to-defend exposed routes along the Australian coast. New oils finds could, however, rapidly alter defence circumstances.

Conclusions

While Australia at the moment is one of the most vulnerable countries of the world in relation to oil supply, requiring a high proportion of its throughput from abroad delivered over long, undefended, ocean distances, the discovery of substantial indigenous reserves promises a solution from 1971 onwards. But the change in circumstances is not as dramatic as a superficial examination of the figures suggests. Even with an apparently complete self-sufficiency of oil production the unusual character of Australian crudes, and the long exposures of the Australian coastline, ensure that only half of refining capacity is relieved of serious defence problems. Thus, some of the above analysis for the contemporary situation will continue to be valid after 1971. One can forget plans to diversify sources of crude away from the Middle East and Indonesia. Uncertainty of supply sources was never a real problem. And the relatively small quantities which must come from overseas, 140,000 to 170,000 B.P.D., will always be obtainable from some area. In order to transport the foreign component there is no great advantage in having even a small Australian tanker fleet for defence emergencies (unless it can be combined with a profitable, foreign-exchange earning, operation as part of the international fleet of ocean-going tankers). The provision of storage capacity in all re-

finery centres (mainly for foreign crudes) to give, say, thirty to sixty days operation free from supply problems, would, however, seem to be a useful form of insurance. It would be wise also to conserve fields conveniently located to refinery centres which otherwise must be supplied by sea. For example the Moonie fields, which give only a small flow and cannot be expected to last for more than ten years at present rates, should be purchased and their production shut in or reduced to a fraction of normal commercial operation in order to provide a strategic emergency supply for the Brisbane refineries. And the construction of a pipeline from the Gippsland fields to Sydney refineries (subsidized if necessary to take account of the extra costs of pipelines over efficient tanker operations) would appear to be a *sine qua non* of defence policy in relation to oil supply considerations.

All the above analysis assumes that ocean tanker routes—particularly in the Indian Ocean—are in danger of interdiction in the coming decade. This may not be so.

The Transformation in Australia's Foreign Trade

PETER DRYSDALE

The restructuring of its economic relations with the rest of the world was among the most powerful influences shaping Australia's international political interests in post-war years. Political action is frequently a necessary pre-condition to opening up the channels of trade and commerce, but economic realities can also provide a strong inducement to political action. Nowhere is this more strikingly illustrated than in the growth of economic relations between Australia and Japan, and it was the growth of trade with Japan and the Asian-Pacific region that dominated the transformation of Australia's specialization in the world economy in post-war years.

The year 1966 must rank among the most significant in the history of Australia's international commerce. Japan became Australia's largest export market—the first occasion that any country surpassed the United Kingdom in its annual purchases of Australian produce. Less noticed, but no less significant, the United States replaced Britain as Australia's major supplier of imports—again the first occasion that any country's annual sales to Australia have been larger than those of the United Kingdom. These developments underline the significant restructuring that has taken place in Australia's economic relations with the rest of the world, largely through the remarkable shift in the geographic distribution of its commodity trade away from Britain and Europe towards the Pacific and Asia. In 1969 over 45% of Australia's foreign trade was with advanced Pacific countries—Japan, the United States, Canada, and New Zealand. The United States alone supplied 26% of all Australian imports and Japan took 24% of total exports. Around 60% of export trade and 50% of import trade was with the Asian-Pacific region (see Tables 4 and 5).

Several important questions arise. What were the origins of these large-scale shifts in the geographic structure of Australia's trade? In

TABLE 4

Australia: Distribution of Exports by Major Trading Region
(Percentage of total value)

Destination	1950	1955	1960	1961	1962	1963	1964	1965	1966	1967[a]	1968	1969
Pacific:	18.79	23.46	33.14	35.73	37.60	39.59	38.73	38.17	41.27	43.00	45.81	50.13
United States	8.09	6.77	8.10	7.48	10.12	12.35	10.09	9.96	12.44	11.87	13.23	14.31
Japan	3.91	7.57	14.36	16.67	17.35	16.09	17.53	16.62	17.29	19.39	21.10	24.44
New Zealand	3.47	4.88	5.80	6.40	5.46	6.09	5.98	5.97	6.29	5.84	5.12	4.71
Canada	1.47	1.36	1.48	1.76	1.63	1.77	1.81	1.51	1.59	1.71	1.76	2.00
Asia:[b]	7.29	5.48	4.98	8.01	10.66	10.27	9.41	9.62	7.37	10.13	8.61	5.57
China	.08	.35	1.72	4.11	6.12	6.01	6.04	5.12	3.92	4.33	4.21	1.99
South-East Asia:[b]	3.67	5.34	5.44	5.37	5.41	5.81	5.31	6.29	6.77	7.77	8.41	9.11
Malaysia and Singapore	2.22	2.58	2.52	2.64	2.69	2.95	2.48	3.13	3.08	3.91	3.81	3.82
Indonesia	.08	.48	.34	.61	.40	.29	.35	.28	.20	.23	.50	.61
United Kingdom	38.71	36.88	26.37	23.90	19.16	18.66	18.40	19.47	17.40	13.34	13.82	12.62
Western Europe:[b]	22.05	24.05	20.54	18.02	19.31	17.45	17.26	16.31	17.89	15.52	13.60	14.46
France	6.63	8.27	6.43	5.27	4.83	4.92	4.94	4.22	4.35	3.34	2.91	3.41
Germany (Fed. Rep.)	—	4.11	4.09	2.76	3.79	3.18	3.30	3.16	3.69	2.47	3.00	3.00
Italy	3.16	4.64	4.97	4.93	4.84	4.09	3.90	3.21	4.05	4.19	2.92	3.22
All other	9.49	4.79	9.53	8.97	7.86	8.22	10.89	10.14	9.30	10.24	9.75	8.11
Total Australian exports ($Am)	1,228	1,548	1,876	1,938	2,155	2,152	2,782	2,651	2,721	3,035	3,411	3,773

[a] Years end 30 June.   [b] Trading regions as defined in *Vernon Report*, p. 1000.

Source: Commonwealth of Australia, *Oversea Trade* (various issues), Canberra.

TABLE 5

Australia: Distribution of Imports by Major Trading Region
(Percentage of total value)

Origin	1950	1955	1960	1961	1962	1963	1964	1965	1966	1967[a]	1968	1969
Pacific:	15.34	19.20	27.19	33.10	32.33	34.56	37.18	39.79	40.03	42.23	43.58	45.74
United States	9.71	12.11	16.15	19.96	19.68	21.27	22.86	23.83	23.94	25.68	25.69	25.62
Japan	1.30	2.18	4.48	6.02	5.59	5.98	6.85	8.90	9.53	9.72	10.50	11.95
New Zealand	.92	.95	1.71	1.60	1.54	1.64	1.89	1.60	1.59	1.55	1.89	2.16
Canada	2.47	2.83	3.20	4.20	3.86	4.25	4.04	4.03	3.67	3.84	4.30	4.42
Asia:[b]	5.77	3.84	3.36	3.53	3.62	3.43	3.54	3.50	3.42	3.68	3.32	3.45
China	.27	.21	.48	.37	.43	.52	.69	.79	.80	.86	.70	.85
South-East Asia:[b]	7.58	8.68	8.28	6.38	7.28	6.05	5.31	5.19	4.57	4.24	4.40	4.48
Malaysia and Singapore	2.27	1.81	2.09	2.70	2.03	1.90	1.54	1.80	1.21	1.20	1.20	1.22
Indonesia	2.74	2.67	3.18	2.63	3.03	2.68	2.34	2.20	2.10	1.86	1.70	1.73
United Kingdom	51.81	44.88	35.61	31.31	30.06	30.45	27.78	26.21	25.81	23.74	22.11	21.58
Western Europe:[b]	9.22	14.76	16.25	16.50	16.51	15.68	16.06	16.63	17.51	16.98	17.40	16.67
France	1.98	1.74	1.48	1.54	1.25	1.64	1.69	2.30	3.12	3.05	2.70	1.80
Germany (Fed. Rep.)	1.22	3.65	5.81	6.09	5.86	5.42	5.51	5.54	5.72	5.20	5.80	5.82
Italy	1.68	1.39	1.40	1.45	1.59	1.81	1.69	1.74	1.69	1.74	2.20	2.28
All other	10.28	8.64	9.31	9.18	10.20	9.83	10.13	8.68	8.66	9.13	9.19	8.08
Total Australian imports ($Am)	1,076	1,688	1,852	2,175	1,769	2,163	2,373	2,905	2,939	3,049	3,661	3,881

[a] Years end 30 June.   [b] Trading regions as defined in *Vernon Report*, p. 1000.

Source: Commonwealth of Australia, *Oversea Trade* (various issues), Canberra.

particular, what were the causes of the vastly increased importance of Japan? How should Australia's international economic policy be cast in the light of these fundamental changes in its economic relations with the rest of the world? And what is the relationship between attaining these economic and other no less important political objectives?

Australia's specialization in international trade

Australia's economic prosperity depends vitally upon its specialization in the world economy. It is a relatively small economy, and though remote from major world markets in the past, its dependence on trade has always been high. Trade dependence fell considerably in the decade or so following the Second World War, but in the 1960s it tended to rise again and imports of goods and services accounted for between 14% and 15% of the Gross National Product by 1969.

The essential features of Australia's commodity specialization in world trade are well known. But the pattern of export specialization in raw materials and foodstuffs and import specialization in manufactures was modified substantially in the two decades after the war. The growth of Australia's export specialization in manufactures was accompanied by the remarkable growth of export specialization in minerals and metals. In the first place, these changes reflected the growing international competitiveness of the domestic manufacturing sector. In the second place, they reflected the spectacular development of huge and in large part newly discovered mineral resources for international markets.[1] On the other hand, producer materials and equipment increasingly dominated import specialization. Australia's post-war economic growth was characterized by the large-scale immigration of labour and capital from the United Kingdom, Europe and North America, and factor migration was stimulated by trade restraints which encouraged the expansion of the import-competing manufacturing sector. Hence, the effect of factor migration and forced industrialization superimposed itself upon the effect of basic resource endowments in the development of the structure of production and trade that prevailed in Australia in the second half of the 1960s. Although protectionism encouraged the expansion of some highly inefficient industrial activity, it also assisted the establishment of a relatively efficient industrial base centred on steel, metals, motor vehicles and engineering.

The most notable development in the geographic restructuring of trade was undoubtedly in Japanese-Australian trade relations.[2] Between 1950 and 1969 Japan's share in Australian exports alone rose from 4%-24%, whilst the United Kingdom's share fell from 39%-

13%. In the same period, Japan's share in Australian imports rose from 1%-12%, whilst the United Kingdom's share fell from 52%-22%. These key shifts in the geographic structure of Australian trade resulted from three broad sets of factors: the relatively rapid growth of Japan's share in world trade; the underlying complementarity between the structure of Japanese and Australian trade; and factors affecting the geographical, political, and historical closeness of the two economies.

Two countries trade more or less intensively with each other than they do with the rest of the world because of the particular commodity composition of their trade in relation to world trade—this may be called the degree of complementarity in bilateral trade—and because of their geographical proximity and special institutional and historical ties—this may be called the degree of special country bias in bilateral trade. The degree of complementarity and the degree of special country bias jointly determine the intensity of trade between two trading partners.[3]

The results of a detailed study of complementarity, special country bias, and intensity in Japanese-Australian trade flows are presented in Table 6. The general picture that emerges is that during post-war years, there was always a high degree of complementarity in trade between Japan and Australia. Although the index of complementarity in Japan's export trade with Australia declined noticeably in later years, this trend—which became evident during an intermediate stage in the post-war transformation of Japanese export specialization away from strong specialization in light industrial exports towards stronger specialization in heavy industrial exports—had begun to reverse. At the same time the structures of Australia's export specialization and Japan's import specialization were highly complementary, although the index of complementarity in that trade flow declined slightly in the early 1960s.

In short, the intensity of Japan's export trade with Australia and Australia's export trade with Japan rose significantly in post-war years, first, because complementarity in both trade flows remained high; and second, because there was a marked increase in the degree of special country bias in both trade flows.

It was the high intensity of Japan's export and import trade with Australia that has given the extraordinary post-war growth in Japanese foreign trade such significance for Australia. Japan's share in world trade has grown rapidly, while that of many other countries whose trade is of significance for Australia has lagged. The shift in the relative positions of Japan and the United Kingdom in Australia's trade that has taken place in the 1960s should be seen as

TABLE 6

Complementarity, Special Country Bias and Intensity in
Japanese-Australian Trade[a]

Exports from \ Exports to		Japan			Australia		
		1953	1958	1966	1953	1958	1966
Japan	c		—		166	140	148
	b				27	95	135
	i				45	132	200
Australia	c	209	214	186		—	
	b	129	220	216			
	i	270	471	401			

[a] Row i measures the intensity of trade. An index of 100 indicates that one country exports (imports) exactly that proportion of its total exports to (imports from) another country as that country's share in world trade. Row i equals row c, complementarity in trade, multiplied by row b, special country bias in trade, divided by 100. The methods by which these indexes were calculated and a brief description of the data upon which the calculations were based, are presented in Drysdale, 'Japan, Australia, New Zealand: The Prospect for Western Pacific Economic Integration', *Economic Record* (September 1969). For example, consider Australia's export trade with Japan in 1953. The results of this study reveal that, simply because of the character of Australian export specialization and Japanese import specialization in world trade in 1953, Japan's share in Australia's export trade should have been over twice as large as its share in world imports, further, that Japan's share in Australian exports was almost one and a third times as large as might be expected from both countries' shares in world trade of each commodity; and that, therefore, Japan's share in Australia's export trade was almost two and three quarter times as large as might have been expected from its share in world imports. That is, the degree of complementarity in Australia's export trade with Japan was 209, the degree of special country bias was 129, and the intensity of trade was 270.

Source: Peter Drysdale, 'Japan, Australia, New Zealand: The Prospect for Western Pacific Economic Integration', *Economic Record* (September 1969); and Peter Drysdale, Japanese-Australian Trade, Australian National University, unpublished thesis, 1967.

reflecting the different trade growth rates of two countries with which Australia trades intensively.

The impact of Japanese growth on the Australian economy

The growth of Japanese-Australian trading relations deserves more detailed examination. In the first place, the increased importance of the Japanese market to Australia derived from Japan's very high rates of economic growth, and its vastly increased share in

world trade. By 1969 Japan accounted for almost 6% of total world commodity trade.

In the second place, the high degree of complementarity between the Japanese and Australian economies ensured that Japan's overall trade growth stimulated proportionately larger purchases from and sales to Australia.[4] In the earlier phases of post-war Japanese growth increased import demand was heavily concentrated on textile raw materials and provided new outlets for exports of Australian wool. In later phases, accelerated heavy industrialization and new patterns of consumer demand associated with higher income levels strengthened Japanese import demand for fuel and minerals, such as coal, iron ore, copper, bauxite and alumina, and foodstuffs such as wheat, meat and dairy products.

On the other hand, Japan specialized in the export of manufactured goods for which Australia's import demand has always been relatively strong. In the past the degree of complementarity between the structure of Japanese exports and Australian imports within these broad commodity categories was not so strong as the degree of complementarity between the structure of Australian exports and Japanese imports—one factor which helps account for persistent bilateral imbalance in Japanese-Australian trade. But the growing share of capital equipment and machinery in Japanese exports and their predominance in Australian imports is likely to strengthen complementarity in that trade flow.

In the third place, geographical proximity always favoured Japanese-Australian trade. Some commodities, especially manufactured goods, can, of course, be delivered to distant markets at relatively small cost so that the location of foreign markets does not much affect the geographic distribution of their export—another factor which accounts for bilateral imbalances in Japanese-Australian trade. On the other hand, low value to weight bulk commodities, like fuels and mineral ores, are generally expensive to transport and near-by sources of supply offer distinct cost advantages to international buyers. Much of the special country bias in Australia's export trade with Japan is accounted for by the special nature of Australia's trade with Japan in raw wool and the influence of transport costs. As for the former, it is interesting that the reorientation of New Zealand's economic relations away from traditional markets in the United Kingdom and Europe towards nearer growth markets in the Pacific and Asia proceeded at a much slower pace than did Australia's. This is partly explained by institutional factors and the greater stress placed on British ties in New Zealand; but it was also partly a consequence of the fact that the structure of New Zealand's export specialization,

notably in coarser carpet wools and dairy products, was less immediately tuned to the growth of Asian-Pacific trade.[5] The latter factor
prompted Japan's participation in the development of Australia's
huge deposits of high quality and accessible coal, iron ore, bauxite
and copper.[6] For Japan Australia promised to be the most adequate
and stable source of supply of these materials for many years, especially because of increased political uncertainties in mainland China.
Japan has contracted to buy large quantities of iron ore, coal, bauxite
and alumina during the 1970s and 1980s. Indeed, Japanese demand
played a major role in developing Australia's new and stronger
advantage in the export of mineral products. By the mid-1970s they
will have effected a complete transformation in Australia's whole
specialization in the world economy and far-reaching changes in the
whole fabric of Australia's political economy when minerals and
associated manufactures replace wool as Australia's chief export
earner.

Institutional factors and trade policy have not always favoured a
large trade between Japan and Australia. As is well known, they positively inhibited it. Significantly, it was the breakdown of special institutional and policy biases against trade between the two countries
that permitted its remarkable expansion in post-war years. Australia's
earlier reluctance to foster freer trading relations with Japan stemmed from strong economic, cultural and political ties with the United
Kingdom, fears of 'cheap labour' competition and the hangover of
war, and its trading policy discriminated severely against imports
from Japan until 1957. The conclusion of a trade agreement between
the two countries in that year was the major watershed in Japanese-
Australian trading relations after the war. Under the agreement,
Australia accorded Japan most-favoured-nation treatment, which
involved substantial reductions in tariffs on textiles and other consumer goods and non-discriminatory treatment under import licens-
ing arrangements. Japan allowed freer access to its markets for Australian agricultural exports and it undertook not to impose a duty
on the import of wool. In 1963 the threat of early British entry into
the European Common Market added point to renewal and extension of the agreement. Australia relinquished its right under Article
35 of G.A.T.T. to discriminate specifically against Japanese imports.
In return, Japan made new concessions in its import policy towards
Australian wool, foodstuffs and motor vehicles.

It is impossible to over-stress the role these trade agreements played
in establishing freer and fuller economic relations between Japan and
Australia. A complete transformation of each country's interest in
the other has been effected under their aegis. The direct impact on

trade growth was reinforced by a combination of indirect dynamic effects on trade and investment flows.

For example, one obstacle to the development of Japanese-Australian trading relations was the quite general difficulty encountered in all trading with foreign countries where business rapport must be established carefully and slowly. Perhaps in some ways this factor posed a great problem for Australians who were not used in the past to dealing with nations very different in language and customs from their own. But in other ways it posed a far greater problem for the Japanese. The nature of the merchandise which Japanese exporters were newly trying to sell in Australian markets demanded more direct contact with Australian businessmen and knowledge of Australian industrial conditions. In this connection the establishment of the Japan-Australia Business Co-operation Committee in 1963 proved valuable, not only to Japanese businessmen in their understanding of the character and potential of the Australian economy, but also to Australian businessmen in their understanding of the mutual benefits to be derived from trade with Japan, and their vision of the international economy, both of which have been considerably enhanced by the dialogue with their Japanese counterparts. To those who remember the chilly reception which Australian manufacturing interests gave the first trade agreement in 1957, this development must rank among the most satisfying in the history of post-war Japanese-Australian relations.

The changes in the relative magnitude of Japanese-Australian trade, and their explanation, only begin to tell the full story. For growth and trade between Japan and Australia had significance beyond anything its mere proportions suggest. It was one factor in the complete reorientation of Australia's economic and political relations away from Britain and Europe towards Asia and the Pacific—a realignment of consequence not only to Australia's economy but also to its whole international outlook. It contributed to fundamental changes in Australian attitudes to international and commercial affairs.

Australia in the Asian-Pacific economic community

The developments in United States-Australian trade hardly seem less noteworthy than those in Japanese-Australian trade. Between 1950 and 1969 the United States' share in Australian exports rose from 8%-14%. In the same period, its share in Australian imports rose from 10%-26%. But this development did not have the same impact on the public mind as the development of trade with Japan.

Other questions, mainly political and strategic, have dominated United States-Australian relations.

On the other hand, American investment in the Australian economy has been the subject of considerable public discussion. And the role of American investment in Australia's post-war industrial transformation is intimately bound up with the changes in the geographic structure of Australian trade. There has been relatively large-scale American investment in new Australian industrial and mining activity throughout the whole post-war period.[7] Firms in new industries have a very high propensity to import equipment and supplies which are commonly not available domestically. American private investors, through their firms, subsidiaries and associates, tended to buy equipment and producer materials from their home country (if not their home firm), thus boosting the proportion of imports originating in the United States, over two-thirds of which consist of machinery, equipment and producer materials. In the mid-1960s the degree of complementarity (125) was high for the United States' export trade with Australia, and the degree of special country bias (110) and trade intensity (137) were also high.

Growth in the share of Australian exports destined for the United States was far less impressive. Significantly, this resulted from the persistence and effectiveness of protectionist pressures in the United States against Australia's principal exports, wool, minerals and foodstuffs, all of which were subject at some time to high tariff duties or import quota restrictions.

Both New Zealand and Canada were also increasingly important trade partners to Australia, although their share in Australian trade was still relatively small. Between 1950 and 1969 New Zealand's share in Australia's exports grew from 3%-5% and Canada's rose from 1%-2%. Throughout the same period New Zealand's share in Australian imports rose from 1%-2% per cent and Canada's grew from 2%-4%. In the mid-1960s complementarity in Australia's export trade with New Zealand (58), whilst still low, was perhaps larger than might have been expected from a superficial consideration of the broad structures of the two economies. The index of complementarity for this trade flow indicates Australia's stronger export specialization in manufactures, as well as New Zealand's strong import specialization in wheat, sugar, and other foodstuffs in which Australia's export specialization has always been strong. Special country bias in Australia's export trade with New Zealand (2104) and trade intensity were both extremely high. The extremely high degree of special country bias in export trade with New Zealand resulted from geographical nearness, preferred tariff arrangements

o

under the Commonwealth Preference Scheme and the New Zealand-Australia Free Trade Agreement and market homogeneity and familiarity. Australia's manufactured exports are heavily concentrated in the New Zealand market. The degree of complementarity in Australia's import trade with New Zealand (20) was extremely low, though special country bias (1400) and, therefore, trade intensity (280) were very high. As might be expected, the extremely high special country bias in import trade with New Zealand was a product of the same institutional factors which acted to stimulate bilateral trade in the reverse direction. The intensity of Australia's trade with Canada was not high, but the growing importance of Canada in the world economy stimulated Canadian-Australian trade expansion.

Alongside developments in Australia's trade with the Pacific area was the growing importance of Australia's trade with Asia. Between 1950 and 1969 Australian exports destined for Asia rose from 11%-15%. There were increased exports of manufactured goods to the region. In 1967 Asia accounted for 18%, importantly because of large wheat sales to China. Exports to developing countries in Asia and the Pacific, excluding mainland China, comprised about 17% of total Australian exports in 1969. The propinquity of Asian markets and certain similarities in the structure of Australian and Asian demand for industrial goods have facilitated this new trade. Trade in manufactures with Asia and New Zealand assumed special importance in policy designed to strengthen Australia's industrial base through the expansion of export markets.

Imports from developing countries in Asia and the Pacific, excluding mainland China, fell from 13% of total Australian imports in 1950 to only 8% of total Australian imports in 1969. The falling share of Asian imports largely resulted from reduced demand for raw materials. But the performance of Asian exporters in Australian markets was variable. Some Asian countries were increasingly competitive suppliers of textiles and light manufactures and their share in Australian markets for those products tended to grow at the expense of the United Kingdom and Japan. In the mid-1960s complementarity in Australia's export trade with developing countries in Asia and the Pacific was generally low but not so low as might be expected.[8] Special country bias in Australian export trade with the region was commonly very high. Interestingly, there was inverse variation in the high special country biases in Australian and Japanese export trade with Asian-Pacific countries, closely correlated as it was with the political and institutional closeness of countries with British connections and with the facts of geography. Intensities in Australian import trade with the region revealed considerable varia-

tion. The intensity of import trade with near-by suppliers of raw materials, such as Indonesia and New Guinea, was extremely high because of special country bias in trade. At the same time, the intensity of trade with exporters of light manufactures and processed raw materials, such as Hong Kong and Singapore, was quite high because of complementarity in trade.[9] Linked by high complementarity in import trade with some Asian developing countries, and high special country bias in import and export trade with more, Australia's trading interests in the region are proportionately much more important than they are in the world at large. Indeed, Australia has weighty political, as well as economic, interests in this developing region's prosperity.

Issues in Australia's international economic policy

How might these major shifts in the geographic structure of Australian trade shape the future evolution of Australia's commercial policy? And have they any wider significance?

In the late 1960s there was a rapid change in Australian sentiment in relation to the protection of high cost secondary industries. There was more widespread criticism of the extent and structure of tariff protection, not least by the Australian Tariff Board itself, both because of the growing strength and more diverse interests of the Australian industrial sector.[10] This raises important questions about the desirable course for Australia's international economic policy. Critics of past tariff policy have argued that there are powerful reasons for moves in the direction of tariff rationalization, since the main concern now should be to ensure efficiency in the use of national resources.[11] Despite these changing attitudes, it is recognized that any modification of past tariff practices would have to be extremely gradual so that people and resources displaced from inefficient industrial operations could be absorbed into more efficient growth industries. But a strong case can be made for unilateral action by the Australian government, on the advice of the Tariff Board, to proceed with the gradual restructuring of Australian tariffs in order to promote industrial efficiency. This represents the first course Australian commercial policy could take. Indeed, it is the course most frequently advocated by critics of Australian tariff policy.

A second course seems open. Clearly, any reduction of Australian tariff barriers is internationally negotiable. Moreover, an exchange of tariff concessions between Australia and the rest of the world, within the General Agreement on Tariffs and Trade or under Kennedy Round-type negotiations, would yield extra trade and income gains. But in the past it has been, and it is likely to continue to be, extremely

difficult for major primary exporters such as Australia to engage in meaningful multilateral trade negotiations through G.A.T.T. or under Kennedy Round-type negotiations because of the intransigence of European and United States agricultural protectionism. The prospect of Australian participation in useful multilateral trade negotiations involving trade in agricultural commodities appears remote.

There is a third course that Australian commercial policy could take. Australia could opt for the regional approach to a rearrangement of tariff and other trade barriers. Australia's trade interests now lie squarely in the Asia-Pacific region and it seems sensible to seek an exchange of concessions within that region.[12] But Asian developing countries are hardly in a position to exchange many commercial concessions: indeed, Australia, in a limited but pragmatic way, helped establish the principle of extending non-reciprocal tariff concessions to developing countries for the purpose of stimulating growth in their export earnings.[13] So that any mutual exchange of trade concessions within the region of greatest importance to the Australian economy must principally involve the five advanced Pacific basin countries alone.

The exchange of trade concessions and closer economic integration among the advanced Pacific nations could take any of several forms. Some ambitious plans for a Pacific Free Trade Area have already received a good deal of thought from Japanese government authorities, academics and business people.[14] Australian participation in a Pacific Free Trade Area would have benefits associated with a significant move towards freer trade. Incomes would rise as a result of the direct effects on trade volumes. There would also be important dynamic benefits, through improved access to international capital and technology. The main costs of Australian involvement in a Pacific Free Trade Area would be the costs of trade diversion from outside trading partners; the costs of adjustment resulting from the need to reallocate labour, capital and other resources out of less efficient import-competing industries into more efficient domestic production; the costs in terms of capital movements; and the political costs of any shift of emphasis in international relations.[15]

Australian reactions to the idea of a free trade area in the Pacific are likely to be conditioned by three important factors: by old established protectionist attitudes; by opposition to integration with Pacific countries at the expense of traditional ties with the United Kingdom; and by opposition to integration with advanced Pacific countries at the expense of growing ties with South-East Asian countries.

Protectionist attitudes have changed considerably but they would

not yet permit a significant move towards regional free trade. Protection for genuine infant industries would have to be assured. And it is difficult to foresee the acceptance in the near future of comprehensive regional trade concessions by Australia. On the other hand, trade relations with the United Kingdom are becoming less important, and they will become still less important if Britain gains entry to the European Economic Community. If it does not join the E.E.C., a freer trading association with it through a link between the Pacific and Atlantic trading areas might be viewed sympathetically by Australians.

Finally, the idea of trade between the rich countries of the Pacific burgeoning at the expense of the economic interests of other Asian and South-East Asian countries is antipathetic to a strong and growing part of Australian sentiment and policy. Proposals for a Pacific Free Trade Area are, however, commonly linked with proposals for accommodating the trade and aid needs of the less-developed countries in Asia through concerted regional action. In so far as the trade needs of near-by less-developed countries were accommodated by the extension of tariff preferences, and there was increased provision of developmental assistance by the five advanced Pacific basin countries, Australia's growing ties with South-East Asia would not be placed in jeopardy. Quite the reverse. It can be argued with some justification that the only real chance of significant trade and development assistance to less-developed countries in Asia is for a group of directly interested advanced countries, such as those in the Pacific, to couple the granting of unilateral concessions to developing countries with a mutual exchange of trade concessions among themselves. In that way, there will be some sharing of the burden of concessions and some promise of reciprocal trade gains, both of which should make the operation slightly more palatable to domestic electorates and consequently feasible. In particular, the American electorate will have to be persuaded that it will not bear all the burdens if new aid programmes are begun or even perhaps if the line is to be held on assistance programmes currently in operation.

But what of the interests of other Pacific trading partners? Each country has its own special position in world trade and its own particular economic and political objectives.

The trading interests of the United States are worldwide. To a large degree the evolution of international commercial policy since the Second World War has been dominated by relations between the United States on the one side, and the European countries on the other, relations strongly conditioned in the immediate post-war period by the Cold War between the United States and the Soviet

Union. During the post-war period United States international economic policy has shifted from pursuit of the objective of multilateral non-discriminatory tariff reductions within G.A.T.T. to the encouragement of European integration, and then back again to the non-discriminatory liberalization of world trade as a means of containing the regionalizing and discriminatory forces that had been let loose in Europe.[16] The conclusion of the Kennedy Round of tariff negotiations represented only limited success in moving towards this last objective. The mood of the outgoing Johnson administration was to press on with the endeavour of promoting multilateral trade liberalization and suppressing the forces of protectionism when they gathered strength at home. Involvement in regional trading arrangements was unacceptable on wider political grounds, too, since it was likely to evoke ill will in the many countries to which the United States would remain important in trade but which were excluded from membership of any particular free trade area arrangement. The overt political stance of the Nixon administration has been more protectionist, and at the same time more sympathetic to restrictive regional economic arrangements. But no major change in policy has yet taken place. It is possible that in this context, and in view of the mounting short-term economic problems in the United States, there could be a revival of the discussion of the North Atlantic Free Trade proposal as an alternative to multilateral reduction in trade barriers.[17]

Trade growth in the Pacific region, which overlaps the North Atlantic region through the inclusion in both of the United States and Canada, has changed the configuration of world trade. Further, the political environment in which commercial policy is fashioned has also been changing. The world role of the United States has become less crucial as the United States and Russia have achieved a kind of *détente*, and China has emerged as a rival power. Given a satisfactory solution to Britain's problem in Europe, the United States might recognize opportunities for commercial policy leadership in the Pacific and Asian region.

Like the United States, Japan too has worldwide trading interests and its commercial policy is aimed at the expansion and freeing of trade with every trading region. But the limited success of multilateral moves to freer trade, the possibility of a larger and more inward-looking European community, and the danger of growing American protectionism, have recommended a Pacific Free Trade Area approach to it. Like Australia, Japan's economic and political interests are greatest in the Asian-Pacific region. The establishment of a Pacific Free Trade Area would probably yield the largest static trade gains for Japan.[18] Japan's exports would increase and its balance of

trade with the region would improve. It would benefit from Pacific free trade through the import of cheaper foodstuffs and raw materials (though the costs of adjustment in its agricultural sector would be large), through the expansion of its exports of light manufactures, and through the promotion of horizontal trade in heavy manufactures and chemicals. Furthermore, Japan's geopolitical interests would be well served by involvement in Pacific economic integration and the encouragement of regional co-operation in assistance for development and trade growth in Asian countries.

Canada's interests in the Pacific hinge on its special trade and economic relations with the United States. There appears to be a reasonably strong case for further rationalization of the pattern of Canadian protection as the economy approaches industrial maturity, but this largely involves considerations of its competitiveness in the North American market. Nonetheless, Canada's growing trade with Asia and its liberal stance in world diplomacy give it added interest in the proposals for Pacific integration as a means of pushing a collective programme of development assistance.

New Zealand's interests in some measure parallel those of Australia. Perhaps more than any of the other Pacific nations, it is now in search of a new approach in its international trade policy. It has not yet effected so complete a reorientation in its trade towards the Pacific and Asia as Australia, but its trade links with Australia, the United States and Japan have intensified. Despite British assurances, New Zealand's special trade tie with the United Kingdom would be unlikely to survive British entry into the European Economic Community for long.

It may well prove possible to attain most of the benefits of a Pacific Free Trade Area coupled with special arrangements for less-developed countries, and avoid many of the costs, if a more gradualist approach were adopted. For example, there is adequate scope for regional negotiations on trade barriers on a most-favoured-nation basis. The discriminatory effects of the exchange of trade concessions around the Pacific could thus be avoided. Moreover, even if the United States and Canada were reluctant to come to the party Japan, Australia and New Zealand could profitably take the initiative in such moves. In the short term, the formation of an inter-governmental Organisation for Pacific Trade Aid and Development, including the latter three countries or all five advanced Pacific countries with participation by less developed countries would seem a useful policy objective.[19] It could provide the same kind of stimulus to Pacific economic co-operation and growth as the O.E.C.D. provided for European economic co-operation and growth.

The constellation of circumstances which might drive the advanced Pacific countries into very much closer economic co-operation certainly no longer seems wildly improbable. Indeed, there is growing evidence that government circles in Australia and Canada, as well as Japan, accept the importance of working in that direction. On 8 November 1968 the Australian Treasurer, in an address to the Australian-American Association, said quite explicitly that

> . . . if progess is to be made in the matter of peaceful economic cooperation in the Pacific area, we really ought to start with the freer flow of trade between the advanced countries of the region. If the advanced countries cannot give some sort of lead in this matter we can hardly expect the developing countries to have much faith in us.[20]

What of the politics of Pacific economic integration, in any of its forms? It may be instructive to summarize them briefly as they are sometimes seen in Japan. For Japan the development of Pacific economic co-operation would lessen bilateral dependence in what often appears to Japanese to be a one-sided United States-Japanese relationship without risking any of its benefits. Moreover, it would provide a secure Pacific economic framework from within which Japan could play a less suspect and more useful role of conciliation towards communist China. And finally, regionalization of the development assistance effort would prevent Japan's own growing relations with the less-developed countries from becoming too lop-sided.

There is a certain urgency about the formulation of alternative economic strategies to ensure progress and stability in the Asian-Pacific region. The potential fluidity of post-Vietnam commercial and foreign policies within the region underlines that urgency. Japan and Australia, in particular, will probably have to take the initiative if a more forthright approach towards trade and economic relations between advanced countries around the Pacific and between these countries and developing countries in Asia is to be adopted.

CHAPTER 14

Capital Inflow and Australia's Defence Commitment

IAN POTTER

Growing significance of defence expenditure

In the year 1969-70 it is estimated by the Federal Treasurer that Australia is spending $A1,104 million on defence. While this amount is about 5% less than the previous year's expenditure, it is significant that the amount expended abroad amounts to $A243 million, or some 22% of the total. In 1968-69 the figure was even higher: some $A330 million was expended overseas on defence. In two years, therefore, a total of $A573 million has been spent abroad for this purpose.

These facts are indicative of several important changes in Australia's defence policy. First, the 1968-69 amount was 4.3% of Gross National Product which continues the substantial build-up of defence spending which began in 1963-64. In money terms expenditure has almost doubled in the past four years.

In the late 1950s Australia's defence expenditure absorbed about 3% of G.N.P. which put it among the smaller defence spenders in the western world. Since then, the position has changed dramatically. In the earlier period the prevailing philosophy was that Australia's greatest contribution to the defence of the South-West Pacific Area was the development and population of its own country. The acceleration of the war in Vietnam and the imminent withdrawal of British forces from Malaysia and Singapore has ended its attitude of almost complete dependence for its defence upon help from abroad.

Growth in defence expenditure has involved changes in terms of economic growth, but the overall rate of growth in Australia's G.N.P. (some $5\frac{1}{2}$% in real terms) has made the achievement of greater defence expenditure relatively easy. There has over the past few years been a constant increase in all categories of personal consumption and capital formation but the rate of increase in some categories could clearly have been greater had defence expenditure remained static. It can be said that the cost is in terms of schools, hospitals or high-

ways forgone but if national productivity continues to rise many of these other needs can and will be met.

As was recently pointed out by Professor H. R. Edwards,

> the possibilities which growth *per se* opens up are very substantial. If real G.N.P. continues to grow at the order of $5\frac{1}{2}\%$ per annum as in recent years, then ten years on, in 1977/78 it will amount to the order of $42,000 millions (at present prices). At 5% of G.N.P. defence spending would be $2,100 millions—nearly double the 1967/68 level of expenditure.[1]

In relation to capital inflow, however, the second factor from the Budget Speech (i.e. defence expenditure overseas) registers the influence of defence on the balance of payments. No discussion on capital can overlook the fact that of the $A330 million spent overseas on defence in 1968-69, less than one-third was financed by term loans from abroad. The rest was mainly a burden upon capital inflow.

Effects on capital inflow

Just how important is capital inflow for Australia? Table 7 shows the sources and use of funds in the National Capital Account over the past four years and a projection for 1976-77.

It will be seen that net apparent capital inflow has provided about 10%-15% of Australia's invested funds in recent years. Also such sums have averaged about 4% of G.N.P. over the last few years. But despite these small percentages the capital thus provided has enabled a dynamic development of resources that could not have been achieved by internal savings alone. In addition, the capital brought with it managerial skills and technical know-how. In terms of the use of human resources, capital inflow has ensured the success of a large migration programme—Australia having accepted no less than 3 million new settlers since the end of the Second World War, including in the early years, large numbers of displaced persons. In an international political sense, the emigration from Europe of which these new settlers were an important part, played a significant role in the creation and maintenance of stability on that continent.

In Table 7 a projection is made of capital needs in 1976-77, based on 1966-67 figures and projected at a modest 5% *per annum* increase in G.N.P. in real terms. Capital inflow in 1976-77 measured as a constant 3% of G.N.P. would need to be a little over $A1,000 million or actually less than it was in 1968-69. This projection method has limited authenticity but as a rough measure it does indicate that by 1976-77 Australia will still need to import 10% of its capital from overseas but that on current indications it may not be difficult to obtain.

During the intervening years, however, tax and interest rate policies

TABLE 7

National Capital Account

	$A Million				Estimate
	1965–66	1966–67	1967–68	1968–69	1976–77[a]
Personal saving	1,161	1,525	1,023	1,835	2,609
Public authority surplus on current account	1,282	1,213	1,318	1,670	1,986
Deficit on current account with overseas—					
Withdrawal from overseas monetary reserve	−59	120	−81	−154	
Net apparent capital inflow	939	531	1,208	1,154	1,030
Other savings including depreciation allowances	2,676	3,037	3,227	3,587	4,514
Total capital funds accruing	5,999	6,426	6,695	8,092	10,139
Total gross fixed capital expenditure	5,678	5,959	6,488	7,226	9,740
Increase in value of stocks	240	497	219	858	388
Total use of funds	5,918	6,456	6,707	8,084	10,128
Statistical discrepancy	81	−30	−12	8	11
Total capital funds accruing	5,999	6,426	6,695	8,092	10,139

[a] Projected at 5% growth in G.N.P. at 1966–67 prices.

Source: Quarterly Estimates of National Income and Expenditure.

may cause a different configuration in the savings habits of the community. What is more likely to augment domestic resources is an improved capital market where local funds are marshalled together for developmental investment. Greater mobility in the financial mechanism which is now being achieved will ensure that better use is derived from the command of capital. Australia can only reduce its dependence upon overseas capital if its productivity is so increased that every dollar works harder and thus the marginal efficiency of capital is increased.

Why is it that Australia cannot provide all its own capital? The answer, at present, must be: the money supply can easily be increased by the banks lending more for capital needs, but as such a policy would cause excessive demand for scarce physical resources of manpower and material, inflation would soon cancel out our efforts. It is also true that Australia will always need to import some of its capital equipment and raw materials as these are not available in Australia— or at least not at economic prices.

Capital inflow is therefore an essential balancing factor in its National Capital Account. Quite apart from its importance in the development of new resources, it clearly will be needed for some years to supplement domestic savings if it is to maintain its current rate of growth.

Defence spending and the balance of payments

Reference has been made to the marked growth in defence expenditure in recent years. The impact of this expenditure upon G.N.P. is still below 5%. But if we look at the effect of defence spending upon the balance of payments we obtain quite a different picture. Since 1964-65 direct overseas defence outlays have, as a percentage of overall defence spending, risen from 22%-29% in 1968-69. Though estimated to have fallen to 22% in 1969-70 due to special circumstances the overseas element in defence expenditure clearly continues to be significant. If we add to these outlays the indirect import content of domestic defence spending, then it is evident that the acceleration of Australia's overall defence expenditure has had an important impact upon its balance of payments. In effect, defence would have absorbed 35%-40% of capital inflow in recent years, were it not for the special long-term credits provided by the United States which, in 1968-69, provided some $A91 million. A further $A51 million of such credits was available in 1969-70.

Some relief from the adverse effects of overseas defence outlays upon Australia's balance of payments may come from an increased Australian content in defence equipment purchases. Apart from this direct economic effect further benefits should arise from the encouragement so provided for technological development in Australian industry. Important steps are now being taken in this direction.

Consistent with the reorganization of the Defence Department, which began in July 1968, is the newly formed Defence Industrial Committee led by Sir Ian McLennan.[2] This committee of businessmen will advise the government on

> industrial war potential, consider means by which the private sector can be encouraged to participate more extensively in research and development and production for Australian and overseas defence needs, and generally co-ordinate the planning and industrial capability to meet requirements of an emergency.

No doubt the Committee will consider such expedients as subsidies, grants for equipment and taxation concessions. Such aid is already an inherent part of economic policy (e.g. in the fostering of exports) and

worthwhile incentives should have significant results in the defence area also.

Factors affecting capital inflow: Economic and political considerations

The question of capital inflow into Australia has passed through many stages of controversy over the last decade. Perhaps at no previous time, however, has it become such a question of national significance. Some of the causes of this controversy are outlined below, but at this stage it must be emphasized that the main considerations that have emerged in current discussions on the desirability of overseas capital are very largely political. This contrasts markedly with the background of discussions in the period before 1960. Then, the main arguments for and against overseas investment in Australia were economic. As Australia emerged from the war period, expectations of great economic growth, and the parallel desire to become a manufacturing country, were predominant in the arguments. Since all political parties were committed to a policy of immigration and rapid development, very few voices were raised against capital imports. The general consensus of opinion was very strongly favourable to the maximum stimulation of overseas investment in Australia.

In the last three or four years, however, the argument about overseas investment has assumed a greater political emphasis. This, in part, is due to the great degree of industrialization that has occurred in Australia since the war, to the point where almost every important manufacturing industry is now established. But perhaps a more important factor has been the substantial improvement in the last five years in Australia's external position, as shown by the stability of the country's balance of payments, and by the vast changes in the prospects for the Australian economy, largely because of the development of mineral resources and the discovery of substantial reserves of crude oil. This has meant that the economic pressures on Australia have very materially relaxed and psychologically Australians have assumed a highly optimistic attitude towards their future.

This attitude differs profoundly from the uncertainties of the 1950s and the early 1960s, when Australia was faced recurrently with periods of external instability due to passing phases of stress in the balance of payments, and the close correlation between official domestic economic policy and the state, either actual or prospective, of the country's international balances.

Australia's economic progress during the mid-1960s culminated in the decision in 1967 not to devalue the Australian dollar concurrently with the devaluation of the pound sterling. This, more than anything

else, brought home to Australians the fact that in the area of international finance their country had achieved viability. Furthermore, with the prospective development of mineral resources, especially in iron ore, bauxite and nickel, Australians realized that the strength underlying the decision not to devalue was not likely to be easily shaken in the next decade unless new and at present unforeseeable circumstances emerged. Official estimates that Australian mineral exports would be trebled within a short period, rising to $A2,000 million yearly, was in itself profoundly significant. The discovery of major oil reserves foreshadowed a further improvement by import replacement in the order of some further $A400 million. These alone provided ample evidence that Australia was not likely to slip back easily into the old uncertainties of the previous decade.

This new economic status was quickly reflected in the field of politics. There had always been some element of political thinking strongly opposed to overseas investment. Some of this thinking was caught up in clear cut lines of policy with ideological overtones. A great deal of such opposition as existed in the early post-war period stemmed from the traditional Labor Party reservations concerning the United States—the main source of post-war direct investment. On the other hand, the Leader of the Country Party, Mr McEwen, had always qualified his support for overseas investment and frequently found himself at variance with his Liberal Party associates in government, although such differences were never so profound as to create fears of major disagreement.

Undoubtedly, the biggest element in recent changes in political thinking on capital imports into Australia has been the desire to retain for Australians a substantial part in the exploitation of newly discovered mining wealth. The political posture that Australia should not become a 'quarry for the World' finds its place in the political views of all Australian parties.

This attitude, furthermore, has recently spread into the question of the ownership of industrial enterprises. A spate of takeovers of established Australian commercial companies by overseas interests has brought the question of capital inflow into the very centre of the political scene. As a result, the Prime Minister has himself taken a major part in the controversy, thus taking it out of the realm of departmental, especially Treasury, interest into the broad sweep of Australia's overall future development.

The position today

This series of events leads to a number of major questions which Australia must now face and decide:

1   Has it reached the stage of economic development at which overseas capital is unimportant; and, if so, on what basis can it accept capital in the future?

2   If it is still partially dependent on overseas capital (as most would argue), is it practicable or desirable for it to impose restrictions or conditions on capital inflow?

3   Should such conditions be limited to the extractive industries only, leaving an open field for industrial development as in the past?

4   What limitations, if any, should be imposed on the acquisition of controlling interests in existing Australian companies?

5   What scope exists, legally or politically, to force Australian participation in existing enterprises owned abroad?

Apart from general statements of policy the only positive act has been the promulgation of 'guide-lines' that limit the capacity of overseas companies to borrow on the Australian market. There is little strength in the political opposition to capital inflow at any cost. The Prime Minister during his period in office has appeared to change his emphasis and now upholds the promotion of capital inflow, provided that it can be achieved on Australia's own terms. A common factor in all the Prime Minister's statements has been that Australians should be offered participation in the equity of enterprises established here with overseas capital. Another view that is given less emphasis is that some difficulties should be placed in the way of the acquisition of control of existing Australian enterprises by overseas interests. The Prime Minister himself took the lead in introducing legislation to prevent the control of the M.L.C., a well-known life insurance company, from passing into the hands of a British company. In this case, since the M.L.C. was registered in Canberra, he was able to act under Federal law, but this limits the scope for Commonwealth action. Wide-scale action of a similar nature would require the co-operation of the State governments. Since the States have led the promotion of capital inflow, it is unlikely that their agreement to the general application of such a means of limiting the acquisition of Australian businesses by overseas interests would be forthcoming.

Under pressure from the Federal government, the Australian stock exchanges are considering the amendment of their listing requirements to allow for differential voting rights for overseas and local shareholders. This could mean that in order to protect themselves from takeover by overseas interests, directors of Australian companies could seek the authority of their shareholders to cancel or restrict the voting rights attaching to shares beneficially acquired by non-Australian shareholders. This step could place major difficulty in the

way of the takeover of Australian companies, although there is no certainty that directors would submit such a proposal to shareholders, or that the requisite majority (75%) of shareholders would accept it if they did. Most shareholders are normally motivated by self-interest and could be won over by a generous takeover bid, thus effectively thwarting public policy.

Reference has been made to the limitations on the use of Australian borrowed funds in effecting overseas investments. The so-called 'guide-lines' policy has had some effect in reducing the demands by overseas companies on the Australian money market but it is doubtful whether it has had any important effect so far in inducing overseas companies to offer Australians some participation in these ventures. The result has been mainly to augment the inflow of borrowed funds from abroad (in substitution for Australian borrowing).

One of the difficulties about making participation a matter of public policy is that Australians may not be attracted to invest in such ventures, and if they did, the payments for each acquisition may be a burden upon the balance of payments. The argument for participation is strongest in mining ventures. In these cases, both State and Federal governments have important and effective power to require the offer of participation to Australians when granting mining licences to overseas interests.

Perhaps the most effective instrument to implement policy in regard to capital inflow would be a simple uncomplicated statement of the government's objectives and targets. Few, if any, overseas companies would attempt to defeat or to circumvent such a policy, especially if it provided for elasticity and modification as dictated by time or circumstance.

As evidence of the government's sincerity of its desire to see greater participation in Australian development, it has announced its intention to establish a new Industrial Development Corporation for the avowed purpose of marshalling Australian (and a proportion of overseas) resources for this purpose.

Defence aspects of Australia's capital inflow: Political identity is important

Two main aspects emerge when we consider capital inflow in its relation to Australia's defence policy. The first of these is the kind of international posture that Australia may have to assume in order to ensure that capital is forthcoming from overseas. This involves more than the goodwill of the governments of the countries from which capital may come, as in many cases this capital will be of private

origin. Where, however, the capital is raised on an inter-governmental basis or through a governmental agency, then the goodwill of the lending country is basic. Creditor countries prefer recipient countries to have similar views in the sphere of international military strategy. Their investment interest in countries with contrary views in this field must be minimal.

Even where the funds are of private origin, and especially where the funds are to be devoted to permanent direct investment, the international political orientation of the borrowing country is of great relevance. It is only too apparent that countries which have a leftish image in the political scene will be much less attractive as an avenue for overseas investment by western countries than would a country that is more right wing in its political orientation. There have been, of course, some cases of international investment designed to sway the recipient country toward the military strategy of the investing country, but these cases have been of diminishing importance as international strategic lines have crystallized. Within broad lines the degree of urgency of the needs of the recipient country in regard to overseas capital will have an important bearing upon its political attitudes and upon the utterances of its political leaders.

So far as Australia is concerned, its record in this connection has been relatively uncomplicated as the main political persuasion of Australian governments, especially in the Federal sphere, has been right wing for twenty years. Consequently, the only question that has been raised concerning the political aspects of investment in Australia has been about the likelihood of possible future political changes and the effect that these would have upon the attractiveness of investment in Australia.

The Australian Labor Party, following its unsuccessful attempts at nationalization in the early post-war years, has carefully avoided public advocacy of socialization, although it still remains an inherent part of Labor's long-range policy. Unless the party should finally abandon this plank in its platform, the election of a Labor government in the Federal sphere is likely to reduce the attractiveness of Australia as an area for investment by western countries.

The Labor Party line on this subject has been to seek Australian participation of up to 30% of the equity in all enterprises owned abroad. More recently the Federal Leader of the Labor Party (Mr Gough Whitlam) has advocated joint enterprises between the Australian government and overseas investors. This proposed marriage between socialization and private overseas investment seems to be a compromise forced on Mr Whitlam by the paradox of maintaining party policy on the one hand and a recognition that Australia's

213

P

development in the foreseeable future will continue to depend upon capital inflow.

If the analysis is carried further into the sphere of State governments we find that the political factor has little influence in investment decisions as between one State and another. Indeed, Australian States with Labor governments have expended almost as much effort in attracting capital as have the essentially right-wing States. This is largely due to competition between States in attracting industry with its consequential influence upon industrial development. There are, of course, sometimes advantages to a left-wing government in stimulating industrial development, since this creates or encourages the industrial economy and labour force which are on balance, likely to benefit a left-wing political outlook. Consequently, we have seen the strong competition between the States of Victoria and New South Wales, initiated in the first place by the efforts of a right-wing Premier (Sir Henry Bolte), leading to competitive efforts over many years by a Labor government in the adjoining State.

But it is in the Federal sphere that these considerations are really of importance to overseas investors. To the extent that recent changes in the attitude of the Australian government on the subject of overseas capital in general show a greater degree of robustness, it can perhaps be assumed that Australia's anxiety to obtain overseas capital is somewhat less pressing than it was a few years ago. Whether this greater independence of attitude will be reflected in similar independence in defence policy remains to be seen.

It can at least be assumed that the need to maintain capital inflow will have less influence in the future than it has in the past in deciding Australia's defence policy. On the other hand, greater Australian independence, whether in regard to capital, or defence, or in any other significant area, will probably tend to stimulate rather than to lessen interest in Australia as an area for permanent investment. Such robustness is in itself a desirable quality in the recipient country.

Protection of investment

Another important defence aspect of overseas investment in Australia is the influence of such capital inflow in creating an interest on the part of the investing country in preserving the invulnerability of the countries in which substantial investments are made. We can go back to the beginnings of history for our examples. The ancient empires were largely maintained by defence of their colonies and of trade routes. This has been true of all colonial systems of the past. How relevant is it in today's conditions? Obviously, countries like the United States and Great Britain with large investments abroad upon

which they rely for income and for basic materials, will show more than a passing interest in the defence of such countries. Both of these countries have invested something over $A2,500 million in Australian manufacturing between 1948-65 and the American content of overseas capital inflow has substantially increased in the recent crescendo in overseas investment in Australian mining ventures.

Furthermore, a great deal of the recent increase in American investment in Australia is related to the growth of the Japanese economy in which the United States has a very great political and economic interest. Therefore, even though the old colonial attitudes have disappeared, the security of overseas investment, particularly on the scale now reached in Australia, must clearly have some important bearing in determining America's interest in Australian defence.

The sources of capital: Predominance of Britain and America

It has already been noted that by far the greatest elements in overseas investment in Australia have originated from the United Kingdom and the United States. The latest figures available, for 1965, show that of an accumulated total of $A5,300 million of foreign investment in Australian manufacturing industries, approximately 92% came from Britain or the United States. Of this amount of some $A5,000 million, a little less than half came from America, British investments at that time still being the largest element in capital inflow. Since less than 10% of Australia's capital inflow has come from countries other than Britain or America, there is no scope for extending our inquiry beyond these two.

In some respects, the maintained inflow of British capital into Australia is surprising, in view of the economic problems which have faced Great Britain since the post-war period. Despite these difficulties, however, outflow of long-term private capital into this country from Great Britain has actually steadily increased. It is one of the paradoxes of the British situation that, in spite of the short-term difficulties in its balance of payments, Britain has been able to maintain a steady outflow of long-term capital.

If we analyse the British flow of capital into Australia we find that a significant proportion has been derived from the undistributed income of British companies operating there. The ratio of undistributed income to other investment has, naturally, varied since the latter is a much more dynamic factor. Nevertheless, undistributed income has at times represented as much as 80% of the annual inflow, falling in some years to as low as 20%. If the last two to three years be excluded, the element represented by undistributed income has shown a tendency to increase, both relatively and absolutely.

Examination of capital inflow into Australia during 1968-69 reveals some trends that may have future significance. Retained profits of all overseas companies operating here nearly trebled over the past three years. This applies equally to British and American companies, and is no doubt a reflection of restrictions imposed by those countries upon the export of capital for direct investment.

Direct investment in Australia, however, has recently undergone some considerable changes that were quite dissimilar as between Britain and America. Over the past three years direct investment by British companies has averaged only $A38 million including a withdrawal of $A3 million in 1967-68, compared with an average inflow of direct investment over the previous three years of $A146 million. American direct investment on the other hand rose to an average level of $A203 million in the last three years, compared with an average of $A160 million in the previous three years.

These figures are a significant reflection of the direct investment policies of the two investing countries. They emphasize the contrast between the dynamic expansion of American direct investment, mainly no doubt in mining activities and the contraction of new investment in enterprises directly operated by British companies.

But more extraordinary still has been the movement during 1967-68 and 1968-69 in portfolio investment and institutional loans made by these two countries in Australia. British investment in this category in these two years was $A268 million and $A244 million respectively, compared with an average of only $A24 million in the previous four years. American portfolio investment in the last two years has been $A59 million and $A5 million respectively, compared with an average in the previous four years of $A55 million.

Does this mean that the contraction of direct investment by Britain is just a change of emphasis, that industrial or mining activity has merely yielded place to financial enterprise? Unfortunately, British portfolio investment hardly merits such a positive classification. Its very size and suddenness suggests that it is based on a negative philosophy that has none of the elements of direct permanent investment made by Britain in the past.

What has prompted this change in British outlook? An answer to that question may give some lead to British military policy East of Suez. A brief examination of British investment policy since the war is of some interest in considering this question.

During the war period the United Kingdom incurred a current account deficit of some £10,000 million which was met in part by the sale of a considerable proportion of overseas assets. During the war and in the immediate post-war period Britain is understood to have

liquidated approximately £1,600 million of overseas investment, which in itself represented a substantial reduction in its overseas holdings. Nevertheless there is no evidence for the view which was current for years after the war that the United Kingdom had lost all or even the greater part of its overseas investments. Britain was able to retain at least three-quarters of the total and ended the war period with some £3,500 million of long-term investments abroad. This accounts for the ease with which Britain's earnings on interest profits and dividends recovered after the war.

Almost throughout the post-war period Britain was able to augment still further its overseas investments even in periods in which it showed substantial deficits on current account. For example, between 1945-61 Britain's gross external investment amounted to more than £1,600 million of which some 80% was in the form of private investment. This amount was far in excess of foreign private investment in Great Britain and was made in a period when the average deficit on current account exceeded £135 million *per annum*. This net outflow of long-term capital from the United Kingdom continued throughout the post-war period except for the year 1961. The year-to-year amounts have not been large, but over a long period, and particularly in recent years, they have added considerably to the problems on current account. Apart from the quantitative aspects of the export of British capital, considerable significance attaches to the direction in which the investment has been made. In recent years it is apparent that on the average about 60% of the total direct private investment went to the sterling area and, although no precise particulars are available, most of the investment up to about five years ago went to Australia, South Africa, New Zealand and Rhodesia. A small proportion— approximately 30%—was invested in developing countries like India and Pakistan. British investment capital since the war has, in fact, gone mainly to countries which have already attained a relatively high degree of development.

There are serious doubts as to whether the United Kingdom can really afford so large an outflow of long-term capital as that achieved over the last fifteen years. The main disadvantages appear to be twofold. First, capital exports have had a short-term adverse effect upon Britain's international reserves, which are still under considerable strain despite some recent improvement. Secondly, the capital could be better used to augment Britain's domestic capital formation which is generally held to be inadequate if it is to attain the accepted target rate of growth of $3\frac{1}{2}$%.

Consequently, there is a growing view that the outflow of capital from Britain should be reduced until the current balance shows a

permanent improvement. The United Kingdom, in short, cannot expect to maintain its role as an exporter of long-term capital without a flexible policy of controls which would reduce or encourage investment overseas according to the state of current accounts.

Only a relatively small proportion of British long-term private capital goes to developing countries, which consequently would not be affected by the reduction in capital outflow. Moreover, investment in developed countries such as Australia produces a lower return to the United Kingdom than capital invested in developing countries or at home and the reduction in capital outflow to the former would be a logical step. This thinking has led to the view that there may be some advantages to Britain in selling a part of the portfolio assets held abroad in order to achieve the current target surplus on the basic balance of payments over the next few years.

If account is taken of these factors by the British authorities, it is possible that the capital inflow into Australia from the United Kingdom may be expected to remain static over the next few years. Having regard to the large inflow of portfolio investment into Australia over the last year or so, such an expectation seems to be unrealistic but continuance of recent balance of payments difficulties may well lead to a change in British policy. In any event, the downtrend in direct investment seems likely to continue.

Any substantial disinvestment abroad by the United Kingdom may be expected to have a significant influence upon defence policy, both in the United Kingdom and in the countries from which capital is withdrawn, which are likely to include Australia. Britain's preoccupation with Europe as a natural goal, both economic and political, would logically promote a diversion of investment in order to match its overall effort toward European development with its future partners in the E.E.C.

The basic difference between American capital investment in Australia and British is, as one might expect, related to the historical industrial expansion in each of the investing countries. British investment goes back into the past century and recent growth is rather the natural development of that investment.

American investment on the other hand is directly related to the enormous industrial expansion in the U.S., especially during the Second World War. Whereas Britain had difficulties in maintaining production adequate to its own needs, United States industrial expansion, linked with a favourable balance of payments, gave it the resources and the techniques to expand industrial investment abroad. Since many countries found their industrial potential either destroyed or seriously impaired by war, there was a natural vacuum for American

capital to fill in almost the whole of the western world. As a result, whole new industries were established in such countries (including Australia) by American enterprise. Much of this investment has been highly significant in certain areas of the Australian economy, especially in oil refining, motor vehicles, agricultural equipment and pharmaceuticals.

British investment, on the other hand, is much more widely spread. It is still significant in some of the areas in which American investment has predominated. Nevertheless, American investment is, for example, about 50% greater than British in oil refining and some five times greater in motor vehicle manufacture.

A corollary of this growth in American investment has been the predominant part played in it by large American corporations. Another feature has been the almost complete absence of Australian participation in any of the major American enterprises operating in Australia. Companies such as General Motors have made it abundantly clear that they do not intend to deviate from this policy.

The consequence of such an attitude is that American investment in Australia has at times shown a tendency to pursue policies that are based upon the corporate interest of the companies involved without always having regard to the national viewpoint or the policies of Australian governments. This has demonstrated itself in several ways. Inadequate development of exports is one, although in recent years a much greater degree of co-operation has been achieved in this regard.

The tendency for American corporations operating in Australia to adopt a rugged attitude in the preservation of their own interests is not an uncommon feature in international company policy, regardless of nationality of ownership. In the case of the United States, however, it is probably prompted by the relations that exist between American corporations and their own government. Few countries in the world take such great interest in the affairs of their corporations. The framing and administration of such legislation as the U.S. Anti-Trust laws has led to internal policies in American corporations that are reflected in the attitudes and activities of those companies throughout the world.

In turn, this involvement between U.S. business and government is not always negative. A feature of this relationship is a strong defensive attitude by the U.S. government toward American business, as exemplified by the frequent occasions on which the State Department has intervened to obtain restitution for American companies affected by the action of foreign governments.

The extent to which the U.S. government is prepared to go in defence of American corporations however, is by no means certain.

There were times, as in the case of the Mexican Eagle Co., when economic relations were adversely affected for many years, and even military action was threatened. But as time has gone by, overt action has given place to diplomatic pressure. The very magnitude of America's military striking power has been a deterrent to action on its part to protect the interests of American corporations affected by arbitrary government action, especially in the developing countries. Events in Central and South America and in Indonesia all point to the fact that military factors no longer have any major influence upon the fate of American corporations.

Therefore the influence of defence considerations upon the flow of American capital is limited. The basic element in protecting capital already invested is no longer military power but the necessity of the recipient country to ensure continuing aid or capital inflow from the United States. In the case of Indonesia we have recently seen the reversal of the antagonism to foreign investment which had led to the expropriation of British and American companies, a reversal based entirely on the desire to gain continuing economic support in the future.

When we consider Australia's position in this connection, it is relatively uncomplicated. The chance of expropriation of foreign companies as such, is nil. Australia's only concern is to maintain its place as a recipient of American investment and whatever changes in Australian defence policy may occur, they are unlikely to affect the general attractiveness of investment there.

The argument in fact is rather the other way around because of America's growing involvement in the development of the Australian continent as a source of raw materials for its industrial needs and for those of Japan. Its interest in the strategic integrity of Australia is likely to be maintained. Whatever limitations may be imposed upon the inflow of American capital they are unlikely to place serious strain upon this relationship.

Summary

The overall impression derived from the foregoing considerations is that the degree of correlation between Australia's defence policy and its need for capital inflow is relatively small. Several important considerations emerge from the analysis.

First, in historic terms, capital inflow over the past years has played a basic part in establishing the Australian economic structure. This has enabled Australia to reach a stage of industrial maturity and to augment its population to a degree that has enabled the country in the last few years to mount a great increase in defence effort.

Secondly, capital inflow has, especially in recent years, sustained the balance of payments in periods when Australian defence expenditure abroad was rapidly increasing, both for equipment and overseas military spending.

Because of the growing strength of the Australian economy, its need for capital inflow is substantially reduced. It is unlikely therefore, that the need to maintain capital inflow will in the future have to weigh so heavily in any consideration of defence policy.

Australia's present political situation is such that it would appear to have considerable flexibility in its relations with other countries, especially with the United States in matters affecting defence. This political stability by far outweighs any economic question in its defence negotiations.

Britain's partial retreat to West of Suez coincides with diminishing direct investment in Australia, and probably also in other countries in this area. Although both tendencies probably stem from the same cause, they will not necessarily continue on the same course. Britain's withdrawal into Europe may continue, and may prompt a diversion of British capital outflow there from Australia but the recent considerable increase in British portfolio investment in Australia indicates a potential for a revival of direct investment as and when Britain's present balance of payments difficulties are overcome.

Finally, so far as the United States is concerned, everything points to the likelihood that capital inflow from that source will stimulate interest in Australian defence. Consequently, its defence posture is not likely to require modification in order to maintain American capital inflow. Considerations of defence posture and capital supply are not interdependent. Its defence problem will be to live with a global U.S. military posture designed in Washington rather than to adjust defence policy to meet capital needs as such.

CHAPTER 15

Australian Capabilities— Telecommunications and Space

A. J. SEYLER

Introduction

The large size of the Australian continent, and its remoteness from other world centres, have meant that distance has always been one of the major problems of national development. Australia therefore is and has been vitally concerned with telecommunications.*

It is not only the size of this continent, which in area is comparable to that of the U.S.A., and the associated distances, but also the particular population distribution which determines the communication problems to be solved. On 30 June 1968 of a total population of 12 million just over 62% lived in the capital city areas, 13% in other principal cities and towns and the remaining 25% were scattered over the rest of the continent as individual settlers and/or small communities.[1]

Economically and technologically the provision of telecommunication facilities within the metropolitan areas presents no problems which differ greatly from those in other countries. The provision of economical inter-city business and personal communication services over hundreds of miles, with very low density *en route* tributary traffic, although already taxing the current state of the art of telecommunications technology is a problem also found in other parts of the world.

The most challenging of the Australian communication problems

* *Editor's Note*: The telecommunications facilities controlled by the Australian Postmaster-General, which are discussed in this paper, comprise almost the whole of the nation's facilities in the field. With the exception of some minor radio networks operated by the Australian Armed Services, there are no important military or diplomatic communications networks separate from the general network of Post Office facilities. It may be that this development is partly due to the fact that telecommunications in Australia is a government monopoly and not, as in some other countries, a commercial enterprise. No detailed information or figures are available as to what segments or percentage of Australia's total facilities are pre-empted by service or diplomatic needs.

is the provision of services to the widely scattered rural population at a standard befitting a modern, technically developed community. (This problem may be comparable to that of providing tactical communication services for modern highly mobile and dispersed defence services.)

This 'rural population' consists of individual homesteads, where often the nearest neighbour is between 50 and 100 miles away; of small farming communities containing perhaps a score of families; and, more recently, of mobile mining exploration teams and of mining centres developing around significant mineral deposits, all far removed from any of the main urban centres.

Thus within Australia there are basically three categories of communication capabilities:

1 Short distance (2-100 miles) very high capacity transmission systems, say, up to and between 10,000 and 100,000 telephone channels or their equivalent;

2 Long distance (500-2,500 miles) medium capacity routes of between 600 and 2,700 telephone channels with provision for television and high speed data transmission; and

3 Long distance low capacity routes between one and perhaps sixty telephone channels to remote settlers and widely scattered rural and mining centres.

Any communications services abroad must, of course, be transoceanic. To the east the nearest neighbour is New Zealand. Fiji and Hawaii are major stepping stations to the North and South American continents. To the north lie the Territory of Papua and New Guinea, Indonesia and beyond, the mainland of East Asia with focal points ranging from Singapore to Japan. Across the Indian Ocean lie India and Pakistan, the Middle East and Africa. The communication facilities to these countries must at the same time carry through-traffic to Europe and the United Kingdom, in the same way as the trans-Pacific routes are loaded with traffic to the east coasts of Canada and the U.S.A. and across the Atlantic, to Europe and the United Kingdom. Conversely, Australia serves as a crossroads and transit centre for communications between these countries. These intercontinental telecommunications facilities give direct support to the whole network of Australia's trading and financial relationships.

The provision and operation of telecommunication services is the responsibility of the Federal Postmaster-General (a cabinet minister) to whom the Australian Post Office (A.P.O.) is responsible for intra-Australian communication and under whose direction the Overseas

Telecommunications Commission (O.T.C.) operates and maintains the international services.

The latter was established in 1946 by Act of Parliament following the recommendations of the 1945 Empire Telecommunications Conference in London at which it was agreed to transfer from private to public ownership all overseas cable and wireless installations in the British Commonwealth of Nations. Thus after acquisition by the Australian government of the Australian assets and installations of Cable and Wireless Ltd. and of Amalgamated Wireless (Australia) Ltd., O.T.C. became the Australian National Body acting in unison with its Commonwealth partners in creating a technically and administratively unified external telecommunication system.

Intra-Australian capabilities

An Australian postal service developed in the first half of last century and the first telegraph services came into being, administratively integrated with it, about the middle of the last century. By the 1870s a continent-wide telegraph network linked the colonies to each other and by submarine cable to the outside world.

Two years after the invention of the telephone the first services came into operation in 1873 and the earlier pattern of inter-colony telegraph service development repeated itself in the telephone service over the next decades. The Federation of the Colonies in 1901 caused the creation of the Federal Postmaster-General's Department, bringing all the State Post and Telegraph authorities under one administration.

The year 1907 saw the establishing of the first interstate trunk circuit between Sydney and Melbourne and 1912 the first automatic telephone exchange in the southern hemisphere had been installed in Geelong in Victoria. From this grew four networks of telecommunication services which today form the largest integrated business undertaking of the country.

Telephone services

In the short span of 70 years, and following the two World Wars, telephone services had grown to 577,777 in 1945 and by 1969 2,511,231 services were in operation (3,598,692 instruments), their number having practically doubled every ten years. 1,548,479 services were then installed in the metropolitan areas and 962,752 in country areas, 89% being connected to automatic exchanges, only 30% of the country services still operating from manual exchanges. 2,614 million telephone calls were made by subscribers in 1969 of which 172.2 million were trunk line calls. It is clear that to service this trunk traffic

requires the provision of an automatic trunk exchange system which must penetrate throughout the provincial areas of Australia.

To provide an orderly development of the expanding services the National Community Telephone Plan was formulated and adopted in 1960. This plan sets down the principles to be followed in the growth of the telephone system up to the year 2010 and in its complete conversion and integration into nation-wide automatic working. Several new automatic trunk exchanges were commissioned in 1967, providing the beginning of automatic Subscriber Trunk Dialling services with a penetration of 33.7% of all trunk calls in 1969. Planning targets for the further development of S.T.D. services aim for a penetration of 66% by 1975. At the same time the current figure of 89% of all subscribers being served by automatic exchanges is expected to reach 94%.

As part of the overall development of telecommunications telegraph, Telex and photo transmission services have shown movements which roughly parallel the development of telephone services.

Telegraphic services

Telecommunication by telegraphy was, of course, the earliest form of all electrical communication; but during the last decade internal telegraph traffic figures have remained about steady. The number of telegrams sent was 22.7 million in 1955, 20 million in 1960 and about 21 million in 1969. Yet it would be an oversimplification to say that in communications the written word is being replaced by the spoken one. Private teleprinter services (Telex) have increased from a mere 95 subscribers in 1955 and 684 in 1960 to 5,067 in 1969. Still more significant is the traffic increase from 410,744 messages in 1960 to 7,362,084 in 1969, a growth of more than three times since the conversion to automatic working in 1966.

But despite the growth of other telecommunication services and the diminution of traffic since its peak during the Second World War, the volume of the Australian public telegraph service remains one of the largest in the world, exceeding that of such major countries as Great Britain and West Germany. This is undoubtedly due to the population distribution, and shows up even more clearly in the Telex traffic pattern, where 75% of traffic is over distances greater than 400 miles.

Data transmission

With the advent of electronic computers and their increasing use in all kinds of administrative and technical operations, data processing and dissemination, the need for communication to, from and be-

tween computers has created the need for a new type of telecommunication service. As an electrical signal, data transmission is basically telegraphic in nature, i.e., information is transmitted in time and amplitude-discrete form. In fact, for direct communication between 'man and machine' the basic teletype terminal serves as an interface input-output device; whereby it is obvious that even a moderately sized computer is orders of magnitude faster in accepting and processing information than is the human being communicating with the machine. This speed imbalance has brought about a mode of operation known as 'time-sharing', in which many such slow input-output terminals communicate, as it appears, simultaneously, but in fact in a time-multiplex (inter-leaved in time) mode, with the electronic partner. The first such service was established in Australia in 1968 by one of the major computer manufacturers and a rapid growth, as indicated by the American precedents, must be expected in this area.

This comparatively slow type of information transmission will eventually require substantial channel capacity in the form of multi-channel data traffic. But direct communication between machines and to and from fast non-human terminals will demand individual channels of higher capacity than that of single telegraph or telephone channels.

But for this new service neither the technology nor the operating policy of public communication carriers are as yet easily predictable. The technology seems to be moving towards increasing speed, possibly requiring channels of the order of, or greater than, present-day television channels, a development already well within the capabilities of current communication electronics. Likely operating policy, however, is much less definable at this stage. The crucial question seems to be whether a new and independent data network should be created in juxtaposition with the conventional telegraph and telephone network, or whether all types of telecommunication services will share the same transmission and distribution facilities.

In Australia the Post Office decided in 1966 to provide and maintain interface devices—known as MODEMS—between the customer's terminal equipment and the Department's telephone transmission facilities, covering the speed range between 200 and 600/1,200 bits per second. (A 'bit' means binary digit, the basic unit of information.) The adoption of this policy followed the establishment of the first international standards recommended by the C.C.I.T.T., (see section on *International Relations*, below) and is intended to avoid the development and use of equipment not meeting such standards. In this way the A.P.O. is able to assume responsibility for the main-

taining of satisfactory operating standards for the whole data transmission system and its orderly development.

Some flexibility has, however, been built into the relevant regulations to prevent the stifling of technological progress in this new field, and privately owned interface units catering for facilities not provided by the A.P.O. will be permitted, subject to type approval. This qualification is essential to prevent interference with other services and to ensure compatibility with existing transmission facilities. This variation clause is especially designed to facilitate higher speed transmission (e.g., over packets of twelve telephone channels or multiples thereof) for inter-computer communications and for bulk data transmission.

The internal transmission network

To meet the growing needs for telecommunication services after the Second World War, a technologically more advanced transmission network had to be established—analogous to super-highways—known as the Broadband Network.

When in 1970 the east-west microwave route across the Nullarbor desert from Port Pirie in South Australia to Northam in Western Australia was completed, a continuous high capacity trunk network extended from Cairns on the north-east coast via Brisbane, Sydney, Melbourne, Adelaide and Perth to Carnarvon and Port Hedland on the west coast of the continent with a branch-off from Melbourne to Tasmania with an over-water link across 200 miles of Bass Strait.

The development of this mainline network began with the completion in 1962 of the coaxial cable system connecting Sydney-Canberra-Melbourne. A mixed microwave coaxial cable system from Sydney to Brisbane followed soon and was extended by 1967 by a microwave system to Cairns. Apart from carrying internal traffic and television relays this 1,600 miles long Sydney-Cairns route is also serving as the trans-Australia link between the trans-Pacific COMPAC cable through O.T.C.'s international exchange at Paddington (Sydney) and the South-East Asia SEACOM cable terminal at Cairns. The year 1967 also saw the extension of the microwave network from Melbourne to Adelaide and to Hobart.

Map 2 shows the future scope of development of the intra-Australian broadband network, connecting in the early 1970s the inland mining centre of Mt Isa and Darwin on the north coast to the east coast network at Townsville. It is also planned to close the ring in the north from Port Hedland via Derby-Wyndham-Darwin and a transcontinental north-south route via Alice Springs to Adelaide will eventually replace the existing facilities first established nearly 100 years

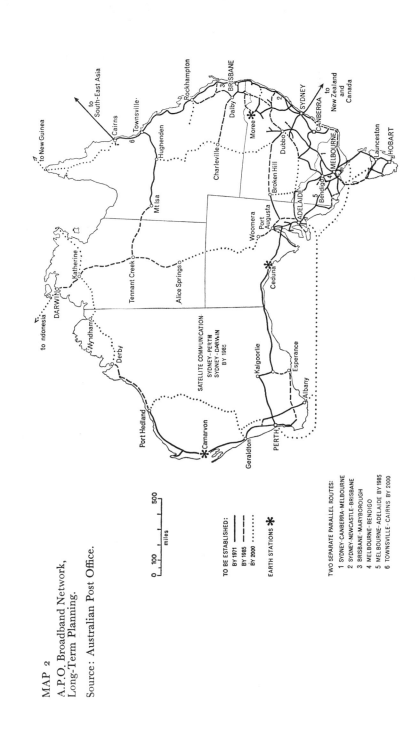

MAP 2

A.P.O. Broadband Network,
Long-Term Planning.

Source: Australian Post Office.

0   100   500
         miles

TO BE ESTABLISHED:

——— BY 1971
– – – BY 1985
········· BY 2000

✳ EARTH STATIONS

TWO SEPARATE PARALLEL ROUTES:

1 SYDNEY-CANBERRA-MELBOURNE
2 SYDNEY-NEWCASTLE-BRISBANE
3 BRISBANE-MARYBOROUGH
4 MELBOURNE-BENDIGO
5 MELBOURNE-ADELAIDE BY 1985
6 TOWNSVILLE-CAIRNS BY 2000

SATELLITE COMMUNICATION:
SYDNEY-PERTH
SYDNEY-DARWIN
BY 1985

ago. Already by 1970 the broadband network with its spur routes between metropolitan areas and provincial centres will cover some 12,500 route miles and represent an investment of about $A150 million.

In providing this network, which today is considered one of the most modern major trunk systems in the world, some notable pioneering work has been done in Australia in the use of broadband techniques. The Brisbane-Cairns radio system over 960 route miles was one of the first systems in the world using mainly solid state circuit techniques in the interests of reliability and low power consumption. The east-west system installed over 1,420 route miles between 1968 and 1970 is solid state throughout. Because of their remoteness the repeater stations are somewhat unorthodox in design. Special building techniques had to be developed to provide a safe environment for the equipment in all seasons with shade temperatures reading up to 125°F in summer. For the power supply, windmill generators of new design are used, to supplement small diesel generators and batteries in order to reduce the amount of fuel which would have to be transported to the more than 50 repeater sites.

The unique meteorological conditions resulting from the interaction between the continental air masses and the surrounding oceans have called for extensive research into the effects of these conditions on the transmission of the electro-magnetic waves used in the long distance microwave systems. It was then possible to design and engineer the over-water link to Tasmania and the desert route to Western Australia so as to ensure reliable systems performance. Already similar studies are being undertaken in inland desert and tropical areas exploring the propagation and equipment design problems for systems extensions planned for the 1970s. New coaxial cable laying techniques have been pioneered which permit an average rate of twenty miles a week, first achieved on the Perth-Carnarvon route, which uses a four-tube cable with buried solid state repeaters.

Also, the channel capacity of broadband systems has been progressively increased. Coaxial cable capacity has grown from 1,260 circuits in the earlier systems to 2,700 in the 12 MHz bandwidth of the new installations. Microwave relay systems capacity has risen from 600 to 1,800 circuits with 2,700 circuits capacity becoming available for special purposes.

Underground cable is mainly used in local distribution to link the subscribers to exchanges and to connect adjacent exchanges. This 'local' cable network contained 19,400,175 single wire miles by 1969. At the same time 1,160,006 single wire miles were carried by 110,943 miles of open wire pole routes. This type of construction still has an

229

economic field of use in lightly populated areas, but is decreasing in relation to the overall network.

The outback problem

While more than 75% of the Australian population lives in six capital cities and urban communities, there remain some 3 million who are scattered over the continent in small settlements and individual homesteads. Clearly, to provide for the highest grade of service everywhere would be prohibitively expensive. The two major interim measures adopted in Australia to provide communication for and with the outback population are based on a co-operative approach between the A.P.O. and the public; these are the Part-Privately-Erected (P.P.E.) and maintained telephone line and the Outpost H.F. Radio communication network.

The former provides for an individual or group of subscribers (in party-line operation) to erect privately an open wire line connecting into a manual exchange. In 1968 36,082 P.P.E. lines were in existence, together making a network of some 150,000 circuit miles, with 900 lines being over 30 miles long and extending to 300 miles in one case.

The second interim communication facility, the outback radio communication network, is a unique Australian feature serving already as a model for a number of other countries in which similar conditions exist or are developing. The current extent of these outback radio services is illustrated by Map 3. Altogether 28 control stations serve as base stations for geographically grouped networks of up to about 100 fixed stations each and a similar number of mobile stations. (The figures for 1969 were 2,772 fixed and 3,455 mobile.) Apart from providing medical aid through the Australian Royal Flying Doctor Service which is supporting most of the network, these stations enable outback children to receive regular schooling through the 'school of the air'. They also serve as communications between homesteads and as a means of exchanging telegrams with the outside world. Where the nearest neighbour may be a hundred miles away, the radio breaks the otherwise overwhelming loneliness and isolation of the outback settler. Stores and provisions for agricultural and personal needs are ordered for delivery by plane or truck and emergency medical, veterinary or technical help may be called on by direct radio consultation with experts. The mobile service facilities not only provide continuing contact between the homestead and the men who may be away for days droving or surveying, but also between prospecting teams and their bases of operation.

Beyond these temporary measures, the A.P.O. is investigating the application of satellite communication techniques which would not

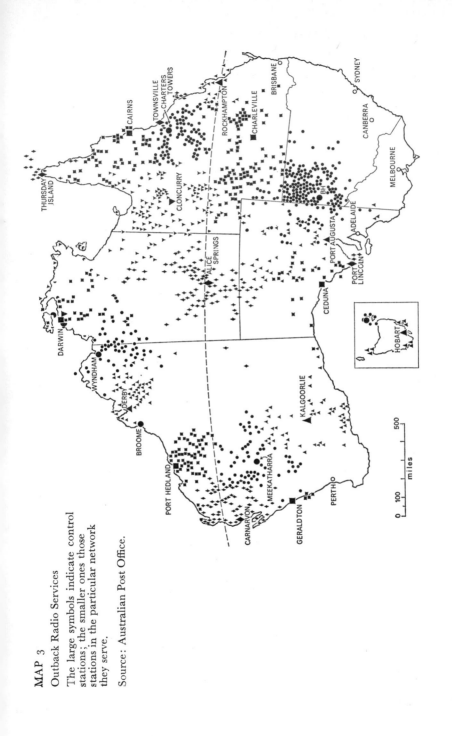

MAP 3

Outback Radio Services

The large symbols indicate control stations; the smaller ones those stations in the particular network they serve.

Source: Australian Post Office.

only integrate the now rudimentary outback services into the general Australian network but might also provide direct broadcasting and television services to the isolated homesteads and small communities.

International communication services

Both because of its physical isolation and its involvement in international trade and politics, first grade international communication capabilities have played and will continue to play a vital role in Australia's national development. Moreover, its very position at the antipodes of the major world centres surrounding the Atlantic have made it the international communications transit point for the South-East Asian, South Pacific and Indian Ocean Countries. (See Map 4.)

Traffic patterns

International telephone traffic in and out of Australia early in the 1960s grew at the rate of nearly 50% *per annum* and its growth was still of the order of 25% by 1968. The total figures for 1966-67 were showing 346,133 outgoing and 320,947 incoming calls respectively. By 1969 the former had grown to 554,531. (See Table 8.)

Whereas until 1963-64 the number of incoming calls generally exceeded that of the outgoing ones, this pattern was reversed in the following year, coinciding with the opening of the COMPAC cable, and it continues to stay this way. Direct automatic number to number calls were introduced in 1968 for service between Australia and the U.S.A. and Canada, permitting a more effective use of the trans-Pacific route and correspondingly reduced charges.

The quadrupling of the international telephone traffic between 1961-62 and 1966-67 has been paralleled by a similar growth in international Telex traffic, which rose from 109,836 calls in 1961-62 to 377,966 in 1966-67. Over the same period telegraph traffic has also increased, from 2,850,332 telegrams in 1961-62 to 4,186,794 in 1966-67, the proportions of outgoing traffic being always slightly higher than the incoming one.

Already before the opening of the SEACOM cable in 1967 25% of the international traffic handled by O.T.C. was transit traffic from and to South-East Asia. In 1968 12% of all telephone, 48% of all Telex and 78% of all telegraph traffic channelled through O.T.C.'s gateway exchange at Paddington was such transit traffic.

Apart from the on demand facilities, leased circuits are made available for organizations such as newspapers and news agencies, diplomatic and defence services, N.A.S.A. and others who have a continuous need for maintaining contact with overseas offices. Typically, early in 1969 N.A.S.A. had leased from the O.T.C. nineteen Voice

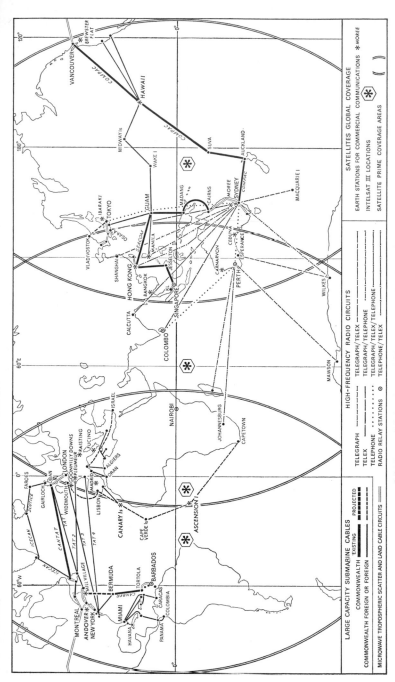

MAP 4 Major World Telecommunications Systems

TABLE 8

Overseas Telecommunications Traffic

Telephone Calls Connected

Country	1963–64 Outgoing	1963–64 Incoming	1964–65 Outgoing	1964–65 Incoming	1965–66 Outgoing	1965–66 Incoming	1966–67 Outgoing	1966–67 Incoming	1967–68 Outgoing	1968–69 Outgoing
U.K. and Europe	39,479	23,346	75,292	43,446	98,157	55,641	119,881	65,100	145,176	174,952
Nth. America	25,192	23,646	39,514	34,139	48,946	41,682	61,093	49,967	83,389	116,511
New Zealand	58,087	76,296	74,863	94,406	90,922	112,418	107,442	139,796	127,283	143,986
Papua and N. Guinea	9,846	15,945	12,813	20,296	16,140	25,688	20,456	31,755	28,633	34,699
Hong Kong	2,992	2,136	4,810	3,452	5,922	4,193	9,274	6,574	14,059	18,232
Japan	2,497	2,197	3,734	3,375	4,782	3,429	5,952	4,454	11,828	15,259
Other countries	9,159	10,850	13,287	15,887	16,971	18,373	22,035	23,301	29,827	40,892
Total calls	147,252	154,416	224,313	215,001	281,840	261,424	346,133	320,947	449,195	554,531

Teleprinter (Telex) calls connected

Country	1963–64 Outgoing	1963–64 Incoming	1964–65 Outgoing	1964–65 Incoming	1965–66 Outgoing	1965–66 Incoming	1966–67 Outgoing	1966–67 Incoming	1967–68 Outgoing	1968–69 Outgoing
U.K. and Europe	30,032	33,190	41,491	50,529	49,997	64,482	65,489	81,190	92,356	187,724
Nth. America	14,684	15,407	21,350	22,186	31,523	34,794	48,619	51,789	69,346	93,664
New Zealand	3,464	4,789	5,932	6,128	10,699	8,977	15,672	11,033	22,952	36,086
Japan	30,107	39,212	36,755	46,248	28,827	32,907	32,083	32,353	41,212	53,119
Hong Kong	2,185	1,952	2,466	2,796	2,756	2,624	4,200	3,942	6,298	8,561
Other countries	3,853	4,035	6,130	8,169	10,430	10,240	15,987	15,609	27,311	34,068
Total calls	84,325	98,585	114,124	136,056	134,232	154,024	182,050	195,916	259,475	413,222

Source: *Financial and Statistical Bulletin*, 1969.

and five Telex circuits through Sydney and twelve and four such circuits respectively through Carnarvon, in order to maintain twenty-four-hour communication between its Australian tracking stations and the U.S. control centres for its space flight operations. At times when critical space flights are in progress, such as the Apollo missions, even more circuits are provided through cable and satellite facilities.

Apart from voice and teleprinter, leased facilities are available for photo telegraph ('facsimile') channels, high quality sound broadcasting channels, data transmission and, most recently, television channels of full colour capability through synchronous satellites.

Transmission capabilities

The continuing increase in demand for overseas telecommunication services had by the 1950s almost saturated the available frequency bandwidth in the short-wave (H.F.) radio band, which apart from the submarine telegraph cables provided the transmission channels for the international services. It needed a breakthrough in technology to overcome this stalemate—the coaxial submarine cable.

After the demonstrated success of the transatlantic TAT 1 cable, which was opened for service in 1956, Britain and Canada agreed on plans to link their two countries by a new transatlantic cable to be known as CANTAT, which came into operation in 1961. In 1958 a Commonwealth Telecommunications Conference was convened to consider the technical and economic feasibility of establishing a global Commonwealth, large capacity, cable network. Following this conference Australia invited other interested governments to consider extending the Commonwealth cable system into the southern hemisphere. Delegates from Britain, Canada and New Zealand met in 1959 in Sydney at the Pacific Cable Conference and set the broad design, construction, ownership and control arrangements. Control of the project was eventually given to a Pacific Cable Management Committee comprising the chief executives of the partner countries' telecommunication authorities.

The laying of the Commonwealth Pacific Cable (COMPAC) began early in 1962 and the first section, from Australia to New Zealand, opened for service in July of that year. Then followed New Zealand-Fiji in December 1962 and the section Fiji-Hawaii-Vancouver in October 1963, linking COMPAC to the transatlantic CANTAT cable by a new microwave system across Canada. Thus a high-grade large-capacity communications system extending from Australia to England over a route distance of 16,251 miles had come into being and opened for service on 3 December 1963. Australia,

through O.T.C., has a share of 25% in the COMPAC cable which cost approximately $A68 million.

By then the extension of COMPAC to South-East Asia was already on its way, having been first recommended by a conference held in Kuala Lumpur in mid-1961. The sponsoring nations apart from those of the COMPAC cable included also the (then) Federation of Malaysia and Singapore. This new South-East Asia Commonwealth Cable (SEACOM) follows the route Singapore-Jesselton (Sabah) (January 1965), Jesselton-Hong Kong (March 1965), Hong Kong-Guam (August 1966), Guam-Madang-Cairns. When the whole system was commissioned in March 1967 a continuous submarine coaxial cable system over 23,000 miles was established.

Moreover, by agreement with U.S.A. communications operators, SEACOM can be interconnected at Guam into the Guam-Philippines-Japan cables and the Wake Island-Midway Island-Hawaii cables, thus giving Australia access into an even wider international telephone network. To accommodate this additional traffic, the capacity of the Cairns-Guam section of SEACOM was increased to 160 two-way voice circuits. The cost of the SEACOM cable was approximately $A59 million, and Australia's share in the ownership is 28%.

When this global Commonwealth coaxial cable system was completed, 86% of all Australian overseas telephone calls were connected over COMPAC and SEACOM, the remaining ones being handled over radio-telephone services.

The coastal radio service

The picture of Australia's present telecommunication capabilities would not be complete without the inclusion of the coastal radio service which is also part of the operations of the O.T.C. Its principal function is to maintain a constant watch for distress signals. In this respect, the service is closely linked with the Commonwealth Search and Rescue Organization organized by the R.A.A.F. O.T.C. is responsible for 25 coastal radio stations around Australia and Papua and New Guinea. Of these 22 are equipped for service to small ships and 10 maintain a continuous twenty-four-hour watch. Coastal radio stations also broadcast weather information at regular intervals, storm and navigation warnings and time signals, and provide a free radio-medical service to ships requiring medical advice.

Communication by radio telegraph and telephone with ships at sea in any part of the world is provided through a long distance H.F. service from O.T.C.'s radio stations in Sydney and Perth. All coastal radio stations provide a public message service for small seagoing craft of all kinds, whether for commerce or pleasure. In remote loca-

tions certain of these stations also perform a dual function in providing a radio telegraph service with extensive networks of mainland and island outpost stations and Australian bases in the Antarctic.

Satellite communications

Just when the technology of submarine coaxial cables was finally established and world-wide large capacity communication facilities had become a matter of course, a new medium of even greater capacity and potential became available: communication satellites.

The speed of the development of satellite technology and application has been spectacular. Within ten years of the launching of SPUTNIK I in 1957, about 1,000 satellites were in space. Some 5% of these were for communications, the remainder for military, meteorological, scientific research and other purposes.

The commercial potential of communication satellites, following some feasibility demonstrations between 1958 and 1960, was first shown in 1962, when the American TELSTAR I (A.T. & T. and N.A.S.A.) carried the first live telecasts between Europe and the U.S.A. as well as relaying for the first time high-quality, two-way voice, data and teleprinter signals. This and the following TELSTAR II and RELAY I and II satellites were launched into non-synchronous orbits requiring continuous tracking. By mid-1963 the first of three SYNCOM satellites was launched by N.A.S.A., demonstrating the practicability of continuous communication over almost one-third of the earth's surface from one repeater in space, 22,300 miles above the equator and rotating at fixed longitude synchronously with the earth. The later SYNCOM III was used in 1964 to televise the Tokyo Olympic Games to the U.S.A. These satellites showed that it was possible to provide virtually world-wide service with three satellites suitably placed over the Atlantic, Pacific and Indian Oceans.

It was then that many countries realized the economic and technical advantages of forming a consortium of nations to create a global satellite communication system, rather than to proceed individually or in small groups. Thus it came about that eleven governments, including Australia, signed two international agreements in Washington in August 1964. These aimed at establishing one commercial satellite system to be shared by, or available to, all nations. Through these agreements the International Telecommunications Satellite Consortium (INTELSAT) came into being. By early 1969 this had 63 member countries and governments, excluding the U.S.S.R. The first agreement set up broad principles to govern the system and created the Interim Communication Satellite Committee (I.C.S.C.), which now has 18 members representing 47 participants.

The second agreement dealt with the financial, technical, operating and contracting principles related to the ownership and function of the global system. The general manager of the O.T.C. represents Australia on the I.C.S.C. which is responsible for the design, development, construction, establishment, maintenance and operation of the space segment of the global system, comprising the satellites and associated tracking and control facilities, and is owned by INTEL-SAT.

At the time of the agreement, a sum of $US200 million was the maximum anticipated cost of the space segment and Australia's share was set at 2.5% ownership of this segment, making it the sixth largest contributor. This represented a move by Australia to enter the field of global satellite communication at the time of its inception and with a substantial financial responsibility.

When these agreements were codified, the target date for the global system was set for 1968. Since then, the system has evolved in stages which in part anticipated these goals. The first INTELSAT I ('Early Bird') satellite, providing 240 two-way voice circuits, was launched in April 1965 and was stationed over the Atlantic. Initially intended to be experimental it soon entered into commercial service, as a result of its high-quality performance and because of the increasing need for additional capacity on the Atlantic route. A further result of Early Bird's success was the decision by I.C.S.C. in 1966 to launch a second series of satellites, named INTELSAT II, as a second step towards the global system. These were initially designed to assist N.A.S.A. in its Apollo space mission, but eventually extended commercial satellite communication to more than two-thirds of the world.

The first INTELSAT II satellite stationed over the Pacific, commenced commercial service in February 1967. This was followed by one over the Atlantic in April 1967 and a second Pacific one in September 1967.

The first satellites providing a truly global telecommunication coverage are those of the INTELSAT III series, which have a capacity for 1,200 two-way voice circuits for all types of international traffic including an 'on-demand' television channel with full-colour TV performance. The first of this series to become operational was stationed over the Atlantic in December 1968, the second over the Pacific in February 1969 and drifted over the Indian Ocean in July 1969 and the third, over the Pacific, in April 1969.

When the Pacific space segment had become operational in February 1967, O.T.C. commissioned the first commercial Australian earth station at Carnarvon in Western Australia, which had been com-

pleted in 1966 at a cost of $A3 million. The station is 2½ miles from a N.A.S.A. tracking station operated by the Department of Supply on N.A.S.A.'s behalf. This is one of the key tracking stations in the manned space flight programme and thus O.T.C.'s earth station was primarily intended to provide a direct communications link between Australia and the U.S.A. in support of N.A.S.A.'s space projects. The station operates through the INTELSAT II and III satellites over the Pacific. Originally it was one of the smaller semi-transportable types, with a fully steerable 42-foot aperture antenna, but since October 1969 has been replaced by a full-scale 90-foot antenna station, the earlier one being employed as a telemetry and control station for INTELSAT satellites. Carnarvon is connected into the Australian broadband network by the Perth-Carnarvon coaxial cable.

Australia's second commercial earth station, costing approximately $A4 million, is located near Moree in New South Wales and is in INTELSAT terms a full-scale station being equipped with a 90-foot parabolic antenna.

The station is linked by a cable to the A.P.O.'s microwave terminal at Moree and thence to the O.T.C. terminal at Paddington. It is designed to handle 600 two-way voice circuits and one television channel simultaneously and to operate through any of the satellites stationed over the Pacific. It provides commercial telecommunications services between Australia and countries surrounding the Pacific including initially the U.S.A., Canada, Japan and Hong Kong.

Since December 1969 the A.P.O. has leased 24 telephone channels between Moree and Carnarvon through the Pacific INTELSAT III satellite to provide direct telephone service connections between Sydney and Perth. Thus Australia became the first country to use communication satellites for domestic telephone traffic within its continental boundaries.

In preparation for the full global system a station of similar function to that at Moree was installed near Ceduna in South Australia in 1969. This earth station located some 500 miles west of Adelaide at the edge of the Nullarbor Plain is operating through an INTELSAT III satellite above the Indian Ocean providing direct links to Britain, Europe, India, Ceylon and East Africa. Connection into the national broadband network is made via a twenty-mile spur into the trans-Australia east-west microwave link which passes through Ceduna.

With these major earth stations, and a direct ownership share and participation through INTELSAT and I.C.S.C. in the development of the global space segment, Australia's space communications capa-

bilities are well established in commercial and public international telecommunications.

Apart from the involvement through O.T.C. in international communications by participation in other international programmes in satellite research and development, Australia has acquired expertise and knowledge in this new medium which will provide the background for the eventual development of domestic, i.e., national satellite communication services.

For some years the Department of Supply, through co-operative programmes with Britain and the United States, has built up considerable expertise and capabilities in the field of space technology and associated support techniques, with substantial consequential benefits for Australian industry. The Department's Woomera range in the South Australian desert has extensive launching and tracking facilities which served as basis for Britain's defence rocket programmes in the Black Knight and Blue Streak series. Also experimental launchings of the European Launcher Development Organization (ELDO) were carried out from Woomera. Upper atmosphere research, using American and British rockets, was and is being pursued there by the Department of Physics of the University of Adelaide and other University researchers.

The Department of Supply is also responsible for the operation, largely by Australian personnel and with support from Australian industry, of tracking stations forming part of N.A.S.A.'s world-wide network. These stations are located at Carnarvon, as already mentioned, in the Woomera complex and at Tidbinbilla, Orroral Valley and Honeysuckle Creek near Canberra and they are playing an important role in the U.S.A.'s manned space flight and deep space research programmes.

In the communication sector the Department of Supply assumed responsibility for the operation on N.A.S.A.'s behalf of the Cooby Creek earth station which was one of the three earth stations in the Applications Technology Satellite (A.T.S.) project of N.A.S.A., the other two being located in the Mojave Desert, California, and at Rosman, North Carolina. Cooby Creek is some 70 miles west of Brisbane in Queensland and has been operating from 1966 to 1970.

Following an invitation by the U.S. government for direct Australian participation in the A.T.S. project the Departments of Supply, Civil Aviation, Interior (Bureau of Meteorology) and the Australian Post Office, which all have a direct interest in satellite applications, had assigned systems engineers to the Cooby Creek earth station to take part with their American colleagues in the experiments scheduled for the A.T.S. project. These began in December 1966 with the

launching of the A.T.S.1 satellite, stationed since then above the Pacific Ocean. This programme provided an excellent opportunity for the training of Australian engineers in the advanced technologies concerned. Moreover, N.A.S.A. encouraged the Australian systems engineers to propose and carry out additional experiments within the A.T.S. programme, and within the field of their specific interest.

This gave the Australian Post Office the opportunity to study satellite communication systems application in the operations of its intra-Australian communications network. A.P.O. experiments were carried out in the fields of data transmission and on the effect on automatic telephone network operations of the transmission delay inevitably associated with synchronous satellites. Of particular significance to Australia were investigations which concerned the operations of small capacity earth stations (down to single voice channel) as applicable to the solution of the outback communication problem. These investigations comprised aspects of a complete system including such problems as network organization, single channel access and interfacing and integration with the terrestrial network, as well as the study of modulation and station hardware techniques.

It is expected that satellites will become part of the intra-Australian communication system in the late 1970s, not only for trunk network operations, but perhaps also as a means of direct audio and television broadcasting for education and entertainment and as a communication facility for the isolated communities and settlers of the outback.

Business and industrial aspects

It is clear that telecommunications is a major business factor in the Australian economy. In fact the Australian Post Office alone is at present absorbing about 9% of all public investment, an amount which is about half the total investment by power and fuel authorities. The value of all A.P.O. assets used in the telecommunication service exceeded $A2,000 million in 1969, and more than $A260 million were being spent on capital investment. To meet the increasing service demands it is estimated that the annual rate of investment will probably exceed $A400 million within five years. To this should be added O.T.C.'s fixed assets, exceeding $A44 million in 1968, including the Commission's share of 28% in the SEACOM and 25% in the COMPAC cables.

In the Australian telecommunications service more than 1,500 professional engineers are employed directing the work of some 36,000 technical staff, and another 12,000 people are engaged as operating personnel involved in providing the wide range of telecommunication services.

In a business operation of this size within a population of 12 million, there are of course continuing pressures of rising costs, particularly for labour. These in turn require a continuing effort and investment in plant automation and more effective methods of manpower utilization. As a result of better plant design, more extensive use of mechanical aids, increasing use of electronic computers in planning, operations, management and business administration, the A.P.O. was able to improve the man-hour productivity of its technical staff at a rate of 4% to 5% *per annum* which compares very favourably with an overall national average of 2.5%.

Apart from equipment and other telecommunications products for the A.P.O., valued at over $A160 million in 1969, Australian telecommunication and electronics industry is supplying an increasing share of the requirements of the armed services through the Department of Supply. The Department of Civil Aviation relies heavily on Australian development and manufacturing capabilities for its instrumentation and communication facilities in air traffic control and navigation. Private intra-office telephone systems, fixed and mobile radio telephone equipment and other kinds of auxiliary electronic systems and process control equipment are being produced for use in public utilities and the oil, gas, mining and manufacturing industries.

Australian telecommunications equipment and materials are also being exported to many countries, including Britain, U.S.A., Europe, New Zealand, South America and South-East Asia. Considering the vigorous competition from equipment manufacturers overseas, the export contribution in this field, though moderate in the overall Australian export trade, shows encouraging potential for future expansion. Among the developing nations, especially in South-East Asia, Australia has assumed the role of a model and guide, having encountered and solved within its own realm many problems in telecommunications which are specific and akin to their own.

The similarity of these problems arises partly from similarities of population distributions and of geographical and climatological factors and partly from the absence of an indigenous telecommunications industry, as during the early Australian development, requiring reliance on overseas suppliers. But the latter is only successful if the particular country has itself a well-informed and effective administration which can translate the needs of the country into technologically efficient solutions.

International relations

Everything else being equal, it is conceivable that there was no need for Australia to become involved in international regulatory

activities relating to the operations and design of its internal communication systems. Its isolation and continental-national entity would suggest much greater freedom in the choice and setting of its own standards than could be tolerated elsewhere. Australia has needed, however, to employ continually the most advanced techniques, especially those applicable to long distance communications, in order to develop facilities and a communication capability commensurate with the nation's economic development and degree of affluence. On the other hand, for many years it had neither the industrial capacity nor the market potential to develop and maintain the highly specialized production facilities for this technology to a degree which would allow it to choose, from the widest possible range of alternatives, those solutions which would best suit its specific problems.

But in order to have still some degree of control over the solutions which it could adopt, two things were necessary: first to have the knowledge of what was possible and needed to solve Australia's problems and secondly to participate actively in the formulation of guidelines and standards to be adopted by the international telecommunications industry and operating bodies. The former is a matter of maintaining a well-informed and competent research and planning force within its own environment, and both these play a considerable role in A.P.O.'s activities. The second made it essential for Australia to establish and maintain its presence on international councils.

The International Telecommunications Union (I.T.U.), a specialized agency of the United Nations, but originally formed over a century ago, and its two Councils, the C.C.I.T.T. (*Conseil Consultatif International des Téléphones et Télégraphes*) and C.C.I.R. (*Conseil Consultatif International du Radio*) with their numerous study groups and working parties, is providing the vehicle for these international relations. Australia's participation in consultations of these bodies at all levels has grown substantially over the years and Australian representatives have been Chairmen of many I.T.U. study groups and working parties and have made major contributions to the solution of world-wide and national problems.

Australia is also playing an active part in the administration of the I.T.U. Since 1959 it has been a member of the Administrative Council which consists of 29 members who meet annually to control and co-ordinate the activities of the Union. In 1965, the centenary year of the I.T.U., an Australian engineer was Chairman of the Council and in 1968 a member of the A.P.O.'s Director-General's staff was elected and appointed to the post of Deputy Secretary-General of the I.T.U.

CHAPTER 16

Australian Defence Procurement

IAN BELLANY AND JAMES RICHARDSON

Introduction

This Chapter will examine Australian defence procurement, paying special attention to the more advanced weapons systems, the focus of controversy in Australia and overseas and increasingly, a subject of systematic study. The most substantial study to date, *Defence, Technology and the Western Alliance,* undertaken by the Institute for Strategic Studies,[1] is mainly concerned with Western Europe's problems, in particular Europe's chances of remaining a producer of sophisticated weaponry. But the study brings out the global context in which Australia's quite different problems arise. The rapid increase in the research and development costs of advanced weapons systems is greatly reducing the ability of European states to develop their own systems, even where the skills and technology are present to a far greater extent than in Australia. The United States, with its much larger orders, can spread the research and development costs more widely. A European government must look to extensive export sales, a precarious basis for sustaining costly defence industries. The trend, then, unless European collaboration becomes far more effective, is towards a decline in the number of states capable of producing advanced weaponry.

The extent of Australia's overseas defence purchases has come to be the major issue in the procurement debate, inevitably dominated by the lengthening shadow of the F-111. There is little awareness of the experience of weapons procurement in the post-war period as a whole, due to a lack of relevant studies and the exceptional secretiveness of Australian governments on defence matters. In the first part of the Chapter, we attempt to set out the main features of Australian defence procurement since 1950: data on costs, in particular, are incomplete and have had to be pieced together from a number of different sources. (See Tables 9 and 10 on pages 267-9.) Subsequently we comment on some of the issues currently under debate.

Some general characteristics

Despite a few notable achievements in research and development, none of the major items of current Australian defence equipment (warships, tanks and combat aircraft) is wholly Australian in origin. The extent of the Australian contribution to their design and manufacture ranges from substantial conversions carried out on the U.S. F-86 Sabre aircraft, including a partly redesigned fuselage and the substitution of a British for the original American jet engine, to the 'off-the-shelf' purchases of British tanks (Centurions) and American guided missile-armed destroyers ('Charles F. Adams' class). Between these two extremes, licence-building of British, French and Italian aircraft with small modifications to the original design and the construction by Australian shipyards of 'Daring' class destroyers and 'River' class (formerly Type 12) destroyer escorts, with small but significant design and armament departures from the original British 'Daring' and 'Type 12' classes, have since the end of the Second World War given work to Australian aircraft factories and naval shipyards.

A feature of the aircraft sector is the tendency for equipment to remain in front-line service with Australian forces for longer than in other advanced countries. Australia is one of the few countries that continues (1970) to have Canberra light bombers in its inventory of front-line combat aircraft:[2] and the subsonic Sabre fighters were removed from front-line service only in 1969. Both of these aircraft first appeared in their original design before the Korean war (the Canberra flew for the first time in 1949, the Sabre in 1948), but the Australian-built versions did not enter service until 1954 and 1956 respectively. The Canberra deliveries were spread over the period 1953-60 and the Sabre from 1954-61.[3] While the individual aircraft may not be exceptionally old, their basic design features, allowing only for subsonic speed and limited pay loads, have classified them apart from most modern military aircraft for virtually a decade (later generation aircraft, the F-104 Starfighter and F-4B Phantom, were delivered to the U.S. Air Force in 1958 and 1960 respectively).

This pattern had already been established by the predecessors of the Canberra and the Sabre. The Lincoln bomber, whose basic design dated from 1941,[4] was not entirely displaced by the Canberra until 1958, having entered service with the R.A.A.F. in 1946. The R.A.A.F. retained the Mustang propeller-driven fighter (design dating from 1941) from 1945 until the beginning of the Korean war when they were replaced on active service by Meteor jet-fighters imported from the United Kingdom.

R

Warships and army ordnance on the other hand have not, since 1950, been subject to the rapid technological changes which have overtaken military aircraft. Great advances in some areas such as nuclear power for ships and anti-tank and anti-aircraft missiles for infantrymen have by no means rendered other forms of marine propulsion obsolete or more traditional defensive artillery useless. Accordingly the Australian Army's Centurions, although bought from the United Kingdom in 1951, can be described as modern tanks; the British have only just begun to replace their own Centurions by the more modern Chieftains. Warships of the Australian navy compare well with ships of a similar class in the navies of the NATO powers. Where Australian naval equipment is deficient is in quantity rather than the quality of individual ships.

The virtual absence of any major weapons of Australian design, and the tendency to obsolescence in the case of aircraft until very recently, are interconnected with, and in part derive from, the smallness of the Australian effort on defence research and development (R and D).

If spending on the joint project with the United Kingdom at Woomera is omitted,[5] the fraction of defence spending devoted to R and D since 1950 has averaged 1% up to 1960 and 1.5% between 1960 and 1968 (see Table 10). This compares with a figure of between 10%-16% for the U.K., France and Sweden, 3% for Germany and between 0.6%-0.9% for Belgium, Italy and the Netherlands.[6] In money terms Australian defence R and D has amounted to an average of $A3.5 million *per annum* over the earlier period of our study, from 1950 to 1960, and $A9.3 million between 1960 and 1968. The size of the Australian effort can be judged when compared with the likely R and D costs of some advanced defence projects; spread over eight or ten years the production of variable geometry aircraft would require an average annual R and D investment of between $A50 and $A130 million, a ground to air missile $A40 to $A50 million and a battle tank $A4 to $A9 million.[7]

In terms of export performance the Jindivik target drone built by the Government Aircraft Factory has been the most successful product of Australian defence R and D; it has been sold in one or other of its many marks to the United Kingdom, Sweden and the United States—overseas sales totalling 213 (out of total sales of 395) by the end of 1967 had accounted for $A17 million out of total sales of $A40 million.[8] Although it is powered by an imported British jet engine (Bristol-Siddeley Viper Mk 201), its overall design is wholly Australian in conception.

The other two products of Australian defence R and D effort

during the period of our study, the Malkara anti-tank missile and the Ikara anti-submarine missile, have also enjoyed some foreign assistance, in the latter case only in the form of financial help. The Malkara,[9] which has entered service only with the British Army (in 1962), was developed in Australia with some design assistance from the U.K. Fighting Vehicle Research and Development Establishment. The Ikara[10] employs an American acoustic homing torpedo and was developed with financial assistance from the United States under the Mutual Weapons Development Agreement of 1950;[11] development of the project began in 1959 and of the $A26 million spent on the project up until 1968, $A4.4 million has been contributed by the Americans.[12] A modified Ikara system for use by the Royal Navy is being developed in Australia. By mid-1968 over $A35 million had been spent on the production and installation of Ikara in Australia's four 'River' class escorts (completed by 1967) and the three 'Charles F. Adams' class destroyers.[13]

From 1953 until 1963 annual procurement spending, including R and D expenditure but excluding Woomera spending, averaged 29% of annual defence spending; from 1963 to mid-1969 annual procurement spending has averaged 35% of annual defence expenditure. (See Table 10.) This is much lower than Sweden and the United Kingdom, which averaged between 40%-50% over both periods, but higher than Belgium and Italy, which spent between 10%-15% up to 1963 and between 15%-25% afterwards (each, however, received substantial U.S. military aid during the 1950s).[14]

Between 1953 and 1963 procurement spending was roughly stationary and was apportioned between the three services, in very round terms, at $A30 million annually to both the Army and the Navy and $A40 million to the Air Force. Over the same period the defence budget remained remarkably stationary somewhat below, and towards the end just above, $A400 million. Overseas defence procurement in the 1950s and early 1960s is difficult to estimate: for the period 1950-60 it probably amounted to about 20% of total procurement spending;[15] between 1960 and 1963 it rose to about 50%, and from 1963 to 1968 to about 54% (see Table 9). The U.K. and Sweden spend only about 10% of their procurement totals overseas, and West Germany is the only European country which has spent abroad during the period 1955-64 a sum approaching 50% of its procurement expenditure.[16] The value of orders for defence equipment placed in Australia by overseas customers (which would partly offset the foreign exchange cost of Australian procurement) has actually decreased from 14% of Australian procurement spending overseas in 1960 to 6% in 1967.[17]

Navy

In 1969 the active strength of the Royal Australian Navy (R.A.N.) was 33 vessels, excluding training and support ships.[18] Of these the flagship, the aircraft carrier *Melbourne*, the submarines and the coastal minesweepers were purchased from the United Kingdom, and the three guided-missile destroyers *Perth*, *Hobart* and *Brisbane* from the United States.

The original cost estimate for the *Melbourne*, and for the *Sydney*, an aircraft carrier of the same Majestic class (but used by the R.A.N. since 1957 as a training ship and troop carrier), was $A8.7 million each, including the cost of initial stores. Both ships were supplied under an apparently generous agreement with the British government which undertook to meet half of the construction cost (originally estimated at $A7.6 million) of both ships. The *Sydney* was accepted for service and arrived in Australia in 1949, her total cost being $A9.8 million, of which Australia paid $A5.1 million. By the time the *Melbourne* arrived in Australia in 1956 she had cost the Australian government $A11.6 million in addition to the British contribution of $A4.1 million.[19]

The increase could be put down in part to the many design changes and the eventual decision to incorporate expensive modifications not carried out on the *Sydney*, such as an angled deck and a steam catapult, which enabled her to carry faster and heavier aircraft; the long period of construction (1949-56) also meant that inflation became significant. One disadvantage of overseas procurement was commented on, viz., the weak control over cost escalation that a small customer could exert. This lesson, however, was obscured by the even more dramatic cost increases over original estimates for the 'Daring' class destroyers and anti-submarine frigates (later called 'River' class destroyer escorts) under construction in Australian shipyards. First ordered in 1946 and 1950 respectively, the estimated unit cost of the destroyers had risen from $2.8 million in 1945 to $9.6 million in 1956 and the frigates from $2.6 million in 1950 to $7.8 million[20] each in 1956.

The government was moved by these figures to the extent of asking for a complete review of shipbuilding and conversion costs to be made twice a year by the Navy and for 'significant variations' to be reported to Cabinet.[21] Costs, however, continued to rise. By 1959 the final cost of the three 'Daring' class destroyers came to $A42 million and the estimate for the four destroyer escorts was $A48 million.[22] By comparison with this $A14 million average figure, the British 'Daring' class destroyers, very similar in design, were built for a cost

of between \$A5 and \$A7 million.[23] Although it is true that the British-built ships were completed, on the average, five years before the Australian-built ones, and cost rises due to inflation must have occurred in the interim, it is surprising that the cost disparity should be as much as 100%. The slight differences in design could make only a minor contribution; armament and displacement are identical,[24] and the Australian ships are inferior in propulsion, being a few knots slower in top speed and with 700 miles less radius of action for the same amount of fuel carried.[25] Britain must have benefited from some economies of scale (eight destroyers to Australia's three), but this was limited in that no two British destroyers were built at the same yard. Perhaps more significant, naval construction was only a small fraction of the work of the British shipyards, whereas it represented a larger part of the work of the Cockatoo Island Dockyard[26] in Sydney and the whole of the construction at H.M.A. Naval Dockyard, Williamstown; hence Australia's overhead charges would be much higher.

In recent years two important technological developments have greatly added to the usefulness and cost of destroyers and frigates: anti-aircraft and anti-submarine missile systems. The Australian-built escorts are equipped with the Australian 'Ikara' anti-submarine system and the British 'Seacat' ship-to-air missile system. The 'Charles F. Adams' class destroyers purchased from the United States[27] are fitted with the 'Ikara' and the American 'Tartar' anti-aircraft (ship-to-air) missile system. Although the precise cost of the 'Charles F. Adams' destroyers is difficult to ascertain, out of a total cost of about \$A40 million per ship between \$A25 and \$A30 million is taken up by the cost of the missiles and associated radars.[28]

The other major naval purchase overseas since 1963 has been the four 'Oberon' class conventional submarines, three of which had been delivered by mid-1969 at a cost of \$A10 million each: submarine building has never been attempted by Australian shipyards. They have been able, however, to meet some of the Navy's less ambitious requirements; orders for 20 Australian-designed patrol boats at a total cost of \$A15 million[29] have been placed with two commercial shipyards in Queensland and all had been delivered by 1970. The destroyer tender *Stalwart* was designed and built in Australia for \$A16 million and delivered in 1968.[30] The aircraft carrier *Melbourne* underwent an extensive refit in 1968 by H.M.A. Naval Dockyard, Sydney, at an estimated cost of \$A7.3 million, mainly to allow her to operate with new carrier aircraft.

The aircraft of the Fleet Air Arm unlike those of the R.A.A.F. have, with the exception of six Mk34 Vampires produced in Aus-

tralia for the R.A.N. by Hawker de Havilland in the late 1950s, always been purchased directly from overseas but they have suffered from the same tendency to have their operational lives extended up to the point of obsolescence. The first aircraft flying off the *Sydney* were the 'Firefly' and 'Sea Fury' both of U.K. Second World War design; they were in service from 1949 to 1956, when they were replaced by 39 Sea Venom (F(AW)Mk 21) and 36 Gannet (AS Mk 4) aircraft bought from the U.K. at a total cost of about $A20 million to fly off the *Melbourne* until 1968.[31] The Sea Venom ceased front-line operation with the Royal Navy in 1961 and the Gannet[32] was replaced in the Royal Navy by helicopters during the late 1950s.

The government's hesitation about the future of the Fleet Air Arm contributed to this obsolescence. Its disbandment was announced in 1959 to take place when the *Melbourne* and her aircraft would need refit and refurbishment (then expected in mid-1963); its partial reprieve was won in 1961 when an anti-submarine helicopter carrying role was suggested[33] and full reprieve came in two stages in 1964 when fourteen anti-submarine 'Trackers' were ordered from the U.S., followed in 1965 by eight 'Skyhawk' attack aircraft. These were delivered in 1967 at a cost of $A36.5 million and $A17 million respectively.[34]

There has been no clear trend in Australian naval procurement policy over the period, except perhaps a veering away from Australian shipyards to overseas yards in the placing of orders for the more complex warships. The high excess costs to be borne, as in the case of the 'Daring' class destroyers and anti-submarine frigates, and the slowness of construction,[35] together with the increasing sophistication of certain naval weapons-systems, have worked against the advantages usually seen in home procurement. The trend towards standardization with the U.S. has not extended to submarines and helicopters.

The high costs of Australian shipbuilding, reflected in the level of protection of the commercial industry,[36] would seem to place limits upon the ability of Australian shipyards to meet future naval requirements for the R.A.N., or for export purposes. The patrol boats ordered in 1965 by the R.A.N. from two Queensland shipyards are, however, an exception to this melancholy rule; they are as cheap or cheaper than near-equivalents built overseas and are being constructed at a fairly rapid rate. Fairly good export opportunities are open for ships of this kind as many countries of small means build their navies around patrol boats.[37]

A limited naval shipbuilding programme of small displacement craft may offer the best course for Australian shipyards; new depart-

ures in warship hull design, the first for almost 50 years, the hover-craft and hydrofoil principles, are at present generally speaking suited only for light craft. Concentration on this sector would not cut off Australian yards from these new techniques. Certainly the projected Australian-designed destroyer foreshadowed in the 1969 defence budget will severely test Australia's capacity to construct major warships at tolerable cost.

Army

In terms of expenditure on large and glamorous items of defence equipment the army is in most countries the Cinderella of the services; the Australian Army is no exception. The pace of technological change on the battlefield (except, of course, in communications) has been far slower than the changes in the air and even at sea: a modern tank, for example, is not so very different from a Second World War tank either in appearance or cost. This slowness of technological change has had two effects on the pattern of Army procurement. Equipment has become obsolescent only very slowly and replacement therefore has been infrequent; and much of the Army's needs are capable of being met from national resources.[38]

The consequences of this have been that from 1958 to 1963 no item of major equipment was procured for the Army from overseas sources and between 1963 and 1968 the total value of the five most costly overseas orders for the Army (about $A30 million) was less than the cost of one 'Charles F. Adams' destroyer.[39] Accordingly in recent years the Army has drawn less from the U.S. credits than either of the other two services, (see Table 9). Outside of procurement spending its foreign exchange requirements are of course large; keeping Australian army units in Vietnam, Malaysia and Singapore accounted for $A34 million in 1967-68,[40] a good proportion of which must have been in foreign currency.

The principal armour of the Australian Army consists of about 120 British Centurion tanks purchased between 1950 and 1959 at an average cost of about $A100,000 each, and the American armoured tracked troop carrier (M113A1), orders for several hundred of which have been placed since 1964 at a cost of about $A30,000 each;[41] up to 1968 $A8.9 million had been spent. Where international comparisons can be made the Australian Army does not seem particularly deficient in quantity of armour. The Canadian Army, with a manpower level of 41,500 men, which is close to the Australian Army of 45,400 men, has a similar inventory of armour.[42]

Australian artillery and guided missile strength includes the air-transportable 'pack' 105 mm howitzer, designed in Italy and adopted

251

by several NATO countries, including the U.K.; it was issued to the Army beginning in 1962, two years after it entered service with the British Army. Total spending on the 'pack' howitzer has been between $A1 and $A2 million. The lack of heavier artillery is a long-standing Army grievance, and could be a serious constraint in any situation where the Army could not, as in Vietnam, call on allied artillery support.

The Army possesses no offensive missiles, i.e. missiles which could participate in an artillery barrage. It possesses, however, an anti-tank missile, the French Entac, and has on order an anti-aircraft missile, the American Redeye, both of which are lightweight weapons and launchable by infantry. The Australian-developed anti-tank missile, the Malkara, was designed specifically for the British Army. It is a good deal heavier than the Entac and requires a one-ton truck for transport and launching; it entered service with the British Army in 1962 and began to be replaced by the British-developed Swingfire in 1967. The cost of the Malkara to the British appears to have been quite low, comparing favourably with the much lighter but equally effective Vigilant missile which entered service with the British in 1963 at a cost of $A1,200 per missile.[43]

The Entac, which is similar to the Vigilant and was developed about the same time, supplements the Army's 84 mm Carl Gustav anti-tank gun which is of Swedish origin. Both were procured during the period 1963-68 at a total cost of over $A0.5 million for each order.[44]

One advantage of the Entac over the Vigilant to Australia is that it is also in service with the American army; the Vigilant has been sold outside the U.K. only to Finland.

The Redeye was ordered from the United States over the same period at a cost of more than $A0.5 million;[45] Australia and Switzerland seem to be the only countries to possess this missile outside the United States where it first entered service in 1966-67.

The Australian Army has the NATO standard rifle, the Belgian FN 7.62 mm (called L1A1 in Australia), which was manufactured in Australia to U.K. design drawings by the government-owned Small Arms Factory at Lithgow (N.S.W.), beginning in 1958.[46] Its ammunition is made at the government-owned Footscray (Victoria) Ammunition Factory. Australia manufactures a variety of other small arms and ammunition.

The electronics requirements of the Army are relatively modest and are limited to radio equipment and tactical radar equipment much of which in recent years has been procured overseas,[47] although more recently still successful attempts have been made by

the Department of Supply to encourage local production of a wide range of components,[48] and items such as the PRC-F1 portable two-way communications set.

Next to the M113A1 armoured troop carriers the biggest overseas Army procurement orders since 1958 have been placed for Bell helicopters (types 47G381 and 47G2) from the United States and Pilatus Porter light aircraft from Switzerland at a total expected cost of $A6.2 million and $A3.7 million respectively.[49] The total number of these light helicopters so far in service with the Army is about 50 and the first four Pilatus light aircraft entered service in 1967-68.[50]

Looked at in the round the pattern of procurement for the Australian Army is notable for three things; the small amount of money spent overseas compared to the other services, the low level of participation by Australian private industry in meeting Army requirements, and the trend towards standardization of equipment with that of the armies of at least some allied countries.

The first of these is not peculiar to Australia. Industrial countries everywhere tend to manufacture their own light and medium arms and as much as possible of their ammunition requirements, the total value of which usually forms a large part of army procurement budgets.

In view of the size of the Australian motor-vehicle industry (340,000 vehicles excluding trucks, produced in 1966-67), it is at first sight surprising that it participates so little in supplying equipment to the armed forces, and to the Army in particular. The private vehicle industry in Italy for example builds tanks and M113A armoured personnel carriers for the Italian army and the Dutch vehicle industry has designed and built personnel carriers for the Dutch army.[51] Part of the reason may lie in the relative smallness of potential Army orders, but this has not deterred the International Harvester Company from supplying a range of trucks to Army specification.[52] The foreign ownership of the entire Australian vehicle industry may be another influential factor.

According to the 1965 *Defence Report* a major requirement of Army equipment is that it should be standardized or at least compatible with that of Australia's allies. Australia entered into a 'Basic Standardisation Agreement' with the U.K., the United States, Canada and New Zealand in 1963;[53] seldom since then has Australia ordered Army equipment which is not also in service with either or both the British and Americans. While this is partly a natural consequence of the Australian tendency to order from British or American suppliers and the tendency of NATO members in recent years towards standardization in small arms and artillery amongst them-

selves, the production of the Australian-designed 9 mm sub-machine gun was held up (somewhat belatedly) for design changes to meet standardization needs.[54]

It is possible that the Army may in future obtain an even larger fraction of its procurement needs inside Australia. On the whole, however, it seems reasonable to assume that any government effort to increase home procurement is likely to be directed more towards the other two services which are far greater consumers of foreign exchange and which, in recent years, have been buying 50% or more of their equipment overseas.

Air Force

The combat aircraft of the Australian Air Force included in 1969 40 Canberra BMk20 light jet bombers, 100 Mirage III-0 jet fighters and 60 Sabre (Commonwealth) jet fighters, together with 10 P-3B Orion anti-submarine 'search and strike' aircraft and 12 P-2H Neptune anti-submarine and anti-shipping patrol bombers. Only one squadron of Canberras remained in the front-line force and the Sabres had been replaced as front-line aircraft by Mirages. In addition it possessed 51 Macchi Mb326 jet trainers, 49 transport aircraft, C-130 Hercules and CV-2B Caribou, and 2 UY-1B Iroquois helicopter squadrons.[55]

The Canberra, Sabre, Mirage and Macchi were built in Australia under licence from their original manufacturers, with different degrees of design modification and with different proportions of locally manufactured to imported components.

Two aircraft factories, the government-owned Government Aircraft Factory (G.A.F.) and the privately owned Commonwealth Aircraft Corporation (C.A.C.),[56] have been responsible for all four production programmes. The Hawker de Havilland Company, a wholly owned Australian subsidiary of the British Hawker Siddeley Group, is a major sub-contractor for the production of the Macchi trainer. Earlier, Hawker de Havilland built the Vampire jet: 80 fighters were built between 1948 and 1953, and 109 trainers when production ceased in 1961.[57]

Since 1950 new orders placed inside Australia for military aircraft have been apportioned almost equally between the G.A.F. and the C.A.C., both of which companies are dependent upon government contracts, with as much regard for the preservation in being of each company as for its suitability as a contractor: the G.A.F. has tended to specialize in airframe construction and testing, the C.A.C. in engine production.

The Canberra bomber was built by the G.A.F. over the period 1950-58 under licence from the original maufacturers, the English Electric Company: in all 48 were built,[58] with little departure from the original English design, except for changes to the cockpit interior.[59] Tools and jigs were produced substantially in Australia, and body and wing components were manufactured locally. The Chrysler motor works of Adelaide made sheet metal pressed parts and the workshops of both South Australian and N.S.W. government railways also rendered assistance.[60]

The engines (Rolls-Royce Avon 111), and those of the Sabre which are closely similar but not identical (Avon 20s and later Avon 26s), were built by the C.A.C., with some parts imported, but at a cost well in excess of that of importing complete engines from the U.K.[61]

The building rate was slow: the last aircraft was completed only three years before the British removed the Canberra from the R.A.F. Bomber Command; and the cost of the aircraft was rather high in spite of the low production rate.[62] The most precise official estimate put the average cost per aircraft at $A950,000.[63] The British sold six of a later version of the Canberra, the B(1)12, to Peru in 1968 for $US4.8 million[64] or $A720,000 per aircraft; the cost of a British-produced Canberra in 1953 was variously reported to be $A400,000 and $A500,000.[65]

Orders for the Sabre were placed with the C.A.C. in 1951. The Australian-built Sabre was substantially different in design from the original North American aircraft in that a Rolls-Royce Avon engine was substituted for the General Electric (J47-G6-27), and more powerful armament was installed.[66] Tools and jigs and large quantities of airframe components were, however, purchased directly from the American manufacturers.

A total of 112 Sabres were built in Australia in three batches, each batch with slightly different design details initially but later all aircraft were standardized to the final mark, Mk 32. Uncertainty and hesitation over the choice of an aircraft to succeed the Sabre, which was not resolved until 1960, were largely responsible for the spinning out of the Sabre production until 1961.

The Sabre represents the peak of participation by Australian industry in the design of a military aircraft since the end of the Second World War. The design modifications met their limited objectives, and the C.A.C. Sabre is faster (but still subsonic), and more heavily armed than the American original. But in return for these gains, sacrifices were made both in cost and in speed of entering service. An official estimate of cost made in 1956 (when about 60 Sabres had been produced) was $A510,000 each,[67] which according to an opposi-

tion spokesman was $A160,000 more than the cost of buying the admittedly inferior standard Sabre abroad.

When the C.A.C. Sabre entered service with the R.A.A.F. in 1956, the supersonic version, the Supersabre, had already been in service with the U.S.A.F. for three years. This slowness of Australian aircraft production was particularly disadvantageous in the circumstances of the 1950s: military aircraft were evolving very rapidly, supersonic aircraft, particularly fighters, rendered subsonic types such as the Sabre obsolete in some respects almost overnight; the introduction of supersonic interceptor aircraft and surface-to-air missiles (S.A.M.s) over the same period much reduced the efficacy of subsonic medium bombers such as the Canberra.[68] It is arguable that in the light of the defence commitments of the R.A.A.F. this obsolescence could be tolerated: the British, alongside whom the R.A.A.F. operated in Malaysia and Singapore, retained their subsonic fighters, Gloster Javelins, in Malaysia until 1966. But this meant that the R.A.A.F.'s role would be severely limited in any war where the opponent was supplied with supersonic aircraft.

As Sabre production was wound down in 1961, preparations began for production under licence of the French Dassault Mirage III-0 supersonic fighter aircraft for which the G.A.F. was appointed the prime contractor and overseeing body, with C.A.C. a major subcontractor. It is difficult to establish how much of the Mirage engine and body components are actually made, as against merely assembled, in Australia. The C.A.C. 'produces' the engine, wings, fins and tail assembly and G.A.F. 'produces' the fuselage, but the foreign exchange cost of the 100 Mirages is officially estimated as $A193.7 million,[69] which probably includes the cost of the Matra R530 air-to-air missile, some $A20 million.[70] The total cost of the project, excluding the missile, is estimated at $A246 million, and expenditure by the Department of Supply within Australia was $A74.6 million up to June 1968.[71] It is claimed that 90% of the Mirage engine, by value, is locally manufactured, which rather suggests that most of the rest of the aircraft must be merely assembled. The extent of Australia's dependence on French suppliers has been little recognized.

The Macchi trainers, however, which are simpler aircraft than the Mirage, appear to have a higher Australian-produced content; out of a total estimated cost of $A64.7 million for 107 aircraft only $A21.6 million worth of components and completed aircraft were imported from the Italian mother factory.[72] Orders were placed with the C.A.C. in 1965 for a total of 97 Macchi to be completed in three batches, one of 75, the others of twelve and ten in the period 1965-71,

these last ten for the R.A.N. (the first twelve were wholly imported from Italy).[73]

The only aircraft to be built by Australian industry entirely to Australian specifications since the Second World War were the Winjeel trainer and the Jindivik target drone; the Winjeel was built by the C.A.C. from 1955 to 1958. The Jindivik, built by the G.A.F., was designed in 1948, first flew in 1952, and has been in continuous production since then: it is the sole export of the Australian aircraft industry since its founding in 1936.[74]

With the order of the F-111C (October 1963) Australia for the first time committed itself to purchase an aircraft in the forefront of advanced technology: there could be no danger of early obsolescence, but Australia has had the misfortune to be initiated into the world of escalating R and D costs at a time when further advances in aircraft have become more difficult and uncertain, as well as more costly than ever before. This is not the place to argue whether the government's bold risk—far bolder than it realized—had any justification, though much of the subsequent difficulty was due to the haste with which the government entered into the contract. But several aspects of the decision are relevant to this study.

The government had been under heavy criticism for its failure to replace the Canberras, especially after Indonesia had received Badger medium bombers from the Soviet Union in 1961. The announcement of the F-111 order and the American offer (not taken up) to supply B-47s as an interim measure, turned a potential electoral liability into an asset, especially when the government announced the 'bargain' price of $A112 million after a price of $A200 million had been widely rumoured. There was a striking absence of public discussion of the implications of rising costs and technological complexity, or of Australia's need for this rather limited form of 'deterrent'.

The lack of informed public debate saved the government's cost claims from any searching scrutiny. A year before the F-111 order, the journal *Aircraft* had estimated that a new bomber would cost at least $A5 million, and that two squadrons of the A3J Vigilante, the strike aircraft most widely mentioned, would cost $A220 million, an estimate of the 'programme cost' of the aircraft, including a full stock of spares.[75] The $A112 million for two squadrons of F-111, it was revealed much later, included only one year's spares.[76] $A112 million was not unreasonable in relation to the American estimates at that time ($US4.6 million per aircraft, a little less than the $US5.2 million for the Australian aircraft).[77] Since a large part of the subsequent cost 'escalation' represents the cost of a long-term inventory of spares, the basic aircraft cost having increased by about one-third, a realistic

257

estimate of the 'programme cost' in 1963 would have led to a figure much closer to the $A220 million suggested in *Aircraft* in 1962, and might well have provoked discussion of the merits of purchasing a Canberra replacement at such a cost. The 1968 cost estimate of $A267 ($US300 million) was made up as follows: aircraft, $US143 million; changes ordered by the R.A.A.F., $US3 million; supporting equipment and spares, $US120 million; conversion of six aircraft for reconnaissance, $US34 million.[78]

The 1969 cost estimate of $A299 million, announced in Parliament on 23 September, when Australia reaffirmed its intention to purchase the aircraft after a period of uncertainty, included a further $A32 million, essentially a rise in the basic aircraft price, attributed to rises in the cost of materials and labour and modifications accepted by Australia, or especially required for the Australian version.

In addition to the F-111, small numbers of specialized aircraft and missiles have been purchased overseas; the maritime aircraft Orion and Neptune have been bought from the United States at a total estimated cost of $A59.3 million and $A20.5 million respectively; transport aircraft and helicopters have been bought from the United States and Canada for a total cost of around $A100 million between 1958 and 1968.[79]

In addition one squadron of Bloodhound MkI surface-to-air missiles was purchased from the U.K., between 1959 and 1962 at a cost of $A5.2 million, and Sidewinder air-to-air missiles were procured from the United States, beginning in 1959, to arm the C.A.C. Sabre, at a cost probably not much in excess of $A1 million.

There are several noteworthy characteristics of aircraft procurement policies over the period. First is the continuing lack of standardization, even after a major policy statement of April 1957 calling for standardization as far as possible with the U.S.[80] Secondly, except where very small numbers are involved, combat aircraft have been built in Australia under licence in preference to purchase overseas. The trend since the Second World War, culminating in the Mirage, has, however, been toward increasing overseas supplies of key components, as aircraft become more complex and the importance of electronic systems, for example, increases. This trend clearly goes a long way toward undermining one of the traditional arguments for local defence industries, viz., that they can meet future requirements for spare parts, which would be especially important if the supplier withdrew the item from service while Australia wished to maintain it.[81]

It is clear that the manufacture and even the assembly of aircraft in Australia carry penalties of cost and delays in production. The available data do not permit a reliable estimate of the cost penalty, partly

because of incompleteness but mainly because it is seldom made clear, in Australian or overseas data, how much of any given figure refers to spares and related items over and above the basic cost of the aircraft. There are several reasons, however, why Australian costs might be expected to be relatively high. These include the high cost of locally produced materials and components, high wages (relative to the U.K., but not the U.S.), high overhead costs on plant designed to enable the rate of production to be expanded in an emergency, the smallness of the companies and their shelter from competition. Experience suggests that unit costs in Australia in the case of a production run of 200 would be about 60% of those in a production run of 50.[82]

Despite a number of parliamentary denials of delays in the production of the Canberra and Sabre, Prime Minister Menzies remarked in 1955 that 'on the production rate and cost of producing planes in Australia we would all be getting pretty elderly by the time we got a first-class Air Force'.[83] A clearer picture emerged from the evidence of Sir Frederick Shedden, Secretary of the Department of Defence, to the Public Accounts Committee in 1956:[84] one of the locally produced aircraft initially fell considerably behind schedule, but eventually the planned rate of production was nearly achieved, a pattern which was to be reproduced in the case of the Mirage.[85]

What scope might the future offer for a small-scale military aircraft industry like the Australian? A merger of aircraft companies may improve the efficiency of licence-built production[86] in the future, perhaps to the extent of making exports possible. Australian-designed projects would still have to be on a small scale to match the small Australian R and D capacity; a development of the Jindivik drone to provide a cruise missile is one possibility; a similar conversion has been done by the French who have modified the Nord CT20 target drone to become a surface-to-sea and sea-to-sea missile. The possibility of co-operative projects with allied or friendly countries, with the benefits of shared R and D costs, and larger markets, could also be explored.

Discontinuities

Two principal criticisms have been levelled at Australia's procurement policies. First, they are criticized for their haphazardness, their apparently stop-gap character, their neglect of long-term planning, manifested in delays in reaching and implementing decisions, in sudden reversals of policy, and failure to achieve stated policy goals. These deficiencies are frequently attributed to faulty organization—an old-fashioned defence structure which magnified inter-service

rivalries while subjecting the services to arbitrary financial controls, arbitrary in the sense that they were not related to the consideration of strategic options, and thus prevented the effective co-ordination of defence policy.[87] Secondly, throughout the period of Liberal rule, but more especially in the defence build-up of the 1960s, Labor spokesmen in particular have criticized the extent of overseas procurement.

There is no lack of examples of delays and reversals of policy, but whether these are correctly attributed to faulty organization is more debatable. A few examples may bring out the diversity of problems associated with policy discontinuities; the delays in aircraft production seem to reflect mainly the inevitable difficulties of a small industry in meeting technological advance, and the deliberate stretching out of production in order to keep the industry alive.

Delays in decision-making, notably on replacements for the Sabre and Canberra, are of greater interest. Official references to the replacements began as early in 1954, and the first of four missions to evaluate new aircraft visited the U.S. and the U.K. the following year. By 1957 the government had given many indications that it would acquire the Starfighter, F-104, as a successor to the Sabre.[88] There were reported disagreements between the R.A.A.F. and the aircraft industry on whether the F-104, like the Sabre, should be modified to be fitted with a Rolls-Royce engine.[89] In his defence statement of 4 April 1957 Prime Minister Menzies said that:

> Our present planning and preparations are proceeding on the basis of an operational contribution to allied strategy of highly trained men armed with the most modern conventional weapons and equipment.

The Air Force was to be equipped with 'an aircraft equivalent in performance to that of the Lockheed F-104'.[90]

The decision, announced in September 1957, not to acquire the F-104 was justified mainly on the ground that it was too specialized for the R.A.A.F. (a rather unconvincing argument in view of the diversity of roles it has been assigned in Europe, and one which surely applied equally to the Mirage, let alone the F-111). But irrespective of the merits of the decision, it reversed the stated policy of equipping the Australian forces with the most modern weapons.

The F-104 decision was the most remarkable instance of changes in apparent governmental intentions and discontinuity between the stated aim of defence policy and the weapons actually provided.[91] Resounding declarations of strategic purpose counted for little against the cost, which must have involved the breaching of the $A400 million ceiling on the defence budget. It is difficult to avoid the conclusion that this was the decisive consideration.

Furthermore, the government failed to fulfil even a modest version of its programme (establishing a professional force capable of rapid deployment overseas, even if lacking the more advanced air support) as the need to introduce conscription to meet the Malaysian and Vietnam emergencies was to demonstrate. The weaknesses of the procurement policies of the later 1950s were not *sui generis*, but were part of the wider failure to think through to a consistent conception of the functions of the Australian forces, and to act on such a conception. Questions of organization were secondary. There is no reason, for example, to attribute changes of mind over the F-104 to organizational weaknesses and, more generally, there is no reason to suppose that the government was unaware of the deficiencies which kept the forces below strength and operational readiness, or of service proposals to remedy the latter.[92] Rather it was prepared to tolerate deficiencies of a kind which had been normal in peacetime in the past, but were no longer normal elsewhere with the heavy defence spending of the present.

Australian versus overseas procurement

The domestic defence industry was vital to Australia in the Second World War, since not even the United States was in a position to give a high priority to supplying Australia. It was the policy of the post-war Labor government, followed by the Liberal governments, to maintain the nucleus of a naval shipbuilding and military aircraft industry which could be expanded in an emergency. To an increasing extent, however, the more sophisticated items have been purchased overseas. In the five years 1962-63 to 1966-67, orders placed overseas amounted to $A1,040 million, nearly 50% more than orders placed in Australia ($A713 million).[93]

The Labor Party has traditionally been critical of overseas defence procurement and has called for support for the local defence industries, increasingly so with the recent high import levels. In reply, the government argued that many weapons either could not be produced in Australia, or could be produced only with too great a delay or at undue cost, e.g. when only small numbers of an item are required. There has recently been a tendency, however, for the positions of government and opposition spokesmen to converge. Deputy Labor Leader Lance Barnard has formulated a more closely reasoned version of the traditional Labor position, and Defence Minister Allen Fairhall in many speeches in 1968-69 spelled out a new approach aimed at encouraging greater local procurement and Australian participation through subcontracting in overseas weapons projects.

Mr Barnard argues for a policy of stimulating Australian defence

S

industry through an upgrading of defence R and D, which was relatively high under the five-year plan of the post-war Labor government (13.5% of the defence budget, admittedly mostly for Woomera). Such a policy should not be over-ambitious but rather 'a modest programme limited essentially to Australian tactical requirements'.[94] Even though Australia could not hope to produce the most complex weapons systems, it should make subsystems wherever possible, and should insist on offset arrangements in other cases.

The new approach formulated by Mr Fairhall, similar in outline, was more fully developed, especially with regard to the use of defence contracts as an incentive to raise the technological and managerial level of Australian industry.[95] The new approach has four aspects. First, local procurement is to be encouraged directly by greater liaison with industry in the formulation of equipment plans. One of the tasks of the new Defence Science organization in the Defence Department is to work with the Department of Supply and the services to this end.[96] A \$A600,000 contract with Amalgamated Wireless (Australasia) Ltd. for the development of micro-electronic technology, in May 1968, pointed to a new willingness—although on a limited scale—to support industrial research relevant to defence. In March 1969 a Defence Industrial Committee, with senior business and official membership, was established with wide terms of reference, including the power to recommend industrial participation in research, development and production for overseas as well as Australian defence needs and to advise on all aspects of Australian as against overseas procurement.[97]

Secondly, Australia will seek offset arrangements as part of any future major overseas procurement purchases. On one occasion this was formulated in terms of local projects equal to the foreign-exchange costs of the overseas purchase, but typically, and more realistically, the amount of the offset has been left unspecified. This general policy brings Australia into line with most major arms purchasers.

Thirdly, offset is envisaged largely in terms of subcontracting either within the project ordered by Australia or any other defence project in which Australian industry can supply relevant items. This broadening of the field of possible offset projects has the effect of establishing defence subcontracting as an area of industrial opportunity in its own right, especially in view of the widely reported attitude of American firms—a willingness to make use of comparative cost advantages wherever they find them, but reluctance to make any special provision for any particular overseas suppliers.[98]

Fourthly, the strands of the 'Fairhall doctrine' are drawn together in the suggestion that governmental stimulus (e.g. through research

and development projects), competition for subcontracts in the very demanding American environment, and the incentive of wider home and export markets may induce Australian firms to advance more rapidly, technologically and managerially. The indications are that Mr Fairhall's successor as Defence Minister, Mr Malcolm Fraser, will seek to maintain the same general policy towards procurement.

The problems for the new policy are not far to seek. The most basic issue is whether Australian industry has sufficient resources or sophistication to play the role assigned to it, except on a very modest scale. If Western Europe is preoccupied with the 'technology gap', what prospect has Australia of bridging it? Some indication of Australia's position with respect to advanced technology is given by comparative data for research and development carried out by business enterprises (as distinct from defence R and D discussed earlier). For Australia, this has recently been estimated as $A35 million *per annum*, or 0.15% of the G.N.P.[99] For certain O.E.C.D. members closest to Australia in G.N.P., industrial R and D for 1963 was as follows (in $US):[100]

Belgium	$ 95 million	(0.68% G.N.P.)
Canada	$212 million	(0.53% G.N.P.)
Netherlands	$195 million	(1.34% G.N.P.)
Sweden	$175 million	(1.09% G.N.P.)

Data for the electronics industry, the key industry for advanced weapons systems, are not available, but some impression of Australia's position may be gained by comparing Australia's estimated $A5.6 million R and D expenditure in the electronic and light electrical field in 1967, with Belgium's $A14.4 million and Sweden's $A38.2 million expenditure on R and D in the electrical machinery and apparatus field in 1963.[101]

Such data serve to suggest how far Australian industry falls short of the capacity to develop advanced weapons systems, and throw some light on the trend, observed above, towards an increased import content in Australian-produced items such as aircraft. They suggest probable limits to the scope for subcontracting in major projects. It seems likely, however, that Australia could produce a wider range of systems, or at least subsystems, under licence, even in the electronic field. Several of the smaller European countries took part in the production under licence of Hawk, Sidewinder and Bullpup missiles, some with a smaller industrial base than Australia.[102]

Industrial spokesmen at times make large claims on behalf of Australian industry. For example, a spokesman for an electronics firm stated in 1965 that local industry could supply 75% of Australia's

needs in this field.[103] This is unlikely, bearing in mind the heavy cost of electronics in the most expensive recent purchases—the Mirage, the F-111 and the 'Charles F Adams' destroyers, all close to the frontier of development in avionics, control and guidance systems. A more plausible view is that of Alex Hunter:

> One is forced to conclude that the further Australian defence moves into electronically sophisticated weaponry, radar detection and communications, the less the contribution local industry can make to these important, but expensive innovations.[104]

While this suggests major limits to Australia's defence potential, it does not rule out the possibility of offset arrangements of a more modest kind, or indeed the gradual diversification of Australian defence industry within these limits. In relation to the United States labour costs in the construction of aircraft components are in Australia's favour. Given all the other variables likely to enter into the decisions of an American firm, these are not often likely to be decisive except where there is the added incentive of a major sale.

Australia's chances of obtaining offset or licence arrangements, on the other hand, will be related to the extent of competition to supply the item in question, as may be illustrated from the new procurement decisions announced in March 1970. The $A23 million order for a light helicopter would depend, it was stated, on the prospects for local manufacture and commercial sales: either of two types (the Bell OH 58A or the Westland-Sud SA 341) was technically satisfactory.[105] On the other hand, the order for two additional submarines ($A37 million) could scarcely have been other than for the existing type, the U.K. Oberon class which cannot be constructed in Australia, giving little leverage for offset negotiations.

It is too early to measure the new policy against the yardstick of actual experience. There has been a hiatus in major defence orders for several years, a consequence of the earlier heavy purchasing and, possibly, delays imposed by the new organization and planning procedures. Precedents have been made in subcontracting, so far on a very small scale.[106] Two Australian-based firms, Philips Industries and Hawker de Havilland, have entered into arrangements with the government of Singapore, the former to manage a new electronics company, the latter to undertake the maintenance of Singapore's military aircraft, thus pointing to a new means by which the defence industries may contribute to the balance of payments.[107]

In the period since the Second World War the *rationale* for Australian defence industry has changed fundamentally, and now calls for rethinking. Technological change has ruled out the degree of self-

sufficiency that was possible, and necessary, during the Second World War, and a protracted non-nuclear war of that nature now seems a remote contingency. A danger which has become evident in the 1960s, however, is that foreign arms suppliers may exploit a purchaser's need for spare parts, ammunition or specialized maintenance equipment, to control the policy of dependent countries—a danger that has been dramatized by the India-Pakistan war of 1965 and Franco-Israeli relations. Australia has been conscious of this danger in the case of the Mirage, and has even met with attempts by Switzerland to restrict the use of the Pilatus Porter light aircraft in Vietnam. This danger can be reduced, but never wholly eliminated, by acquiring large stocks of spares and maintenance and repair facilities: combat use of aircraft, for example, will use up spares more rapidly than peacetime use. Australia tends for logistic reasons to hold unusually large stocks of spares. But the cost of wartime stocks (which could be only imperfectly estimated) would place too heavy a burden on defence budgets. In practice these considerations may lead Australia to rely more heavily on the United States for advanced weapons, and certainly to avoid such unpredictable suppliers as France. It is difficult to imagine Australia's becoming involved in any war unless it has the general support of the United States. Logistic dependence is secondary to broader strategic dependence.

If self-sufficiency is an unrealistic objective, what are the advantages of Australian defence production? The most obvious objective is to reduce the balance of payments cost of defence procurement. This has to be formulated with some care, since there is a good *prima facie* case for extensive defence imports. Advanced equipment, requiring heavy R and D investment and technologies scarcely present in Australia, is a field in which comparative costs strongly favour overseas suppliers, as some of the earlier examples indicate. There is little to be said for paying very high costs to produce part of an advanced weapons system, if vital components must still come from overseas. It is sound on broad strategic grounds, however, to incur some extra costs for local production (at least up to the level of protection of comparable civilian industry). The trade balance will not always be favourable, and defence purchases, being one of the imports directly in the hands of the government, are likely to suffer in times of balance of payments difficulties, especially if they constitute a very large item. Present policies, provided they are implemented effectively, are well directed towards the general aim of maximizing local production within the scope of Australia's present industrial technology.

The second advantage of local defence production would be its

influence as a stimulus to Australian industry. Provided the aspirations here remain realistic, there is everything to be said for a policy which presses industry to become more competitive instead of having recourse to tariff protection. Perhaps the main question to be raised in this context is whether the government should not be envisaging rather more direct intervention to upgrade industry's potential to compete more effectively for subcontracts and exports. The $A600,000 contract for microelectronics stands alone as an example of what might be involved.

The period studied here falls naturally into three phases. In the first, up till the early 1960s, defence procurement was constrained by the $A400 million budget ceiling, which in the early 1950s appeared sufficient for modest peacetime and small-war forces but by the early 1960s fell far short of this. In the heightened tension of the mid-1960s the Government responded to the new technological environment by large-scale, hasty and at times ill-judged overseas purchases. In the breathing-space at the end of the decade, no longer constrained by an unchanging budget ceiling or pressure for an immediate build-up, it has formulated a general policy and reorganized the procurement process with a view to achieving more integrated weapons choices and a much greater Australian content. The new policies appear to be soundly conceived but geography and technology render Australia's procurement choices more difficult than those, for example, of a small European state. Whether Australia rises to the challenge or succumbs to the difficulties will depend in a large measure on the skill of its political leaders, but certainly it will not be assisted by turning a blind eye on the difficulties.

TABLE 9

Overseas Spending*

	1960-61	1961-62	1962-63	1963-64	1964-65	1965-66	1966-67	1967-68	1968-69
(1) Overseas spending[a] on defence equipment ($A million)	53.2	59.7	66.9	110.0	110.8	130.6	106.7	170.8	n.a.[b]
As a percentage of total procurement spending	47.1	51.6	52.7	59.0	55.4	53.9	44.1	57.4	n.a.
(2) Value of equipment purchased through borrowing from U.S. credits† ($A million)									
Navy	—	—	—	—	—	—	18.1	32.4	15.7
Army	—	—	—	—	—	—	14.2	15.6	13.8
Air Force	—	—	—	—	—	—	53.2	80.9	61.0
TOTAL	—	—	—	—	—	—	85.5	128.9	90.5
(3) Actual repayments of borrowings from U.S. credits ($A million)	—	—	—	—	—	—	1.3	20.6	48.2
(4) Value of orders placed with Department of Supply from overseas for defence equipment ($A million)	2.8	3.0	1.6	5.7	2.6	3.4	5.1	n.a.	n.a.

* Official defence statistics are strewn with pitfalls for the unwary. In particular care must be exercised here when dealing with R and D spending since 1963, and with spending from the U.S. Credits, which began in 1966-67. R and D totals as they appear in Department of Supply statistics have, since 1963, included the U.K. contribution to Woomera *as well as* the Australian, and official defence statistics since 1966 (e.g. *C.P.D. (H. of R.)*, 26 November, 1968, p. 3285, and 5 November, p. 2463) have, in accordance with normal government practice, usually combined the amounts withdrawn from the U.S. credits, which are loans, with actual spending, thus causing the defence total, and its fraction spent overseas, to appear larger than the actual expenditures in the year in question. We have followed this practice in Table 10 while identifying the U.S. credit procurement content in Table 9.

† Between 1965 and 1967 the Australian government entered into various agreements with the United States government whereby the Export-Import Bank of Washington agreed to finance payments to the U.S. Department of Defense and other suppliers of defence equipment and services. In 1965 Australia arranged a credit of $US350 million repayable over seven years at 4⅜% *per annum*; in 1966 $US20 million repayable over 5 years with interest at 5⅛% and $US80 million repayable over 5 years at 4% *per annum*. In 1967 additional credits were obtained: $US110 million repayable over 7 years at 4⅜%; $US14.7 million repayable over 5 years at 5⅛%; and $US35 million repayable over 5 years at 4%. At 30 June 1969 Australia owed $US294.4 million under the agreements.

[a] Does *not* include spending from U.S. credits but does include interest and principal repayments on the credits.

[b] Not available.

Sources: (1) *C.P.D. (H. of R.)*, 26 November 1968, p. 3285; (2) and (3) *Reports of the Auditor-General*, 1965-1969; (4) *C.P.D. (H. of R.)*, 14 August 1968, p. 209.

N.B. Figures for (1) and (4) include as defence equipment items such as clothing, fuel and medical supplies which are not normally counted as items of military procurement.

TABLE 10

Defence Procurement Spending
(All costs are in $Australian million)

	1950–51	1951–52	1952–53	1953–54	1954–55	1955–56	1956–57	1957–58	1958–59	1959–60	1960–61	1961–62	1962–63	1963–64	1964–65	1965–66	1966–67	1967–68	1968–69
Army—																			
Weapons	10.8	35.8	52.4	30.4	36.8	32.8	28.2	27.8	37.8	31.8	34.7	33.7	34.4	45.4	58.4	63.8	80.2	91.2	86.3
Ammunition															48.6[b]	47.0	56.9	67.1	63.0
Communications																			
Transport and Engineering																			
Clothing[a]																			
Navy—																			
Aircraft	10.7	26.8	34.0	34.2	39.6	37.8	22.4	29.6	25.6	27.0	30.6	30.8	34.8	42.0	52.4	73.0	93.4	105.5	95.1
Armament																			
Ships																			
Electronics, electrical stores																			
Air Force—																			
Airframe, engines	21.4	40.6	44.6	41.0	41.2	42.8	42.4	41.0	46.4	49.6	42.2	45.0	48.5	88.6	77.2	94.6	146.9	221.9	196.
Armament																			
Aircraft																			
Communications																			

Defence R and D (i)	1.8	2.2	2.4	3.4	3.6	4.4	4.2	4.4	4.4	4.6	5.4	6.2	9.2	10.4	12.0	10.7	10.9	12.1	12.9
Defence R and D (ii) plus Australian spending on Joint Long Range Weapons Project at Woomera	13.6	14.0	15.2	16.8	19.8	23.8	23.4	23.8	23.4	23.6	24.4	25.2	24.4	27.2	27.2	25.4	25.6	26.8	21.0
Total procurement including R and D (i)	44.7	105.4	133.4	109.0	121.2	117.8	97.2	102.8	114.2	113.0	112.9	115.7	126.9	186.4	200.0[c]	242.1	331.4	430.7	390.6
Total defence	207.2	340.2	432.0	357.2[d]	357.6[d]	383.2	379.4	372.6	380.7	389.6	401.3	409.4	432.3	518.7	598.1	741.9	950.1	1,109.5	1,164.7
R and D (i) as percentage of defence (excludes Woomera)	0.9	0.6	0.6	1.0	1.0	1.1	1.1	1.2	1.2	1.2	1.3	1.5	2.1	2.0	2.0	1.4	1.1	1.1	1.1
Procurement as percentage of defence	21.6	31.0	30.9	30.5	33.9	30.7	25.6	27.6	30.0	29.0	28.1	28.3	29.4	35.9	33.4	32.6	34.8	39.4	33.8
G.N.P. (market prices) $million	7,200	7,700	8,400	9,000	9,700	10,600	11,500	11,600	12,500	13,800	14,600	15,000	16,200	18,000	19,800	20,900	22,800	24,200	27,100
Defence as percentage of G.N.P.	2.9	4.4	5.1	4.0	3.7	3.6	3.3	3.2	3.0	2.8	2.7	2.7	2.7	2.9	3.0	3.6	3.7	4.0	4.3

[a] Clothing and medical supplies are not normally considered procurement items and we have omitted them from the Navy and Air Force figures but published data are insufficient to allow us to follow the same procedure with respect to the Army over the whole period covered by the table.

[b] Army procurement *excluding* clothing etc.

[c] Total *includes* Army spending on clothing etc.

[d] Excluding money paid into the Defence Equipment and Supplies Trust Account.

CHAPTER 17

The Administration of Defence

D. E. KENNEDY

Plans, programmes and 'the disadvantages of separatism'

In 1949 Mr Menzies stated in a policy speech that 'we stand for adequate national preparedness for defence'. From the outset, national preparedness was a feature of the defence outlook of the Liberal-Country Party government, which achieved power in December 1949. The first defence programme of the Menzies government was presented to Parliament in 1950 and, early in March 1951, the Prime Minister warned Australia that it had three years in which to prepare for war. The government's programmes would make the country ready for mobilization by 1953. There was a manifest sense of urgency and a determination to ensure that the nation was prepared for a grave crisis, shortly expected. The government called upon the Australian people 'for the greatest effort at defence preparation, and the most realistic approach to the nature of a threatened war ever undertaken here in time of peace'.[1]

The main features of the defence outlook, since the government came to power, were explained by the Minister for Defence, Sir Philip McBride, during a budget debate in September 1956.[2] They were, first, 'the intensification of the cold war and the inherent danger of global war'; secondly, 'the subsequent recession of the threat of global war'; and thirdly, 'the effect on the pattern of future defence preparations of the existence of the deterrent weapon, and the development of other new weapons, and their means of delivery'. The Cold War, the Korean war and the deterioration of the international outlook were reasons why, in 1950, emphasis was placed on preparedness by 1953. The government stepped up the 'tempo of preparedness' and expenditure on defence rose from £54 million ($A108 million) (1949-50) to a peak of £215 million ($A430 million) (1952-53).

By 1954 the outlook had changed. It was believed that the danger of global war had receded and the basis of defence policy was transformed from preparedness by a 'critical date, to maintaining it at a

level that could reasonably be sustained for a "long haul" '. The method, not the objective, was modified. The government, accordingly, in 1954 approved measures designed to rebalance the defence programme. The defence vote was maintained at a level not exceeding £200 million ($A400 million), apparently despite opposition from the Defence Committee.[3] In August of that year the three-year programme from 1954-55 to 1956-57 was adopted, during which the defence vote fell to £190 million ($A380 million) in the last two years of the triennium.

Already by this defence triennium characteristics of the government's approach to defence planning were apparent. A very high priority was given as a rule to the international situation, which helped to define the required or appropriate degree of preparedness, 'the strength and composition of the forces being governed by the related strategic plans which determine Australia's role'. The state of the national economy and its capacity to sustain the defence vote while maintaining stability, together with the question of national development, (including immigration, seen as 'long-term defence'), were associated considerations. These were the factors scrutinized by the government in determining the size of a defence programme, the extent to which the prescribed objectives could be achieved each year and the amount of the defence vote. The defence vote, the government insisted, was not determined arbitrarily.[4]

The objectives of defence planning were in practice to be achieved through the defence programmes, 'each usually extending over a period of three years, to ensure proper planning and authorization of expenditure, and to achieve continuity in those projects which extend over a period of years'.[5] The government held that a five-year programme, such as that proposed by the Labor Party in 1947, was unrealistic. Its arrangements continued to be made in three-year terms until 1968, when Prime Minister Gorton explained their nature at a point when they were assumed to be breaking down. Mr Gorton described them as 'rolling' programmes.[6] The Minister for Defence announced in May of that year that, while the content of a further three-year programme had been studied, it was undesirable 'to go firm on the future' at that stage.

The 1965-66 to 1967-68 programme ended in June 1968 before planning for the next triennium was established, and by December 1968 it appeared that the 'old three-year cycle of procurement planning has apparently been abandoned—but a continued desire to put off any long-term planning on the part of the Cabinet has failed to replace it with anything else'. On this view, 'unless pressure from the U.S. and other countries forces the Gorton Government into some

firm decisions, Australian defence planning will continue indefinitely on an even more variable ad hoc basis than it has ever done in the past'.[7] At that point in time, it was argued, the policy and the programme of defence had ceased to have a viable relationship.

The administration of Australian defence during the 1950s and 1960s was marked by the apparent disparity between the policy, which defines the objectives, and the programme, which provides the means to achieve them. The ministerial statements on defence, sometimes presented by the Prime Minister rather than the Minister for Defence, distinguish policy from planning, and make interesting reading as attempts to match one with the other. Mr Calwell pointedly observed of the Prime Minister's statement on defence in November 1964, that

> ... there is just no connection between the first four pages of the Prime Minister's statement—his essay on the South East Asian situation—and the rest of the statement which deals with what the Government actually proposes to do.[8]

The government recognized certain problems of defence planning after its first years in office. As Mr Menzies acknowledged in April 1957,

> ... we have for some time been greatly disturbed by the fact that an undue proportion of our annual expenditure has been laid out upon the maintenance of existing forces, the bulk of whom are only partially trained, while too small a proportion of our expenditure has been available for equipment. We have, quite frankly, disturbing deficiencies on the equipment side.[9]

The Joint Committee of Public Accounts noted in 1956 that the Service departments expended about 75% of their expenditure each year upon maintenance.[10] The paradox was that the planning and preparations for defence were, at the same time, based upon 'an operational contribution to allied strategy of highly trained men armed with the most modern conventional weapons and equipment'.

Forces so trained and armed were to pursue what the Minister for the Army described as a 'phased' defence programme. A limited or even global war could break out with little notice. To meet this exigency defence was planned in two phases: first, to stop the aggressor at a certain point—'the idea not being to defeat him there but to hold him'; secondly, to stop him and roll him back. Australia, the Minister stated, 'is mainly concerned at this point [October 1957] in the preparations for the second phase'.[11]

It was a bold plan, and the government responded to criticisms of

its defence programmes. Sir Philip McBride answered such criticisms in a fashion that illustrated the problems to which Mr Menzies had referred. He explained that of the £1,200 million ($A2,400 million) expended by the government on defence since 1950-51, 62% had been used for maintaining the defence forces and 19% of the total was spent an aircraft, ships, weapons and other equipment. The expansion of production capacity and the replacement and modernization of existing facilities absorbed some 5%.[12]

During this period interest was given to the defence question by views expressed before the Joint Committee of Public Accounts in August 1956, by Sir Frederick Shedden, Secretary of the Department of Defence. The Secretary opined that Australia was not ready for mobilization by 1953—the original critical date—or by 1956, during the long haul.[13] There was disagreement about the meaning and the value of his evidence. To the Prime Minister, 'it is a pretty stimulating account of the dynamic approach that has been made towards Australian defences . . . with a revamping and rebalancing of our defence programme'. To a Labor speaker, 'It should be sufficient to force the Government to resign'.[14] The discussion of this question in Parliament was spasmodic and on the whole ineffective: there was hardly a storm for the government to weather.

On 4 October 1956, two days after his statement that 'the defences of this country were never in better shape in time of peace in the history of Australia', the Prime Minister announced that the government proposed to make a thorough revision of its defence programme.

This important decision was revealed casually in response to a question 'whether any changes in defence planning . . . are contemplated'. Mr Menzies said,

> . . . when I returned from abroad I had accumulated a certain amount of information and some ideas on the question of future defence policy. I took the opportunity to sort out my ideas over the week-end. I had a long conference with the Minister for Defence on Monday afternoon last and long discussions with Cabinet on Tuesday night, in consequence of which it has been agreed that the whole defence programme is to be reviewed in the light of certain circumstances. That, as we arranged on Tuesday night, will begin at a conference between the Minister for Defence, the three service Ministers, the three Chiefs of Staff and myself on Wednesday of next week. The whole purpose of that will be to have a complete revision from top to bottom of the ideas underlying the defence programme in the light of the circumstances now existing in the world.[15]

Some conclusions emerged on 4 April 1957 from the Prime Minister's statement on defence, the result of a Cabinet review following a comprehensive examination by the Defence Committee and the

departments concerned. The government initiated a move to Canberra, planned initially for 1959, of 'those elements in defence which deal with policy'. Before this development the headquarters of the Department of Defence and other departments in the defence group were in Melbourne.

Changes were made in the Higher Defence Machinery. First, the Defence Committee (then comprising the Secretary of the Department of Defence and the three Chiefs of Staff) was enlarged to include the Secretaries of the Prime Minister's Department, which had developed a policy-making role, including defence, since the Second World War, and of the Departments of the Treasury and External Affairs.[16] The practice of co-opting representatives of interested departments and expert advisers when appropriate was continued. Secondly, while the Chiefs of Staff would continue to attend at Cabinet and Cabinet Committee meetings on defence questions and consult their own Service Ministers and the Minister for Defence, they would as a committee meet regularly on purely military matters. The object was to ensure that 'there may be no restraint placed on the expression of professional military views'.[17]

A further ministerial statement on defence on 19 September 1957 developed the account of the Government's strategic thinking. Mr Menzies confirmed in December that the comprehensive review was completed; but the process of organizational revision had been continued by the appointment in November of a committee chaired by Lieutenant-General Sir Leslie Morshead and including the Chairman of the Public Service Board, the Secretary of the Department of Defence[18] and the Assistant Secretary of the Prime Minister's Department.

The proposed terms of reference help define the problems as the government saw them. The committee examined the organization of the defence group of departments 'in order to avoid overlapping . . . to produce a greater measure of consultation at all levels and . . . to produce a more efficient result'. It also considered the situation in 'places in which civil and military production are conducted in the same department, to see whether any improvement to make that system better organized and more economical can be effected'. It did not deal at all with sources of equipment where deficiencies were disturbing.[19]

The committee reported in December 1957 and February 1958. The report, of which there were apparently three versions, original, revised and authorized, was not tabled, ostensibly because government officials had given evidence before the committee, though Shedden's evidence was printed. Its recommendations were, however, described

by the Prime Minister in March 1958 as falling into two groups.[20] The first group suggested that the Departments of Defence, Navy, Army and Air be amalgamated into one Defence Department under a single Minister for Defence. This Minister would be assisted by two associate ministers, each with functional duties (for example, logistics and personnel), as well as their separate non-defence ministerial portfolios.[21]

The second group included the advice to amalgamate the Departments of Supply and Defence Production into a single department under one Minister, and proposed 'various devices for improving efficiency, reducing overlapping, encouraging the development of common services, defining the responsibility of service chiefs, and strengthening the overall authority and control of the Minister for Defence'.

Proposals along similar lines had previously been made in Parliament. The Member for Darebin anticipated the committee's broad suggestions about co-ordinating the Service departments as well as combining the Departments of Supply and Defence Production; the Member for Indi recommended the amalgamation of the departments and suggested a role for assistant ministers.[22]

At first greatly attracted to the concept of an integrated Department of Defence, the government rejected this proposal as not feasible and saw constitutional difficulties in the way of appointing associate ministers. The Departments of Supply and Defence Production, which had acted under one minister and outside the overall authority of the Department of Defence, were joined into a single Department of Supply, subject in policy to the authority of the Department of Defence. The government acknowledged that there had been 'divergence between the views of the Service departments and the two supplying departments on matters of defence supply and production', and conceded that 'there may be some overlapping or duplication of services which might be common services'.

The Prime Minister drew attention to general shortcomings in defence administration. The authority of the Department of Defence, whose 'vital business' concerned the 'great problems of constant strategic thinking and overall planning', was in some respects 'uncertain'. Therefore, the government proposed by an administrative directive to establish the Department's complete superiority in the field of policy —by authority if persuasion failed. Within the Service departments it proved difficult to obtain 'truly unified joint service views', including the allocation of annual defence votes: what emerged could be an 'uneasy compromise' offered to the Minister for submission to Cabinet.

The Chiefs of Staff had probably not met sufficiently 'without civilian intervention', a problem recognized earlier. The association between them and the Minister for Defence, and their formulation of joint professional advice, needed 'material improvement'. To assist the Minister, a military chairman was added to the Chiefs of Staff Committee, replacing the civilian chairman, Secretary of the Department of Defence. This new chairman would attend the Defence Committee meetings: there was little break in continuity.[23] In sum, these measures, hopefully, would improve administrative efficiency within the Service departments and 'go a long way towards eliminating the disadvantages of separatism which are inherent in the present system'. The disadvantages were manifest in the next ten years.[24]

The Higher Defence Machinery and the problems of co-ordination

During the first two defence programmes the Higher Defence Machinery was shown to be deficient, particularly in regard to co-ordination of the several elements at the ministerial level and below. Both on the upward movement of policy discussions to the highest levels and the downward transmission of decisions to the executive departments there were, in addition to the overlapping and duplication noticed by the government, problems of diffusion of authority, information and responsibility. It had not required the Morshead Committee to point out the disadvantages of separatism inherent in the system. The Joint Committee of Public Accounts, whose reports were tabled, had documented the problems.

The Public Accounts Committee believed that deficiencies in co-ordination within the defence group of departments were 'inevitable' when there were a co-ordinating department (Defence), three Service departments (Navy, Army, Air) and three construction and supply organizations (Supply, Defence Production and Works). This Committee 'inescapably' concluded that there was a 'serious absence of co-ordination' between the Departments of Defence and Works whenever they had to co-operate. For example, at least in 1954-55, the defence works estimates prepared by the Department of Works 'were either ignored or by-passed or both' by the Department of Defence: the defence works programme was £9,500,000 ($A19 million); the Department of Works expended £8,621,000 ($A17,242,000), and was allocated (by means unknown to it) the sum of £13,144,000 ($A26,288,000).[25]

The Department of Defence did not have direct control over the expenditures of the Service departments, and the Supply departments worked outside its authority. But it scrutinized the financial commit-

ments incurred by the departments and, for their guidance, issued a series of rules, beginning 'That first things come first'. The *Twenty-Ninth Report* stated (para. 85) that despite Shedden's claim that insufficient funds were provided for carrying out the full defence programme during the long haul, there were 'heavy under-expenditures, especially on the equipment votes for the Services', that is, during a triennium when the Prime Minister expressed concern over the 'disturbing deficiencies on the equipment side'. *Fronti nulla fides.*

The Committee thought 'deplorable' what it described as the almost grotesque examples of over-estimating during the previous two years, regarding them as showing a 'lack of realism' in the financial sections of the defence departments and their procurement experts. It drew attention to four examples, in works, equipment, stores, arms and armament, where overestimates as a percentage of the estimates ranged from 34% to 40%.[26] To obtain a satisfactory explanation of this kind of divergence the Committee examined the preparation of the defence service estimates.

Parliament did not as a rule approve these estimates until some four months after the new financial year began. The Defence Preparations Committee usually met in October or November to consider expenditure, so the defence establishment could not begin capital expenditures until the financial year was from one-third to one-half over, unless approval was given by the Treasurer and the Minister for Defence. A Treasury Minute (1961) on this point stated that, as the Minister for Defence and the Treasurer early in the new financial year could approve authorization under the programme and up to a specified percentage, conditional upon such authorized expenditure being a first charge upon the vote, the tardiness of the annual Appropriation Bill caused little or no disruption of the defence programme.[27]

The submissions concerned the need for reform *inter alia* of financial direction at the executive level: the Committee eschewed the policy matters raised in its report. The three Services had been part of the Department of Defence until the Second World War. When the Department of Defence was divided, the major constituent of its financial section was also removed, to become the Defence Division of the Treasury. The functions of this Treasury division included the financial aspects of defence, policy, review, budgetary and accounting within the Defence complex. In consequence, the responsibility for the financial administration of the defence programmes rested with the Treasurer and the Service departments. The Minister for Defence was henceforth responsible simply for the financial requirements of defence policy and the distribution of funds made available to im-

T

plement it. When such questions were before the Defence Committee, the Assistant Secretary of the Treasury was co-opted.

This analysis of the problems and responses can be appreciated in terms of the workings of the unreformed Higher Defence Machinery.[28] The machinery was a committee system. At the highest level was a sub-committee of Cabinet, the Defence Preparations Committee, one of the three principal Standing Committees in 1958.[29] It was regarded as the final authority in defence matters. Commenting on the government's administrative directive strengthening the authority of the Minister for Defence, an ex-member of this Committee indicated the problems encountered in obtaining appreciations of the situation to help define their objectives. There was 'great difficulty' in making decisions, the appreciations 'always remained a mirage amongst . . . unrelated details'.[30]

The programmes of the three Service and three Supply departments, originally prepared in those departments, were reviewed by the Defence Committee to ensure a balanced development of policy, then submitted to the Minister for Defence and the Defence Preparations Committee for approval, subject to annual review in the light of the defence vote available each financial year.

The preparation of the defence services estimates followed this timetable: (a) the definition of the defence programme as an expression of policy; (b) the authorization of expenditure upon the projects required to give effect to the programme; (c) the preparation of the draft estimates; (d) the Cabinet review of the draft estimates; (e) the establishment of the estimates and their presentation; and (f) the review of the programme by the Defence Preparations Committee. When the government had approved the programme, the Defence Preparations Committee, and under it the Defence Committee, reviewed progress from time to time. Within the Higher Defence Machinery, two committees—the Board of Business Administration, appointed to give advice on the business aspects of such matters as supplies and works, and the Joint War Production Committee which had four sub-committees—had special functions in financial matters.[31]

The Defence Committee was the major committee below the ministerial level and occupied a key place in the Higher Defence Machinery as the link with the Principal Subordinate Committees. Constituted under the Defence Committee Regulations 1946-52, it served the Defence Preparations Committee and the Minister for Defence as an advisory and consultative body. The Minister was empowered by the regulations to appoint the chairman, and chose the Secretary of the Department of Defence. The Committee could,

with the Minister's approval, co-opt any person, and additional members, including the Secretary of the Department of External Affairs, sat fairly regularly with the Committee.

As stated above, the Committee was expanded in 1957, incorporating members previously co-opted, as from the Treasury and External Affairs. A former naval Chairman of the Chiefs of Staff Committee described the enlarged Committee as a 'vast improvement' over its predecessor, but added that

> it should be chaired by a Cabinet Minister, the Minister for Defence—at least when important defence matters are under discussion. The Minister would then obtain a far more intimate understanding of the difficult problems that confront the committee and would hear the views of its individual members at first hand.[32]

The Defence Committee advised the Minister for Defence on defence policy as a whole and on matters of principle and important questions with a joint Service or inter-departmental aspect. (The officers of the Secretariat of Joint Service and Inter-Departmental Advisory Machinery were responsible to the several departmental Assistant Secretaries for administrative advice.) The work of this committee was 'continuous and voluminous'. Shedden described it as meeting every Thursday almost without exception: it was, he said, 'like a board of directors'. Six Principal Subordinate Committees, with twenty sub-committees, operated under the Defence Committee: the Defence Research and Development Policy Committee, the Principal Administrative Officers' Committees (Personnel, Maintenance and Materiel), the Joint Planning Committee, the Joint Administrative Planning Committee and the Joint Intelligence Committee.

It is clear that the administrative innovations that followed the Morshead Report did not radically alter the structure of the Higher Defence Machinery, though the Government, like the Committee, believed that the structure needed 'material improvement'. Supply departments outside that structure were joined and placed under the direction of the Department of Defence. The authority of this Department was to be enhanced by fiat and made less uncertain. Consultation between bodies and within bodies was to be improved. The Chiefs of Staff were to have a military chairman who would rise above the interests of his own Service, and who would improve the liaison between his colleagues and the Minister for Defence. The 'paramount responsibility' for eliminating overlapping, co-ordinating activities and developing common services remained with the strengthened Department of Defence.

Steps to improve joint Service and inter-departmental relationships were taken during the next decade. They may be summarized as a background to the major reconsiderations of policy and planning in the late 1960s. The Minister for Defence announced in August 1958 that all the recommendations of the Morshead Committee concerning various common services were under consideration by his department and the Service departments. Senior appointments in the Department of Defence were rearranged to provide a unit to review appropriate activities of the armed Services and administer any joint service organization that might be established. An investigation was begun into the prospects of co-ordinating design and inspection services in the Service departments, together with the rationalization of canteen services. An Exploratory Committee was set up in October 1958 to consider the introduction of electronic data processing into the armed Services. The government decided in February 1961 to proceed with this technique.[33]

A Director-General of Inspection Services was appointed by 1959,[34] the co-ordinating unit for Design and Inspection Services had achieved economies in manpower, Army and Air Force canteens were merged and a central cataloguing authority established to standardize the cataloguing of stores in the Service departments. The major item in the Defence Department's programme in 1962 was the provision for an electronic data processing proving and training centre at Russell Hill, Canberra, where the first computers had been installed. Electronic data processing systems were to be developed for each of the Services, beginning with the Air Force in 1964.[35]

Liaison between Services and supply officers and industrialists was organized by the Department of Defence through annual Industrial Mobilization courses. The Board of Business Administration became the Defence Business Board in 1959, with restated terms of reference under the same chairman. The industrial advisory committees were reconsidered during 1963-64, and early in 1964 the Minister of Supply announced a proposed reorganization. Emphasis was placed where practicable on the representation of particular areas of industry rather than on the end-products of war material, for example, 'light' and 'heavy' engineering instead of 'weapons' and 'ammunition'. A meeting in March 1965 was to be the forerunner of annual combined meetings of all committees and advisers, and the committees were to meet each year about three times.[36]

On 22 January 1963 a new Cabinet Standing Committee, the Defence and Foreign Affairs Committee, was constituted. Three committees were added to the Higher Defence Machinery as defined by the Secretary of the Department of Defence in 1956. The Joint Ser-

vice and Inter-Departmental Advisory Machinery included in 1961 a Defence Administration Committee, chaired by the Secretary of the Department of Defence. Its members were then the Secretaries of the Departments of the Navy, Army, Air and Supply, the Assistant-Secretary of the Treasury (Defence Division) and the Deputy Chiefs of Staff of the three Services. This committee was to review regularly the progress of the defence programmes, investigating bottlenecks, to arrange and determine priorities for investigation in the Defence Departments and the armed Services of the integration and co-ordination of activities, and generally consider management practices to introduce improvements.[37]

Two committees were incorporated into the Principal Subordinate Committees. First, a Joint Warfare Committee, under the chairmanship of the Director, Joint Service Plans, was responsible to the Chiefs of Staff Committee for the formulation and review of joint service policy, doctrine and the standardization of techniques for joint warfare operations and training. Secondly, a Defence Medical Services Committee, hitherto a sub-committee of the Principal Administrative Officers' Committee (Personnel), emerged by 1968 as a committee in its own right, with two sub-committees.[38]

The announcement in January 1968 of the accelerated British withdrawal from South-East Asia gave reason for further reassessment of Australia's forward role in the area of primary strategic interest. Without going 'firm on the future', the Minister for Defence outlined some planning considerations in May 1968. Overseas trends towards service integration, especially in Canada, were being studied. There were plans for two colleges; a joint service college to provide tertiary education for officer cadets in the three Services, and an Australian Service Staff College, offering both joint and single service staff training. Mr Fairhall also announced that seminal changes in the joint planning arrangements were under consideration: much of the work undertaken by committees would be done better in future by 'planning and executive staffs of mixed civilian and Service composition—with the tours of duty of the Service personnel being rather longer than the present two year rule'. A working party studied ways to improve joint intelligence arrangements.[39]

The press at this stage reported divisions within the government and Cabinet between the supporters of 'forward defence' and those disabused with the concept. It was felt that the beginnings of a genuine debate on future Australian defence was becoming apparent, though the government's thinking was difficult to gauge and the question of Australia's military role in the Malaysian area remained undecided after the five power conference at Kuala Lumpur in June

1968.[40] Later that month, in a report to the nation, the new Prime Minister, Mr Gorton, announced a complete review of Australia's defence strategy. There had been, he said, a 'fundamental change' in the basis on which Australian defence planning had rested for more than two decades.[41]

On 30 June Mr Fairhall announced a far-reaching reorganization of the planning and staff arrangements in the Department of Defence, along lines he indicated in May. The four main objectives of the new planning arrangements were

> ... to provide for a larger defence planning component within the Department of Defence which will bring to planning continuity of application and a melding of service expertise and civilian experience in a wide range of disciplines; to provide a greater capacity for the examination and consideration of longer term planning and policy issues; to achieve greater flexibility and speedier decision-making procedures by substituting full time staffs for formal committees; to provide more positive arrangements for the full impact of scientific, political, technological, economic and psychological factors etc. in military planning.[42]

This was a wholesome acknowledgement of 'the disadvantages of separatism', ten years after Mr Menzies used the phrase.

The joint Service committee structure, with thirteen main committees in 1968, and twenty-one sub-committees, was to be replaced by a series of joint planning staffs under a Director, Joint Staff (of Major-General level or the equivalent from the other Services), who would have three directors to assist him and supervise the work of the planning staffs. The activities of the planning staffs would be subject to review by the existing Joint Planning Committee, with the Director as Chairman. The Director and planning staff would serve the Secretary of the Department of Defence (Sir Henry Bland) and, on military matters, the Chairman of the Chiefs of Staff Committee and that Committee. The first Director was announced as Rear-Admiral W. J. Dovers, previously Director, Joint Service Plans, and Chairman both of the Joint Planning Committee and the new Joint Warfare Committee.

Each of the planning staffs would be composed of Service personnel seconded to the Department of Defence on a full-time basis and of civilians drawn from the Departments of Defence and External Affairs as appropriate. The Department of Defence would invite the Services to submit nominations against criteria related to the tasks to be accomplished. The selected officers would normally be seconded for a period of three years: the filling of posts on the basis of a Service rotation would not be the prime consideration. The conceptual approach underlying the present organization would be maintained,

namely that those involved in Department of Defence planning would have to execute the plans in their own Services. Though Service officers would belong to the Department of Defence during the period of their appointment, they would have full access to their own Services and Service papers. Plans prepared by the joint staffs would, in turn, be remitted to the Services for comment.

The planning staffs would examine long-term defence policy and planning particularly in the strategic field, equipment requirements, joint welfare, joint operations, joint operational logistics, and joint Services communications. The Director or his delegate would convene as necessary working parties from the Services and other authorities. These arrangements, the Minister for Defence announced, were expected to be fully functioning by 1 October 1968. A new emphasis was placed in the 1968 Defence Report on defence science. The nucleus of a Defence Science organization existed within the Department of Defence to co-ordinate research and development for the Services. A four-year agreement negotiated with the United Kingdom over the Joint Project enabled a progressive reallocation of scientific capabilities to Australian defence requirements. Consultations with United States experts were held in order to develop co-operation in this field.

Mr Fairhall described the new system as the first stage of the reorganization of the defence machinery. The 1968 Defence Report hinted at further change in its reference to the world-wide trend drawing fighting Services together in commands, operations and administration, but averred that in current Australian conditions the separate identities of the three Services would be retained. The Minister was earlier quoted as saying that 'From here on, whatever military commitments Australia faces will be joint service commitments, and the emphasis must be increasingly on joint service planning and co-operation'. The administrative changes introduced in 1968 took account of the 'need to develop strategic concepts and policies appropriate to our defence responsibilities'.[43]

The Gorton government had not received the Defence Committee's paper on the strategic situation by 15 August 1968, though the new defence programme—after an interval of one year—was to extend from 1969-70 to 1971-72. The survey, completed by the end of the month, was not discussed in Cabinet until December, during the parliamentary recess and some six months after the new financial year began. An interim programme for defence procurement was therefore to commence in 1969.[44] After considering the Defence Committee's strategic assessment, the government took basic decisions 'on what the defence services require in order to be able to have the capacity we seek after 1971'.[45]

The themes of this study form a confluence in the administrative decisions concerning defence in 1968. In the official view, the strategic situation, a prime factor in defence programming, deteriorated after 1953, when the country was not ready to meet the anticipated crisis. Conflict could occur at any time, with little notice, and the disadvantages of separatism were acknowledged at the close of the period by adjusting the committee structure in which they inhered. The Higher Defence Machinery was changed to meet the requirements of the emerging Australian role in Asia, defined however reluctantly: it became the victim of its own attributes. In retrospect, the raising of the joint planning bodies to a central place appears a logical outcome of the strategic assessments after the threat of a Third World War receded, when government thinking on defence nevertheless combined apprehensions and complacency.

But the logic appeared to operate only at a certain level. The Prime Minister indicated that decisions about the future joint service capacities of the forces were taken before a policy could be clarified. The political aspects of strategy—what Clausewitz described as 'the standard for determining both the aim of the military force and also the amount of effort to be made'—remained undefined amid the imponderables affirmed by the Prime Minister. It looked as if the means were clearer than the ends. Hitherto, the strategic appraisals were the most vigorous parts of the statements on defence, no doubt because they were drawn in black and white. By 1968 such sharp definition no longer seemed appropriate. In 1969 it was not thought feasible, even in an election year.

Mr Fairhall's Defence Report of August 1969, his last to Parliament, witnessed to this development. This report in conjunction with his April speech in Sydney to the Imperial Service Club provides a clear account of the reforms associated with Fairhall and Bland, then in the last months of their combined effort. The Sydney address, which anticipated the report in form and detail and which was printed as an official statement, is the more revealing evidence. It employs the ritual language of the Cold War but is in fact much more relaxed than previous ministerial statements in this field, 'there is presently no assessed threat of overt aggression against the country or its interests'. While rehearsing the subsequent report, this speech adds the Minister's judgements on the problem of reorganization: 'Twelve months ago we had, frankly too many committees in the higher defence machinery. . . . The Committees consumed time, generated paper, produced an undue share of compromise.'[46]

The two documents record other changes in the committee system. For example, the Principal Administrative Officers Committee

(Maintenance and Materiel) and the Joint War Production Committee were replaced by a Defence (Industrial) Committee, and the Defence Business Board was reconstructed. The report stated that a new Joint Intelligence Organization would soon function; it was formed from elements of the Joint Intelligence Bureau of the Department of Defence and the Service Intelligence Directorates, with some participation by the Department of External Affairs. A National Intelligence Committee, with the Director, Joint Intelligence Organization, as chairman, would replace the Joint Intelligence Committee and be responsible to the Defence Committee for 'the production of national intelligence to support Australian national security policy'.[47]

To the ex-servicemen Mr Fairhall scouted the 'apparent break in our defence preparations' as a genuine source of concern, adding that 'A new programme will begin to appear with the new financial year, and the old idea that there was something sacred about a three year defence programme will give way to a continuing programme'. The Defence Report returned to the point. Programming was now subject to systems analysis—it was argued elsewhere that the abolition of the old forms was almost a prerequisite for the introduction of the new— and the earlier practice of 'period' defence programming had given way to the 'continuing programme, reviewed and up-dated annually or more frequently as necessary'.[48]

Shortly after Mr Fairhall's departure, when Sir Henry Bland announced his resignation, 'a sudden loss of spirit and direction in defence planning' was remarked by a newspaper which had followed the changes closely; this editorial note contrasted with the optimism of the previous year.[49] The 'apparent break' had become a matter for concern. The Prime Minister referred in an interview to the 'hiatus' in the Department of Defence: 'He refused to elaborate, beyond saying that the "hiatus" probably had been caused by Sir Henry Bland's institution of valuable new planning systems'. A similar point was made previously by the new Minister for Defence, Mr Fraser.[50] It appeared at the end of 1969 that a reformed system existed but that it had not been made to work.

A sense of clarity and purpose was restored to parliamentary discussions of defence by Mr Fraser's statement in March 1970. It was reminiscent of the 1969 Defence Report in that the strategic analysis was relaxed and matter-of-fact, and the five-year rolling programmes initiated by Mr Fairhall were endorsed. The functions, organization and activities of the defence group of departments were to be scrutinized in the interests of efficiency by a special studies branch within the Department of Defence. The statement affirmed that the reformation was to proceed.[51]

Judgement must wait upon the event. The prolonged efforts to overcome the disadvantages of separatism inherent in the system and to improve joint planning will be cumulative in effect. More might be achieved in the long run by a new joint service mentality than by administrative changes. In that respect the revised administrative system at the close of the 1960s was far more sensitive to its own defaults than the previous system had been, and it was specifically designed to correct them. Thus, the authority of the Department of Defence was asserted over the three Services in the planning sphere, and the military members seconded to the Department for three years were, in Mr Fairhall's words, 'to that extent, detached from the interests of a single service'. The objective of the new system, as stated by the Minister for Defence in April 1969, contains a key criticism of the old: 'service planning must be oriented more to total defence than to the individual service'.[52]

Appendixes
Parliamentary Statements

I

Defence and Scientific Establishments in Australia, operated jointly with other nations, September 1969.

In the House of Representatives, the Leader of the Opposition, Mr E. G. Whitlam, Q.C., M.P. (Australian Labor Party) asked the Prime Minister, the Rt Hon. John Gorton, M.P., the following questions upon notice:

(1) What (a) defence and (b) scientific installations and facilities are operating in Australia and her overseas territories under the (i) joint control of Australia and another country or (ii) sole control of another country?

(2) What such installations and facilities are (a) under construction or (b) projected?

(3) What is the purpose of each institution and facility?

(4) Which is the other country concerned in each instance?

On 9 September 1969 the Prime Minister gave the following replies:

The following schedule of installations operating under governmental agreement has been compiled from information supplied to me by the Ministers concerned:

[The schedule begins overleaf]

Defence and scientific installations and facilities	Control	Current status	Purpose	Other country concerned
Trials Wing, Weapons Research Establishment, Salisbury, SA and Missile Range and Support Facilities, Woomera, SA	The programme is mutually agreed by Australia and the United Kingdom. Australia has sole control over the operation and management of the Trials Wing within the jointly approved programme	Existing . . .	Plan and direct firings and launchings at Woomera of missiles and vehicles under development as part of the United Kingdom/Australia Joint Project or as mutually agreed for third parties other countries or international organisations	United Kingdom
Joint Tropical Research Unit, Innisfail, Qld	The programme of the Unit is a joint responsibility with the United Kingdom Government. The Unit is under the operational direction of Australia	Existing . . .	Exposure and storage of materials and selected military and other stores under tropical conditions, assessment of deterioration and research into causes and prevention	United Kingdom
ELDO launching facility, Woomera, SA	The programme of this facility is determined by ELDO of which Australia is a member. The management of the facility is under the sole control of Australia as Range Authority	Existing . . .	Provide launching and tracking facilities for ELDO vehicles	Member countries of ELDO, United Kingdom, France, Germany, Belgium, Italy and the Netherlands

Station	Australia's responsibility	Status	Purpose	Country
ELDO Down Range Guidance and Telemetry Station, Gove, NT	The station's programme is determined by ELDO. Australia is responsible for the operation and management of the Station	Existing . . .	Provide down-range guidance and telemetry for ELDO launchings at Woomera	Member countries of ELDO (see above)
US National Aeronautics and Space Administration Tracking Stations: Deep Space Station 41, Island Lagoon (Woomera), SA; Deep Space Station 42, Tidbinbilla, ACT; Carnarvon Tracking and Data Acquisition Station, Carnarvon, WA; Honeysuckle Creek, ACT; Space Tracking and Data Acquisition Network Station, Orroral Valley, ACT; Applications Technology Satellite Station, Cooby Creek, Qld; Baker-Nunn Camera SC23, Island Lagoon (Woomera), SA	Australia is responsible for the operation and management of the stations	Existing. In addition a 210-ft antenna will be added to the facilities at Deep Space Station 42, Tidbinbilla, ACT	Provide support for NASA's programme of space exploration	United States of America
Tranet Tracking Station, Smithfield, SA	Australia is responsible for the operation and management of the station	Existing . . .	Support for the US geodetic satellite observation programme on behalf of US Navy Pacific Missile Range	United States of America

Defence and scientific installations and facilities	Control	Current status	Purpose	Other country concerned
Project Hibal Balloon Launching Station, Mildura, Vic.	The station is managed and operated by Australia	Existing . . .	To monitor the level of radioactivity in the upper atmosphere on behalf of US Atomic Energy Commission. Upper atmosphere research experiments are also flown on behalf of United States and Australian universities and research institutions	United States of America
USAF Geological and Geophysical Research Station, Alice Springs, NT	This station is managed and operated at present by the USAF. Australia has the entitlement to participate in the work of the station	Existing . . .	Long term geological and geophysical studies, including studies of earthquakes and attendant phenomena	United States of America
USAF Radio Receiving Station, Norfolk Island	This station is at present operated by a contractor to the US Government. Australia has the entitlement to participate in the work of the station	Existing . . .	Temporary station assisting the USAF in a research programme involving the study of ionospheric propagation in relation to long range radio paths	United States of America

		Existing except as noted		United States of America
US Geodetic Satellite Observation Programme. Optical Tracking Stations (BC4 cameras) at Culgoora, NSW, Perth, Cocos Island, Heard Island, Mawson and Casey. A Doppler Tracking System is in use at Smithfield, SA, SECOR stations at Darwin, NT, and Manus Island	Operated by the US Army	Existing except as noted	Temporary stations operated as part of the US geodetic satellite observation programme	United States of America
A BC4 camera is planned for Thursday Island and a Doppler Tracking System is planned for Heard Island				
Joint Defence Space Communications Station, Woomera, SA	The facility will be operated jointly with the United States of America	Projected ...	The facility will be a ground terminal for defence space communications involving satellites	United States of America
US Naval Communications Station 'Harold E. Holt', North West Cape, WA	The station is under the operational control of the US Navy. Its facilities are available to the Australian armed forces and the station cannot be used for other than defence communication without the agreement of the Australian Government	Existing ...	Defence Communications	United States of America

Defence and scientific installations and facilities	Control	Current status	Purpose	Other country concerned
US Research Station, RAAF Base, Amberley, Qld	This station is managed and operated by the USAF. Australia has the entitlement to participate in the work of the station	Existing . . .	Joint research programme for the study of physical effects of disturbances in the atmosphere or space, with particular emphasis on their effect on radio communications	United States of America
Nuclear Test Ban Monitoring Station, RAAF Base, Pearce, WA	Operated by the UK Atomic Energy Authority	Existing . . .	Monitoring of the Partial Nuclear Test Ban Treaty (1963)	United Kingdom
Joint Defence Space Research Facility, Alice Springs, NT	Jointly controlled by Australia and United States of America	Under construction	To carry out a variety of defence space research projects with the results being made available to both countries	United States of America
Anglo-Australian 150-in telescope, Siding Springs, NSW	Jointly controlled by Australia and United Kingdom	Under construction	Research in the field of astronomy	United Kingdom
Seismic Array, Warramunga, NT	Operated by the Australian National University on behalf of the UK Atomic Energy Authority	Existing . . .	To study the frequency of natural earthquakes in certain areas, and the possibility of distinguishing these from artificial explosions. Also general seismological research	United Kingdom

Source: *Current Notes on International Affairs*, Department of External Affairs, September 1969, pp. 547-9.

II

Statement on Nuclear Non-Proliferation Treaty
By the Rt Hon. John Gorton, M.P., Prime Minister—
18 February 1970, House of Representatives

Cabinet this morning gave full consideration to the question of whether Australia should sign the Nuclear Non-Proliferation Treaty.

We have decided that it would be in Australia's interests to sign—but with reservations. Signature will enable us to join with other like-minded signatories, such as West Germany and Japan to achieve those interpretations, assurances, and qualifications which we regard as important.

We have always supported the proposal for a Treaty designed to limit the further spread of nuclear weapons among the nations of the world.

But we have wished to be satisfied that such a Treaty was effective, and did not damage Australia's interests.

We do not believe that as yet sufficient nations have signed or ratified the Treaty to render it fully effective. But the recent signatures—with reservations—of Japan and West Germany have undoubtedly made it possible for the Treaty to be much more effective than it was.

Further, although the questions of inspection and the safeguard provisions of the Treaty have not yet been resolved to our satisfaction progress has been made towards a solution.

It is clear, too, that the Treaty will not inhibit but will assist the application of atomic energy for peaceful purposes in Australia.

In these circumstances the Government believes that the time has come to sign the Treaty—and hopes that this action will encourage other countries to do the same.

Our decision is an expression of our earnest hope that a fully satisfactory Treaty can be achieved. It is also an expression of our desire to help—and above all not to hinder—such an achievement.

However we wish to make it plain that our decision to sign is not to be taken in any way as a decision to ratify the Treaty, and of course, the Treaty is not binding on us until it is ratified.

As was the case with Japan and West Germany our signature will be accompanied by a statement of our reservations—and we do not propose to ratify the Treaty until the matters of concern to us have been clarified to our satisfaction.

On 27 February 1970, the Minister for External Affairs, the Rt Hon. William McMahon, M.P., said that the Australian heads of mission in London, Washington and Moscow would sign the treaty for the non-proliferation of nuclear weapons on behalf of the Australian Government.

The statement by the Government on the occasion of the signing of the Treaty on 27 February 1970 was being communicated by Australian heads of mission to the Governments to which they were accredited.

U

STATEMENT BY THE GOVERNMENT OF AUSTRALIA ON THE
OCCASION OF THE SIGNING OF THE NUCLEAR
NON-PROLIFERATION TREATY

The Government of Australia:

(1) Supports effective international measures to counter the spread of nuclear weapons and weapons of mass destruction. In April 1968 when the treaty to prevent the further spread of nuclear weapons was introduced in the United Nations General Assembly, Australia supported the resolution commending the treaty for the consideration of governments.

(2) Is conscious of the fact that in the long run the security of the world as a whole will depend upon effective measures to control the nuclear arms race and to bring about general and complete disarmament. The Government therefore welcomes the call in Article VI of the treaty for negotiations to achieve these ends.

(3) Hopes that the treaty will be effective in its operation and will lead to improved relationships and enhanced co-operation between the nations of the world, and in particular between the nations of the Asian and Pacific region.

(4) Believes that a condition of an effective treaty is that it should attract a necessary degree of support. Some progress in this direction has been made but the Government will nevertheless want to be assured that there is a sufficient degree of support for the treaty.

(5) Regards it as essential that the treaty should not affect continuing security commitments under existing treaties of mutual security.

(6) Attaches weight to the statements by the governments of the United States, United Kingdom and the Soviet Union declaring their intention to seek immediate Security Council action to provide help to any non-nuclear weapons state party to the treaty that is subject to aggression or the threat of aggression with nuclear weapons. At the same time the Government reaffirms its adherence to the principle, contained in Article 51 of the Charter of the United Nations, of the right of individual or collective self-defence if an armed attack occurs against a member of the United Nations, until the Security Council has taken measures necessary to maintain international peace and security.

(7) Notes that Article 10 of the treaty provides that any party has the right to withdraw in circumstances that jeopardised its supreme interests.

(8) Notes that the treaty will in no way inhibit and is in fact designed to assist non-nuclear weapon States in their research, development and use of nuclear energy and nuclear explosions for peaceful purposes either individually or collectively; nor must it discriminate against any State or States in their peaceful pursuits in nuclear activities.

(9) Considers that the safeguards agreement to be concluded by Australia with the International Atomic Energy Agency in accordance with Treaty Article III must in no way subject Australia to treatment less favourable

than is accorded to other States which, individually or collectively, conclude safeguards agreements with that Agency.

(10) Considers it essential that the inspection and safeguards arrangements should not burden research, development, production and use of nuclear energy for peaceful purposes; that they should not constitute an obstacle to a nation's economic development, commercial interests and trade; and that they should be effective in ensuring that any breaches of the treaty would be detected.

(11) Attaches importance to a review of the IAEA safeguards system and procedures to clarify those issues of importance to Australia.

(12) Welcomes the fact that the treaty in Articles four and five provides for international co-operation for the development of the peaceful uses of nuclear energy and the peaceful applications of nuclear explosions; notes the assurances that under the treaty the supply of knowledge, materials and equipment would not be denied to any party; and considers it important that no nuclear development should be prohibited except when such activities would have no other purpose than the manufacture of nuclear weapons or other nuclear explosive devices.

(13) Will co-operate closely with other governments in seeking clarifications and understandings in relation to those matters which must be resolved before Australia could proceed to ratification, being convinced that a treaty which was truly effective in preventing the further proliferation of nuclear weapons would be a major contribution to the security of the world as a whole.

Reprinted from *Current Notes on International Affairs*, Department of External Affairs, Canberra, February 1970, pp. 70-1.

III

Statement on Defence
By the Hon. Malcolm Fraser, M.P., Minister for Defence,
House of Representatives, 10 March 1970

I propose in the course of my remarks to provide a broad view of our defence policy and the considerations that have contributed to it. I shall refer to the Government's defence objectives and to our planning arrangements which support them; to the capacity of our armed forces and to our proposals to increase that capacity.

I will set the Services' capability against the roles we have assigned them. I shall also mention the organisational changes which are still continuing in the defence structure which, I believe, are important in helping the Government to come to decisions in defence matters. Some of what I say will not be new but I feel it would be useful if the House could have as full a view as possible of our approach to Defence policy.

Defence policies and the decisions we take to give effect to them must have meaning not only for the immediate present; they must also fit the situation that we assess will face us in the future. This task is not easy. There is a dynamic in the policies, the economic and the social changes of the countries of our region. The rapidity of technological and scientific development introduces yet another dimension. Yet if we are to take the right decisions, we must have a defence organisation which is equipped to analyse all the facts, and perceive as best it may what lies ahead.

My colleague, the Right Honourable the Minister for External Affairs, will, in the course of this Session, be giving the House a survey of the international situation and of Australia's external policies. I shall confine myself to describing in brief terms the strategic setting against which the Government has made certain decisions and in the context of which we are elaborating our Defence policies.

STRATEGIC SETTING

The world wars of this century had their roots in political conflict in Europe. 1945 heralded the end of European dominance. In the time since then the two themes of over-riding importance in world affairs have been the pre-eminence of the continental superpowers in North America and Eurasia and the dramatic end of European colonial rule over much of the rest of the world.

In 1945, apart from New Zealand, there were three sovereign states within five thousand miles of Australia. Today there are seven times that number in the same distance.

In retrospect we can discern the distinctive characteristics of the last 25 years. We need now to recognise that we are entering a new era. Since 1945, we have had a longer period of what is imprecisely called peace than prevailed between the two World Wars. A generation which neither created

nor experienced the last Great War has matured in, or in spite of, its after-math. In what are still called the "newly independent" countries, the first fully post-colonial generation has already emerged.

Many nations, whose policies and roles are important to us and interact with our own, are now in a process of transition and reappraisal.

In Indonesia,—our nearest neighbour and not so long ago a cause of concern to us—remarkable changes have been worked in favour of modera-tion and national rehabilitation. A large part of the world—certainly our part of the world—cannot but be interested in the way the new generation of Indonesian leaders further shape their country's future.

In mainland China, the so-called Cultural Revolution was intended to mobilise the new generation in support of Mao Tse-tung's extreme radical and nationalistic policies. The Cultural Revolution was conceived in ideo-logy: its purpose was to perpetuate the revolutionary spirit of early Com-munism. Its immediate results are difficult to ascertain, let alone assess. But you cannot turn inside out a society so large, and on average so young, as the Chinese, without there being many consequences within, if not beyond, the borders of China. The Chinese have been taught to see themselves as the sole repository of the true Communist doctrine and practice. China is developing a nuclear capability. She continues to give encouragement and support to revolutionary movements in neighbouring countries. She has border disputes with India. She maintains pressure on Burma. She is engaged in building roads in northern Laos that could facilitate activities directed against Thailand. How much her border arguments and ideological disputes with Russia will affect the future history of Asia it is impossible yet to predict.

Japan is now the world's third industrial power. Japan's defence forces are of no mean dimension and there is currently a programme to expand them. It is unlikely that the Japan of the coming decades—an economic giant confident in its technological sophistication and advanced standards of living—will have the same outlook as the Japan of the 50's and 60's. Indeed there is already wide agreement, including among the Japanese themselves, that some kind of break with the postwar era is developing. Japan in the 70's and 80's will have great opportunities to play a progressive and con-structive part in Asia. She has a substantial interest in the stability of the area because much of her trade, upon which her industrial growth and high living standards depend, originates in the South East Asian region or is funnelled through its narrow seas.

For twenty-five years the United States has carried the main burden of defence of the free world. Today it is a matter of public record that a re-appraisal is taking place of the manner in which American commitments might be discharged in the future. That re-appraisal focusses largely on Asia. The Nixon doctrine, first enunciated at Guam, is full of meaning for the countries to our north and to us. American help will be more readily forthcoming to those countries that help themselves; insurgency situations are expected to be contained—better still, prevented from developing—without U.S. combat manpower. It is to be expected that there will be

some contraction of total U.S. forces and installations. However, the Americans have proclaimed that they will stand by their Treaty obligations. Two of these are of major concern to us—ANZUS and SEATO.

Turning to the Soviet Union, her Far East fleet is growing and honourable members will be aware of the increasing Russian interest in the Indian and Pacific Oceans and in the South East Asian region. Likewise she has sought to expand the scope of her diplomatic and trade relations with South East Asian and other nations touching the Indian Ocean. She has placed great emphasis on the development of a world-wide maritime capability, both merchant and naval, which are closely co-ordinated. We have recently had demonstrations of this capability, close to our shores. We have noted her ability to maintain groups of vessels at sea for unusually long periods. This extension of Soviet maritime interest, particularly in the Indian Ocean is not something we can afford to be disinterested in. I have already said Australia cannot confront the Soviet Union, but we must take account of her Indian Ocean activities in our defence policies and planning.

I refer now to Great Britain. The United Kingdom has been searching for a new kind of role. Economic problems and what she regards as the necessity of her future, are leading her to Europe and the Common Market. Her present intention is not to maintain forces in her areas of traditional responsibility in Singapore and Malaysia. Nevertheless, her economic and commercial interests in this region are widespread. She intends to demonstrate her capacity to transport forces to Malaysia and Singapore quickly and she has undertaken to train and exercise in the area after 1971. Her present plans to have no forces permanently based in Malaysia/Singapore and particularly no naval forces, add to the significance that we must attach to the increasing Russian activities in the Indian Ocean.

India, on the northern shores of the Indian Ocean, maintains one of the world's largest armies and some significant air and naval power backed by a growing economy. India strives to create a productive system which will provide one-seventh of the human race with better living standards. In the next ten years the Indian population will almost certainly exceed 700 million. Australian interests cannot fail to be affected by India's success or failure in solving its problems with its neighbours and in building on the foundations of a great independent democracy.

What total situation will emerge from all of this we cannot foresee. Clearly, forces working around the world are going to affect South East Asia and Australia. While we must not fear change, and indeed social change is necessary in many countries, it would be foolish to act as if we had assumed the overall thrust of future events will automatically enhance our security. We must note that of the seven major countries mentioned, Indonesia is our closest neighbour. Changing policies of the others are certain to have a cumulative impact on the region of our strategic interest.

In addition, our region of particular concern has its own problems of divisions between and within states. There is, of course, promise in countries which are marching boldy towards a better future for their citizens. At the same time, ethnic, religious and political tensions and the pressure of rising

populations, not matched by economic and social development, must cause concern.

Another point has to be made. The very nature of war has changed. We now have to contend with a variety of politico/military situations. These include subversion, confrontation, guerilla wars, "Revolutionary Warfare" and other limited conventional operations short of a "declared" war. Propaganda is an important weapon in these situations.

OUR BASIC APPROACH TO DEFENCE POLICY

Against the strategic background I have sketched, two basic approaches were available to us.

We, on the periphery of the region, might have sought to avoid its uncertainties and imponderables. Some might have taken the view that our growing wealth, our high productivity, our advanced technology and our geographical advantages, equipped us to take care of ourselves except against nuclear attack or a large-scale invasion, and that no additional effort was required. This is a strange, odd, concept. It smacks of Australia being in the region but not of it; of Australia passively waiting to be overtaken by events. It would be an attempt to have all the advantages at no risk. This surely is not the way to a viable meaningful community of friendly nations devoted to economic growth and development in an environment of stability and security.

The Australian Government has consistently engaged itself in political policies and in trade, financial and developmental aid activities which are designed to make an effective Australian contribution to the economic growth and political stability of the region to which we belong. It would be irrational for us to pursue these policy objectives while at the same time refusing to contribute to military security and to creating an environment of confidence which is indispensable for countries embarking on long range developmental plans.

If a policy of isolating ourselves ever made any sense, which I deny, the Nixon doctrine to which I have alluded makes it a complete nonsense. Considered from the narrowest military ground a policy with isolation as its central concept would pose one inescapable question: how long could we stand aloof in armed—or unarmed—detachment from our environment? One can only guess—probably a decade—perhaps a generation. There might be comfort in that for us—less for our next generation perhaps. For you do not make South East Asia or the Indian Ocean disappear by turning your back on them. The region of South East Asia and the surrounding Pacific and Indian Ocean waters comprise our environment: we are as well a part of the environment of the other nations in our region. If that environment is going to change we want to be able to play a meaningful part in the changes—not work out a relationship after the region had been transformed by processes with which we were not associated and of which we had accumulated little knowledge or experience.

Of course we and other countries hope that by diplomacy and policies of aid we will reduce and ultimately eliminate threats to the region so that

we may all devote our energies to improving the standard of life of our people. Military isolation on Australia's part would obstruct this objective. Military co-operation is designed to establish security so that the governments concerned can work for their own people without hindrance.

We reject the concept of detachment. We accept the risks and opportunities of involvement, within the limits of the Prime Minister's statement of the 25th February last year, because we believe isolation would lead to greater risks both for the region and for Australia. We do not believe there is any security in isolation. We believe there will be no permanent security for any of the small countries of the region until there is permanent security for all. This being the case, within our resources our military capability must be geared for deployment in the region of which Australia is a part when in our judgment we conclude that this is demanded by our concept of regional security as well as for the obvious purpose of meeting possible threats to Australian territory.

This is the only proper conclusion, to which an analysis of our basic situation should lead us.

It should be noted also any other course would involve the denial of our Treaty obligations. It would mean the elimination of our SEATO associations. It would be incompatible with ANZUS which some tend to suggest wrongly is a Treaty of one way obligation. ANZUS does not mean merely that other people should prepare themselves to defend Australia's national interests.

A policy based in isolation would have meant a different response from the one we gave the Malaysian and Singaporean requests that Australia continue to maintain forces in their countries. For the future it would mean standing aside from other forms of regional co-operation in Defence. If anyone imagines that we could effectively maintain a broad ranging co-operation with the region but without forces capable of fulfilling a regional role then I can only say that such a policy would earn no response from our friends in the area. Politically it would lack credibility. In purely military terms, it would be impracticable. To be fully effective a regional policy at present requires deployment of forces in the area.

The decision the Government has taken concerning involvement in South East Asia and the maintenance of a force from our three Services in Singapore/Malaysia might appear superficially to represent little change from previous policy. But I hope I have said enough about the changing strategic setting to demonstrate that, if our decision is one for continuing involvement, it is also one for involvement in a new set of circumstances.

So far as the region of South East Asia is concerned, the withdrawal of Britain as a power with major forces permanently stationed in the region is irreversible: the U.S. is re-appraising the nature of its involvement: Soviet political and strategic policies impinge progressively upon the region: a changing Japan must feel its interests in security and stability affected by developments in the region: while China continues in a position of self-imposed isolation and of intransigence towards all non-compliant regimes in its vicinity.

It is against this background of change that we are moving from a situation in which we have been supporting commitments of major powers, to a position of partnership with other regional countries which must now accept greater responsibility for their own defence.

The familiar forces which have influenced international events for the past 20 years are changing in directions which we cannot yet fully foresee. We are developing Defence policies designed to serve us into the 80's in a situation where we are faced with formidable uncertainties about the world in which we will be living.

It follows that Australia will be required to show initiative and flexibility in the execution of her Defence policies.

At the same time our commitments must be related at all times to our capabilities and it must be clearly understood that there are limits on both.

MALAYSIA/SINGAPORE

I want to refer in more detail to our relationship with Malaysia and Singapore. Since the early 1950's Australia has had a tradition of co-operation with, and of assistance to, these countries. We provided military help at the time of communist emergency; we provided help during confrontation; and now when the British have announced a decision no longer to station forces in the region, we have said that, providing the two Governments continue to desire our presence, we will maintain Forces in the Malaysia/ Singapore area after 1971.

This commitment should be judged against the spirit of co-operation and assistance that has prevailed over a great number of years. Governments nowadays do not sign blank cheques saying automatically that if something happens their troops will march. Our friends in Malaysia and Singapore will judge us by the pattern of past relationships. The past could give them no cause for doubt or hesitation as to where Australia would stand. They understand fully, that decisions about the actual commitment of our troops at any particular time, and in any particular situation, must be just as much the prerogative of the Australian Government, as would be decisions by them affecting their forces.

The arrangements we are developing with these two countries both in the context of the Five Power arrangements, and separately, are well known. There have been Five Power meetings in Kuala Lumpur and Canberra at Ministerial level and at Kuala Lumpur at senior official level. As well, the many details involved, including those connected with the proposed new Air defence system, are being worked out in four Advisory Groups dealing with Naval, Army, Air and Joint Service matters.

In a variety of ways we have done much to strengthen the defence capability of Malaysia and Singapore; the Sabres for Malaysia is a well known example. Discussions continue with the Malaysians about the co-location of RMAF units with ours at Butterworth and with the Singaporeans about the final location of our forces there now that their move from Terandak has been completed.

301

VIETNAM

The Governor-General's speech reiterated the Australian and allied purpose in Vietnam to oppose aggression and to seek to establish the circumstances in which the citizens of South Vietnam can live under a Government of their choice.

The Governor-General's speech went on—

> My Government is glad to note that the increasing capacity of the South Vietnamese to defend themselves has already permitted the withdrawal of some Allied Forces. Should the future situation permit a further substantial withdrawal of troops—beyond those announced by President Nixon on 16 December 1969—then in consultation with the Government of the Republic of Vietnam and the Government of the United States, some Australian troops will be included, at some stage, in the numbers scheduled for such withdrawal.

My Department, the Department of the Army and others have been examining the situation closely so we will be in a position to discuss the matter with the Governments of South Vietnam, the United States and New Zealand.

GUIDING PRINCIPLES FOR THE DEVELOPMENT
OF DEFENCE CAPABILITY

Our strategic situation coupled with our basic approach to regional defence leads to certain broad principles in developing our Defence capability. They are—

(a) we seek the maximum of strategic flexibility;
(b) we see Australian security as intimately tied in with regional security;
(c) we wish our forces to be organised, equipped and trained so that they can be effectively employed in the region of which Australia is a part as well as for the direct defence of Australia;
(d) we see our forces as not being too closely tailored to particular requirements but versatile and flexible and capable of rapid deployment over a wide range of situations;
(e) we see our forces as being capable of a rapid response, with an offensive capability that would be an effective deterrent because it would enable us to reach out to an enemy;
(f) we see a need for our forces to be more self contained with a high degree of strategic and tactical mobility;
(g) we believe our forces must have reasonable compatibility of weapons and equipment with those of the U.S. and New Zealand;
(h) we see our forces requiring a sound infrastructure in Australia and its Territories, adequate to support the operations of our forces wherever they may be.

THE DEFENCE ORGANISATION

The development of Defence capability is a much more complicated procedure than was once the case; we need the professional military advice of

our most senior officers; we need the best possible political and military intelligence; we need the best possible scientific and technical input; we need procedures for assessing our requirements for complicated equipments; we need to be able to question and probe effectively to make sure that the best possible solution to a particular military need is achieved. We need planning and preparations for the development of our Forces based on joint concepts and plans to meet the various situations that may confront us. We need to ensure that each of the services prepares for the same kind of conflicts, in the same places and in the same time scale.

We must not be bound by tradition. If a matter has been pursued in a certain way that in itself is no argument for continuing in the old way. On the other hand, before tried and proven methods are abandoned, we must be sure that new ways and techniques will be better. Above all change for its own sake is to be avoided.

The factors that we need to have in mind are twofold. First there are the likely circumstances for which we need to raise, train and equip forces. We have to project a view about this as far ahead as is sensibly possible. Secondly there are the technological developments that are likely to bear on our choice of weapons systems.

I propose now to deal with the organisational changes we have made to aid our decision making.

Joint Staff

I want first to refer to the new Joint Staff arrangements established in the Department of Defence by my predecessor. The Joint Staff replaces most of the numerous Committees which previously existed to which people were allocated by the individual Services. The Service members of the Committees had a dual responsibility: to the Committee and to their Service Chief.

Now senior officers from each of the Services are seconded to the Defence Department generally for a three year period to work on the Joint Staff along with selected officers of the Departments of Defence and External Affairs with responsibility only for the Joint Staff function. By this means members see problems as defence, not individual Service, problems. At the same time each gains an insight into, and invaluable experience of, the totality of Defence planning, which should later stand him in good stead in his own Service.

The Joint Staff represents an integration within the Defence Department of the best Army, Navy and Air Force expertise. The Department also provides for the co-ordinated examination of military, political, scientific and economic factors. The Joint Staff provides more effective support for the Joint Planning Committee and the Chiefs of Staff Committee. Its work is essential to consideration by the Defence Committee, the Minister for Defence, and, where appropriate, the Cabinet.

Intelligence Arrangements

Australia must have intelligence arrangements of the highest order to

ensure the availability of the best political, strategic and tactical information relevant to our interests.

The House is aware of the recent changes in our intelligence arrangements. We have amalgamated within the Defence Department, in a Joint Intelligence Organisation, the former Joint Intelligence Bureau with sections of the three Services Directorates of Intelligence. We have provided for the full participation of the Department of External Affairs. The purpose is to provide a unified environment for the quick and complete pooling of information and the consideration of the diverse factors that have to be weighed at the national or strategic level of assessment. Matters that must be considered include strategic, political, military, economic and scientific factors. Within this framework the former Joint Intelligence Committee has been replaced by a National Intelligence Committee at a higher level. It will include representatives from the Department of External Affairs as well as from the Joint Intelligence Organisation. It will be responsible for broad assessments and projections relevant to the planning of national security policy. I add that each of the Services remains responsible for meeting its own operational intelligence requirements.

Defence Science Arrangements

To provide the necessary scientific input, organisational changes have been made in my Department and the whole Defence Group. In the first place, there is now in the Defence Department an appropriate and active Defence Science Branch headed by a Chief Defence Scientist. Through the Defence Research and Development Policy Committee, all scientific research in the Department of Defence and the three Services and the Department of Supply is co-ordinated. The number of scientific advisers seconded to the Services and the scope of their responsibilities have been increased.

Considerable support continues to be provided by the Research and Development Establishments in the Department of Supply. These laboratories maintain a high level of scientific competence over a wide range of disciplines, and are able to provide direct scientific assistance in solving many problems which arise from time to time in defence activity. The resources and facilities at Weapons Research Establishment formerly allocated to the development and support of the Joint Project operations at Woomera have progressively been re-oriented to meet the needs of Australian Defence. A new Central Studies Unit has been established in Supply to engage in operational research studies on behalf of the Defence Group of Departments and the Armed Services. Its role will complement the operational analysis activities being undertaken within Defence and Service Departments and within other Establishments of the Department of Supply.

A number of project development tasks are in progress designed to provide solutions to specific local defence needs, and if successful some of these could lead to production of various items of defence equipment.

Policy and Analysis

The Policy and Analysis sections of the Department have been greatly strengthened.

A Policy Planning Branch has been established to ensure that proper attention is given to the more fundamental and long range issues in the strategic field that impinge on our security.

In addition, proposals for equipment and major works coming from the Services are submitted to the Department of Defence for examination. The critical task is to make sure that regardless of individual Service interest, the best "Defence" solutions are found and the best allocation is made of those resources which are available to Defence.

To assist in this decision making, we have established another group within the Department whose task it is to examine proposals and possible alternatives, taking account of the benefits and costs of each. Provided that our military requirements will satisfactorily be met, a proposal that will contribute to our industrial or technological skills in Australia, or put broader, to our economic and national development, is more attractive than one that will not.

Costs cover more than the price tag on prime equipment. So we require the identification and costing of all ancillaries—for example the cost of support facilities, manpower, training and maintenance.

The Services will adopt the same techniques.

The procurement of Defence equipment is so important that it is my firm belief that all techniques must be used and exploited to ensure that our military needs are most effectively and economically met.

Special Studies Branch

A Special Studies Branch has been established in the Defence Department to examine aspects of the functions, organisation and activities of the Defence Group of Departments so that we may achieve the most effective use of existing resources.

Rationalisation or integration will not be pursued for their own sake; traditions have a value that should not be hastily discounted. But, if rationalisation or integration or co-location, or single-service management, or the standardisation of equipment, methods and procedures can achieve savings in manpower or in money without affecting efficiency, then those changes must be pursued. Within this context a number of studies are being undertaken. I shall refer to these later.

DEFENCE AND INDUSTRY

We recognise industry as the "fourth arm of defence". With this in mind, we have promulgated guiding principles for the procurement of Defence equipment. They aim to ensure that the scope for Australian production is considered in the early stages of a Service requirement.

It is in the interests of our allies as well as our own that the Australian industrial base is sound, diversified and technologically competent. Much credit is due to my predecessor for being the first to enunciate the policy of offset arrangements. It remains to see that those arrangements work. A mission concerned with these matters recently visited the United States led by Sir Ian McLennan who is also Chairman of the Defence (Industrial) Committee.

This committee was established and the Business Board restructured to give my Department the best possible advice on the capability of Australian industry and the best means of harnessing Australian production to the Defence effort. The businessmen members of this Committee and Board have already, in their examination of some matters of major importance, contributed much. We look to them playing a vital role in the general development of Australia's defence capacity and in aiding us to get the greatest value for every defence dollar.

In this context I should also note the general logistic arrangements that my predecessor concluded with New Zealand.

PLANNING FOR THE FUTURE

Within the new Defence organisation we are looking at a number of long term problems. In these studies special emphasis has been given to Joint Service-Civilian participation to make the best use of available knowledge, military experience and analytical ability.

Where possible, our efforts are directed to ensure that defence and national development march together. This applies not only to our relationships with industry to which I have referred, but also to the infrastructure required for military purposes—for example, airfields and dockyards. Wherever we can, we aim to develop facilities which will equally serve civil and national development objectives.

Army Establishment

In recent years modern barrack accommodation has been built for six battalions. After Vietnam, additional accommodation will be required. There is a joint Defence/Army examination of this matter.

Naval Dockyards

We have under study the whole gamut of our requirements for naval dockyard facilities. Considering the withdrawal of the Royal Navy from the Indian Ocean, it is no longer wise to concentrate all naval support facilities in the Eastern States. A major question concerns the facilities that we should provide in Cockburn Sound that might earlier have been considered for Sydney or Melbourne.

Inter-Relationship between Naval and Air Power

There is the highly complex problem of the inter-relationship of naval and air-power embracing the character and place of naval platform and land-based aircraft. It is to be remembered that Melbourne has a life expectancy only until about 1980. So we have under study the whole complex of problems that relate to the place of carriers in our force structure.

Armed Forces of Papua and New Guinea

We have under study the kinds of forces that ought to be developed in Papua and New Guinea to meet the needs of an emerging independent community. Whatever may lie in the future, we have a responsibility to ensure,

as far as we may, that the forces in Papua and New Guinea will enable their future governments to meet their longer term defence needs.

Manpower

We are making a full examination of the total service manpower problems including National Service. In our full employment society, whatever other countries in their circumstances believe possible about fully volunteer forces, I see no likelihood that we will be able to sustain the forces required without National Service in Australia. The purpose of this survey is not only to assess manpower requirements but also to ensure that we make the most effective use of available manpower, not only for the regular forces, but also for the reserve and citizen forces which are a vital element in our total defence capability.

Medical Services

The examination of the scope for rationalisation of overall medical services of our Armed Forces including the military hospital facilities required and the use that might be made of the hospital and rehabilitation facilities provided by the Repatriation Commission is well advanced.

Procurement

The organisations, functions and practices of the three Service Departments and the Department of Supply in relation to procurement matters generally, both in Australia and overseas, are under study. The questions concern the degree to which the Department of Supply can be made responsible for Defence procurement—an area where much has already been achieved—and the scope for extension of the single-manager concept in respect of control of stores.

Flying Training

An overall review of flying training for the three Services is in progress. In particular, consideration is being given to the possibility of establishing a Joint Service Helicopter Training Centre.

Service Communications

The scope for rationalisation of Service communications is under review. These assume great importance because we have, in many ways, entered a new era in communications and if we are to march in harmony with the many exciting technological developments in this field in a coherent and economical way, a unified Defence approach will be essential.

Standardisation of Inventories

As a result of early studies, conversion of the inventories of defence equipment—some 1,300,000 items of supply—to a Defence Cataloguing System common to the three Services, and the Department of Supply and also to systems in the U.S. and NATO countries has made much progress. Considerable savings will result from reduced stock holdings, and by continual screening of apparently new items.

Organisation of the Army

To conclude my remarks in this section, Mr. Speaker, I might refer to the study which the Army, in agreement with my Department, is about to undertake of the present Command structure and of the functions of the various Branches at Headquarters level. Our present structure, as is well known, is largely based on State boundaries: it is rooted in the past: it goes back to the circumstances of the first decade of this century. The examination will determine, for example whether the geographic Army Command structure should be maintained or whether other arrangements should be made. My Department will be associated with Army's study to watch particularly for implications on our total defence organisation.

PERSONNEL

Time will not permit me to say as much as I should like about the importance of personnel policies. Our economic and social circumstances are such that there is fierce competition for manpower. Defence is of the highest importance. Our Services require officers and men of the highest calibre. To obtain them, and retain them, we must have personnel policies in tune with our rapidly changing social attitudes and economic standards, in tune with the character of a democratic society in the latter part of the twentieth century.

Tri-Service Academy

I now have the Report of the Committee headed by Sir Leslie Martin which was appointed by my predecessor to develop a plan for the establishment of one Armed Forces Academy which would provide education at the tertiary level for officer cadets of all three Services. This report is being processed by my Department and the Service Departments and I am preparing a Submission for Cabinet.

Australian Services Staff College

In January this year, the first course commenced at the Joint Service Wing of the Australian Services Staff College. The Wing is located in temporary premises in Canberra pending the eventual co-location in Canberra of the single Service wings of the College which, for the present, are located in separate Service establishments. The objective of the Joint Service Wing is, broadly speaking, to train selected officers from the Armed Services for Joint Service Staff and Command appointments. Senior officers of the Public Service concerned with Defence also attend the course. The six months course places emphasis upon Joint Service planning and operations and the wider aspects of Australia's defence and foreign policies.

Pay and Conditions of Service

It is clear that matters relating to pay and other conditions of service cannot be divorced from the total stream of Services personnel administration, for example, such items as recruitment policies, duration of engagement, housing and so on.

As I announced a few months ago, we have established a Pay and Conditions of Service Branch in my Department. A new high level Committee, the Defence (Conditions of Service) Committee, has assumed the functions previously discharged by the Treasury Finance Committee. This means that pay and conditions of service will, for the future, be considered by a Committee having equal status with the other top level committees of the Higher Defence Machinery and within a Defence environment.

I want to mention two matters in particular which have an impact on Servicemen.

The first concerns housing. That much progress has been made in providing housing for our servicemen is quickly apparent. In 1964 we had some 11,000 houses for the Services. By the end of June next, we should have about 20,000 houses available. In addition, approximately another 1,000 will be under construction, or programmed for early commencement. In the meantime, of course, our forces have grown, but housing has more than kept pace with that expansion.

I believe that no aspect of service life gives rise to more dissatisfaction than the lack of certainty about the availability of housing at a new posting. So we intend to improve the housing position. We will continue vigorously with the major housing programme and we will be looking to see whether there are other practicable methods of cutting down delays, where they do occur, in a married serviceman becoming eligible for a married quarter after posting.

Associated with housing is the frequency of postings. Too frequent moves are particularly unsettling for families and for school aged children. While the Services are giving much attention to reducing the frequency of postings, I shall be looking for even better results. A solution is not necessarily as easy as it seems. Particularly am I thinking of Army, so long as its obligations in Vietnam continue, which call for one year tours of duty.

These two matters are of great importance. I am sure that they bear directly on the high turnover of personnel the Army and Navy have been experiencing. That turnover, of course, requires an all too great diversion of personnel to training functions.

PROGRAMMING

My predecessor told the Parliament last year that the Government had decided to move from fixed three year defence programmes to what he described as a five year rolling programme. I think the latter concept is not yet clearly understood: especially because the word "programme" tends to indicate some immediately ascertainable series of items that are going to be purchased over any given period of five years.

The fixed period programmes of the past tended to lead to an uneven development of defence policy. Put broadly, unless some new factor emerged, proposals not included in one period programme were postponed to the next.

We have now chosen a five year span for planning purposes. This we see as a realistic period permitting us a reasonable assessment of international political trends, while not being too short to allow for the long lead times

involved in acquiring modern defence equipment. Here I should make the point that much time may elapse between the initial formulation of a Service requirement and the actual decision to acquire the equipment sought.

Under the new concept the practice will be to review each year the future requirements of the Services over a forward period of five years against—

First, the current assessment of our strategic situation which itself attempts to look forward over a ten year period;

Second, consideration of the outlook for the capabilities and characteristics of the forces over the next five year period;

Third, against the progress being made with studies in the Services and my Department of the most effective means of providing such capabilities as are needed; and

Fourth, against the technological developments in sight.

Normally under these arrangements, defence equipment proposals will come forward at Budget time. So there will be announced, each year, additional proposals whether for needed expansion or replacement purposes. There will not be one momentous announcement once every five years but an announcement every year, in the setting I have described. I might illustrate this. At the beginning of any five year period there may be a certain piece of equipment that is believed necessary for a particular Service. Research and development may not be sufficiently far advanced for firm decisions to be made, but in 18 months or two years we may be in a position to make such decisions. Under our new programming concept there will be no inhibitions about this.

Thus, unlike the three year programme, the five year forward look will provide a continuing ability to respond to the progressive emergence of new equipment and techniques and the progressive development of defence planning and policy.

This new concept will not remove problems of selection. Indeed we will always have to be careful that we do not, at any given stage, make decisions about new projects, important though they may be, that because of their cost might shut out higher priority items which will not be ready for decision for one, two or three years.

THE ROLES AND CAPABILITY OF OUR DEFENCE FORCES

I have spoken about the changes in my Department, to which I give full credit to my predecessor and the previous Secretary. I have indicated that these changes will be continuing—we are not in a static position. But organisation is nothing if it does not produce the desired results, that is, strong viable defence forces directed to meet the needs of Australia.

I want to indicate in more precise terms the roles that we expect our defence forces to be able to fill, either in joint service operations or in a single service basis. I want to indicate in the broadest terms the present capacities of our forces and then I will tell the House how the decisions we have now made will add to that capacity.

Force Roles

Earlier I mentioned the guiding principles for the development of Defence capability.

We are committed to regional defence. We are committed to the maintenance, under present circumstances, of forces overseas. We are committed to the protection of the Australian mainland and Territories. In conjunction with our friends and allies we must contribute to the security of our trade routes and our lines of communication. These commitments require that we pay particular regard to the development of certain areas of our overall defence capability. While these point to certain roles for all three Services, they are better viewed in a functional setting because the roles of the individual Services are seldom exclusive; generally any function involves more than one Service.

To start with, we need a greater maritime capability in the waters around Australia, the Pacific and Indian Oceans and the seas to our north. This involves both the Navy and the Air Force.

We need greater strategic and tactical mobility, the capability to move forces quickly with adequate logistic support, the capability to bring to bear maximum fire power. We need to be able to maintain forces that we deploy abroad. We need the capacity for emergency air-lift of troops and reinforcements and for subsequent support by sea. We have made much progress in this area and the announcements that I will shortly make will add to it. It does not mean that this capability should be exclusively Service provided. It includes making provision for harnessing commercial transport, maritime and air, if ever the need arises.

Next there is scope for increasing our offensive capability.

I now come to the new decisions. The figures quoted represent for the most part the estimated capital cost of the projects.

	$m.
Light Destroyer (Patrol) Detailed Design	5.0
Eighty four Observation Helicopters	
(Light Helicopters)	23.0
Forty two Utility Helicopters	31.6
Eleven VTOL Aircraft for Fire Support	
(Helicopter Gunships)	13.2
Naval Communications Station, Darwin—	
New Receiving Facilities	3.8
Overhaul and Modernisation of gun mounts	
for the Guided Missile Destroyers	8.1
Two Oberon-class Submarines	37.2
Six Low Cover Radars	6.0
One Logistic Cargo Ship	10.0
Ten Additional Skyhawks	20.0
Two Twin-engined Support and Training aircraft	8.0

The estimated total capital project costs of these various items is $165.9m. I recall that the estimated capital project costs of the major items announced

by my predecessor last year was $140m. And let me add immediately that these figures do not include the ultimate cost of the facilities that may be developed at Cockburn Sound—merely the estimated cost of the first stage, the causeway—or the full cost of designing the light destroyer, let alone any element of cost for the destroyers that may ultimately be ordered.

I wish to indicate on a functional basis the importance of these decisions.

Our maritime capability will be enhanced by the two additional Oberon-class submarines and by the new Naval Communications Station at Darwin. Our aim in pressing forward with the design studies for the new class of light destroyers, announced by my predecessor, is also to add to our maritime capability.

Strategic mobility will be improved by the construction of a Logistic Cargo Ship. This will be capable of carrying the Army's landing craft, vehicles, equipment and stores to areas of operation and of unloading them without recourse to developed ports. While this ship will be designed to serve the Army's needs, it will, when not required for defence purposes, be available for efficient commercial operation by the Australian National Line. It should be noted that the decision made last year to construct a Fast Combat Support ship in Australia at the cost of $42 million was also directly related to the improvement of our strategic mobility.

Our tactical mobility, and at the same time fire power and battle-field surveillance of our forces, will be improved by the acquisition of 11 helicopter gunships and we will also buy 42 Utility helicopters and 84 Light helicopters which will provide for replacement of the existing equipment over its period of service and also add to the eventual strength. The final decision about the type of gunship should be made in April. The choice remains between the Huey Cobra and the Armed Iroquois. There are two possibilities for the light observation helicopter. They are the Bell OH 58A and the Westland Sud SA341. There are no technical considerations which would bias the decision for their required military purposes. The final selection will be made on the basis of the best prospects for local manufacture, including commercial sales. It will be recalled that last year we decided to buy twelve medium lift helicopters and eight heavy landing craft, directed to the same end—the improvement of our tactical mobility.

Our offensive capability will be improved, not only by the purchase of the two Oberon Submarines which I have mentioned, but also by the doubling of the Skyhawk strength of the R.A.N. to twenty aircraft. This purchase is subject to the proviso that we can get early deliveries and therefore a high utilisation during the remaining life of "Melbourne".

To improve the *general capability of the Army*, Cabinet last year gave Army permission to enter into commitments for capital equipment which would bring expenditure up to a level of $60m. for the year 1970-71. Cabinet has now approved Army entering into additional commitments up to the same level for the year 1971-72. These authorisations will enable the Army to take full advantage of forward ordering for long lead items. A great deal of Army equipment concerns very important but unspectacular items. In addition to the equipments I have specially mentioned, items now to be

procured include additional Armoured Personnel Carriers, trucks cargo 3/4 ton and other load carrying vehicles, lightweight man-pack radio sets and other communications equipment, engineering equipment, large quantities of ammunition of various calibres, tentage and shelters. These new authorisations will also enable more and better equipment to be made available to the Citizen Military Forces, which I regard as a matter of great importance. Procurement of new equipment planned to satisfy C.M.F. needs includes increasingly items of operational standard such as personnel carriers of the type in use in Vietnam and man-pack radio sets.

The Government is also well aware that there are other requirements that must be met in future but on which decisions are not yet possible: in some cases because testing and evaluation has not yet proceeded far enough, in some cases because further research and development is necessary, in others because our studies are not far enough advanced. Vehicles, tanks, surface to air missiles for the Army are illustrations: maritime reconnaissance and strategic airlift aircraft for the R.A.A.F. are others. Further ahead are problems associated with the replacement of the Mirages.

As we enter a new decade I believe it would be instructive to glance backward for a moment and see how far we have come since 1960. While I do not wish to weary the House with a detailed comparison of our forces today with those of ten years ago, may I illustrate our progress including the impact of present decisions, again in functional terms.

Our maritime capability has been built up by the addition of three guided missile destroyers, all of which have performed intensive service in Vietnam; four Oberon-class submarines, thus restoring this versatile weapon system to an important place in the structure of the R.A.N.; a major modernisation of H.M.A.S. Melbourne and its re-equipment with Tracker, Skyhawk and Wessex aircraft, the re-equipment of an R.A.A.F. Neptune squadron with Orion aircraft; 20 patrol boats essential for surveillance and control of coastal waters both of Australia and the Territory of Papua and New Guinea; and the replacement of "Q" class and Tribal class frigates with six River class Destroyer Escorts, the last of which we will commission later this year. As well, our oceanographic and hydrographic capability so necessary to successful maritime operations, is being developed with modern survey and hydrographic ships and an oceanographic research ship. The new Oberons and later the light destroyers will add further to maritime capability.

Our strategic mobility has been enhanced by the conversion of the former carrier SYDNEY to a Fast Troop Transport; the acquisition of a second squadron of HERCULES transport aircraft; the addition of a Fast Fleet Tanker, H.M.A.S. Supply, and the Australian built Destroyer maintenance Ship, H.M.A.S. Stalwart; and now the construction of a Fast Combat Support Ship approved last August; and the Army Logistic Ship, announced tonight.

Great strides have been made in *tactical mobility*. In 1960 the Army was still operating much as it had in World War II. Now it is aided by two squadrons of Caribou short take off and landing aircraft, numbers of utility

and light helicopters, a whole new range of armoured personnel carriers and related vehicles, and water craft of various kinds. The Army Aviation Corps has been established and is progressively expanding. Further purchases announced last year include Medium Lift Helicopters and eight Landing Craft Heavy. The choice for the Medium Lift Helicopter remains between the Boeing Vertol and Sikorsky. Tonight's announcement of additional Observation Helicopters, of 42 Utility Helicopters and of 11 Helicopter Gunships adds greatly to this capacity.

While there has been an increase in our *offensive capabilities*, there are yet unresolved problems concerning the strike aircraft. New equipment in service or on order includes 4 squadrons of Mirage aircraft, which are also effective in the ground support role, the Oberon-class submarines which I have already mentioned, the Skyhawk aircraft embarked on Melbourne, and the fire support capabilities of the guided missile destroyers. Tonight's announcement of the decision to procure two more Oberons and ten additional Skyhawks provides significant additions.

Our general Army capability has been vastly improved, both by the introduction of National Service and by the procurement of large quantities of modern and effective equipment. Today we have nine battle-proved battalions and in addition, three squadrons of highly trained SAS.

Over the last ten years the Army has in large measure been re-equipped. More modern howitzers, anti-tank weapons, mortars, machine guns and rifles and radio sets have been purchased in large numbers. Stocks of light, medium and heavy trucks have been greatly improved. The $2\frac{1}{2}$ ton and 5 ton trucks have been designed and constructed in Australia and contracts have been let for the prototype of a 1-ton general purpose vehicle which will replace the $\frac{3}{4}$-ton truck over a period of years.

More modern water transport vehicles and additional landing craft of various sizes have been obtained and in the last Budget authorisation was provided for 8 Landing Craft Heavy to replace the aging LSMs. The effect of the purchases made in recent years is to increase the range of modern weapons and equipment available to the C.M.F. both during home training and particularly whilst in camp.

Manpower

The manpower of the regular forces has been built up considerably over the last ten years from 48,000 in January 1960 to 84,700 in January 1970. Of this total the Navy strength has grown from 10,600 to 17,400; the Army from 21,900 to 44,500 and the R.A.A.F. from 15,500 to 22,800. In the same ten year period the Pacific Island Regiment has increased from 600 to 2,500.

INFRASTRUCTURE

Much has been done to build up the infrastructure upon which the efficiency of our Services depends.

The last decade has seen the greatest building programme for the Services

in Australian history. Extensive Army establishments have been built at Swanbourne, W.A.; Puckapunyal, Victoria; Holdsworthy, Kapooka and Singleton in New South Wales; Enoggera and Townsville in Queensland; while barracks for the Pacific Island Regiment have been completed at Port Moresby, Lae, Wewak and Goldie River.

For the Navy, major refitting facilities for submarines, barracks, ammunition depot extensions and patrol craft facilities have been built in the Sydney area. Very large improvements have been carried out at the training centres at H.M.A.S. Leeuwin (Fremantle); H.M.A.S. Cerberus (Flinders) and H.M.A.S. Nirimba (Schofields). Improvements have also been carried out to the dockyards at Garden Island, Cockatoo Island and Williamstown.

Many millions of dollars have also been spent on the rehabilitation and development of R.A.A.F. bases throughout Australia.

The modernisation and improvement to Department of Supply factories has continued. A new plant for the production of TNT is nearing completion at the Albion Explosives factory.

New works under construction or approved include the development of the R.A.A.F. airfield at Learmonth, the construction of the access causeway at Cockburn Sound in Western Australia, the establishment of the Army Aviation Centre at Oakey in Queensland, erection of a new clothing factory at Coburg in Victoria and construction of storage facilities for the Department of Supply at St. Mary's, N.S.W. Also in hand is the provision of personnel accommodation for the R.A.N. at Nowra, whilst new CMF depots are programmed for Blacktown and Armidale in New South Wales, and Sunshine, Clayton and Oakleigh in Victoria. Other major works proposals are under consideration.

Over the past ten years, the Government has spent $413m. on capital works and real estate procurement programmes for the Services and the Supply Department and $56m. on the provision of houses for servicemen under the Commonwealth/States Housing Agreement. In the current financial year additional amounts of $49m. and $10m. respectively will be spent.

THE CITIZEN FORCES

No statement of the character I am making would be complete without mention of our Citizen Forces.

There has, I believe, been a tendency in recent years for the public to overlook the vital importance of the Citizen Forces to Australia's defence capacity and posture. In the case of the C.M.F. factors tending to influence this have been the growth of the Regular Army, the introduction and development of the National Service Scheme, our involvement in the Vietnam war, and the publicity which all of them have had.

Many people have come to think of the Regular Army supplemented by the National Service Scheme being all that we need for the Army to be able satisfactorily to fulfil its role. The success of our Army component in its role in Vietnam may itself engender such notions.

This must be corrected. We must plan for many contingencies. Some require forces in excess of the sort of Regular Army we can foresee as being

reasonably within our capacity as a nation to man, equip and maintain in peace.

If our planning is to have credibility and substance, it must be backed up by realistic and practicable methods of providing follow-up forces for the Regular Army.

So, in general, the role of the C.M.F. is twofold—

(1) to provide back up forces for the Regular Army in times of Defence emergency;

(2) to provide for expansion in the event of mobilisation if that should ever again be upon us.

In spite of the operational requirements of the Regular Army the overall equipment position for the C.M.F. is as good as, if not better than, it has ever been before. There are, however, some recognised deficiencies, particularly in Armour and Signals, which will be overcome.

Good progress has been made in the provision of new training depots and the replacement of old style or temporary buildings for the C.M.F. in all Commands, and significant provision is being made in this field for the future. The new type depots are designed according to the functional needs of units under modern conditions of training.

It is in the field of training that the greatest advances have been made. Far greater emphasis is now placed upon centralised rather than unit training for the production and subsequent promotion of officers, the training of non-commissioned officers and specialists, and the basic training of recruits.

The present size and structure of the C.M.F. provides a sound basis for future planning. Such matters as organisation, equipment and training will be examined along with similar features of the regular forces—for the regular and C.M.F. components cannot be considered in isolation.

If I have in my remarks devoted major attention to the C.M.F. I would not like it thought that I am unmindful of the needs of the Naval Reserve and Citizen Air Force units. These also are being given attention.

CONCLUSION

I believe it is important that the House should know, that the Australian people should know, as much as can be, of what we are doing in the defence field. I have tried to depict the total picture but necessarily many of the matters have been mentioned only in the briefest terms.

While I have mentioned in the broadest possible terms the kinds of roles our forces have to fulfil, and the functional areas calling for particular attention, the level of forces necessary for these tasks and the equipment provided for them have to be decided by the Government after weighing all considerations. The Services requirements are first subjected to the kind of examination I have outlined. But when these requirements have been reviewed, it falls to the Government of the day to decide the resources that can be devoted to defence. There are in our sort of society "constraints" on what can be done in any area. We have learned long ago that defence needs cannot be divorced from other community needs. No country can meet

every possible defence contingency. So it falls to the Government, having weighed the best advice it can get from its military and civilian advisers, to judge the likely threats and the likely tasks that will fall to our forces at any one time. The Government has to judge what must be done to enable them to be discharged, and weigh the cost against the other demands that our community makes upon resources.

There is no scope for complacency about what we must do to ensure the future security of Australia. I have indicated that in the circumstances of the British withdrawal from our North, and of American re-appraisal, Australia will be required to put forth a greater effort embodying greater independence. I envisage the capability of our forces being continuously improved in the years ahead. I do not suggest that we can afford to devote resources to defence, unmindful of Australia's needs in other areas. We must hope to establish circumstances by diplomacy, by policies of economic assistance, by policies of regional security, in which the countries of our region will be able to devote their full resources to improving the standard of life of their own people.

While this must be and will remain our objective we will be naive to think that less will be required of us in the future. Any assessment of our circumstances points to the need for a greater effort. The shape and the structure of our forces at the present time have served Australia well. For the future they will provide a basis on which further development can take place.

Source: Ministry of Defence text.

Notes

Chapter 1
AUSTRALIA AND CHINA (page 3)

1 H. G. Gelber, 'Problems of Australian Foreign Policy: January-June 1967', *The Australian Journal of Politics and History* (December 1967), p. 316.

2 For example, see John Wilkes (ed.), *Communism in Asia: A Threat to Australia?* (Angus & Robertson, Sydney, 1967); Henry S. Albinski, *Australian Policies and Attitudes Toward China* (Princeton University Press, Princeton, 1965); Gregory Clark, *In Fear of China* (Lansdowne Press, Melbourne, 1967).

3 Alastair Buchan, *China and the Peace of Asia* (Frederick A. Praeger, New York, 1965), p. 206; Coral Bell, 'Australia and China: Power Balance and Policy', in A. M. Halpern (ed.), *Policies Toward China* (McGraw-Hill Book Co., New York, 1965), pp. 197-8.

4 Donald C. Hellman, *Japan in the Postwar East Asian International System* (Research Analysis Corp. (Report RAC-R-46-2), McLean, Virginia, 1969), pp. 19-30; Robert Trumbull, 'Australians Worried by Growing Japanese Role in Economy', *New York Times*, 25 December 1968.

5 John Davenport, 'Japan's Competitive Cutting Edge', *Fortune*, 1 September 1968, pp. 90-128.

6 See, for example, 'Japanese Expansion in Asia Condemned', New China News Agency (N.C.N.A.), Peking Broadcast, 10 March 1968; 'Sato Economic Expansion in Indonesia Reported', N.C.N.A., Peking Broadcast, 11 March 1968; 'Japanese Monopoly Capital Steps up Economic Expansion in Southeast Asia', N.C.N.A. release, Peking, 5 August 1968; 'Japanese Expand Markets in Southeast Asia', N.C.N.A., Peking Broadcast, 24 September 1968.

7 Marshall D. Shulman, Soviet Policy in Asia (unpublished paper prepared for Japanese-American Seminar at Wingspread, Racine, Wisconsin, 6-9 January 1969).

8 'Communiqué of 11th Plenary Session of 8th Central Committee of China', Survey of China Mainland Press, No. 3762, 17 August 1966; 'CCP Central Committee Holds its 12th Session', N.C.N.A., Peking Broadcast, 1 November 1968; 'U.S., Sato try to Revive Japanese Militarism', N.C.N.A., Peking Broadcast, 27 June 1968.

9 'Japan, India, Others to Form Anti-China Bloc', N.C.N.A., Peking Broadcast, 8 August 1968; 'USSR Offers Japan Soviet Far East Resources', N.C.N.A., Peking Broadcast, 13 December 1968.

10 'Militarization of Economy Spells Sato's Doom', N.C.N.A., Peking Broadcast, 17 August 1968.

Chapter 2
INDIA (page 19)

1 It would be easier for an authoritarian regime in India to impose heavy sacrifices on its people in order to pursue adventurist foreign policies; among the factors which make it likely that India's international conduct

will remain peaceable is the fact that the democratic system makes it incumbent upon the government to attach the highest priority to internal development and people's welfare.

2   Questions of security of the region apart, the problems of national unity and cohesion in India, Pakistan and Ceylon are inextricably interlinked. The growth of Tamil or Bengali separatism in India would create serious strains for Ceylon and Pakistan.

3   The emphasis on world reforms in the early years of India's foreign policy yielded place to an emphasis on internal development in the second half of the 1950s; since the Chinese attack of 1962, defence and security have emerged as the most important considerations shaping India's foreign policy.

4   Although India is in many ways a *status quo* power and is primarily interested in peace and stability in the world, its role in the context of the north-south problems is bound to be reformist. For a clear exposition of this aspect of India's world role see: Nehru's conversation with Karanjia in R. K. Karanjia, *The Philosophy of Mr Nehru* (George Allen & Unwin, 1966), pp. 56-67.

5   A number of books and articles published after the Sino-Indian conflict have discussed the historical validity of the Indian and the Chinese claims regarding their boundaries. While helping the clarification of certain issues in Sino-Indian relations, this has obscured the fact that the origin of the conflict is best explained in political terms and not in terms of the respective merits of the two cases regarding the border.

6   Mr Nehru said in the Indian Parliament in 1949: 'Europe has a legacy of conflicts of power and of problems which come from the possession of power. . . . In Asia, at the present moment at least, there is no such legacy. . . . That is a very great advantage for Asia . . .', *India's Foreign Policy* (The Publications Division, Government of India, 1961), pp. 22-3.

7   For a discussion of India's defence problems in the late 1960s see: D. Mukerjee, 'India's Defence Perspectives', *International Affairs* (London, October 1968).

8   In many ways the course of the Sino-Indian conflict has been determined by the trends in Sino-Soviet relations. For a discussion of the interconnection between Sino-Indian and Sino-Soviet conflicts see: Sisir Gupta, 'India and the Soviet Union', *Current History* (March 1963).

9   It is not improbable that the U.S.A. and/or the U.S.S.R. will try to accommodate China as an 'adverse partner' by tolerating the spread of its influence in certain regions of Southern Asia. A 'pragmatic' China may well decide to press its claims against its weaker neighbours while 'normalizing' its relations with the Super Powers. Again, one or both of the Super Powers might regard it as necessary to satisfy Pakistan's aspirations *vis-à-vis* India in order to wean it away from China.

10   *India's Foreign Policy, op. cit.*, p. 249.

11   It is of some importance that both India and Australia regarded the Indonesian policy of 'confrontation' with Malaysia as unjustifiable and that both extended moral and material support to Malaysia during the period of strained relationship between it and Indonesia.

12   Foreign Minister Dinesh Singh elaborated these views in an interview with a foreign correspondent in New Delhi in early March 1969. See report in the *Australian*, 5 March 1969. Mrs Gandhi had earlier expressed the hope that 'the Indian Ocean would always remain an area of peace and a bridge of understanding between the littoral states whose nationalism and independence were the best safeguards for the progress and tranquility of the region', *Times of India*, 24 October 1968.

13   See Bruce Grant's commentary on Indo-Australian relations in the *Age*, Melbourne, 21 May 1968. Also R. G. Neale, 'Australia's Changing Relations with India' in J. D. B. Miller (ed.), *India, Japan, Australia: Partners in Asia?* (Australian National University Press, 1968), pp. 67-89.

14 *Jawaharlal Nehru's Speeches (1953-1957)* (Government of India, New Delhi, 1957), pp. 290-1.

15 *ibid.*, p. 294.

16 The monthly *Newsletter* of the Indian Investment Centre of 15 June 1968 surveyed Australian assistance to India and wrote:
An important feature of Australian aid to India is that it is all in the form of grants. Australian aid to India under the Colombo Plan amounted to Rs. 274 million till the end of 1967, which was nearly a quarter of the total aid given by Australia to all the developing countries. This has embraced many fields of development and various projects including the supply of diesel rail cars and rail wagons to Indian Railways; transmitting and other equipment for All India Radio; electrical equipment for the Ramagundam Thermal Power Scheme in Andhra Pradesh; earth moving equipment for Tungabhadra Dam; port equipment for Kandla and Visakhapatnam; paper for school text books; equipment for the Bombay Milk Scheme; and heavy duty trucks for the Rajasthan Canal Authority. Six automatic bakery units are being set up in Delhi, Bombay, Calcutta, Ernakulam, Madras and Ahmadabad from Australian aid. Under the Technical Assistance Programme, Australia has so far given training to a total of 824 Indians in different fields including industry, agriculture, public administration, nursing, science, medicine and health and engineering and has also made available the services of 63 technical experts. To help India overcome the food shortage, over and above the assistance under the Colombo Plan, Australia made four emergency gifts of wheat worth approximately Rs. 295 million during the last three years. In November 1965, Australia offered a gift of four million lbs. of greasy wool worth Rs. 22.8 million to form a revolving stockpile to enable India to increase her exports of woollen textiles.

17 *Age*, Melbourne, 21 May 1968, concluded its editorial on Mrs Gandhi's visit to Australia by drawing attention to this: 'now might be the appropriate time to consider ways in which the pattern of trade between the two countries could begin to work productively in India's favour'.

18 See Dinesh Singh (Indian Minister of Commerce), 'Australia Proves a Friend' in the special *India Survey* of the *Sydney Morning Herald*, 24 May 1968.

Chapter 3
INDONESIA AND AUSTRALIA (page 32)

1 The only systematic discussion by an Indonesian of Indonesian-Australian relations that I have encountered is an unpublished paper by the *Antara* news-agency representative in Canberra, Mr Ronnie Muntu, given to the Indonesian Study Group of the Australian National University in August 1968, 'Indonesian-Australian Relations: Possible Obstacles and Pitfalls' (A modified version of this was later published in the series entitled 'Pacific Signposts: 6) Australia's Regional Role in Asia: a Clear Necessity', *Meanjin* (Winter 1969), pp. 184-93. A much earlier and more general Indonesian book about Australia by Arif Effendi, *Demikianlah Australia* (This is Australia) (Djakarta, 1954), has been briefly summarized by Herbert Feith in *News and Views, Indonesia*, Special Independence Day Anniversary Issue (Indonesian Embassy, Canberra, 1965), pp. 27-9.

2 A useful survey of Indonesia's foreign policy in the post-Soekarno era, particularly in relation to the South-East Asian region (but only marginally to Australia), was given in the Dyason Memorial lecture for 1967 by Soedjatmoko, 'Indonesia and the World', *Australian Outlook*, Vol. XXI, No. 3 (December 1967). A good comprehensive study of Indonesian foreign policy over the past fifteen years is still lacking.

3   See, for example, Benedict Anderson's analysis of 'The Javanese Concept
     of Power' in Claire Holt, *The Cultural Roots of Indonesian Politics*
     (Ithaca, Cornell University Press, forthcoming).
4   See J. A. C. Mackie, 'Australia and Indonesia 1945-60' in Gordon Green-
     wood and Norman Harper (eds), *Australia in World Affairs 1956-60*
     (F. W. Cheshire for the Australian Institute of International Affairs,
     Melbourne, 1963), pp. 272-83.
5   The Army-sponsored (but then rather radical) National Front for the
     Liberation of Irian Barat, Bogor branch, was responsible for the publica-
     tion in 1958 of an Indonesian translation of R. K. Karanjia, *SEATO—
     Security or Menace* (Blitz Publications (Private), Bombay, 1956). On
     American involvement in the regional rebellions, there is a useful survey
     by Daniel S. Lev, 'America, Indonesia and the Rebellion of 1958', *United
     Asia* (July-August, 1965), pp. 305-9.
6   See Dr Subandrio's account to the Indonesian parliament of this negoti-
     ation with the Australian government in February 1959 in *Current Notes
     on International Affairs*, Department of External Affairs, Canberra Vol.
     XXX, No. 2 (February 1959), pp. 92-7.
7   A good account of Soekarno's manipulation of American diplomatic
     pressure in the West Irian dispute is given in Frederick Bunnell, 'Guided
     Democracy Foreign Policy, 1960-65', *Indonesia*, Cornell University
     Modern Indonesian Project, Vol. II (October 1966), pp. 50-4.
8   Hanno Weisbrod, 'Sir Garfield Barwick and Dutch New Guinea', *Aus-
     tralian Quarterly* (June 1967), pp. 24-36.
9   See George Modelski, *The New Emerging Forces, Documents on the
     Ideology of Indonesian Foreign Policy* (Australian National University,
     Department of International Relations, Canberra, 1963). For a more
     comprehensive study of the Indonesia-Malaysia conflict see J. A. C.
     Mackie, *Confrontation: the Indonesia-Malaysia Conflict 1963-66*, forth-
     coming.
10   For background information on Soekarno's views of Australia in 1963-65
     I am indebted to Mr K. C. O. Shann, former Australian Ambassador in
     Djakarta; he is not responsible, however, for the wording of the summary
     given here.
11   The idea of Maphilindo originated from the proposal for an association
     of the three nations of predominantly Malay race, Malaya, Philippines
     and Indonesia (the acronym being formed from these names), which was
     a central feature of the Manila Agreements of June-August 1963 signed
     by the three Heads of Government concerned.
12   See statements by the Australian Minister for External Affairs to Parlia-
     ment on 18 August 1966 and 17 August 1967 in *Current Notes*, Vol.
     XXXVII, No. 8 (August 1966), pp. 485-6; and Vol. XXXVIII, No. 8
     (August 1967), p. 315.
13   A gloomy picture of the trade between Australia and Indonesia, and of its
     prospects of development in the immediate future, is given by H. W.
     Arndt, 'Trade Relations between Australia and Indonesia', *Economic
     Record*, Vol. XLIV, No. 106 (June 1968), pp. 168-93.
14   Charles Coppel, 'Indonesia: Freezing Relations with China', *Australia's
     Neighbours*, Fourth Series, Nos. 54-5 (March-April 1968), pp. 5-8.
15   See Muntu, *op. cit.*, p. 7.
16   *ibid.*, p. 6 (quoting *Kompas*, the Catholic Party newspaper in Djakarta).
17   Australian forces in Malaysia in 1967 consisted of two squadrons of
     R.A.A.F. Mirage aircraft at Butterworth and one Australian battalion
     attached to the Commonwealth Brigade at Terendak, near Malacca.
18   Muntu, *op. cit.*, pp. 12-13.
19   The progress of the border delineation operation in 1966-68 is reported
     in D. Cook, J. C. Macartney and P. M. Scott, 'Where is the Border?'
     Australian External Territories, Vol. XIII, No. 5 (October 1968),
     pp. 7-18.

20 See Peter Hastings, 'West Irian 1969', *New Guinea and Australia, the Pacific and Southeast Asia*, Vol. III, No. 3 (September-October 1968), pp. 12-22. Hastings has subsequently published a fuller discussion of recent and future developments in West Irian in his *New Guinea Problems and Prospects* (F. W. Cheshire for the Australian Institute of International Affairs, Melbourne, 1969), Chapter 6.

21 Christine Goode, 'Papua and New Guinea's Relations with West Irian: a review of 1969', *Australian External Territories*, Vol. X, No. 1 (February 1970), pp. 25-31.

22 Visits to Papua-New Guinea by successive Indonesian Ambassadors to Australia have been few and far between. An Indonesian parliamentary delegation paid a brief visit in mid-1968 and the military commander for West Irian, Brig.-Gen. Sarwo Edhie, in February 1969.

Chapter 4
AUSTRALIA AND JAPAN (page 53)

1 *Australia Rikugun Shoshi* (Short History of the *Australian Army*) (Anonym.) in *Gunji Kenkyu* (Military Study) (September 1967); Masabumi Nagae, *Australia-Kironi tatsu Kokubo-seisaku* (Australia's Defence Policy at a Crossroad) in *Sekai Shuho* (World Weekly), Vol. 49 (1968); Masao Miyawaki, *Igirisu-no Indo-yo karano Tettaito Australia-no Boei-mondai* (British Withdrawal from the Indian Ocean and Australia's Defence Problems) in *Reference* (Parliamentary Library) (May 1969).

2 Data from the files of the *Yomiuri Shimbun* where clippings of newspaper stories are collected from the *Yomiuri*, the *Asahi*, the *Mainichi*, the *Nikkei*, the *Sankei* and the *Tokyo* newspapers.

3 Kajima Peace Research Institute (ed.), *Australia and New Guinea* (Kajima P.R.I., Tokyo, 1968), p. 191.

4 T. B. Millar, *Australia's Defence* (Melbourne University Press, Melbourne, 1965), p. 49.

5 *Australia and New Guinea*, *op. cit.*, p. 193.

6 *ibid.*, p. 193.

7 Hachio Iwasaki, *Australia-no Keizai* (Australia's Economy), (Asia Keizai Kenkyujo, Tokyo, 1967), p. 169.

8 *Australia and New Guinea*, *op. cit.*, p. 206.

9 M. Yasuda, 'Japan Must Avoid State of Hostility with US' in the *Daily Yomiuri*, 13 January 1970, p. 5.

10 M. Yasuda, 'Reality of Built-in Weakness, Basis of New Defense Buildup' in the *Daily Yomiuri*, 23 November 1969, p. 5.

11 Japan's constitution prohibits 'the threat or use of force as means of settling international disputes' in Article IX. Accordingly, the successive conservative governments have repeatedly pledged in the Diet that no armed forces or personnel would be deployed overseas.

12 Fred Greene, *US Policy and the Security of Asia* (McGraw-Hill, New York, 1968), pp. 296-7.

13 *ibid.*

14 Akio Doi, *Shin-senryaku-to Nihon* (The Jiji Press, Tokyo, 1968), p. 65. An Australian-Japanese 'nuclear co-operation' is advocated there. Such an opinion, however, remains in the minority in contemporary Japan. Technically, too, it is not clear how close Japan is to a nuclear capability. Its natural uranium deposits are estimated at about 3,000 tons, of which only several hundred tons can be actually explored to produce enough ore to be processed into $U235$ and eventually to a total of 'about 200 to 300 (nominal) atomic bombs', according to *Nihon-no Anzen-Hosho* (Japan's National Security) (1968 edition), p. 299. Its fast breeder reactor programme will not be decided upon before 1975. Even if $U235$ is available

(possibly through Japan's own technological breakthrough in the field of centrifugal processes), the nation still lacks space to build earthquake-proof bomb plants and, above all, testing grounds. Most importantly, Japan lacks strategic survivability due to its small and densely populated area. A tactical nuclear programme requires extremely sophisticated technological know-how which may be available only from the U.S. As it is impossible to think of a situation where the U.S. withdraws its nuclear protection from Japan while offering it technological help in nuclear matters, an independent Japanese nuclear programme is virtually inconceivable—unless Australia should replace the U.S., presumably by going nuclear first.

Chapter 5

GREAT BRITAIN AND AUSTRALIA (page 65)

1 My friend and colleague, Trevor Reese, is notable as the only English-born and based academic who specializes in the study of recent Australian history and politics and writes books and articles about these subjects, helped no doubt by his Australian wife. But even he has not written specifically about British-Australian relations. Among recent notable contributions from Australia must be numbered Oscar Spate and Harry Gelber, who are emigré Englishmen now living in Australia. The writings of Coral Bell, Hedley Bull, Arthur Lee Burns, Sir Keith Hancock, T. B. Millar, J. D. B. Miller, J. L. Richardson and Sir Alan Watt provide much illumination of this theme; they are all Australians.

2 See the *Daily Telegraph*, 23 June 1970.

3 For a succinct discussion and appraisal see Peter Samuel, 'Population and Immigration Policy' in *Australia, New Zealand and the South Pacific. A Handbook*, edited by Charles Osborne (Blond, London, 1969), pp. 240-7.

4 For some aspects of this theme see Craig McGregor, *Profile of Australia* (Penguin, 1968); and a stoutly Anglophilic article by Arthur Lee Burns 'Who are the Australians? Class Attitudes without the Classes' in *The Round Table*, No. 238 (April 1970), pp. 145-52, which concludes that 'in Australia there is no major tradition, no native wisdom in politics, that does not derive from the peoples of the British isles'.

5 In *The Round Table*, No. 232 (October 1968), pp. 365-8 Sir Robert referred briefly to changes between Britain and Australia as regards (a) the monarchy (b) the Commonwealth (c) trade and (d) defence. He lamented that 'one finds oneself struggling to create an organization, a British-Australian Association that would serve to strengthen ties between the two countries, ties which only a few years ago did not need to be defined or built upon. This is indeed something of a setback.'

6 As reported, mostly verbatim, in the *Sunday Times*, 7 June 1970, with very little comment by the paper's diplomatic correspondent. The headline was 'Australian envoy makes astonishing [*sic*] attack on Labour Britain'.

7 This is a distinction first invented in and applied to the politics of the United States by Robert A. Dahl in his *A Preface to Democratic Theory* (Chicago, 1956).

8 See J. O. N. Perkins, *Australia in the World Economy* (Sun Books, Melbourne, 1968), especially p. 29. See also *Commonwealth Trade 1968*, prepared by the Commonwealth Secretariat (London, 1969), for detailed statistics of composition and direction of trade. The Treasurer, Mr William McMahon, said in the House of Representatives on 17 June 1968 that Britain's devaluation the previous November had lost Australia $A113 million but 'we have not engaged in a policy of deliberate shifts of our overseas holdings from the U.K. to the currencies of other countries'.

9 On ANZAM, the informal Anglo, Australian, New Zealand arrangement for defence of the Malayan area, which originated in 1949, see *Collective Defence in South East Asia* (Oxford University Press for the Royal Institute for International Affairs, 1958), p. 20; and Sir Alan Watt, *The Evolution of Australia's Foreign Policy 1938-1965* (Cambridge University Press, 1967), pp. 163-6.

10 See Peter Lyon, *War and Peace in South East Asia* (Oxford University Press for the Royal Institute for International Affairs, 1969), pp. 16, 19, 115-19.

11 For example, Philip de Zulueta, 'The East of Suez Game' in the *Spectator*, 18 February 1966; Sir Robert Scott, *Major Theatre of Conflict: British Policy in East Asia* (London, Atlantic Trade Study 1968); F. S. Northedge, 'British Foreign Policy' in *The Foreign Policies of the Powers*, edited by F. S. Northedge, (Faber & Faber, 1968), especially pp. 179-85; Neville Brown, *British Arms & Strategy 1970-80* (for Royal United Services Institution, London, May 1969); L. W. Martin, *British Defence Policy: The Long Recessional* (Adelphi Paper No. 61, Institute for Strategic Studies, London, November 1969); the present writer has discussed this subject for the November 1970 issue of *The British Survey*; the most compact, many-sided, and concise Australian assessment is Thomas B. Millar (ed.), *Britain's Withdrawal From Asia: its implications for Australia*, Proceedings of a seminar conducted by the Strategic and Defence Studies Centre, Australian National University, 29-30 September 1967.

12 5 March 1970, House of Commons Debates, Vol. 627, Columns 750-2.

13 For Mr Heath's views on these issues see especially his article in the *Daily Mail*, 9 January 1970, where he costed his East-of-Suez programme at £100 million a year (+ or − £10 m.); and *The Times*, 19 January 1970. See also the *Economist* of 10 January 1970, p. 15; and Ian Colvin, 'East of Suez: what is the cost?' in the *Daily Telegraph*, 10 February 1970.

14 See especially two articles by Sir Alec Douglas-Home in the *Daily Telegraph*, 6 February 1970 and 20 April 1970, the first just before and the second just after his first visit to Australia for twelve years. The first was entitled, 'Cold War: the next decade' and the second 'Australia: the confidence and the fears'.

Chapter 6

U.S.A. AND AUSTRALIA (page 77)

1 So amply have the U.S.S.R. and China fulfilled American wishes in this matter in recent years that some U.S. observers have been tempted to classify acute Sino-Soviet hostility as a permanent feature of the international scene.

2 The American impatience with the Vietnam commitment seems to be closely connected with the belief that the U.S. is alone there; that it has clients in this affair but no real allies and that most of its traditional friends would like it to get out of Vietnam. Similarly, the pressures in Washington for a smaller U.S. presence in Western Europe are closely connected with a growing belief that what began as an effort to achieve collective security has become a way for Western Europe to be comfortable and prosperous at American expense.

3 It is clear that 'vertical proliferation' has postponed and will continue to postpone the time when the U.S. and the U.S.S.R. may have to pay the price for such new arrangements to new nuclear powers like China. It is not yet clear whether the payment can be avoided altogether.

4 Cf. Morton H. Halperin, 'After Vietnam: Security and Intervention in Asia', *Journal of International Affairs*, Vol. 22, No. 2 (1968), pp. 236-46.

5 The *Spectator*, 3 January 1970, p. 14.

6 Steven J. Kelman, 'Youth and Foreign Policy', *Foreign Affairs*, Vol. 48, No. 3 (April 1970), p. 419.

7   There is, for example, Professor J. K. Galbraith's remark that if the U.S.
were not in Vietnam 'all that part of the world would be enjoying the
obscurity it so richly deserves'. Quoted in *Time*, 16 February 1968. And
Senator J. William Fulbright has spoken of 'the myth that Vietnam ever
really mattered to the security of the United States' and declared roundly
that 'It simply does not matter very much for the United States . . . who
rules the states of Indo-China'. *New York Times*, 3 April 1970, p. 11.

8   Its evolution has gone through several stages. See, for example, Mr Nixon's
'Asia After Vietnam', *Foreign Affairs*, Vol. 46, No. 1 (October 1967),
pp. 111-25; his interview with the *Washington Post*, 8 December 1968,
p. B3; his news conference at Guam on 25 July 1969, *New York Times*,
26 July 1969, pp. 1, 9; and his report to Congress, *A New Strategy for
Peace*, Office of the White House Press Secretary, 18 February 1970.

9   Charles A. Beard, *Giddy Minds and Foreign Quarrels* (1939). Also J.
William Fulbright, *The Arrogance of Power* (Random House, New York,
1966).

10   *New York Times*, 2 March 1949.

11   D. D. Eisenhower, *The White House Years: Mandate for Change 1953-
1956* (Doubleday, New York, 1963), pp. 446-7.

12   News conference of 5 January 1949. Dean Acheson, *Present at the Creation* (Norton, New York, 1969), pp. 351-2.

13   The phrase is Henry Brandon's, *The Atlantic Monthly*, Vol. 225, No. 3
(March 1970), p. 16.

14   Nixon, *A New Strategy for Peace, op. cit.*, pp. 40-1.

15   The U.S. has in any case been edging towards an understanding with the
Russians on a 'no first use' of nuclear weapons. It has, for example, become
American policy to maintain strategic forces explicitly in order to deter
'a deliberate nuclear attack on the United States' or its allies. See *The 1970
Defense Budget and Defense Program for Fiscal Years 1970-74*, Statement
by Secretary of Defense Clark M. Clifford, Washington, 15 January 1969,
p. 47. It is therefore not clear what the United States response would be
in the event of any hostile action not unambiguously classifiable as a
'deliberate nuclear attack'.

16   For an interesting general analysis, see Edward L. Morse, 'The Transformation of Foreign Policies: Modernization, Interdependence and Ex-
ternalization', *World Politics*, Vol. 22, No. 3 (April 1970), pp. 371-92.

17   As the Rev. Alan Booth has put it:
. . . we prefer private enterprise and the banding together of social
groups and individuals by common consent to do and dare at the barri-
cades, rather than docile enlistment in a military service to carry out
operations and policies with which we may have little personal identification.
'The Limitations of Military Power', in 'Soviet-American Relations and
World Order: The Two and the Many', *Adelphi Papers*, No. 66 (Institute for Strategic Studies, London, March 1970), p. 155.

18   The literature on this is, of course, considerable. See, for example, Ray-
mond Vernon, 'Economic Sovereignty at Bay', *Foreign Affairs*, Vol. 47,
No. 1 (October 1968), pp. 110-22; Raymond Vernon, 'Antitrust and
International Business', *Harvard Business Review* (September-October
1968), pp. 78-87; S. Rolfe and W. Damm (eds), *The Multi-national
Corporation in the World Economy* (Praeger, New York, 1970); Peter
Kenen, 'The International Position of the Dollar in a changing World',
International Organization, Vol. 23, No. 3 (Summer, 1969), pp. 705-18.

19   It may be that the attitude of a Bismarck towards Austria after 1866 is
an essentially aristocratic one, impossible for the leaders of a mass democracy.

W

20 The shortcomings of such an absolutist attitude to international relations have been much commented upon, never more effectively than by George Kennan, *American Diplomacy 1900-1950* (Secker and Warburg, London, 1952), especially Chapters 5 and 6.

21 It seems likely, for example, that Vice-President Spiro Agnew's repeated attacks upon the press and the media indicate his belief that there is a considerable constituency in the nation which finds his views appealing. It would be rash to conclude that his judgement on this point is necessarily mistaken or that his political opponents can afford to disregard the constituency in question.

22 Samuel A. Stouffer *et al.*, *The American Soldier: Combat and its Aftermath* (New York, 1949), p. 149.

23 E. Mesthene, *Technological Change: Its Impact on Man and Society* (Harvard University Press, Cambridge, Mass., 1970), pp. 68-9.

24 L. S. Finkelstein, 'International Cooperation in a Changing World: A Challenge to United States Foreign Policy', *International Organization*, Vol. 23, No. 3 (Summer 1969), p. 587.

25 As McGeorge Bundy put it bluntly, 'The future of European foreign policy is no longer outside Europe. . . . Europe can now have no decisive foreign policy except that of the future of Europe'. 'America's enduring links with Europe', *The Round Table*, No. 237 (January 1970), pp. 7-16.

26 See, for example, Carl Kaysen, 'Military Strategy, Military Forces and Arms Control', in Kermit Gordon (ed.), *Agenda for the Nation* (The Brookings Institution, Washington, 1968), pp. 549-84.

27 Mr Nixon has been explicit about this. 'The principles underlying our relations with Communist China are similar to those governing our policies toward the USSR.' And, with respect to Japan, 'we consider our security inseparable from theirs'. *A New Strategy for Peace, op. cit.*, pp. 105, 109.

28 Nixon, *A New Strategy for Peace, op. cit.*, p. 4.

29 Congressional and public interest in foreign aid has, of course, markedly declined during the last few years.

30 This is by no means a new idea. It is, in fact, a description of the dilemma of Queen Elizabeth I, compelled to fight Spain but confronted by a House of Commons exceedingly reluctant to behave (or grant taxes) as if England were really at War. See Garrett Mattingly, *The Defeat of the Spanish Armada* (Penguin Books, Harmondsworth, 1962), p. 413.
   As Dean Acheson once said, in foreign affairs there are very few new ideas, and most of those are bad.

31 Acheson, *Present at the Creation, op. cit.*, p. 728.

32 Alastair Buchan, *Crisis Management: The New Diplomacy* (Atlantic Institute, Paris, 1966), pp. 47-8.

33 Professor J. D. B. Miller has commented upon the remarkable Australian incomprehension of America, even within the civil service. See his 1969 Alfred Deakin Lecture, 'The Conduct of Australian Foreign Policy', *The Australian University*, Vol. 7, No. 2 (August 1969), p. 150.

34 For one (not universally accepted) analysis of the way in which Australian protest about Vietnam has seen matters through the eyes of American anti-war groups, see Gerard Henderson, 'Vietnam and the Victorian Universities', *20th Century* (September 1969), pp. 5-20.

35 'A civilization of pioneers', Michael Oakeshott once explained, 'is, almost unavoidably, a civilization of self-consciously self-made men', *Rationalism in Politics; and other essays* (Methuen, London, 1962), p. 27.

36 This needs qualification. But, as one would expect, it is precisely among Australian professional men, academics and other groups where these American characteristics are being most closely imitated, that political and economic criticisms of America are strongest. By contrast, Australian workmen and artisans, the lower middle class, smaller farmers and some returned servicemen, all of whom have in various ways retained a broad

tolerance of and respect for the 'underachiever', tend to be groups among whom the American alliance is most firmly accepted. It is, however, also true that America is resented among some of the wealthy or right-of-centre—whether by those serving officers or civil servants who argue that following its display of weakness over Vietnam the U.S. cannot be relied upon, or those groups which harbour cultural resentments of various kinds.

37   This is not, of course, because the Australian political system is beyond the reach of American moral objections. It is rather that one of two factors operates to protect the Australians. Either they are too unimportant a target for the critics. Or else, for all the technical and constitutional differences between the two political systems, the ways in which Australians fall short of perfection are quite similar to many of the faults of the U.S. system. Consequently Australia is a secondary and therefore uninviting object of criticism.

38   Sometimes in oblique ways. The Australian effort at the Djakarta conference on Cambodia in May 1970, for example, was clearly very much in line with President Nixon's wish to involve South-East Asian states more fully in security efforts—preferably collective—in the region. Whether an attempt to secure regional co-operation in such terms was sensible, or likely to be productive, is of course debatable. For the conference *communiqué* see Department of External Affairs, Canberra, *News Release*, D/31 of 17 May 1970. For one sceptical American comment on the conference, see George W. Ball, 'Cambodian Retrospective', *Newsweek*, 22 June 1970, p. 72.

39   The procurement aspects are discussed in Chapter 16. The degree of Australian procurement dependence upon the U.S. may be influenced by the need to reconcile the Australian government's tendency to encourage domestic arms and equipment production with the continuing inability of Australia to produce sophisticated categories of weapons at acceptable cost, and perhaps by the stronger American arms sales effort which is likely to accompany the pursuit of the Guam doctrine. Cf. *Congressional Quarterly*, Weekly Report, Vol. 28, No. 1, 6 March 1970, pp. 698-701.
   In the past the U.S. has also succeeded in imposing considerable restrictions upon the technical and strategic freedom of movement of its allies by imposing conditions upon aid in weapons development, cf. the Australian-American Mutual Weapons Development Programme agreement of 23 August 1960, text in T. B. Millar, *Australia's Foreign Policy* (Angus and Robertson, Sydney, 1968), Appendix A, pp. 293-8. See especially Article 8. On the other hand, the United States has not always insisted on maintaining a technical or legal advantage whe ·h· might be damaging in terms of a larger alliance relationship. Se   n concessions on the F-111 agreement as explained by th   Minister of Defence, Mr Malcolm Fraser, *C.P.D. (H. of R.)*   ), pp. 1985-97. Also the critique by the Deputy Leader of   tion, Mr L. Barnard, *ibid.*, pp. 1997-2000.

40   There are grounds for believing that one impor   for the close alignment of the governments of Sir Robert Me   Holt and Mr Gorton with the Vietnam policies of the Johnson   n administrations was the simple fact that both governments   much the same intelligence information. They therefore tended   to very similar policy conclusions.

41   According to the Prime Minister, Mr Gorton, t   is a partner in twelve joint defence and scientific establishmer   ustralia. One of these complexes (of NASA facilities) itself has a n   f sub-stations in various parts of the continent. See Mr Gorton's   entary reply of 9 September 1969, reprinted as Appendix I; also   vernment statement of 10 November 1969, *Current Notes on*   *national Affairs* (November 1969), p. 650.

W

42 The proportion of U.S. investment has probably risen somewhat since then. See Chapter 14.

43 See Chapter 13.

44 It was reaffirmed by Dean Rusk at the Canberra meeting of the ANZUS Council in 1962 and Averell Harriman at Wellington in the following year. Mr Nixon has emphasized America's intention to stand by its commitments, for example in *A New Strategy for Peace, op. cit.*, pp. 6-7.

45 Both these points are well discussed in Sir Alan Watt's 'The ANZUS treaty: Past, Present and Future', *Australian Outlook*, Vol. 24, No. 1 (April 1970), especially pp. 24-31. For the fullest examination of the treaty, see J. G. Starke, *The ANZUS Treaty Alliance* (Melbourne University Press, Melbourne, 1965).

46 Cf. *C.P.D. (H. of R.)*, 20 April 1955, pp. 52-3.

47 Mr Menzies, for example, assured Parliament in April 1964 that the U.S. approved the dispatch of Australian troops to Borneo and added, not unambiguously, that America would stand by its treaty obligations. The Leader of the Opposition, Mr Arthur Calwell, objected that he had been told by Mr Averell Harriman that U.S. protection did not apply to Australian troops in Borneo. *C.P.D. (H. of R.)*, Vol. 42, 21 April 1964, pp. 1231-5, 1274, 1280; 22 April 1964, p. 1303. For a general discussion of these uncertainties, see Trevor R. Reese, *Australia, New Zealand and the United States: A Survey of International Relations 1941-1968* (Oxford University Press, London, 1969), pp. 218-25.

48 One of the arguments during 1969-70 for retaining Australian troops in Malaysia beyond 1971 was that though there was no certainty of American support, the risk that it might be given would itself suffice to deter an aggressor.

49 McGeorge Bundy, 'The End of Either/Or', *Foreign Affairs*, Vol. 45, No. 2 (January 1967), p. 190.

50 House of Representatives, 8 June 1950, *Current Notes on International Affairs*, June 1950. See also Mr Paul Hasluck's discussion of the reasons for the Australian participation in Vietnam, *C.P.D. (H. of R.)*, 31 March 1966, Vol. 50, p. 866.

51 The point has been forcibly made by Clark M. Clifford who has explained his own growing disillusionment with a Vietnam involvement in which the U.S. was given inadequate support by its allies. Cf. 'A Vietnam Reappraisal', *Foreign Affairs*, Vol. 47, No. 4 (July 1969), pp. 601-22.

Chapter 7
MALAYSIA AND SINGAPORE (page 97)

1 Institute for Strategic Studies, *The Military Balance 1969-1970* (London, 1969), p. 49.

2 Singapore's G.N.P. in 1964 was $US813 million: *Malaysia, Official Year Book 1964* (Kuala Lumpur, 1966), p. 213.

3 *Malaysia, Official Year Book 1967*, p. 49. The 1967 Year Book is the most recent available (February 1970) as the 1968 year book was withdrawn because of errors.

4 A small holding in Malaya is generally defined as from 1-99 acres, although the average size in 1952 was 4.11 acres: James C. Jackson, 'Smallholding Cultivation of Cash Crops', in Wang Gungwu (ed.), *Malaysia, A Survey* (Cheshire, Melbourne, 1964), p. 247.

5 K. T. Joseph, 'Problems of Agriculture' in Wang Gungwu, *Malaysia, A Survey, op. cit.*, p. 275; and *Malaysia, Official Year Book 1967*, p. 12.

6 *Malaysia, Official Year Book 1964*, p. 214. By comparison Australia's population density in 1966 was 3.89 persons per square mile.

7 *ibid.*, and *Singapore 1969 Facts and Pictures*, Singapore Government Publication, p. 5.

8 *ibid.*

9   *ibid.* For 1960 and 1964 figures see T. G. McGee, 'Population: A Pre-liminary Analysis' in Wang Gungwu, *Malaysia, A Survey, op. cit.*
10 Between 1953 and 1960 yearly rates of increase were: Malaya 3.0%, Sabah 3.6%, Sarawak 3.3%, Singapore 4.6%. T. G. McGee, *op. cit.,* p. 73.
11 *Malaysia, Official Year Book 1967,* p. 276.
12 Yip Yat Hoong, 'The Mining Industry', in Wang Gungwu, *Malaysia, A Survey, op. cit.,* p. 299.
13 T. B. Millar, *Australia's Defence* (Melbourne University Press, Melbourne, 1965), p. 80. See also the second edition (1969), pp. 62-3.
14 The figures relating to the defence forces of Malaysia and Singapore are taken from *The Military Balance 1969-1970, op. cit.*

Chapter 8

AUSTRALIAN MARITIME STRATEGY (page 107)

1   Bureau of Census and Statistics, *Transport and Communications Bulletin,* No. 59, 1967-68. Australia's exports of goods (f.o.b.) in 1967 amounted to 13.0% of the G.N.P., which may be compared with 13.2% for the U.K., 9.1% for Japan and 3.9% for the U.S.A. Figures for Australia from *Quarterly Estimates of National Income and Expenditure* published by the Commonwealth Statistician. Figures for other countries from O.E.C.D., *Observer* (February 1969).
2   World ocean-borne trade has grown at an average annual rate of 7.4% since 1950, and in 1966 totalled 1,700 million tons. A study prepared by Litton Systems Inc. for the U.S. Department of Transportation predicts a twenty-fold increase in world ocean-borne trade by 2043. *Weekly Bulletin,* Shipbuilders' Council of America, 15 August 1968.
3   Bureau of Census and Statistics, *Transport and Communications Bulletin,* No. 59.
4   Bureau of Census and Statistics, *Transport and Communications Bulletin,* No. 59; and *Commonwealth of Australia Year Book* (1967).
5   See 'Flags of Whose Convenience?', *U.S. Naval Institute Proceedings* (October 1968).
6   See, for example, Department of Defence, Canberra, *Defence Report 1968,* which refers to 'the detection and destruction of enemy forces which threaten our control of the sea areas'.
7   R. V. B. Blackman (ed.), *Jane's Fighting Ships, 1968-69* (London), p. 54.
8   *ibid.,* p. 137.
9   *ibid.,* p. 482; *The Military Balance 1969-1970* (Institute for Strategic Studies, London, 1969), p. 8.
10 Article V of the Security Treaty between Australia, New Zealand and the U.S.A. states: 'An armed attack on any of the parties is deemed to include an armed attack on the metropolitan territory of any of the parties, or on the island territories under its jurisdiction in the Pacific or on its armed forces, public vessels or aircraft in the Pacific'. Department of External Affairs, Canberra *Treaty Series* 1952-53.
11 *Jane's Fighting Ships, 1968-69, op. cit.,* p. 54.
12 *Jane's Fighting Ships, 1968-69, op. cit.,* gives the radius (presumably meaning the range) as 13,000 to 16,000 miles. Allowing for a ten-day patrol, and a reasonable fuel margin on return to base, it seems unlikely that the operational radius would exceed 4,000 miles. It is 3,200 miles from South China to the eastern end of New Guinea.
13 High power, very low frequency (V.L.F.) transmissions can be read by a submarine while fully submerged. The submarine has to reveal an aerial above the surface (with the consequent risk of detection by radar-fitted aircraft) in order to receive medium or high frequency transmissions.

14 The German Navy had only 28 ocean-going U-boats available in August 1939, although they had been increasing their strength as rapidly as possible for six years, and had the advantage of having many officers who had taken part in the First World War submarine offensive. See S. W. Roskill, *The War at Sea*, Vol. 1 (Her Majesty's Stationery Office, London, 1954), pp. 58-9.

15 At the time of Pearl Harbor, Japan possessed 60 fully operational submarines, 46 of which were of the I class and 14 of the smaller Ro class. During the war 127 submarines were built and in addition Japan took over 8 German U-boats; 130 were sunk and 4 were scrapped, leaving a total force of 61 in August 1945. See S. D. Waters, *The Royal New Zealand Navy* (War History Branch, Wellington, 1956), pp. 211-21; and George Odgers, *Air War Against Japan* (Canberra, 1958), p. 153.

16 G. Hermon Gill, *Royal Australian Navy, 1942-45* (Canberra, 1968), pp. 257-62.

17 The submarine is in fact a very limited weapon, restricted to a depth not much greater than the length of a ship. Its great quality is its invisibility. If a new technical device were to be produced which destroyed this invisibility—enabling a submarine to be detected reliably at long range—the effectiveness of the submarine as a weapon would be destroyed. For an assessment, see 'The National Insurance Policy— A.S.W. Coverage', *U.S. Naval Institute Proceedings* (May 1968).

18 Roskill, *The War at Sea*, Vol. 1, *op. cit.*, p. 10.

19 Some modern anti-submarine destroyers, two or three submarines, and a number of anti-submarine helicopters and fixed wing aircraft, which could be based ashore.

20 *Jane's Fighting Ships, 1968-69, op. cit.; The Military Balance 1969-1970, op. cit.*, p. 8. There are also 25 nuclear and 22 diesel-electric submarines armed with cruise missiles, with ranges up to 300 miles.

21 *Jane's Fighting Ships, 1968-69, op. cit.*, p. 54; *The Military Balance 1969-1970, op. cit.*, p. 40.

22 This is true for Soviet Y class submarines, whose missiles are roughly equivalent to the American Polaris A-2s. The range of the U.S.N. Polaris A-3 missile is 2,850 miles, and the new missile being introduced, the Poseidon, will have a similar range. (*Jane's Fighting Ships, 1968-69, op. cit.*, p. 344.) It must be assumed that the U.S.S.R. is capable of producing missiles of comparable performance in time.

23 Even a conventionally powered submarine would not have great difficulty in eluding the shadowing efforts of several nuclear submarines. Sonar jammers and decoys, skilfully used, would make shadowing difficult for even the most efficient submarines. The risk of detection is so much higher for a conventionally powered submarine, however, that they cannot be regarded as more than interim missile-firers, to be replaced by nuclear-powered submarines as rapidly as possible.

24 Within a decade or so it may be possible to arrange for continuous radar surveillance of the oceans by satellites. This would make the operations of non-nuclear submarines much more hazardous, for while using their snort masts they would always be vulnerable to attack by aircraft directed to their position as located by the satellite. Of course, on many occasions there would be no aircraft suitably placed to take advantage of the satellite detection, but the submarine could rarely be sure of this, for the aircraft would not have to reveal their presence by using their own radar. By the time such a satellite surveillance system could be available, however, all missile firing (and most anti-shipping) submarines are likely to be nuclear-powered and invulnerable to radar detection.

25 J. R. M. Butler, *Grand Strategy*, Vol. 1 (H.M.S.O., London, 1964), p. 470.

26   In addition to posing a threat of invasion, a hostile Indonesia could provide bases for submarines which could operate effectively against Australia's coastal and overseas shipping routes. An invasion of Australia would nevertheless remain a formidable undertaking, and at the present time it is not clear what possible gains there could be for Indonesia to justify the high risks involved. But, at the very least, it seems certain that a hostile Indonesia would cause Australia to increase greatly its armed forces.

27   The extent to which the Indonesian government had gained the loyalty of the people, and whether a relatively small Australian military commitment would be both necessary and effective, would be critical judgements. It would be disastrous for Australia to enter into an open-ended commitment to an unwinnable war.

28   *Jane's Fighting Ships, 1968-69, op. cit.*, p. 418, gives the following characteristics for one of the U.S.N. amphibious assault ships:

Displacement	17,000
Sustained speed	20 knots
Helicopters	20-24 medium
	4 heavy
	4 observation
Troops	2,090

29   A cost-effectiveness study compares two or more methods of achieving a desired result. In the case of the comparison between aircraft carriers and shore airfields the actual effectiveness of air attack is not quantified, since this is common to both alternatives. The effectiveness of air attack is very difficult to determine, and despite the lessons of the Second World War and the Korean war there is a strong tendency to exaggerate its likely effects, particularly when aircraft are employed on 'strategic' bombing.

30   A 50,000-ton aircraft carrier would accommodate twice as many aircraft as a 35,000-ton vessel, but would only cost 25% more, assuming a twenty-year life span. Considerable research and experience went into the British Navy's attempt to build the most cost-effective carrier, to be known as CVA 01. This was a ship of 53,000 tons, but the project was cancelled in 1966. See 'Phantom Carrier', *U.S. Naval Institute Proceedings* (February 1967).

31   The Australian Fleet Air Arm was formed in 1947 and its organization was based on that of the Royal Navy, whose Air Arm had been part of the R.A.F. from 1918 until 1937. In both Australia and Britain the responsibility for all shore-based aircraft (other than disembarked carrier squadrons and training aircraft) remained with the Air Force. It is true that the effectiveness of the British Fleet Air Arm for most of the Second World War was low, but there were several reasons for this apart from R.A.F. control in the inter-war years. The efficiency of the R.A.A.F.'s shore-based anti-submarine squadrons is at least as high as the Navy's carrier-based squadrons—and probably rather higher than its U.S.N. equivalents—so it is unlikely that efficiency would fall if the carrier squadrons were manned by the R.A.A.F.

32   *Jane's Fighting Ships, 1968-69, op. cit.*, pp. 137-40 lists the following:

Cruiser	1	(ex-Soviet)
Destroyers	7	(ex-Soviet)
Frigates	11	(7 of them ex-Soviet)
Patrol Vessels	12	
Torpedo Boats	31	
Patrol Boats	6	
Motor Gunboats	21	

See also *The Military Balance 1969-1970, op. cit.*, p. 44.
There is no sign of a new building programme, and one is most unlikely

in the present state of Indonesia's finances. The Russian-built ships are ageing and spare parts will become an increasing problem.

33   *Jane's Fighting Ships, 1968-69, op. cit.,* p. 141, lists the following:
     Tank Landing Ships   6 (ex-U.S.N. Second World War)
     Tank Landing Craft   7 (3 U.S.N. Second World War
                                     4 built in Yugoslavia)

34   Fourteen Tracker anti-submarine aircraft were ordered for the *Melbourne* in the U.S.A. in 1966, and at the same time the modernization of twenty-three Wessex anti-submarine helicopters was approved. Ten Skyhawk fighter-bombers have been received, but two of these are of the two-seater trainer version; a further twelve are to be ordered. The New Zealand Air Force has also ordered Skyhawks, and it is conceivable that these might operate from the carrier *Melbourne*.

35   *Jane's Fighting Ships, 1968-69, op. cit.,* p. 18, gives the speed as 21-24 knots.

36   *Defence Report 1968,* pp. 20-1, lists the following:
     Guided missile destroyers   3
     Daring class destroyers   3
     River class destroyer escorts   4 (with two building)
     Type 15 destroyer escort   1 (with two in reserve)
     Battle class destroyer   1 (with one in reserve)

37   The U.S.N. is extremely skilled in the long-range deployment of fleets. The Sixth Fleet in the Mediterranean, for instance, is based on the east coast of America, and while on station replenishes at sea, only visiting Mediterranean ports for flag-showing and recreation.
     East of Suez, however, the distances are vast, and it would be difficult to maintain a fleet in the Indian Ocean from a base in Hawaii, even if an advanced base in the Philippines were still available. If the U.S. deployed a fleet to the Indian Ocean, an anchorage for repair ships would almost certainly be required. The Chagos Archipelago, in the centre of the Indian Ocean, would seem an ideal location, since it is reasonably close to all the probable operating areas.
     It is unlikely that the U.S.N. would be interested in Fremantle except as a recreation port; nor would there seem to be much requirement for a base there for the Australian Navy. Fuel, provisions and ammunition are already available in the Fremantle area, and to extend the facilities to cater for repairs and overhauls would not be justified at present. The equipment needed for overhauling a modern ship is complex and extremely costly. The existing overhaul yards on the east coast (Sydney and Williamstown) are working far below their full capacity (they are not yet even on shift work, for instance), and it would be most uneconomic to provide another overhaul base until the existing ones are fully used.

38   Thirty-seven countries, including Australia, U.S.A., U.K., Japan and Malaysia have ratified the 'Convention on the Territorial Sea and the Contiguous Zone'. The Soviet Union has reservations on the right of passage of warships through territorial waters. Communist China and Indonesia are not signatories of the Convention. *United Nations Treaty Series,* issued by the Department of External Affairs (Canberra), pp. 319-20.

39   32.5% by value in 1967. (Japan External Trade Organisation pamphlet, 'Trade and Industry of Japan, No. 129'.)

40   A study prepared by Litton Systems Inc. for the U.S. Department of Transportation predicts that, by 1983, tankers in the 400,000-600,000 D.W.T. category will comprise 10% of world tonnage; the largest dry bulk carrier is likely to be 200,000 D.W.T. Shipbuilders' Council of America, *Weekly Bulletin* (15 August 1968).

41 In the hypothetical situation of all of mainland South-East Asia having become communist, it is impossible to predict what the relations of the communist parties of Malaysia and Singapore will be with the P.K.I. But if there were communist insurrections in Sumatra and Borneo they would be well placed to assist.

42 The forces to be left in Singapore and Malaysia after 1971 are:
    2 squadrons of fighter aircraft (at Butterworth)
    1 destroyer (based on Singapore)
    1,200 troops (most of them in Singapore)
(Statement by the Prime Minister, *Hansard*, 25 February 1969.)

43 An assessment of the contribution of aircraft carriers to the war in Vietnam is given in the October 1967 edition of the *U.S. Naval Institute Proceedings*.

44 The U.S. force level of fifteen attack carriers was predicated on having two attack carriers employed in the Mediterranean and three in the Western Pacific. The requirement for *five* attack carriers in the Western Pacific during the Vietnam war was met by reducing the number of carriers in the Atlantic, and by employing the anti-submarine carrier *Intrepid* as a 'limited' attack carrier in South-East Asia.

The current strength of fifteen attack carriers is made up of the nuclear-powered carrier *Enterprise*, seven ships of the Forrestal class, two Midway class, and five modified Essex class. The Essex class are of Second World War design and are really too small. By current plans, in the mid-1970s the U.S.N. will have four nuclear and eight conventional attack carriers of post-war design, plus three extensively modernized Midway class ships (originally completed 1945-47). See 'Carrier employment since 1950', *U.S. Naval Institute Proceedings* (November 1964); and *Jane's Fighting Ships, 1968-69, op. cit.*, p. 352.

45 The maximum desirable distance is affected not only by the transit time of the aircraft but also by their endurance on task once they arrive.

46 During intensive operations ships are likely to stay at sea for periods of 30-100 days, refuelling from a tanker every three or four days, and replenishing with ammunition and provisions from storeships. Supplies of fuel and provisions present no problems, and ships carry sufficient equipment spares to last for several months. (If a serious equipment breakdown occurred, the ship would have to return to a base port, and any necessary spare parts could be air-freighted there while the ship was in transit.) The real problem is with ammunition, which may be used in large quantities. Ammunition manufacture in Australia does not reduce the difficulty significantly, because the problem is one of distribution rather than production.

47 The present Australian Navy has been designed for the defence of shipping, and many of the ships are not suitable or economical for employment in counter-insurgency wars. It is very doubtful whether a single small, slow carrier such as the *Melbourne* is a worthwhile long-term proposition. If carriers are to be provided at all, at least two 50,000-ton vessels would seem to be the minimum useful force. Of the fifteen destroyers and destroyer escorts, five are obsolete and are either in reserve or used for training. Of the ten modern vessels, only three—the American-built D.D.G.s—are capable of using U.S. ammunition supplies. The others use British or Australian weapons and, should the British depart, the deployment of these ships in South-East Asian waters will become difficult.

The twenty patrol boats are useful for inshore patrols, but they are lightly armed and not really fast enough. They need support from faster and more heavily armed vessels.

The six minesweepers are adequate for their task at present, but would not be capable of keeping more than a single port open in the face of a serious mining campaign.

333

The four submarines are an adequate—even lavish—provision for anti-submarine training. It is not clear what useful operational role they could perform at present.

The support ships consist of one tanker and one repair ship. They are quite inadequate for the support of the fighting ships whose operations are likely to be dispersed over thousands of miles. In the past the Australian Navy has sustained its operations through the assistance of British or American support ships. It seems urgent that more support ships should be provided.

Chapter 10
CONTROLLING SMALL WARS (page 132)

1   For a statement of such reasons, see Paul Kecskemeti, *Insurgency as a Strategic Problem*, The Rand Corporation, RM-5160 (Santa Monica, February 1967).

2   The following discussion, as well as some of the preceding comments, draws freely on the more extensive treatment in a forthcoming book by Nathan Leites and Charles Wolf, Jr, *Rebellion and Authority: An Analytic Essay on Insurgent Conflicts*.

3   Despite frequent rhetoric to the contrary, a probably more typical, but not more accurate, military viewpoint was expressed by General Earle G. Wheeler in 1962 *before* he became Chairman of the Joint Chiefs of Staff:

It is fashionable in some quarters to say that the problems in Southeast Asia are primarily political and economic rather than military. I do not agree. The essence of the problem in Vietnam is military.

Quoted by Alastair Buchan, 'Questions about Vietnam', *Encounter* (January 1968), p. 7. The reason this formulation is no more accurate than the other is that it focuses on the amount and the priority of force (the opposing view focuses on the amount and the priority of politics). Both views neglect the more important questions concerning the types of force and the types of politics.

4   Leites and Wolf, *Rebellion and Authority: An Analytic Essay on Insurgent Conflicts, op. cit.*, Chapter II.

5   See Wolf, 'Insurgency and Counterinsurgency: New Myths and Old Realities', *The Yale Review*, Vol. LVI, No. 2 (Winter 1967), pp. 225-41.

6   Leites and Wolf, *op. cit.*, Chapter VII.

7   For a fuller discussion, see Leites and Wolf, *op. cit.*, Chapter IV.

8   Robert Grainger Ker Thompson, *Defeating Communist Insurgency: Experiences from Malaya and Vietnam* (Chatto and Windus, London, 1966), p. 48.

9   Below some theshold value. Unless the response time is at least quicker than some minimum value, it may make no difference.

10 See Wolf, 'Insurgency and Counterinsurgency', *op. cit.*

Chapter 11
AUSTRALIA AND THE NUCLEAR BALANCE (page 144)

1   See A. L. Burns 'A "Regional" Problem: the American Signalling Station in Western Australia', *Disarmament and Arms Control*, Vol. 2, No. 1 (1964), pp. 23-33.

2   This party, electorally supported mainly in Queensland and in Victoria where it has on occasion polled 17%, holds the balance in the Senate and until recently, it has in practice been able to prevent the election of an A.L.P. government. It has done this by exploiting the preferential voting system: it has directed D.L.P. second preference votes away from the A.L.P.

3   *Current Notes on International Affairs*, Department of External Affairs, Canberra (August 1969), p. 419.
4   *The Times*, Supplement on Australia, 31 March 1970, p. xv, by Christopher Jay.
5   For example by Alan Wood in *Australian Financial Review*, 19 February 1970.
6   See Christopher Jay, *loc. cit.*
7   *Australian Financial Review*, 24 August 1970.
8   'Nuclear Arms for Australia', *Current Affairs Bulletin*, Vol. 46, No. 1 (June 1970), Department of Adult Education, University of Sydney.
9   The general Australian public either took the film as a literal view of a possible future; or it drew a contrary moral, which could have been derived from a jibe attributed to the leading actress: she had been making a film about the end of the world in Melbourne, Australia, and couldn't think of a more appropriate place for it!
10 J. Wilkes (ed.), *Australia's Defence and Foreign Policy* (Australian Institute of Political Science, Angus and Robertson, Sydney, 1964), pp. 26-7.
11 *Current Notes, op. cit.* (August 1969), p. 414.
12 Though he probably lost it for domestic, indeed local, reasons.
13 See Appendix I for a catalogue of facilities in Australia shared with other countries. Of the explicitly military, two are shared with the United Kingdom, and seven with the United States.
14 Morton A. Kaplan, *System and Process in International Politics* (New York, 1957), p. 50.

Chapter 12
OIL AND DEFENCE (page 169)

1   The work in this study was originally completed for *Canberra Papers on Strategy and Defence No. I*, entitled *Oil Supply in Australia's Defence Strategy* (Australian National University Press, Canberra, 1968). This Chapter is a revised version of that argument.
2   Fuel Branch, Department of National Development, estimates published in Petroleum Information Bureau, *Oil and Australia 1967*.
3   John F. Jacobs and Co. Ltd., *World Tanker Fleet Review* (London, 1969); and *Analysis of World Tank Ship Fleet* (Sun Oil Co., Philadelphia, 1969).
4   And this tanker problem is, of course, one which would exist even if there were no Australian refinery industry or if the present one were destroyed.
5   See Hunter, *Oil Supply in Australia's Defence Strategy, op. cit.*
6   Dr Mossadegh's intervention into Anglo-Iranian operations in 1951-54 succeeded only in halting production in Iran, transferring export markets to Kuwait and Saudi Arabia and losing Iran the commercial leadership of the Middle-East group of oil countries. No destination country suffered a shortage of supplies.
7   See R. V. B. Blackman (ed.), *Jane's Fighting Ships* (1967-68 and 1969-70). The U.S.S.R. has 385 operational submarines in a four-theatre fleet (Baltic, Black Sea and Atlantic and Pacific Oceans). Half of them are ocean-going and some 80 of the latter have guided-missile systems possessing operating ranges of from 200 to 600 miles for so-called 'cruise' missiles. Some of the latest, with Polaris-type missiles, have considerably greater ranges for their nuclear war-heads. The Chinese People's Republic has only one conventional (diesel-electric) long-range (28,000 miles) submarine capable of firing missiles; 29 medium range (9,000-16,000 miles); and a few coastal protection and training vessels. It is

reported that the U.S.S.R. has a high scrap rate for its older vessels and there are 30 new types under construction. The new-building performance of China in submarines is uncertain. Although it is intended to construct in Chinese yards, the present fleet is of U.S.S.R. origin or the boats' components came from that country.

8 Jacobs, *World Tanker Fleet Review*; and British Petroleum, *Statistical Review of the World Oil Industry*. The same is true, broadly, of all ocean-going ships although they are less essential for the continued operation of most industrial economies. The Soviet Union-East Europe-China group of countries operate only 8% of the non-tanker shipping of the world—but the share of the Soviet bloc is growing.

9 Expressed as *per annum* costs and counting in costs of maintenance, depreciation of the installations, interest on the investment and interest on the funds outlaid on purchasing the crude, the *per annum* cost of financing one tank is around $A250,000. So, for thirty days supply the annual cost would be $A6 million; for sixty days supply $A12 million; and for ninety days $A18 million. (All figures in this passage are rounded for convenience.)

10 The Middle East problem deserves more intensive treatment. See Hunter, *Oil Supply in Australia's Defence Strategy, op. cit.*

11 The considerations touching control of tankers—ownership of the present ocean-going fleet, the connection with refining and producing companies, their probable disposition in wartime, is dealt with in more detail in Hunter, *Oil Supply in Australia's Defence Strategy, op. cit.*

12 *ibid.*

13 Further, such alterations in the refinery structure are not costless. Most of the expense will fall on the refinery companies in the first place. Eventually the consuming public will pay through higher prices for petrols, kerosines, diesels and the heavy oils. The costs of using indigenous crude were even greater under the Commonwealth's scheme of compulsory purchase at $US3.50 per barrel between 1965 and 1969. Fortunately this degree of support for local production has been abandoned in favour of a formula, coming fully into operation in September 1970, which modifies compulsory purchase. Indigenous crudes will now be sold to refining companies at the import-parity values obtaining in October 1968; and this arrangement will last for five years. Thus local crude prices, delivered at refinery, while higher than international equivalents, are closely connected with them and in September 1975 may well be adjusted to the average of the foreign crudes displaced or some such appropriate formula. For comment on this aspect of indigenous crude production see Alex Hunter, *Petroleum Product Prices in Australia and Indigenous Crude Oil* (a report prepared for the Australian Automobile Association, Sydney, 1968), Parts II and III.

14 See Hunter, *Petroleum Product Prices in Australia and Indigenous Crude Oil, op. cit.*; and *Oil Supply in Australia's Defence Strategy, op. cit.*

Chapter 13

TRANSFORMATION IN FOREIGN TRADE (page 188)

1 Peter Drysdale, 'Minerals and Metals in Japanese-Australian Trade', *Papers of Annual Conference of the Australian Institute of Mining and Metallurgy* (Sydney, August 1969).

2 Peter Drysdale, Japanese-Australian Trade, Australian National University, unpublished thesis, 1967.

3 Peter Drysdale, 'Japan, Australia, New Zealand: The Prospect for Western Pacific Economic Integration', *Economic Record* (September 1969).

4 Peter Drysdale, 'Japan and Australia: The Prospect for Closer Economic Integration', *Economic Papers* (February-December, 1969).

5 I. A. McDougall, 'The Prospects of the Economic Integration of Japan, Australia and New Zealand', in Kiyoshi Kojima (ed.), *Pacific Trade and Development* (Japan Economic Research Center, Tokyo, February 1968).

6 Drysdale, 'Minerals and Metals in Japanese-Australian Trade', *op. cit.*

7 D. T. Brash, *American Investment in Australian Industry* (Australian National University Press, Canberra, 1966).

8 Drysdale, 'Japan, Australia, New Zealand: The Prospect for Western Pacific Economic Integration', *op. cit.*

9 *loc. cit.*

10 Commonwealth of Australia, *Tariff Board Report: Annual Report for Year 1967-68* (Canberra, August 1968); G. A. Rattigan, *The Tariff Board Today*, address to Associated Chambers of Commerce (Perth, May 1967).

11 Rattigan, *The Tariff Board Today*, *op. cit.*

12 J. G. Crawford, *The Development of Australian Trade Policy*, Shann Memorial Lecture (University of Western Australia, October 1968); Drysdale, 'Japan, Australia, New Zealand: The Prospect for Western Pacific Economic Integration', *op. cit.*

13 Commonwealth of Australia, *The Australian System of Tariff Preferences for Developing Countries* (Department of Trade and Industry, Canberra, January 1968).

14 Drysdale, 'Japan and Australia: The Prospect for Closer Economic Integration', *op. cit.*

15 Kiyoshi Kojima (ed.), *Pacific Trade and Development* (Japan Economic Research Center, Tokyo, February 1968).

16 Harry G. Johnson, 'World Trade Policy in the Post-Kennedy Round Era: A Survey of Alternatives, with Special Reference to the Position of the Pacific and Asian Regions', *Economic Record* (June 1968).

17 Kiyoshi Kojima (ed.), *Pacific Trade and Development*, *op. cit.*

18 *loc. cit.*

19 Drysdale, 'Japan, Australia, New Zealand: The Prospect for Western Pacific Economic Integration', *op. cit.*

20 W. McMahon, Speech to the Australian-American Association, Sydney, *Commonwealth Treasury Press Release No. 96* (8 November 1968).

Chapter 14
CAPITAL INFLOW AND DEFENCE COMMITMENT
(page 205)

1 'Defence and the Australian Economy', *Economic Papers No. 29* (November 1968).

2 Sir Ian McLennan is Managing Director of Australia's largest company, Broken Hill Proprietary Ltd.

Chapter 15
TELECOMMUNICATIONS AND SPACE (page 222)

1 Australian Commonwealth Bureau of Census and Statistics.

BIBLIOGRAPHY

Australian Year Book. 1967.
Annual Report of the Postmaster-General. 1969.
Financial and Statistical Bulletin. 1969. Postmaster-General's Department. Australia.
Planning Review. June 1967. Planning and Research Division. Postmaster-General's Department. Australia.

'The Overseas Telecommunications Commission (Australia)'.
'The Southeast Asia Commonwealth Cable'.
'O.T.C. links Australia and the World via Satellites'.
(Publications of the Overseas Telecommunications Commission)
'Australian Telecommunications 1969' published by the Australian Telecommunications Development Association.
Fixed Outpost Radio Communication Stations. Radio Branch. Postmaster-General's Department. Australia. 1965.

Chapter 16
DEFENCE PROCUREMENT (page 244)

1 Published by the Institute as six separate studies in 1967. For previous accounts of Australian defence procurement see T. B. Millar, *Australia's Defence* (Melbourne University Press, 1965), Chapter 5; and H. G. Gelber, *The Australian-American Alliance* (Penguin, Harmondsworth, 1968), pp. 34-9.
2 A squadron of Canberras is on active service in Vietnam. (Commonwealth of Australia, *Defence Report 1969*, p. 38.)
3 The decision to equip the R.A.A.F. with these aircraft had been taken in 1950.
4 It was derived from the Lancaster bomber which was first delivered to the R.A.F. in 1941: the Lincoln went out of service in Australia as a maritime reconnaissance aircraft.
5 According to a special defence section in the *Commonwealth Year Book 1955*, pp. 985, 1108, 'the long-range weapons project at Woomera is a joint UK-Australia one, the UK being responsible for the development of guided weapons systems and Australia providing the facilities necessary for the testing of such weapons'. Woomera appears to have contributed very little to the Australian services.
6 These figures are for the year 1964 and can be expected to have risen slightly since then. They are independent estimates, since national defence statistics follow extremely divergent principles in classifying R and D. See C. J. E. Harlow, *The European Armaments Base: A Survey*, Parts 1 and 2 (Institute for Strategic Studies, London, 1967), *passim.*
7 Harlow, *The European Armaments Base: A Survey, op. cit.*, Part 1, p. 22; he gives somewhat higher figures for the variable geometry aircraft.
8 T. L. Shelton, 'Further Progress with Jindivik', *Aircraft* (Melbourne, November 1967), pp. 16-18.
9 For a full description see S. Pugh, *Fighting Vehicles and Weapons of the Modern British Army* (Macdonald, London, 1962), p. 58.
10 A description can be found in R. V. B. Blackman (ed.), *Jane's Fighting Ships 1967-68* (London) p. 506.
11 T. B. Millar, 'Australia's Defence, 1945-1965', in G. Greenwood & N. Harper (eds), *Australia in World Affairs 1961-1965* (F. W. Cheshire, Melbourne, 1968), p. 292.
12 Commonwealth of Australia, *Report of the Auditor-General 1967-68*, p. 307.
13 *ibid.*, p. 279. The Minister for the Navy claimed that $A20 million could be saved by the decision not to install Ikara in the two 'Daring' class destroyers, which would seem an overestimate. *Sydney Morning Herald*, 25 August 1967.
14 Harlow, *The European Armaments Base: A Survey, op. cit.*, Part 1, p. 7, and Part 2 *passim*: the figures for Britain, Sweden, Italy and Belgium begin at 1955 so the comparison with Australian figures from 1953 may not be wholly accurate.

15   This figure is no more than an informed guess based upon known total numbers of aircraft, ships, etc. purchased over the period and upon known figures for Australian production of these items.

16   Harlow, *The European Armaments Base: A Survey, op. cit.*, Part 1, p. 25.

17   *Commonwealth Parliamentary Debates, House of Representatives, [C.P.D. (H. of R.)]*, 14 August 1968, p. 209; and see Table 9.

18   1 carrier, 3 guided-missile destroyers, 3 Daring class destroyers, 4 River class destroyer escorts, 3 coastal minesweepers, 3 submarines and 16 patrol boats (*Defence Report*, 1969, p. 20).

19   *Report of the Auditor-General 1949-1950*, p. 196; and *1955-1956*, pp. 69-70.

20   *Report of the Auditor-General 1955-1956*, pp. 69-70.

21   Another example of weakness in the control and co-ordination of naval procurement was the indecision surrounding the role of the *Hobart*, a cruiser of Second World War vintage. In 1950 it was decided to modernize the *Hobart* as a fighting ship until the 'Daring' class destroyers were completed; in 1952 it was decided to rescind this plan and to develop *Hobart* as a training ship. In 1953 it was decided that it would not be needed in this role, as a result of a decision that only one operational carrier, the *Melbourne*, should be kept in service and that the *Sydney* should then become the training ship. Other roles were canvassed for the *Hobart*, but in 1955 it was decided that she should be mothballed. Expenditure had by this time reached $A2.8 million; a further $A2 million would have been needed to complete the modernization programme.

22   *Report of the Auditor-General 1958-1959*, p. 80. The final average cost of the escorts was $A14 million. The destroyers *Voyager* and *Vendetta*, begun in 1949, were completed in 1957 and 1958 respectively; *Vampire*, begun in 1952, was completed in 1959.

23   R. V. B. Blackman (ed.), *Jane's Fighting Ships 1968-69* (London), p. 300.

24   Except for depth charge mortars: the British use the 'Squid' type, the Australians use the 'Limbo' type.

25   R. V. B. Blackman (ed.), *Jane's Fighting Ships 1968-69, op. cit.*, pp. 14 and 300.

26   Cockatoo Docks and Engineering Co. Pty. Limited (sometimes called Vickers (Australia) Pty. Limited), a wholly owned subsidiary of the British company of Vickers, leases this yard from the Australian government.

27   The *Hobart* and the *Perth*, ordered in 1961, were delivered in 1965; the *Brisbane*, ordered 1963, delivered 1968.

28   The ships themselves were produced for less than the original estimate, but the cost of the shore based spares increased greatly: 'the actual cost of these ships (*Hobart* and *Perth*) has not finally been determined . . .'—*Report of the Auditor-General 1967-68*, p. 277: the figure of $A40 million does *not* include the cost of installing 'Ikara' which might add approximately a further $A7 million to the cost of each ship.

29   Of this cost, $A4.6 million was spent overseas; the engines for example were procured in the U.K. See *C.P.D. (H. of R.)*, 26 November 1968, p. 3285.

30   Its original cost estimate, in 1963, was $A10 million: *Report of the Auditor-General 1967-68*, p. 278.

31   *Report of the Auditor-General 1955-1956*, p. 70.

32   But it remained in service with the German Navy (as a land-based aircraft) until the mid-1960s.

33 27 Westland Wessex Mk. 31A helicopters were ordered for the purpose from the U.K. at total cost of about $A16 million.

34 *C.P.D. (H. of R.)*, 26 November 1968, p. 3285.

35 It is hard to be sure in some instances whether construction is slow or has been slowed to fit in with limits placed on defence expenditure; the construction of the 'Daring' class destroyers, for example, was carried out in the years of the $A400 million defence budget 'ceiling'.

36 The industry is subsidized by the government at a rate of up to one-third of the construction cost on all vessels intended for use in Australia of 200 tons or more; vessels of smaller displacement are protected by tariff. In 1966-67 naval shipbuilding accounted for roughly 15% by value of the total output of Australian yards.

37 Blackman (ed.), *Jane's Fighting Ships 1968-69, op. cit., passim*. The eventual cost of the Australian-built patrol boats is expected to be approximately $A750,000 each (*Report of the Auditor-General 1966-67*, p. 214), although there are some indications that this figure may be somewhat low. The patrol boats sold by the British to Singapore in 1968, which although somewhat faster than the Australian boats have similar dimensions and displacement, cost $A1.5 million each: *The Military Balance 1968-1969* (Institute for Strategic Studies, London, 1968), p. 59.

38 According to *Defence Report 1967* (p. 31) 80% of the Army's needs are being met by Australian production.

39 *C.P.D. (H. of R.)*, 26 November 1968, p. 3285. The orders were for armoured personnel carriers (M113A), Bell helicopters, amphibious vehicles (Larc 5), Pilatus Porter aircraft and 105mm pack howitzers.

40 *Report of the Auditor-General 1967-68*, p. 281.

41 Harlow, *The European Armaments Base: A Survey, op. cit.*, Part 2, pp. 11, 16. The British equivalent, the FV432 Trojan, costs twice as much.

42 *The Military Balance 1968-1969*, p. 21.

43 Neville Brown, *Arms Without Empire* (Penguin, Harmondsworth, 1967), p. 107. It should, however, be borne in mind that the Vigilant needs no support vehicle, and the Malkara is useless without the fairly large support truck which would probably cost an additional several thousand dollars.

44 *C.P.D. (H. of R.)*, 16 October 1968, p. 2048. The cost is likely to have been below $A1 million; items procured or ordered abroad of a total cost in excess of $A1 million are listed in a later *Hansard* (26 November 1968, p. 3285)—neither Entac nor Redeye is on this list.

45 *C.P.D. (H. of R.)*, *loc. cit.* Again the cost is likely to have been below $A1 million. The Swiss paid $A8 million for more than 1,000 Redeye missiles due to enter service in 1969 (*Military Balance 1968-1969*, p. 58).

46 British production began in 1957 and ceased in 1959; Australian production is (1969) only now winding down.

47 *C.P.D. (H. of R.)*, 16 October 1968, p. 2048.

48 *Defence Reports* for 1965-1968. Some preliminary electronics work has also taken place in Australia for Project Mallard. This is the code name for an international military satellite communication system involving Britain, Canada and the United States as well as Australia, due to enter operation by 1975. Private industry and government laboratories within Australia up to 1969 had completed contracts worth about $A500,000 and between 1969 and 1971 are expected to share a further $A1 million worth of development work. The total development cost of the project is about $A113 million and will be mainly borne by the United States and Britain.

(*Editor*: The U.S. withdrew from the project in October 1970.)

49   *C.P.D. (H. of R.)*, 26 November 1968, p. 3286.
50   *The Military Balance, 1968-1969*, p. 34; and *Defence Report 1968*, p. 30.
51   Harlow, *The European Armaments Base: A Survey, op. cit.*, Part 2, p. 64,
     p. 54: India, too, builds tanks (British) under licence.
52   The engine and chassis differences between an army truck and a civilian
     truck may not, however, be as great as those between a private car and
     a 'jeep' or Land Rover-type vehicle.
53   Canada is not formally allied to Australia. The agreement is a statement
     of willingness to co-operate on new military developments and techniques
     with an eye to increasing standardization. See *The Times*, 20 February
     1963.
54   *Supply '66: Activities and Developments* (Commonwealth of Australia,
     Department of Supply, September 1966), p. 31.
55   *The Military Balance 1968-1969*, p. 34; and *Defence Report 1969*,
     pp. 38-9.
56   Prominent shareholders are Broken Hill Proprietary Ltd. and the Electro-
     lytic Zinc Co. together with several Australian subsidiaries of overseas
     firms—Rolls-Royce, I.C.I. and the P.&O. Company.
57   *Jane's All the World's Aircraft 1966-67, op. cit.*, p. 8.
58   J. W. R. Taylor, *Warplanes of the World* (Ian Allen, London, 1966),
     p. 44: the first Australian-built Canberra flew in 1953.
59   Out of a total of 19,300 basic design drawings, 17,000 were of overseas
     origin: *Aircraft* (July 1953), p. 24.
60   *Aircraft, loc. cit.*, p. 26.
61   The Australian engines cost at least 43% more—see *Aircraft* (December
     1956), p. 58.
62   Which for a small total production target favours low costs. See S. G.
     Sturmey, 'Cost Curves in Aircraft Production', *The Economic Journal*,
     Vol. LXXIV, No. 296 (December 1964), pp. 954, 982.
63   Statement by Defence Minister, *C.P.D. (H. of R.)*, 11 September 1956,
     p. 368; a later, but vaguer estimate gave 'in the vicinity of $800,000' as
     the price, *C.P.D. (Senate)*, 8 May 1957, pp. 605, 606. It is unclear
     whether these estimates include any allowance for spare parts.
64   *The Military Balance 1968-1969*, p. 59.
65   *Sydney Morning Herald*, 26 July and 12 August 1953.
66   Only 40% of the original fuselage structure was retained: *Aircraft* (July
     1953), p. 29.
67   Defence Minister, *C.P.D. (H. of R.)*, 11 September 1956, p. 368.
68   Heavy bombers could be equipped with 'stand-off' missiles which per-
     mitted the discharge of bombs outside the range of S.A.M.s.
69   *C.P.D. (H. of R.)*, 26 November 1968, p. 3285.
70   *Air Force Magazine* (January 1965), p. 46.
71   *Report of the Auditor-General 1967-68*, pp. 285, 308. This total foreign
     exchange cost must include payment for a large quantity of spare parts.
     The cost of a Mirage IIIC (similar to the III-0 bought directly from
     the French is given by one source as less than $A900,000: R. Miller and
     D. Sawers, *The Technical Development of Modern Aviation* (Rout-
     ledge and Kegan Paul, London, 1968), p. 273. This is close to the
     estimate of $A1 million given by the Australian Minister for Air in 1960
     for the 'flyaway' cost of the aircraft, which he contrasted with $A2.2
     million for its 'programme cost' (including spares, spare engines, ground
     handling equipment and technical information) (*Aircraft*, January 1961,
     p. 46). The rather similar Mirage 5 has recently been sold by France at
     approximately $US2 million (*The Military Balance 1968-1969*, pp.
     58-9). Australia has bought ten Mirage trainers from France at $A2.4
     million each.
72   *C.P.D. (H. of R.)*, 26 November 1968, p. 3285; and *Report of the
     Auditor-General 1967-68*, p. 289.

73   *Aircraft* (October 1967), p. 24.
74   See the discussion of research and development, above.
75   'Aeronews Roundup', *Aircraft* (September 1962), pp. 42-3. For a comprehensive discussion of the Australian government's decision, see Hanno Weisbrod, 'Australia's Decision to buy the F-111', *Australian Quarterly*, 41, 2 (June 1969).
76   *C.P.D. (H. of R.)*, 2 May 1968, p. 1080.
77   Certain charges, e.g. for ground handling equipment, would be a higher proportion of aircraft costs in the case of a small order such as the Australian. T. Alexander, 'McNamara's Expensive Economy Plane', *Fortune* (June 1967), p. 186, gives data for the original American estimate.
78   *Report of the Auditor-General 1967-68*, p. 289.
79   *C.P.D. (H. of R.)*, 26 November 1968, p. 3286.
80   Speech by Menzies, *C.P.D. (H. of R.)*, 4 April 1957, pp. 571-9.
81   In practice it is difficult to find instances of this; it is interesting that an item for the purchase of spare parts for the Sabre from an American supplier appeared in the 1966-67 defence estimates (*Report of the Auditor-General 1966-67*, p. 232).
82   For a scholarly enquiry into the general problem of aircraft production costs see S. G. Sturmey, 'Cost Curves in Aircraft Production', *loc. cit.*
83   *Sydney Morning Herald*, 13 January 1955, p. 5.
84   Australian Parliament, Joint Committee of Public Accounts, *29th Report*, 1956, Minutes of Evidence, p. 46.
85   *Aircraft*, Vol. 45, No. 6 (March 1966), p. 24.
86   Such a merger would probably be feasible only between C.A.C. and G.A.F.; see *Australian Financial Review*, 14 November 1968, for a discussion of a possible merger.
87   For a forceful critique along these lines, see B. D. Beddie, 'Some Internal Political Problems', in John Wilkes (ed.), *Australia's Defence and Foreign Policy* (Angus and Robertson, for Australian Institute of Political Science, Sydney, 1964).
88   H. Weisbrod, 'Australia's Defence Structure Reorganisation, 1957-58' (Department of International Relations, Australian National University, Work-in-Progress Seminar, 1965), p. 2.
89   *Aircraft* (July 1956), p. 4.
90   *C.P.D. (H. of R.)*, 4 April 1957, pp. 575-6.
91   The changes of mind over the Fleet Air Arm, referred to earlier, represent a more straightforward case of the revision of policy in the light of a loosening up of budgetary restrictions, reassessment of life of existing aircraft, and reassessment of the practicability of flying the next generation of aircraft (Tracker and Skyhawk) from the carrier *Melbourne*.
92   Sir Frederick Shedden (Secretary of the Defence Department), who caused a sensation by stating before the Public Accounts Committee in 1956 that the forces were not ready for mobilization either in 1953 or 1956, went on to say that the government 'is aware and has long been aware of what are the deficiencies of the Services', but had not been willing to meet the cost. Australian Parliament, Joint Committee on Public Accounts, *29th Report*, 1956, *Minutes of Evidence*, pp. 43-4.
93   *C.P.D. (H. of R.)*, 16 October 1968, pp. 2048-9. The figures are for orders placed, not actual expenditure, which would lag behind the orders, but in fact averaged 53% of total procurement for this period (see Table 9).
94   L. H. Barnard, 'Increasing Stresses and Strains in Defence Policy', *Australian Financial Review, Annual Defence Survey* (2 December 1968), p. 17; *Australian Defence-Policy and Programmes*, Victorian Fabian Society Pamphlet 18 (January 1969).
95   See reports in *Australian Financial Review*, 17 October and 7 November 1968, 2 April, 13 May, 8 July and 26 August 1969; *Canberra Times*, 1 February 1969. Also *Defence Report 1969*, p. 11.

96 *Defence Report 1968*, pp. 8-9. Defence Minister Fairhall has elsewhere admitted that there was some force in one of the frequent criticisms of procurement policy: 'in the past insufficient notice has sometimes been given for industry to develop the necessary special skills in a satisfactory time scale . . . I have instituted new procedures whereby appropriate Services requirements are made available to industry advisory committees as soon as they are finalised within the Service concerned', *Australian Financial Review*, Annual Defence Survey, 2 December 1968, p. 14.

97 *Australian* and *Australian Financial Review*, 10 March 1969.

98 See e.g. *Australian Financial Review*, 24 November 1969 (special Defence Survey), and 11 December 1969.

99 'Australia lags behind world in industrial R and D', *Australian Financial Review*, 16 August 1968.

100 *A Study of Resources devoted to R and D in OECD Member Countries in 1963/64* (in series International Statistical Year for Research and Development), O.E.C.D. (Paris, 1968), pp. 156-7.

101 *ibid.*, pp. 156-7.

102 Under the NATO Hawk programme, France, Germany, Italy, the Netherlands and Belgium built 4,000 missiles at a cost of $US667 million, estimated to be 20% higher than the cost of American construction. Belgium, Denmark, Germany, Greece, the Netherlands, Norway, Portugal and Turkey took part in the much smaller Sidewinder programme (5,000 missiles, cost $A25 million). Robert Rhodes James, *Standardisation and Common Production of Weapons in NATO*, Part III of *Defence, Technology and the Western Alliance* (Institute for Strategic Studies, London, 1967).

103 *Aircraft* (January 1966), p. 13.

104 Alex Hunter, 'Industry and Defence in Australia', in T. B. Millar (ed.), *Australian-New Zealand Defence Co-operation* (Australian National University Press, Canberra, 1968), pp. 54-5.

105 *Australian Financial Review*, 11 March 1970.

106 In February 1969 Australia signed a contract to build wings for the General Aircraft Corporation's GAC-100 at the Government Aircraft Factory. In May 1969 Hawker de Havilland won a contract for the manufacture of helicopter tail rotor hub assemblies, and later in the year Litton Industries called for subcontracting bids in Australia for work on a radar defence system.

107 *Australian Financial Review*, 24 February and 3 June 1969.

Chapter 17
ADMINISTRATION OF DEFENCE (page 270)

1 'Defence Call to the Nation', broadcasts by the Prime Minister in September 1950: *Current Notes on International Affairs*, Vol. 21 (1950), p. 659. Civil Defence was the responsibility of the Department of the Interior, a decision taken in 1945. Measures for defence against atomic and biological warfare could not be adequately planned by 1947. By March 1949 a Civil Defence Committee was established. The Department of Defence advised on the military aspects. *The Defence Department and the Higher Defence Machinery. Functions and Organization* (Government Printer, Melbourne, 1947), p. 15; *The Defence Department and the Higher Defence Machinery. National Planning for an Emergency* (Government Printer, Melbourne, 1949), p. 7, both by courtesy of the Defence Group Library, Department of Defence.

2 *Commonwealth Parliamentary Debates, (House of Representatives), C.P.D. (H. of R.)*, Vol. 12, 11 September 1956, p. 367 *et seq.*

3   B. D. Beddie, 'Some Internal Political Problems', in J. Wilkes (ed.), *Australia's Defence and Foreign Policy* (Angus and Robertson, Sydney, 1964), p. 131. This maximum figure was first fixed in 1952-53.

4   *C.P.D. (H. of R.)*, Vol. 17, 22 October 1957, p. 1593.

5   *ibid.*

6   He said that, 'the 3-year programme . . . is not a 3-year programme which has begun at the beginning of a period of 3 years and which runs through to the third year. It is in fact a rolling programme. There is a 3-year programme and when one year passes there are 2 years left and there is a consideration of the following year. This is the way in which this matter has always been treated'. *C.P.D. (H. of R.)*, 20 November 1968, p. 3015.

7   *Australian Financial Review*, 6 December 1968.

8   *C.P.D. (H. of R.)*, Vol. 44, 12 November 1964, p. 2924.

9   *C.P.D. (H. of R.)*, Vol. 14, 4 April 1957, p. 573.

10 *Twenty-Ninth Report. Joint Committee of Public Accounts*, para. 55, in *Papers Presented to Parliament*, 1956-57, Vol. II. Mr Fairhall, Minister for Supply, remarked in 1963 that, depending on the service, some 32%-48% of the entire defence vote was absorbed in pay and civilian support. *C.P.D. (H. of R.)*, Vol. 40, 22 October 1963, p. 2067.

11 *C.P.D. (H. of R.)*, Vol. 17, 23 October 1957, p. 1659.

12 *ibid.*, p. 1593.

13 In view of the argument about this evidence, it is useful to cite the Secretary's own words:
    187. Mr. Leslie — . . . You said that the Prime Minister stated at the outset in connexion with this programming that the proposal was that we were to be ready for mobilization by 1953? Would we have been?
    — (Sir Frederick Shedden) No, sir.
    188. Mr. Leslie — Would we be now? — No, sir.
    Twenty-Ninth Report, p. 43 of Evidence.

14 *C.P.D. (H. of R.)*, Vol. 12, 5 September 1956, pp. 226; 2 October 1956, p. 1002.

15 *C.P.D. (H. of R.)*, Vol. 13, 4 October 1956, pp. 1137-8.

16 It was explained afterwards that these additional members would attend 'when it is required to deal with matters that have a political concept or a concept wider than that of strict defence'. *C.P.D. (H. of R.)*, Vol. 18, 25 March 1958, p. 634.

17 *C.P.D. (H. of R.)*, Vol. 14, 4 April 1956, p. 576.

18 Mr E. W. Hicks. Prior to his retirement, Shedden was commissioned to write a book on Australian defence administration: work began in 1957.

19 *C.P.D. (H. of R.)*, Vol. 17, 19 November 1956, p. 2256; Vol. 19, 2 May 1958, p. 1441.

20 *C.P.D. (H. of R.)*, Vol. 18, 19 March 1958, pp. 433-42; 25 March 1958, p. 645; 27 March 1958, p. 769.

21 In the Menzies government at this time the Postmaster-General was also the Minister for the Navy.

22 *C.P.D. (H. of R.)*, Vol. 15, 7 May 1957, p. 116; Vol. 17, 14 November 1957, pp. 2241-2.

23 E.g., Vice-Admiral Sir Roy Dowling, Chairman of the Chiefs of Staff Committee in 1959, was a member of the Defence Committee between 1955-59 and the Chiefs of Staff Committee between 1955-58. At least four years previously there were attempts to secure the appointment of a chairman: *C.P.D. (H. of R.)*, Vol. 18, 27 March 1958, p. 771.

24 See B. B. Schaffer, 'Policy and System in Defense. The Australian Case', *World Politics*, Vol. XV (1963), pp. 236-61; and 'Decision-Making and the Civil-Military Experience', *Public Administration* (Australia), Vol. XXIII (1964), pp. 328-42.

25 *Twenty-Fifth Report*, paras. 76-81; *Twenty-Ninth Report*, paras. 12-13.

26   *Twenty-Fifth Report*, para. 41, and *n*.

27   *Fifty-Seventh Report. Joint Committee of Public Accounts*, p. 12, *Papers Presented to Parliament*, 1961, Vol. II.

28   See the chart presented by the Secretary of the Department of Defence to the Joint Committee of Public Accounts, and the explication: *Twenty-Ninth Report*, especially Chapter 2, 4 and Appendix 1. A comparison with a chart of the Higher Defence Machinery prepared by the Department of Defence in 1947 (*The Defence Department and the Higher Defence Machinery. Functions and Organisation*, chart No. 1) shows that by 1956 the Defence Preparations Committee replaced the Council of Defence, the Defence Scientific Advisory Committee had gone while the Board of Business Administration and the Joint War Production Committee were added. The Joint War Production Committee was established by 1949. (*The Defence Department and the Higher Defence Machinery. National Planning for an Emergency*, p. 5.) The Principal Subordinate Committees remained, save that the New Weapons and Equipment Development Committee had become the Defence Research and Development Policy Committee, with similar subcommittees (plus Medical Research).

29   Shedden's chart listed the following members: Prime Minister, Treasurer, Ministers for Defence, External Affairs, Navy, Army, Air, Defence Production, Supply and Customs and Excise. Other members evidently attended, *C.P.D. (H. of R.)*, Vol. 18, 27 March 1958, p. 771. This Committee lapsed after replacing the Council of Defence: 'Menzies division of the whole Cabinet into two—an inner Cabinet and the rest—meant, in conjunction with these changes, that no special Cabinet Defence Committee was revived or existed'. B. B. Schaffer, 'Policy and System in Defense, The Australian Case', *op. cit.*, p. 247, *n*. 11.

30   The reason given was that the Minister in charge of one of the junior of the service departments was a senior Minister in Cabinet and could override the Minister for Defence', *C.P.D. (H. of R.)*, Vol. 18, p. 771. This refers to the early 1950s.

31   Sir John Allison (Chairman of the Board of Business Administration and its successor), 'The Contribution of Advisory Bodies to Defence', *Public Administration* (Australia), Vol. XXV (1966), pp. 2-21. Allison served in other capacities, cf. *C.P.D. (H. of R.)*, Vol. 17, 22 October 1957, p. 1597.

32   Vice-Admiral Sir Roy Dowling, in J. Wilkes (ed.), *Australia's Defence and Foreign Policy, op. cit.*, p. 90.

33   *C.P.D. (H. of R.)*, Vol. 20, 27 August 1958, p. 777; Vol. 21, 10 September 1958, p. 1079; E. W. Hicks, Secretary of the Department of Defence, 'The Application of a Large-Scale E.D.P. System', *Public Administration* (Australia), Vol. XXII (1963), pp. 74-88.

34   The appointee subsequently became First Assistant Secretary: Inspection and Design.

35   *C.P.D. (H. of R.)*, Vol. 25, 7 October 1959, p. 1841; Vol. 37, 24 October 1962, p. 1884.

36   Sir John Allison, 'The Contributions of Advisory Bodies to Defence', *op. cit.*, pp. 14-15.

37   *Commonwealth of Australia. Directory*, 1961, p. 60.

38   *ibid.*, 1968, pp. 68-9.

39   *C.P.D. (H. of R.)*, 2 May 1968, pp. 1076, 1083; *Australian*, 3 May 1968.

40   As the *communiqué* stated, 'The arrangements to operate beyond 1971 would depend on a decision to be taken by the Australian Government on the part which Australia would play in the defence of the area after that date'. *Current Notes*, Vol. 39 (1968), p. 249. An editorial in the *Age* (Melbourne), 12 June 1968, described this as 'the purest gobbledygook'.

X

41 *Age* (Melbourne), 21 June 1968.

42 *Defence Report 1968*, p. 7 *et seq.*; *Australia in Facts and Figures*, No. 98, p. 71.

43 *Australian*, 9 August 1968; *Defence Report 1968*, p. 8.

44 *Current Notes*, Vol. 39, 1968, p. 350; *Defence Report 1968*, p. 6; *Age*, (Melbourne), 3 December 1968; *Australian Financial Review*, 6 December 1968.

45 Mr Gorton, interview in the *Australian*, 14 December 1968.

46 *Current Notes*, Vol. 40 (1969), p. 131.

47 *Defence Report 1969*, pp. 7, 9. On page 8 of the Report there is a chart of the Australian Higher Defence Organization, useful to compare with the charts of 1947 and 1956.

48 *Current Notes, loc. cit.*; *Defence Report 1969*, pp. 7, 11; *Australian Financial Review*, 2 April 1969.

49 *Australian*, 18 November 1969. The editorial of 30 September 1968 presaged that the Australian approach to defence might become more than 'a huge drain on our money resources and an echo-chamber so far as ideas are concerned'. 'The real reasons' why the Secretary resigned are discussed by Alan Ramsey in the same paper on 19 November 1969.

50 Interview with Allan Barnes, *Age* (Melbourne), 6 December 1969; *Australian*, 20 November 1969.

51 *Age* (Melbourne), 11 March 1970; *Australian*, 11 March 1970.

52 *Current Notes, loc. cit.*

Notes on Contributors

Dr Ian BELLANY teaches in the Department of Politics, University of Lancaster. He was educated at Oxford, where he took his D.Phil. in atomic physics in 1966. From 1966-68 he served in the Arms Control and Disarmament Unit of the British Foreign Office. From 1968-69 he was a Research Fellow in the Department of International Relations at the Australian National University.

Admiral Arleigh BURKE is Chairman of the Center for Strategic and International Studies of Georgetown University. He is also a member of the Board of Visitors of the Fletcher School of Law and Diplomacy, a member of the executive committee of the Texaco Co. and a director of several companies. He was educated at the U.S. Naval Academy and before his retirement from the U.S. Navy served, from 1955-61, as Chief of Naval Operations.

Professor Arthur L. BURNS is Professor of Political Science in the Institute of Advanced Studies of the Australian National University. He was educated in History, Philosophy and Theology and conducted research in International Relations at Princeton University and the University of Chicago in 1958-59 and 1961. He was with Political and Economic Planning, London, in 1961-62 and spent 1969-70 with the Centre of International Studies at the University of Cambridge.

Dr Peter DRYSDALE is Senior Lecturer in Economics, Australian National University, Canberra. He has also been associated since 1964 with Hitotsubashi University, Tokyo. He is a former consultant to the Asian Development Bank, Manila, on South-East Asian trade problems. Dr Drysdale is a specialist in Japanese-Australian economic relations and trade policy and is presently engaged on a study of Australian economic policy in the Asian Pacific Economic Community for the Australian Institute of International Affairs.

Dr Harry G. GELBER is Reader in Politics, Monash University. He was educated at Cambridge and served for several years as Foreign Correspondent in Europe. His recent research has concentrated on strategic studies. In 1966-67 he held a Visiting Fellowship at the University of California, Los Angeles. In 1969 he was a Fellow of the American Council of Learned Societies and a Research Associate of the Harvard Center for International Affairs.

347

Professor Sisir GUPTA is Professor of Disarmament Studies in the School of International Studies of the Jawaharlal University in New Delhi. Until the end of 1969 he was Senior Research Fellow in the Department of International Relations of the Australian National University. He is a former Research Director of the Indian Council of World Affairs and served on the staff of *The Times* of India.

Captain David HAMER, D.S.C., M.H.R., is Member of Parliament for Isaacs, Victoria. He retired from the Royal Australian Navy after some twenty years' service which included postings as Director of Naval Intelligence and Director of Project Coordination in the Navy Office in Canberra.

Dr Alex HUNTER is Professorial Fellow in the Department of Economics, Institute of Advanced Studies, Australian National University. He was formerly Professor and Head of the Department of Economics in the University of New South Wales. He is a graduate of the University of Glasgow. His most recent research has concentrated on shipping and oil economics.

Dr D. E. KENNEDY is Reader in History at the University of Melbourne. He was educated at the Universities of Melbourne and Cambridge and was awarded the Julian Corbett Prize in Modern Naval History by the University of London in 1958. He has divided his research between seventeenth century naval, political and ecclesiastical history and modern strategic problems and is the author of *The Security of Southern Asia* (London, 1965).

Dr John M. H. LINDBECK is Director of the East Asian Institute, Columbia University. From 1959-67 he was Associate Director of the East Asian Research Center at Harvard University. From 1952-58 he was a member of the State Department with particular responsibilities relating to China and overseas Chinese. He is Chairman of the Joint Committee on Contemporary China of the American Council of Learned Societies and the Social Science Research Council.

Dr Peter LYON is Secretary of the Institute of Commonwealth Studies and Senior Lecturer in Commonwealth Studies in the University of London. He was Lecturer in International Relations at the London School of Economics from 1963-69 and Visiting Associate Professor of Political Science at the University of California, Los Angeles, and a Ford Foundation Fellow in 1967.

Mr J. A. C. MACKIE is Research Director of the Centre of Southeast Asian Studies, Monash University, and a Reader in the Department of History and Politics. He was formerly Reader in charge, Department of Indonesian and Malayan Studies, University of Melbourne. He is a past-President of the Australian-Indonesian Association of Victoria, a member of the Executive Committee of the Australian Institute of International Affairs and review editor of *Australian Outlook*.

Professor Makoto MOMOI is Professor at the National Defense College, Tokyo. During 1968-69 he was Visiting Professor at the University of North Carolina.

Dr Robert O'NEILL is Senior Fellow in the Department of International Relations, Institute of Advanced Studies, Australian National University. He is a graduate of the Royal Military College of Australia and of the Universities of Melbourne and of Oxford, where he was a Rhodes scholar. He served as a regular soldier from 1955-68, ending his service as a Major on the staff of the Royal Military College, Duntroon.

Sir Ian POTTER is a company director and stockbroker. He is founder and Governor of the Ian Potter Foundation and Chairman of the Australian Elizabethan Theatre Trust. From 1935-67 he was principal partner of Ian Potter and Co., Melbourne.

Mr J. L. RICHARDSON is Senior Lecture in the Department of Government, University of Sydney. He was educated at Sydney and Magdalen College, Oxford. He was Student of Nuffield College, Oxford from 1958-61, a Research Associate at the Harvard Center for International Affairs from 1961-63, Research Fellow at Balliol College, Oxford 1963-65 and a member of the Arms Control and Disarmament Research Unit of the British Foreign Office from 1965-66.

Dr Albert SEYLER is Director of the Advanced Techniques Section of the Research Laboratories of the Australian Post Office. He attended the Technische Hochschule, Munich, and received his Master's degree and doctorate from the University of Melbourne. Most of his career has been spent in research. He is a member of the Faculty of Engineering, Monash University, and a Consultant for the Department of Electrical Engineering of the University of Adelaide.

Dr Charles WOLF Jr is Head of the Economics Department of the Rand Corporation, Santa Monica, California. He received his undergraduate and graduate training at Harvard, served with the State Department from 1949-53 and taught at Cornell and Berkeley from 1953-55. Since then he has been with the Rand Corporation. He has served as consultant to several government agencies and is a member of the South-East Asian Development Advisory Group of A.I.D. Most of his published work has been in the fields of economic development, foreign aid and military problems.

Index

Index